Migration and Multiculturalism
in Scandinavia

Migration and Multiculturalism in Scandinavia

Edited by
ERIC EINHORN, SHERRILL HARBISON and
MARKUS HUSS

THE UNIVERSITY OF WISCONSIN PRESS

The University of Wisconsin Press
728 State Street, Suite 443
Madison, Wisconsin 53706
uwpress.wisc.edu

Gray's Inn House, 127 Clerkenwell Road
London EC1R 5DB, United Kingdom
eurospanbookstore.com

Copyright © 2022
The Board of Regents of the University of Wisconsin System
All rights reserved. Except in the case of brief quotations embedded in critical
articles and reviews, no part of this publication may be reproduced, stored in a
retrieval system, transmitted in any format or by any means—digital, electronic,
mechanical, photocopying, recording, or otherwise—or conveyed via the
internet or a website without written permission of the University of Wisconsin
Press. Rights inquiries should be directed to rights@uwpress.wisc.edu.

Printed in the United States of America
This book may be available in a digital edition.

Library of Congress Cataloging-in-Publication Data

Names: Einhorn, Eric S., editor. | Harbison, Sherrill, editor. | Huss, Markus,
    1981– editor.
Title: Migration and multiculturalism in Scandinavia / edited by Eric Einhorn,
    Sherrill Harbison, and Markus Huss.
Description: Madison, Wisconsin : The University of Wisconsin Press, [2022] |
    Includes bibliographical references.
Identifiers: LCCN 2021009784 | ISBN 9780299334802 (hardcover)
Subjects: LCSH: Multiculturalism—Scandinavia. | Cultural pluralism—
    Scandinavia. | Immigrants—Scandinavia. | Scandinavia—Social conditions.
Classification: LCC HN540.Z9 M8455 2022 | DDC 306.44/60948—dc23
LC record available at https://lccn.loc.gov/2021009784

Contents

Acknowledgments	vii
Introduction	3
ERIC EINHORN, SHERRILL HARBISON, and MARKUS HUSS	

THE POLITICS OF IMMIGRATION

Immigration to Scandinavian Welfare States in the Time of Pluralism	31
GRETE BROCHMANN	
Folkhemmet: "The People's Home" as an Expression of Retrotopian Longing for Sweden before the Arrival of Mass Migration	60
ANDREAS ÖNNERFORS	
Racing Home: Swedish Reception of Black/White Identity Politics in the 2016 US Presidential Election	80
BENJAMIN R. TEITELBAUM	
Racist Resurgences: How Neoliberal and Antiracist Lefts Make Space for the Far Right in Sweden and the United States	96
CARLY ELIZABETH SCHALL	

ON THE GROUND

Coming to Terms with Belonging: Unemployed Migrants and Sociocultural Incorporation in Norway	115
KELLY MCKOWEN	
Crisis and Pattern during the 2015–2016 "Refugee Crisis" in Sweden	133
ADMIR SKODO	

Contents

Contesting National Identity as a Racial Signifier: Mixed-Race
Identity in Norway and Sweden   150
SAYAKA OSANAMI TÖRNGREN and TONY SANDSET

Managing Multicultural Tenants: Rental Agreements and Feminist
Qualms in Auður Jónsdóttir's *Deposit* and Vigdis Hjorth's
A House in Norway   170
ELISABETH OXFELDT

Swedish Identity and the Literary Imaginary   191
PETER LEONARD

The Issue of Land Rights in Contemporary Sámi Literature,
Art, and Music   205
ANNE HEITH

Afro-Swedish Renaissance   217
RYAN THOMAS SKINNER

INHERITANCE

Within Our Borders: Sámi Mobilization, the Scandinavian Response,
and World War II   241
ELLEN A. AHLNESS

Denmark in Miniature: The Interplay of Cosmopolitanism,
Nationalism, and Exoticism in Copenhagen's Tivoli   260
JULIE K. ALLEN

"Musicians Find 'Utopia' in Denmark": African American Jazz
Expatriates   281
ETHELENE WHITMIRE

Finnish War Children in Sweden after World War II and Refugee
Children of Today   297
BARBARA MATTSSON

Afterword   311
SHERRILL HARBISON

Contributors   319

Acknowledgments

We wish to give thanks to organizations and individuals who have contributed ideas and organizational effort to this book. Special thanks go to the Barbro Osher Pro Suecia Foundation for providing significant financial support to the project and to the Swedish Fulbright Hildeman exchange program, through which the editors first had the opportunity to meet and work together in the spring of 2017.

Essential practical assistance was provided by doctoral candidate Karolina Hicke, Professor Frank Hugus, Professor Emeritus James E. Cathey, translator Roger Stenlund, and administrative assistant Dolkar Gyaltsen, all in the German and Scandinavian Studies Program at the University of Massachusetts.

Additional financial support was provided by these programs and departments at the University of Massachusetts Amherst: the Department of Languages, Literatures, and Cultures; the College of Humanities and Fine Arts; the College of Social and Behavioral Sciences; the International Programs Office; the Program in Modern European Studies; and the Program in German and Scandinavian Studies.

We especially thank the four readers who cooperated with the University of Wisconsin Press and our editors, Amber Rose Cederström and Holly McArthur, for helping us improve the manuscript and bring it to life.

Migration and Multiculturalism
in Scandinavia

Introduction

ERIC EINHORN, SHERRILL HARBISON,
and MARKUS HUSS

In the early twenty-first century, almost every region of the globe is trying to cope with unprecedented human migration. In the Western European context, this development has been especially dramatic in the Scandinavian countries, which were long sources of emigration but since 1945 have become the destination for an increasingly diverse stream of migrants. In 2015, at the height of the civil conflict in Syria, more than 160,000 asylum seekers, mostly refugees from the Middle East, crossed into Sweden (population approx. ten million), which has more newcomers per capita than any other country in Europe. Sweden's prime minister then defended its open-door policy, despite growing social problems and an increasingly popular Far Right party, declaring, "My Europe doesn't build walls." But only months later, Sweden introduced border checks as it struggled to cope with up to ten thousand new arrivals every week.

In 2016 Denmark passed a notorious "asylum austerity" law, permitting police to search asylum seekers and confiscate cash and most valuables to pay for their accommodation. Because modern Scandinavia has a pronounced tradition of humanitarianism, such harsh measures startled the rest of the world. One aim of the law, a Liberal MP frankly explained, is simply to "make Denmark less attractive to foreigners."

Experiences with and concerns about clashes between religion and culture, discrimination, and crime have pervaded all of the once-relatively homogeneous Nordic states following the arrival of so many migrants and asylum seekers from war-torn countries. As these examples from Sweden and Denmark indicate, national accommodation policies have differed within the region, with Sweden traditionally being the most consistently liberal, Denmark the most volatile and restrictive, and Norway somewhere in between. In terms of economic and social stability, the question is perhaps most closely linked to the extent to which national and cultural belonging is intertwined with the historical legacy of the social democratic welfare state, the world-famous "Nordic Model" (see, e.g., Brochmann and Hagelund 2012; Byström and Frohnert 2013; Schall 2016).

Scholars in Scandinavia and elsewhere have been tackling such questions increasingly, from several different angles, during the past decade, and, given that the challenges of migration are multinational, many of these studies appear in English.[1] A scholarly assessment of the recent demographic, political, and cultural shifts in Scandinavia and how these shifts are intertwined with broader transformations in Europe and beyond is the aim of the current volume. We feel that this conversation, which ranges into so many areas of public and private life, can be most fruitful when enriched by viewpoints and approaches across a variety of disciplines, bringing together humanities and social science viewpoints and considering both theoretical perspectives and personal experiences. Because each discipline has its own intellectual objectives and research protocols, they open new perspectives on shared problems, offering a nuanced, critical understanding of contemporary Scandinavian identities and politics in transition.

This is important, because the challenge to Scandinavia's self-image involves more than numbers. Each country's past speaks to its present, influencing both current social responses and future national policies. For that reason, we have conceived this volume to include historical dimensions of the issue as well as its present dilemmas. Discussions around national belonging in Scandinavia must encompass not just modern immigrants but also the place of older historical minorities, including the indigenous Sámi in the Arctic region.

To handle such complexity, we invited scholars from the social sciences, the humanities, and beyond to share essays for the volume. Specifically, our contributors in social sciences come from political science; sociology; anthropology; human geography; migration, diversity, and welfare; and international affairs. In the humanities, we are represented by Scandinavian studies, Swedish South Asian studies, African American and African studies, culture and media studies, comparative arts and letters, German, Nordic literature, history of sciences and ideas, digital humanities, and ethnomusicology. We also have contributors from medicine and psychology. Such a variety of disciplinary objectives and methods enhances our understanding of the multifaceted social reality of immigration, cultural diversity, and ethnic pluralism

Introduction

in continental Scandinavia. By providing a wider range of disciplinary perspectives on the topic at hand, we hope to be able to inspire scholars and students alike to dig deeper and engage in a multidisciplinary conversation about the past, the present, and the future of Scandinavia in transition. The volume is an editorial project, not a group endeavor, meaning that contributors have not been involved in selecting or shaping the collection. They have spoken directly to readers, not to each other. Where appropriate, we have inserted some cross references in essays that do speak to each other.

THE ORIGINS OF MULTICULTURAL SCANDINAVIA

Even though the number of asylum seekers to Scandinavia reached a historic peak in the fall of 2015, different categories of immigrants have been entering the Scandinavian countries continuously since 1945, and some background is essential.

The nineteenth-century migration pattern that dominated Scandinavia—the predominantly one-way emigration from Europe to North America—has been replaced by much more complex patterns. Modern transportation and communication have had a significant demographic and cultural impact on migration, so that the earlier focus on integrating national minorities, or historic subcultures, has become broader issues of ethnic and cultural heterogeneity, including recent immigrants. Historical practice and experience can give us some insights into how particular Scandinavian societies deal with differences.

Prior to 1945, ethnic and cultural minorities had a long prehistory of interaction with the majority but were often concentrated geographically on the periphery, for example, Germans in southern Denmark (Jutland); Finns in North Bothnia, Sweden; Sámi across northern Norway, Sweden, and Finland. The few groups in cities, such as Jews and other religious minorities, were exceptionally small and had been present for generations. European countries have sought to regulate immigration for the past century when, following World War I, the earlier regime of relatively open borders gave way to much stricter controls. After 1945, all countries in the Western sector allowed unrestricted emigration, while for former authoritarian countries in Central and Eastern Europe, open borders, even for emigrants, is much more recent.

By 1950 the chaos of World War II population displacements had largely subsided, and internal European migration was liberalized in the West.[2] Refugees from the war and later the Cold War could be accommodated. After the 1950s, the system worked fairly smoothly because refugees were fewer and from relatively similar societies. The need for labor was voracious in most of Western Europe once the postwar recovery accelerated, roughly after 1948. Even after accommodating European migrants, most Western European states needed workers for the postwar reconstruction and then the ensuing strong economic expansion between 1950 and 1973. That opened the door to ethnically diverse migration from different regions of Europe and then from outside the continent.[3]

The Scandinavian countries had immediate postwar refugee issues, as will be discussed briefly below, but by the early 1950s that problem had disappeared. Until the 1970s, migration within Scandinavia was mainly from Finland to Sweden. The loss of significant territory to the Soviet Union led to a wave of Finnish refugees (mainly from eastern Karelia) who needed to be resettled at a time of postwar austerity, and the availability of Finnish labor for the dynamic postwar Swedish economy was a boon for both countries.

Cultural Issues in the Context of Immigration

Throughout most of the twentieth century, the Nordic countries were identified as among Europe's most ethnically, religiously, and culturally homogeneous. That homogeneity has been exaggerated. There has always been a distinctly different indigenous Sámi population in Norway, Sweden, and Finland, and the Sámi people have endured cultural deracination programs in all their host countries. Other social cleavages and political divisions in Scandinavia were over economic and class issues, not cultural ones. Even here, however, in each country there were significant divisions. Examples below highlight some of those that put contemporary cultural differences into some broader perspective.

Denmark claims to be Europe's oldest monarchy, but the country's borders have undergone many changes over the centuries. Until the nineteenth century, the Danish realm comprised no fewer than six entities. The "kingdom" of Denmark consisted of Denmark proper and the province of Norway. The latter had been joined to the Danish monarch for centuries until 1814, when the Treaty of Kiel awarded Norway to Sweden. The duchies of Schleswig, Holstein, and Lauenburg consisted of mainly German speakers, with a substantial Danish minority in Schleswig (Slesvig). Schleswig and Holstein were bound by medieval contracts. After 1815 Holstein and Lauenburg belonged to the German confederation, despite having a nominally Danish "duke." Iceland and the Faroe Islands had come to Denmark along with Norway in

Introduction

the Middle Ages and remained part of the kingdom after 1814. Greenland was a Danish colony whose ties to Copenhagen were weak until well into the twentieth century. Finally, Denmark acquired several Caribbean islands (now the US Virgin Islands), a toehold in India, and several trading forts in Africa. Each of these territories possessed its own culture, but only Norway was of significant size, and it produced several major figures that influenced Denmark. Denmark was reduced to its modern boundaries through the loss of Norway (1814), the German duchies (1864), the Virgin Islands (1917), and Iceland (1944). The Faroe Islands (1948) and Greenland (1979 and 2009) gained home rule and remain part of the Danish realm.

The Swedish realm gained Finland in the Middle Ages and the southern Swedish provinces (Skåne, Halland, and Blekinge) from Denmark in the seventeenth century. By the end of the seventeenth century, Sweden had possessions across Scandinavia, northern Germany, and the Baltic states. Norway resisted incorporation into the Swedish kingdom in 1814 but was an autonomous part of a dual monarchy until 1905. Finland was transferred to Russia in 1809, while Sweden's small colonial holdings in North America and the Caribbean disappeared earlier. Sweden's German territories likewise disappeared early in the nineteenth century. Within the Swedish kingdom there remained a small but geographically concentrated population of Sámi and Finns.[4] Between 1850 and 1930, nearly a million Swedes immigrated, mostly to North America but also to Denmark.[5]

Finland had never been an independent country until its liberation from Russian rule in 1917. Ironically, the transfer of Finland from Sweden to the Russian Empire in 1809 gave birth to a Finnish polity and a revival of Finnish culture under the limited sovereignty of the Duchy of Finland. Within Finland a small but powerful Swedish-speaking minority formed much of the country's political and economic elite until well into the twentieth century. Finland lost significant territory to the Soviet Union in 1940 and 1944, with a large population transfer. After a century of Russian rule, there were only a few thousand ethnic Russians in Finland in 1910. That did not prevent late efforts at Russification of the public administration, but turmoil and war in Russia paved the way for Finnish independence (granted by the Bolsheviks). Nevertheless, the Russian Orthodox Church became one of two state-supported religious institutions, despite a membership of less than 2 percent of the population.

Norway kept its cultural identity despite centuries of dynastic union with Denmark and Sweden. Adjustments of border territories with Sweden were

8   ERIC EINHORN, SHERRILL HARBISON, and MARKUS HUSS

often violent but without ethnic significance. Norway's modern culture and politics blossomed through the nineteenth century but were shaped by tension between urban centers with cultures and language close to Denmark and rural and peripheral regions that kept more traditional language and culture. As in Sweden and Finland, a Sámi minority lived in the northern provinces, but the majority perceived cultural distinctions in Norway as between two cultures—rural and urban—and one ethnicity. As discussed in the chapters by Ellen Ahlness and Anne Heith, this goal of national homogeneity neglected Sámi identity and interests in all three of the northern Scandinavian countries.

Iceland has been called Europe's first "new" country after mainly Norwegian settlers moved there in the late ninth century, bringing a smaller population of enslaved captives, mainly from Ireland. Eventually, the island came under the Norwegian king and followed Norway into the arms of Denmark in the thirteenth century. Iceland's small population nevertheless maintained an increasingly autonomous culture. Immigration to Iceland after the Middle Ages was limited to Danish merchants and administrators, while a handful of Icelanders went to Copenhagen for higher education. Democratic reforms in Denmark paved the way for Icelandic self-determination with home rule in 1918 and full independence in 1944. Iceland could truly claim to be Europe's most homogeneous country (all 369,000 citizens) until non-Scandinavian immigration began gradually after 1970.

While a small Scandinavian population settled in Greenland after 980 and maintained a marginal existence until the early fifteenth century, the country remained in the hands of its small Inuit population. Europeans explored the island from the late fifteenth century, but permanent European colonization commenced only in the late eighteenth century, with traders and missionaries dedicated to Christianizing the native population. Greenland remained a Danish colony after 1814 and began to get local government at the end of the nineteenth century. Limited home rule was gained in 1953, after which Denmark slowly expanded training and empowerment of the native population. "Greenlandization" has progressed with only a small Danish cadre (excluding US military personnel, who have manned bases there since World War II). The island continues to receive significant subsidies from Denmark (as do the Faroe Islands). Inuit Greenlanders are nearly 90 percent of the island's population of fifty-six thousand, while some nineteen thousand Greenlanders live in Denmark (Amundsen 2013).

This summary reflects that the definition of Danes, Swedes, Norwegians, and others has evolved. In nineteenth-century Copenhagen, one would have

Introduction

heard various Danish regional dialects, a substantial amount of German and Norwegian, some Swedish, and the occasional Icelandic or Greenlandic. English, German, and French were widely spoken in all major Scandinavian cities. Craftsmen and traders from all over Europe moved freely as guild rules permitted. Only as the ideology of nationalism grew would people question the presence of "outsiders."

The Scandinavian national cultures were shaped by two powerful institutions. The first was the church, particularly post-Reformation Evangelical Lutheran Protestantism. Until recently, all Nordic countries had an established church to which nearly all inhabitants belonged, at least nominally. Religious tolerance, at first quite limited, gradually developed, along with democratic government, over the nineteenth century, but a single dominant religion remained highly influential until the spread of secularism during the past century. The positive aspect of this was the lack of serious religious antagonism, in comparison with much of premodern Europe. To be sure, different forms of Lutheranism in each of the countries, such as fundamentalism versus more cosmopolitan interpretations (e.g., Pietism vs. Grundtvigianism in Denmark), produced periodic cultural struggles.

Religion played a major role in the relatively early spread of mass literacy in Scandinavia. Children had to learn to read the Bible to become confirmed members of the state church, but the church also allowed them to read other things and formed the background for a literate peasantry and urban population in the nineteenth century. Religious tolerance spread slowly. Norway incorporated anti-Jewish and anti-Jesuit articles in the original Norwegian Constitution, composed in Eidsvold in 1814, just as religious toleration was expanded in Denmark to Jews and other minorities. Swedish restrictions on dissenting or different religions were a factor in Sweden's massive nineteenth-century emigration, but tolerance increased after 1860.

The spread of secularism through the twentieth century resulted in the disestablishment of the Norwegian and Swedish state churches in recent decades, although ties continue in Denmark, Finland, and Iceland. Much if not most of traditional Scandinavian folk culture remains closely tied to religious history, and nearly all holidays have a religious origin, even if they rarely elicit broad religious activity. The decline in religious activity has been dramatic, with only a tiny percentage of Scandinavians regularly attending church services.[6] Predictably, the spread of secularism and the liberalization of the traditional Lutheran religion have become factors in Scandinavian discomfort with the culture and politics of religious immigrants, especially Muslims.

The Origins of "Multiculturalism"

Although the term "multiculturalism" is contemporary, the phenomenon is not. It is not merely a demographic or sociological factual description; it implies a collection of history and policies dealing with ethnic, religious, or linguistic pluralism. In the view of some scholars, it may also define an ideology of how a multicultural society should accommodate its various parts. Most commentators assume that multiculturalism should imply an open and tolerant attitude to social group diversity. The chapters in this volume show many facets of these issues.

The historical lack of sharp religious or ethnic antagonism in Scandinavia did not prevent the growth of alternative cultures. Just as religion was beginning to decline, class and regional divisions became more visible and antagonistic.[7] Rural-urban tensions grew throughout the nineteenth and early twentieth centuries.[8] Distrust of "capital city" domination spurred a variety of rural movements, including the folk high schools (*folkehøjskole*) and agrarian cooperatives.[9] In short, cultural difference depended on how groups perceived themselves and their neighbors both within and across national borders. Across nineteenth-century Scandinavia, popular movements (*folkebevægelser*) sprang to life to promote various political, religious, and cultural agendas. As civil rights expanded, a myriad of newspapers and other publications connected the newly literate public. This coincided with the era of mass emigration of Scandinavians, primarily to North America. Many of these social movements had political agendas; others, like the temperance movement, cut across class lines. A special challenge faced the women's movements, which pursued social, economic, and political rights across many traditional social divisions.

The evolution of historic craft guilds into industrial labor unions had become a major force in Scandinavian society by the end of the nineteenth century. Most labor unions were tied to the rising socialist movements, but they became more than mere economic and political agencies. A "workers' culture" took shape following patterns seen earlier by educated peasants. In the first half of the twentieth century, worker organizations became a powerful mass movement, sponsoring newspapers, publishers, music and arts activities, sports, and education. They built urban housing, financial institutions, and consumer cooperatives. Not all labor movements were peaceful, but the increasingly democratic Nordic countries accepted such social and political organizations. Most socialist labor organizations were open to all supporters, just as the social democratic parties—after 1920 consistently the largest parties in Denmark, Norway, and Sweden—formed political coalitions with

Introduction

agrarian and moderate nonsocialist parties. In short, they became part of the mainstream culture as industrialization spread.[10]

The result of decades of social mobilization was in fact an attenuation of class, ethnic, and regional antagonisms. Reform movements secured voting rights, parliamentary democracy, basic social insurance, and industrial regulation. In the context of democratic parliamentary politics, coalitions became a necessity. Issues such as Norwegian independence (1905) and external threats during World War I supported gradual reconciliation. There were, of course, recurrent crises that sharpened social divisions in Scandinavia. The revolutionary events of 1917–20 echoed across the region, producing sporadic confrontations and violence. The short but brutal Finnish civil war was the most significant and would reverberate for two generations. In Sweden, economic strife and material hardship during World War I led to the final breakthrough of parliamentary government in 1918.[11] In Norway, the socialist/labor movement split into revolutionary ("pro-Bolshevik") and evolutionary wings. In Denmark, a similar but smaller split divided the Left.

Again, in the 1930s, economic crisis strained society with fascistic movements arising on the right. The response to these prolonged and severe crises brought about Scandinavia's famous "politics of compromise," which saw pragmatic social democratic parties work with nonsocialist parties to relieve the worst of the Great Depression.[12] The decision of the mainstream social democratic / labor parties to become broader "people's parties" promoted political compromise with a goal of class advancement rather than class struggle. The proportional electoral system adopted after 1920 had already made single-party parliamentary majorities nearly impossible. Most centrist and conservative parties followed suit, but antidemocratic forces remained potent in the form of Stalinist Communist parties and fascist parties. Rightist movements disappeared, at least for a generation, after 1945, while less rigid Marxist parties evolved after the 1950s.

The ethnic dimension of multiculturalism was less visible but not entirely absent in the interwar period. First, the era of mass Scandinavian emigration had been suspended by World War I and scarcely revived in the 1920s. Access to many destinations became more restrictive, especially the United States, with its quotas and ethnically discriminatory immigration laws of 1921 and 1924.[13] Second, by the 1930s economic conditions were bad enough in North America to lead to a modest "reverse immigration." Third, widespread unemployment caused the Scandinavian countries themselves to restrict immigration, so that few non-Scandinavians could obtain entry and work permits. Some political refugees from Soviet Russia and later Nazi Germany were admitted, but ethnic refugees (e.g., Jews from Germany) were admitted only in very small numbers.[14] Nationalism and ethnic chauvinism were rampant, as were policies of social engineering that often included biological theories of eugenics. Sweden implemented some racial hygiene policies, including sterilization practices, that would continue for decades.[15]

World War II changed the status quo. Finland was at war with the Soviet Union from November 1939 to March 1940 and again from June 1941. In April 1940 Denmark and Norway were attacked and occupied by Germany. Prior to the German invasion, some seventy thousand Finnish children were evacuated, mainly to Sweden but also to Norway and Denmark. Sweden's reluctance to accept European refugees was suspended for its Nordic neighbors. During the war some fifty thousand Norwegians escaped to Sweden, including the minority of Norwegian Jews who were not captured by the Germans or by their Norwegian collaborators ("Norway in Exile" 2017). Although the wave of refugees from Denmark started later, about fifteen thousand Danes found safety in Sweden, including 95 percent of the Danish Jewish population (about seventy-five hundred people).

At the end of the war, the movement of displaced and fleeing people grew sharply in this region as elsewhere. In addition to Danes and Norwegians, soldiers and civilians from the Baltic states fled to Sweden. Civilians were accepted as refugees, but military personnel were a problem, given Soviet demands for their repatriation. This was eventually done, with later recriminations. Most Baltic military prisoners received relatively mild punishment (by Soviet standards of the time!), but there were trials and executions of several Baltic officers. In the case of Norwegian and Danish refugees, most returned to their homeland in 1945–46.

About 238,000 German civilians fled to southern Denmark during the war's final weeks. This number amounted to nearly 8 percent of the Danish population (Labourer 2016).[16] Although the Danes were anxious to be rid of these unwelcomed enemy "guests," the Allied powers in Germany could not receive so many displaced persons. It would take years before the refugee camps were closed.

POSTWAR MIGRATION:
THE CALM BEFORE THE STORM

By the early 1950s, most displaced persons had been returned to their homelands or had moved on to third countries. Demographic issues were secondary

Introduction

to postwar reconstruction. Sweden's neutrality prevented the dislocation and destruction that faced Norway and Finland. Denmark had instances of wartime sabotage and destruction, but they were minor. All the Nordic countries depended on European economic reconstruction to energize their traditional export industries. The US European Recovery Program (Marshall Plan) helped Denmark, Norway, Sweden, and, indirectly, Finland. The latter's economy was strongly influenced by large reparation payments and deliveries to the Soviet Union. Emigration was again possible, but there was little immigration to the Nordic countries until well into the 1950s. Finland had to settle thousands of expellees from Karelia (eastern Finland) and other territories seized by the Soviet Union. Both Norway and Denmark had net emigration most years until the 1960s. For example, in 1947–48 and again in 1955–56, Danish emigration reached about thirty-five thousand per year, the highest in a generation. Immigration was around twenty thousand per year, consisting mainly of returning Danes (Danmarks Statistik 2000, 51).

Norway had similar trends, and statistical data show that in 1950 there were 46,562 people in the country who had been born abroad (total population about 3.265 million). The three largest sources were Sweden, the United States, and Denmark. Those born in non-Western countries numbered about 1,000 (but many of them could be of Norwegian ethnicity). Foreign citizens numbered 15,797 (0.48 percent of the population), with the same three countries accounting for more than half (Statistisk Sentralbyrå 1960, 17–18). Postwar Sweden was one of the continent's most prosperous countries and attracted on average thirty-five to forty thousand immigrants per year from 1947 to 1965. Emigration was typically under twenty thousand annually during this period (Statistiska Centralbyrån [SCB] 2008). In 1954 the Nordic countries signed an agreement to allow their citizens to move freely between the countries for work.[17] Initially, the flow was mainly of Finns to Sweden, where economic conditions were considerably better.

From Guest Workers to Permanent Migrants

By the mid-1960s, improved economic conditions in all the Scandinavian countries were beginning to create labor shortages. Already in the late 1940s, Sweden's labor migration policies established a pattern that would become common in northern Europe. A shortage of mainly industrial labor pushed firms to request permission to recruit labor from abroad (consisting mainly of southern Europeans, displaced Germans, and Finns). Labor unions wanted to exploit the shortage to raise wages and guarantee full employment. The compromise would be the flexible recruitment of "guest workers," who were expected to return to their homelands after a few years or when the demand for labor slackened (Svanberg 2017, 156–74). Grete Brochmann's chapter in this volume relates the expansion of this policy over the following three decades and its expansion to Denmark and Norway as well as to most of Western Europe.

In addition to imported labor, the issue of refugees arose as countries such as Chile and Greece and later many Third World countries fell under regimes that violated basic human rights. In 1951 most UN members had signed a refugee convention in Geneva to prevent a repetition of the "closed-door" policies for victims of fascism in the 1930s. The legacy of Baltic and other European refugees in Sweden after World War II set some precedents. Reluctantly, the Swedish government allowed especially Estonian and Jewish refugees to establish various cultural and educational institutions. This was discreet "multiculturalism," but the ethnic minorities otherwise assimilated quickly into the Swedish economic and political mainstream (Wickström 2015, 31–34).

As Brochmann discusses in her chapter, prior to the 1970s the Scandinavian countries had assumed that migrants would follow two courses. Those who were temporary workers (i.e., guest workers) would generally accommodate their home culture to the Scandinavian scene but would stay only for a limited time. Those migrants and refugees who might stay indefinitely were expected to assimilate to their new homeland's culture, as had most of the postwar refugees. At the very least this would mean learning the national language, accepting national laws and customs, and being discreet in celebrating their original culture. It was assumed that assimilation would gradually solve the cultural issues, especially if the number of new entrants was limited. Public policy was mainly focused on providing adequate housing and guaranteeing comparable working conditions and pay. Strong unions made certain that foreign labor could not be unfairly exploited.

It was clear by the 1970s that many migrants had no intention of leaving and instead wanted to bring family members to their new homeland; to keep their native culture, religion, and customs; and, in many cases, to live together with similar migrants. In 1975 Sweden decided to embrace multiculturalism—that is, full acceptance of separate ethnic subcultures—on an indefinite basis (Runblom 1998, 1). Because such a large portion of its recent immigrants came from Finland, a neighboring Nordic country with long historical ties to Sweden, accommodating them was rarely a serious challenge. This meant

Introduction

schooling immigrant children in their parents' native language (as a second language), encouraging their ethnic religious and civil organizations, and creating liberal family reunification policies. Given a housing policy that allowed immigrants to settle where they wished, de facto ghettoization resulted when most chose to live near compatriots.[18]

The Scandinavian countries tightened criteria for economic migration with the economic slowdown of the 1970s, but refugee asylum regimes remained quite liberal for another decade or more. The new populist New Right parties focused and articulated rising anti-immigration sentiment.[19] After 1990 the issue became politically fraught. First, the numbers reached a critical mass in which multicultural communities became increasingly visible in and around larger cities. The disintegration of Yugoslavia, with its ensuing bloody conflicts, produced a wave of migrants toward Northern and Western Europe. The expansion of the European Union brought all the Scandinavian countries into the "open borders" regime by the mid-1990s. The eastward expansion of the EU after 2003 widened the income gap with the new European labor market just as non-European migration accelerated. Political debates over migration, asylum, and integration policies moved up the political agenda, especially in Denmark and Norway.[20]

Although Sweden had by far the largest and longest experience with multiculturalism, the debate was restrained until the sudden appearance of a populist protest party, New Democracy (Ny Demokrati), in 1991. That party was mainly concerned about the social costs of immigrants but became increasingly critical of the size and composition of Sweden's growing immigrant community. The party collapsed in the 1994 elections, and there was no party strongly critical of Swedish immigration and integration policies in parliament until 2010.[21] With the rise of the Sweden Democrats (Sverigedemokraterna), their entry into Parliament in 2010, and their notable gains in 2014 and 2018, Sweden's unique status ended.

Hence in the second decade of the twenty-first century, Scandinavia faced perhaps the largest influx and settlement of non-Scandinavians in its modern history. Comparisons between present and earlier phases of immigration, state policies, and public discourses reveal common concerns, not least regarding the inevitable question of national belonging: Who belongs, and who does not belong, in today's Scandinavian societies? Formal citizenship requirements aside, what are the tacit cultural components of "Swedishness," "Danishness," and "Norwegianness"? Each of the Scandinavian countries keeps detailed population statistics. In Norway and Denmark about 20 percent of the current population either was born abroad or is descended from at least one foreign parent. In Sweden the figure is close to 30 percent. Further details include counts of those of Western or non-Western background, as well as a myriad of educational, occupational, criminal, and other social statistics.[22]

Despite increasingly restrictive policies, Scandinavia, like much of Europe, has a large migration challenge with few signs of abatement. Boatloads of migrants are launched into the Mediterranean nearly daily from North Africa, often as part of human trafficking schemes. Although both international conventions and specific European Union policies have sought to create a legal and political regime for migration, chaos is more apparent than policy. Across Europe, policies range from firmly closed doors in most of central and eastern Europe to desperate attempts to accommodate in Southern and Western Europe. The role of the immigration issue in the June 2016 British referendum to leave the EU (Brexit) was not the first, but it was possibly the loudest thunderclap to date.[23] No issue is more prominent on the European political agenda.

While the past century saw at first roughly fifty years of social convergence of incomes, welfare, and cultures throughout Scandinavia, the last fifty years have seen divergence as immigrant populations have grown to become a substantial portion of the population. The remaining integration issues of second- and even third-generation immigrants suggest a prolonged period of adjustment for the foreseeable future.

The European Context

This overview makes evident how manifold and complex the issue of immigration to Scandinavia has been and continues to be. However, it is also important to remember that Scandinavia remains linked to broader international developments, since the current wave of migration has affected all European countries. Their political responses to this have also been determined in part by historical legacies, especially their experiences of World War II. It was in France, both split and occupied by the Germans, that beginning fifty years ago a number of intellectuals developed the Nouvelle Droite (ND, New Right) political philosophy. Since its first heyday in the late 1970s, it has increasingly permeated the political atmosphere of Europe, including Scandinavia. This variety of thinking was deliberately hard to categorize, an attempt at a "postmodern synthesis" that would replace the traditional Left/Right dichotomy with a revolutionary alternative vision.

The inherent hazard for the Right in Europe is its historical association with fascism, and despite claiming to be "postfascist" and "antiracist," the

Introduction

New Right has not fully distanced itself from this heritage. Fascism (which Sindre Bangstad notes is often used as an "all-purpose term of abuse" [2014, 85]) is a notoriously imprecise and unreliable analytical term, and already in the 1960s French ND theorists made deliberate efforts to cleanse their program of "outdated vocabulary" for the postwar liberal and antifascist context. Their strategy was borrowed from the Marxist theorist Antonio Gramsci, who contended that "political movements needed to attain cultural hegemony in society to be successful" (Bar-On 2013, 5).[24] A right-wing Gramscianism could offer new ways of seeing the world, they reasoned, using a nonviolent, "metapolitical" stance to combat the European social elites and intellectuals, who have been conditioned by negative historical associations with the Right since World War II.

Unlike the neoliberal theorists of the Anglo-American New Right, who focus on accommodating global capitalism, the French ND, which has become the foundation for all European New Right thinking, is opposed to capitalism for its materialism, greed, rampant egoism, and spiritual vacuousness. This suggests a commonality with the New Left, except that the ND is also opposed to socialism, communism, and every other political scheme with eschatological promises and egalitarian aims.

Tamir Bar-On, scholar of the ND, explains that its quest is "Europe for Europeans," and the ideal is the ancient Indo-European "natural" hierarchical social structure, first described by Georges Dumézil in 1929, a tripartite pyramid structure of leaders above warriors, warriors above workers (see Dumézil [1958] 1973, 1959; Haugen 1973). Like Friedrich Nietzsche, the ND blames Christianity for introducing the false goal of egalitarianism, from which, they contest, came the philosophical errors that have plagued the West: "The primordial concerns of the ND for about 45 years have been its idiosyncratic rejection of multiculturalism and the creation of 'rooted,' homogenous, ethnic communities within a pan-European context. In the ND worldview, individual rights, human rights, multiculturalism, liberalism, socialism, capitalism, communism, and administratively imposed equality all seek to destroy local, particular communities worldwide" (Bar-On 2013, 144). The ND's vision of an "alternative modernity" would not give up technical progress or modern conveniences but would reorient Europe to communitarian political systems, "fusing ancient democratic longings with ethnic homogeneity" (145).

Hence, the ND renounces the old colonialist-racist policies of extermination of the Other, as well as contemporary assimilation policies of nation-states, in favor of the "right to difference," an ethnopluralism that at first glance sounds like modern leftist identity politics but also like Johann Gottfried Herder's Romantic notion of "the nation" as an organic entity. This is by design: the old Left/Right political dichotomies are out of date, the ND claims; many of the ND's complaints resemble those of the Marxist revolutionaries of May 1968, from which the ND took inspiration. By focusing on this cultural terrain, the ND has attempted to distance itself from extreme right-wing populist parties, such as those of Marine Le Pen in France and Victor Orban in Hungary, as well as from ultranationalist terrorist movements.

Since the 1990s, transversal issues for Left and Right have included immigration, terrorism, the fate of the secular state, welfare state depletion during economic decline, and concerns about the EU project vis-à-vis national sovereignty (and also the eligibility of Muslim Turkey) (Bar-On 2014). But the chief red flag about immigrants has been cultural. Challenges to liberal values such as free speech (the Danish "cartoon crisis" and the Swedish artist Lars Vilks) and cultural assumptions (eating pork or not as part of food-cultural identity) have produced what Bar-On (2014) calls an emotionally driven "post-political biopolitics" of fear formulated as defense against potential victimization or harassment. A serious flash point has been feminism, a powerful force in Scandinavian public policy for the past 150 years. The clash between Scandinavian norms and Islamic customs about women's dress and domestic status has alarmed Scandinavian women and vexed human rights advocates; this has been exploited by the Scandinavian New Right.

Fear is also raised about ideological Islamic terrorism, which has in fact been rare in Scandinavia. (A more troublesome matter may be alienated Scandinavians with an immigrant family background who are afflicted by "color-blind racism" and who become radicalized at home.) The worst terrorist act in Scandinavia was in fact committed in Oslo and at Utøya in Norway in 2011 by the home-grown ethnic purist and anti-immigrant Anders Behring Breivik, who feared the advent of "Eurabia," or a "reverse Crusades" resulting in the colonization of Europe by Islam (Bangstad 2014, 130). To some Scandinavians caught in this cycle, resentment and nostalgia for old familiar folkways makes the ND's claim that multiculturalism actually undermines the world's richness and diversity—which are properly embodied in "rooted" ethnic communities that must be protected—an easy sell.

Introduction

Increased immigration to Scandinavia has produced different and shifting national policies of acceptance, distribution, and integration, with mixed results. The essays in this volume are grouped in three categories. Part 1, "The Politics of Immigration," explores the political evolution of current national policies. Essays in part 2, "On the Ground," the longest section, address practical challenges in today's multicultural Scandinavian reality from anthropological, sociological, and artistic vantage points. Finally, in part 3, "Inheritance," contributors explain some of the historical experiences of "otherness" in the region that underlie and inform contemporary attitudes.

THE POLITICS OF IMMIGRATION

The volume begins with Grete Brochmann's close analysis of how the three Scandinavian countries' current immigration policies developed so that issues particular to individual countries can be understood in their own context. The Scandinavian welfare state, or Nordic Model, is composed of universal and generous policies in each country, but there are still significant differences between them. All were founded by ethnically homogeneous populations practicing a degree of social engineering with the expectation of full employment. As immigration became increasingly non-Western and economic conditions more precarious, new populist parties arose promoting tighter restrictions and less generous treatment of newcomers, notably in Denmark, less so in Norway, and least in Sweden.

Andreas Önnerfors showcases how the history of the Swedish social democratic welfare state, subsumed under the concept of *folkhemmet* (the people's home), has turned into a contested battle ground of politicocultural memory. In his close reading of Jimmie Åkesson's anti-immigration rhetoric of the right-wing populist party Sverigedemokraterna (the Sweden Democrats), Önnerfors shows how *folkhemmet* is actively used to evoke symbolically charged memories of an uncorrupted golden age based on a highly selective and revisionist account of Swedish history.

The chapter by Benjamin R. Teitelbaum traces the Swedish reception of the 2016 US presidential election, exploring the ways Swedes embrace, reject, translate, and transform American racial discourses for their own purposes. The widespread official Swedish self-image is one of a color-blind society that has abandoned racism to the scrap heap of history. But exposure to American racial politics has opened the possibility that indeed race lives in their own society as well. Teitelbaum examines Swedes' general hesitation to acknowledge domestic racialization in light of political investments in Sweden's status as an enlightened global beacon of moral authority and a liberal, uncontestably open society.

Carly Elizabeth Schall further explores parallels between the American and Swedish experience, specifically the antiracist Left, in the wake of disruptive political events (e.g., the Swedish governmental parliamentary crisis of 2014 and the election of Donald Trump in the United States in 2016). She argues that, despite national variations, investment in neoliberal policies in both Left movements have unwittingly aided in the resurgencies of the Far Right, leaving voids in the battle against more institutional, collective forms of racism.

ON THE GROUND

Kelly McKowen provides an anthropological perspective in Norway, interviewing immigrants to examine their experiences as unemployment benefit recipients with the country's welfare system. He maps the processes by which they identify with, assent to, and contest what they perceive to be societal expectations in their host country. McKowen concludes that the Norwegian welfare state functions as a powerful homogenizing force to shape practices and values about the relationship between work and welfare across multiple ethnic lines.

Admir Skodo provides a comparison between the perspective of the Swedish state during the 2015–16 "refugee crisis" and that of local officials, voluntary workers, and Afghan asylum seekers on the ground. While the state saw the refugee crisis as a national security threat and bureaucratic crisis, the municipalities saw it as a strain on the welfare state bureaucracy that was in fact successfully managed. The lessons and resources of these experiences, he argues, were lost on the government and the state, even as they were establishing new practices to better deal with another mass entry.

Sayaka Osanami Törngren and Tony Sandset study how the mixed population in Norway and Sweden (defined as having one parent who is considered ethnically Nordic and one parent who is seen as an "immigrant") becomes invisible or visible as "foreign" depending on the phenotype. The authors, based on thirty-eight interviews with mixed-race Swedes and Norwegians, illustrate how individuals are ascribed with the immigrant category based on the visibility of mixedness such as phenotype or name, challenging the official, supposedly color-blind categorization of its people into ethnic Norwegian/ Swedes or "immigrants."

Introduction

A great deal of contemporary artistic material deals with the issue of Nordic society and its relationship to immigrants. Elisabeth Oxfeldt discusses examples of contemporary Norwegian and Icelandic literature about majority-minority relations. The novels tell stories of capitalist women belonging to the so-called creative class, sustaining their leisurely freelance existence by renting out property to underprivileged immigrant women. The tales function as allegories, revealing the dark sides of privilege, altruism, capitalism, feminism, and creative ambition as both protagonists metapoetically question their own global engagement without providing clear pointers to where their reflections could lead.

Peter Leonard addresses a new kind of Swedish literature written early in the twenty-first century by authors with at least one immigrant parent. This "second generation," including Jonas Hassen Khemiri, Johannes Anyuru, Marjaneh Bakhtiari, and Alejandro Leiva Wenger, have pushed boundaries of literary language and national belonging, carving out fictive space for speculative forms of identity against a background of assumed homogeneity. Leonard observes both commonality and difference between their authorships and considers their differences from first-generation immigrant writers such as Theodore Kallifatides.

Cultural differences are also at the basis of struggle between Scandinavian nation-states and the indigenous populations, whose concept of land rights is based on seasonal sustainability rather than restrictions and fixed borders. Anne Heith illustrates how Sámi are now employing artistic expression for political activism, focusing on the epic poem *Aednan*, by Linnea Axelsson; visual art by Anders Sunna; and popular music by Sofia Jannok. She analyzes their work against the backdrop of conflicts between Sámi and the Beowulf Mining Company in the Jokkmokk area and the Girjas Sámi village, which is prosecuting the Swedish state over rights to use the mountain areas of their village threatened by mining.

Ryan Thomas Skinner examines the development in Sweden of a dynamic and diverse Afro-diasporic art world, which he calls an "Afro-Swedish social and cultural renaissance," in contemporary Swedish society, manifest in theater, music, film, and literature. Focusing on two pop music artists, a theater director, and a filmmaker, he considers the diasporic legacies that inform this work (from midcentury Harlem to postcolonial Africa), the doubly conscious identities of the artists who make it, and their racially conscious critique of anti-Blackness in the Swedish public sphere.

22 ERIC EINHORN, SHERRILL HARBISON, and MARKUS HUSS

INHERITANCE

World War II negatively affected the indigenous Sámi populations of Norway, Sweden, and Finland. Ellen A. Ahlness studies political obstacles to Sámi efforts to regularize their traditional nomadic mobility across national borders. This movement began in the 1920s but was inhibited during World War II when international oversight was directed elsewhere. The differing situations in Norway (occupied), Sweden (neutral), and Finland (war front) led to different kinds and degrees of internal restriction and conflict over Sámi rights, and Ahlness shows that the greater the level of wartime conflict, the more coercive was domestic repression of the Sámi.

Julie K. Allen explores how, since its opening in 1843, Copenhagen's Tivoli Gardens has been a hybrid of the nationalistic and the exotic that continues to fuel Danish national branding efforts today. The park's Orientalist symbols and imported foods and products were originally meant to bring worldly sophistication to a capital city that felt itself to be "small and dull." Over the generations, Tivoli's combination of "cosmopolitanism and banal nationalism" came to symbolize Denmark as a "pretty tolerant place where everyone should feel welcome," but that reputation is now being tested by the country's controversial policies toward immigrants, especially in the context of its historical engagement with colonialism and imperialism.

Ethelene Whitmire's chapter also turns to Denmark to explore the experiences of African American jazz musicians there during the second half of the twentieth century. Male African American jazz musicians found that Denmark provided an environment where they could work, create big bands and record labels, and have increased productivity as composers and arrangers. Denmark also gave them financial security as artists. Though living in Denmark was not always a utopia, Whitmire shows that a surprisingly large number of noted African American jazz musicians spent the rest of their lives there.

The plight of uprooted migrant children is examined by psychologist Barbara Mattsson using illustrations from the World War II era. Around seventy thousand Finnish children were sent to Sweden during World War II, and seventy-one hundred never returned after the war. Using in-depth interviews of ten Finnish children as adults, Mattsson explores the social and psychological impacts of the transplant on them, showing how their struggle to master their losses was lifelong, even when they succeeded in adapting themselves in Sweden. Her findings can inform the needs and challenges of unaccompanied refugee minors today.

Introduction

The volume is concluded by Sherrill Harbison's synthetizing afterword, in which she identifies the overall tendencies, challenges, and contemporary trajectories of Scandinavian identities in transition.

NOTES

1. Previous scholarship with a multidisciplinary intent appears in *New Dimensions of Diversity in Nordic Culture and Society* (Björklund and Lindqvist 2016). The volume employs a broad definition of diversity, including intersectional approaches (intersections of gender, sex, class, ethnicity, race) to study current Scandinavian societies and cultures. In the volume *Debating Multiculturalism in the Nordic Welfare States*, Peter Kivisto and Östen Wahlbäck identify the Nordic countries as an "important research site for exploring the ways in which the politics of identity and recognition play out in societies that are committed to redistributive politics" (2013, 9). *Crisis in the Nordic Nations and Beyond: At the Intersection of Environment, Finance and Multiculturalism* (Loftsdóttir and Jensen 2014) interrogates the crisis concept as a means of gaining new insights into contemporary Nordic societies against the backdrop of global financial crises, environmental crises, and the widespread notion of a "failed" multiculturalism. Grappling with similar broad societal and political issues connected to today's Nordic multicultural societies, *Literature, Language, and Multiculturalism in Scandinavia and the Low Countries* (Behschnitt, De Mul, and Minnaard 2013) concentrates on artistic expression, addressing multiculturalism as a contested and multifaceted topic in contemporary literature from Sweden, Denmark, Flanders, and the Netherlands. Scholars of critical race studies and critical whiteness studies have produced scholarship of relevance to the current volume also. *Whiteness and Postcolonialism in the Nordic Region: Exceptionalism, Migrant Others and National Identities* (Loftsdóttir and Jensen 2012) interrogates the history of racist pseudoscientific theories in Scandinavia and how these categories came to be used against various national minorities considered to be ethnic and racial "others." The special issue "Nordic Whiteness" of *Scandinavian Studies* from 2017 continues the effort of scrutinizing the historical legacy and contemporary dynamics of tacit racial assumptions behind "Nordicness," in which whiteness is a crucial component. The volume *Afro-Nordic Landscapes: Equality and Race in Northern Europe* (2014), edited by Michael McEachrane, also critically addresses the tendency in Nordic majority societies to regard race as an obsolete and irrelevant concept, as well as the widespread unwillingness to acknowledge everyday racism.

2. One should not minimize the chaos of post-1945 forced and voluntary migrations. An estimated 11.5 million Germans were expelled or fled eastern and central Europe by 1950. By 1959 nine hundred thousand European refugees had been resettled in Europe and nearly one million more in North America, Australia, and elsewhere outside Europe (Wasserstein 2011).

3. This economic migration and its multicultural challenges for Britain, France, Germany, and the Netherlands is discussed in Chin (2017). She does not discuss the Scandinavian countries. The Nordic countries are treated in detail by Wickström (2015).

4. The Finns were concentrated in the Torne Valley district. Their descendants are today referred to as Tornedalians and are recognized as one of Sweden's five national minorities.

5. This was about a quarter of the Swedish population (Westin 2006).

6. A recent survey and analysis of religious attitudes in Denmark and Sweden is Zuckerman (2008).

7. As social scientists would generally agree, "class" is socially constructed. Premodern Europe typically divided society into peasants (the clear majority), the bourgeoisie or middle class, and the aristocracy. Some would add the clergy as a separate class. Nineteenth-century Europe saw the rise of an industrial working class or proletariat, who, like most peasants, owned nothing and lived by their wages. Industrialization came later to Scandinavia than most of Western Europe; as a result, Scandinavian workers were often literate and more likely to have some political influence. See Sejersted (2011).

8. This "center-periphery" tension was most prominent in Norway but can be found in all the Nordic countries. See Rokkan and Urwin (1983).

9. Folk high schools were started in Denmark by pastor and writer N. S. F. Grundtvig (1783–1872) and educator Christen Kold (1816–70) in part as a more liberal, popular strain of Lutheranism and popular culture. Likewise, agricultural cooperatives spread from the dairy sector to many others, including consumer cooperatives. Both became pervasive throughout Scandinavia and democratized both the culture and the economy.

10. The history of Scandinavian social democracy is rich (see Sejersted 2011). Note that Finland and Iceland followed a more complex course. Finland's labor movement was divided by the Finnish civil war of 1918 and continuing violence there. Iceland had little industry before World War II and hence a weaker labor movement. The struggle of independence tended to dominate its political agenda.

11. Despite Sweden's long parliamentary tradition, the supremacy of the Riksdag, especially its Second Chamber, was not solidified until 1918. Similar parliamentary breakthroughs occurred in Norway in 1884 and Denmark in 1901.

12. See Rustow (1955) for a careful study of the Swedish case. Important compromises had shaped Scandinavian politics previously even as class and ideological tensions recurred.

13. The US immigration quota system was first enacted in 1921 and then renewed in 1924 and 1952. The quotas for the Scandinavian countries were large enough to have little restrictive effect.

Introduction

14. Estimates are not precise, but approximately three thousand Jews were admitted to Sweden, with a similar number to Denmark.

15. In 1922 Swedish biologists and medical doctors persuaded the government to establish the Government Institute for Racial Biology (see Björkman and Widmalm 2010). Eugenics in Scandinavia is also treated in Broberg and Roll-Hansen (1996).

16. A thorough review of Danish immigration policy from roughly 1970 to 2010 is Mouritsen and Olsen (2013).

17. In 1952 the Nordic countries established the Nordic Council, principally to promote economic and social cooperation. Some had hoped for more extensive economic integration, but such steps would have to await the European Free Trade Association (1960) and then the expanding European Community (now EU) in the 1970s and 1990s. The labor agreement was further liberalized in 1982, but for the past two decades the European Union regulations on the "free movement of persons" have been the main directives.

18. Ghettos are not formally recognized and have a very negative historical connotation. One might more accurately describe the process as "self-ghettoization" as immigrants choose to live in enclaves or because that is the only housing available. Sweden has tolerated this process more openly than the other Scandinavian countries. During the past decade, the Scandinavian countries have tried to disperse non–Western European immigrants, and recently Denmark has prohibited new refugees and migrants from settling in ghettos.

19. So-called Progress Parties (Fremskridtpartiet in Denmark and Fremskrittspartiet in Norway) arose in the early 1970s as antitax, antibureaucratic, and antiwelfare parties. By the 1990s they or their successor parties, such as Dansk Folkepartiet (the Danish People's Party), have focused on anti-immigration and anti–European Union policies.

20. In her doctoral dissertation, Norwegian scholar Frøy Gudbrandsen (2012, 80–89) traces the evolution of refugee and asylum policies in Norwegian party manifestoes between 1977 and 2005. They reflect, of course, the changing quantity and composition of such immigrant flows.

21. For analysis of the New Democracy Party, see Rydgren (2006).

22. The annual statistical yearbooks collect most of these data, but there are also special series that focus on immigrants. Comparative data for most Western countries is available from the OECD in the *International Migration Outlook* series.

23. Although thorough analyses of the British "Brexit" vote are complex and tentative, clearly immigration played a significant role and was ruthlessly exploited by the "Leave" (UKIP) faction. Ironically, the immigrant "masses" targeted were EU citizens who had exercised their decades-old right to pursue employment in other EU member states.

24. Antonio Gramsci, written in his "Prison Notebooks" while he was incarcerated under Mussolini (Bar-On 2013, 5).

References

Amundsen, Michael. 2013. "Inuit Greenlanders Face Chilly Life in Denmark." *Christian Science Monitor*, January 16, 2013. http://www.csmonitor.com/World/Europe/2013/0116/Inuit-Greenlanders-face-chilly-life-in-Denmark.

Bangstad, Sindre. 2014. *Anders Breivik and the Rise of Islamophobia*. London: Zed Books.

Bar-On, Tamir. 2007. *Where Have All the Fascists Gone?* London: Routledge.

Bar-On, Tamir. 2013. *Rethinking the French New Right: Alternatives to Modernity*. New York: Routledge.

Bar-On, Tamir. 2014. "The French New Right: Neither Right, nor Left?" *Journal for the Study of Radicalism* 8(1): 1–44.

Behschnitt, Wolfgang, Sarah De Mul, and Liesbeth Minnaard, eds. 2013. *Literature, Language, and Multiculturalism in Scandinavia and the Low Countries*. Amsterdam: Rodopi.

Björklund, Jenny, and Ursula Lindqvist, eds. 2016. *New Dimensions of Diversity in Nordic Culture and Society*. Newcastle upon Tyne: Cambridge Scholars Publishing.

Björkman, Maria, and Sven Widmalm. 2010. "Selling Eugenics: The Case of Sweden." *Notes and Record of the Royal Society* 64:379–400.

Broberg, Gunnar, and Nils Roll-Hansen, eds. 1996. *Eugenics and the Welfare State: Sterilization Policy in Denmark, Sweden, Norway, and Finland*. East Lansing: Michigan State University Press.

Brochmann, Grete, and Anniken Hagelund. 2012. *Immigration Policy and the Scandinavian Welfare State 1945–2010*. Basingstoke: Palgrave Macmillan.

Byström, Mikael, and Pär Frohnert, eds. 2013. *Reaching a State of Hope: Refugees, Immigrants and the Swedish Welfare State, 1930–2000*. Lund: Nordic Academic Press.

Chin, Rita. 2017. *The Crisis of Multiculturalism in Europe: A History*. Princeton, NJ: Princeton University Press.

Danmarks Statistik. 2000. *Befolkningen i 150 år*. Copenhagen: Danmarks Statistik.

Dumézil, Georges. (1958) 1973. *L'idéologie tripartite des Indo-Européens*. Brussels: Latomus.

Dumézil, Georges. 1959. *Les dieux des germains: Essai sur la formation de la religion scandinave*. Paris: Presses Universitaires de France.

Gudbrandsen, Frøy. 2012. "Explaining Scandinavian Immigration Policy, 1985–2010." PhD diss., University of Bergen.

Haugen, Einar, ed. and trans. 1973. *Gods of the Ancient Northmen*. Berkeley: University of California Press.

Kivisto, Peter, and Östen Wahlbeck. 2013. "Debating Multiculturalism in the Nordic Welfare States." In *Debating Multiculturalism in the Nordic Welfare States*, edited by Peter Kivisto and Östen Wahlbeck, 1–21. Basingstoke: Palgrave Macmillan.

Labourer, Peter. 2016. "Indvandring til Danmark efter 1945." Danmarkshistorien, Aarhus Universitet. http://danmarkshistorien.dk/leksikon-og-kilder/vis/mate riale/indvandring-til-danmark-efter-1945/?no_cache=1.

Loftsdóttir, Kristín, and Lars Jensen, eds. 2012. *Whiteness and Postcolonialism in the Nordic Region: Exceptionalism, Migrant Others and National Identities*. Farnham: Ashgate.

Loftsdóttir, Kristín, and Lars Jensen, eds. 2014. *Crisis in the Nordic Nations and Beyond: At the Intersection of Environment, Finance and Multiculturalism*. Farnham: Ashgate.

Lundström, Catrin, and Benjamin Teitelbaum. 2017. "Nordic Whiteness: An Introduction." *Scandinavian Studies* 89(2): 151–58.

McEachrane, Michael, ed. 2014. *Afro-Nordic Landscapes: Equality and Race in Northern Europe*. Routledge: Abingdon, Oxon.

Mouritsen, Per, and Tore Vincent Olsen. 2013. "Denmark between Liberalism and Nationalism." *Ethnic and Racial Studies* 36(4): 391–410.

"Norway in Exile." 2017. Norway National Archives. https://www.arkivverket.no/en/using-the-archives/world-war-ii/norway-in-exile.

OECD (Organisation for Economic Co-operation and Development). 2019. *International Migration Outlook*. Paris.

Rokkan, Stein, and Derek W. Urwin. 1983. *Economy, Territory, Identity: Politics of West European Peripheries*. London: Sage.

Runblom, Harald. 1998. "Sweden as a Multicultural Society." Current Sweden, paper no. 418. Swedish Institute, Stockholm.

Rustow, Dankwart. 1955. *Politics of Compromise*. Princeton, NJ: Princeton University Press.

Rydgren, Jens. 2006. *From Tax Populism to Ethnic Nationalism: Radical Right-Wing Populism in Sweden*. New York: Berghahn Books.

Schall, Carly Elizabeth. 2016. *The Rise and Fall of the Miraculous Welfare Machine: Immigration and Social Democracy in Twentieth-Century Sweden*. Ithaca, NY: ILR Press.

Sejersted, Francis. 2011. *The Age of Social Democracy*. Princeton, NJ: Princeton University Press.

Statistiska Centralbyrån (SCB). 2008. *Sveriges befolkningsutveckling 1750–2007*. http://www.scb.se.

Statistisk Sentralbyrå. 1960. *Statistisk årbok for Norge 1960*. Vol. 79. Oslo: Statistisk Sentralbyrå.

Svanberg, Johan. 2017. "Labour Migration and Industrial Relations." In *Labour, Unions and Politics under the North Star: The Nordic Countries 1700–2000*, edited by Mary Hilson, Silke Neunsinger, and Iben Vyff, 156–74. New York: Berghahn.

Wasserstein, Bernard. 2011. "European Refugee Movements after World War Two." BBC, February 17. http://www.bbc.co.uk/history/worldwars/wwtwo/refugees_01.shtml.

Westin, Charles. 2006. *Sweden: Restrictive Immigration and Multiculturalism*. Washington, DC: Migration Policy Institute.

Wickström, Mats. 2015. *The Multicultural Moment*. Turku: Åbo Akademi.

Wikipedia. n.d. "2022 Swedish General Election." Accessed November 2020. https://en.wikipedia.org/wiki/2022_Swedish_general_election#/media/File:Swedish_Opinion_Polling,_30_Day_Moving_Average,_2018-2022.png.

Zuckerman, Phil. 2008. *Society without God: What the Least Religious Nations Can Tell Us about Contentment*. New York: New York University Press.

THE POLITICS OF IMMIGRATION

Immigration to Scandinavian Welfare States in the Time of Pluralism

GRETE BROCHMANN

In a European context, the three Scandinavian countries are often viewed as being new to immigration. This truism needs modification: Norway, Sweden, and Denmark have had different kinds of immigration for centuries, but what is associated with immigration today—so-called new immigration—is a relatively recent phenomenon for all of them. The new immigration has to do with people who come from countries outside the OECD and have largely migrated after the 1960s. It is this new immigration that will be discussed in this chapter.

Why does it make sense to focus on and analyze these three countries together in connection with immigration? There are many good reasons. Since the new immigrants started to come—first to Sweden, somewhat later to Denmark and Norway—all three countries have come a long way in developing modern and comprehensive welfare states.[1] They resemble each other to the extent that the countries are often treated as one in the international literature on welfare states, and the "Nordic Model" has become an established concept in welfare research.[2]

In Scandinavia this welfare model is probably the societal feature with the greatest relevance to issues surrounding immigration. The welfare state framework—normative, institutional, and proactive—was and is basically the same in the three countries. But there are additional features of the region that make it meaningful to evaluate the three countries together. They are all small and, viewed culturally, relatively homogeneous societies on the northern periphery of Europe with shared linguistic and historical identities. After the war, in slightly differing ways, all were strongly influenced by social democratic governments. All three countries rank highest in international evaluations of societal trustworthiness. The type of immigrant to the region has varied in a similar way over time, and the political tools that the governments have used were also very similar for a long time. All three countries were influenced by new thinking in the 1960s and 1970s on the inclusion of newcomers and minorities, thinking that has become known as *integration politics*. Integration politics is a variation of what is internationally called a *multicultural* approach. In Scandinavia this approach has had a two-sided aspect. The state has stood for active governance both to hinder social and economic marginalization of newcomers and to actively promote acceptance of cultural diversity within the existing population.

But there have also been essential differences between the Scandinavian countries.[3] In recent times the three countries have had different economic bases: Norway has become a producer of oil and raw materials; Sweden historically has been a strong industrial country; and Denmark is more characterized by small businesses, especially in agricultural production. Different economic roots have also guaranteed different rhythms regarding economic crises and fluctuations, with varying consequences for welfare and immigration policies.

While in recent times the three countries have shared a distinctive social democratic history, their constellations of power with other political parties have been different. Danish social democrats have often been in the government, but almost always with a nonsocialist majority in the parliament (Folketing). The position of the Swedish social democrats has been more stable, with strong majority governments over long periods of time. This was also the case for the Norwegian social democrats after the war, but since the 1980s nonsocialist and social democratic minority governments have often traded places.

Right-leaning populist parties have had varying degrees of influence in all three countries as well, with notable consequences for public debate and immigration policies. Denmark has had a clearly critical opposition to immigration since the 1970s, first with the Progress Party (Fremskridtspartiet) and then with the Danish People's Party (Dansk Folkeparti). The Norwegian Progress Party (Fremskrittspartiet) got its start only in 1987, when the party proceeded to "politicize" immigration by making it an election issue. Sweden has followed a different path and only with the 2014 election registered significant critical reaction to immigration through the Sweden Democrats (Sverigedemokraterna).

For many years Sweden was the leading immigration country in Scandinavia in duration, scope, and policy development. Postwar immigration, which began in Sweden earlier than in neighboring countries, also had a greater scope over time. This probably explains much of Sweden's role as a pioneer country in the area of integration politics, with a strong effect on the other two countries, especially in an early phase and particularly in Norway. This pattern was less tangible after 1990, when both Denmark and Norway had gone their own ways in many areas of immigration and integration policies.

In certain ways there are also serious differences among the Scandinavian countries in the public debate over immigration. The Danish debate has had a harder tone in recent years, with more prominence of voices critical of immigrants. Since the turn of the millennium, Danish politics have also moved in a more restrictive direction both regarding control of immigration and in social policy. Some similar developments in the debate have also been seen in Norway, if not to the same degree. Sweden has been the exception both in the climate of the debate and in concrete policies. The country has been more reluctant to carry out comprehensive restrictions in immigration policy and has, up to now, had a more moderate tone in the public debate. At the same time, the Swedish welfare state had to undertake more drastic savings than the other two countries after the financial crisis at the beginning of the 1990s, and since then the level of its benefits has been lower than in the neighboring countries.[4]

With regard to external framework provisions, the Scandinavian countries have chosen different forms of association with the European Union. Sweden has complete EU membership (except for the monetary union). Denmark has been an EU member the longest but has opted out of the common immigration policy (justice, freedom, and security), and the country is not a member of the monetary union either. Norway has chosen to remain outside the EU proper but at the same time has joined the borderless Schengen Area (part of the EU structure), which has important implications for immigration policy. European Economic Area (EEA) membership also makes Norway part of the internal market of the EU, with significant consequences for labor migration.

In sum, Scandinavia can be described today as three countries with similar economies, a number of common cultural traits, comparable welfare and labor market models, a high degree of societal trust, yet at the same time different approaches to immigration and integration, particularly as to ideology and the way policies have been legitimized.

Later in this chapter, I will describe and analyze the growth of discord in Scandinavia over the question of immigration. I will use a historical, analytical

approach that combines institutions, norms, and actors in a dynamic interplay in order to understand and explain both continuity and change in the
area of immigration in the three respective countries over time.[5] I explore
policy change as a way to understand substantial changes in society resulting
from immigration and cultural pluralization. Empirically, I want to restrict
the comparisons to three central policy areas: *immigration policy* (control and
access), *integration* (incorporation and facilitation), and *naturalization* (allo-
cation of citizenship—the ideological self-image of the nation-state).

THE NEW IMMIGRATION

Before the new immigration started and before the central welfare institutions were in place, immigration to the Scandinavian countries was dominated by labor migrants. In the time between World War II and the end of the
1960s, some few, relatively modest groups of refugees arrived from eastern
Europe in three waves after the intervention of the Soviet Union in Czechoslovakia in 1948, Hungary in 1956, and Czechoslovakia again in 1968.[6] A common Nordic labor market was established in 1954, which meant that citizens
from the region could freely live and work in another Nordic country without
losing social rights gained at home.

During the 1960s and early 1970s, the first wave of "new immigrants" consisted of labor migrants mainly from countries such as Turkey, Yugoslavia,
Morocco, and Pakistan. Sweden, in addition, had a comprehensive wave of
labor immigrants from Finland during the whole postwar period. This labor
migration occurred under very liberal migration conditions. The strong influence of the United States, not least through the Marshall Plan, contributed to
a prevailing ideology that people should be able to move as freely as possible
across country boundaries in line with market forces. It was only at the end of
the 1960s that the brakes were slowly applied in Western European recipient
countries. Times of financial recession, amplified by the so-called oil crisis
in the early 1970s, dampened the demand for workers, and the receiving
countries began to worry about the results of the influx from abroad. By this
point most European recipient countries had established welfare models that
ensured that people who came, worked, and paid taxes had earned welfare
rights. Thus the "guest worker" system, as it was called in Germany, proved
to be based on weak assumptions: in this arena, market mechanisms failed to
function, as the foreign workers did not pack up and return to their countries
of origin when demand decreased.[7] Thus in the early 1970s a restrictive period
began in all of Western Europe with regulation of immigration, during which

the states tried to restrict further labor migrants at least until some control of this relatively new and confounding phenomenon had been established. The Scandinavian countries also introduced so-called immigration stops—Sweden in 1972, Denmark in 1973, and Norway in 1975.

Immigration stops represented mileposts in Scandinavian immigration policy. They introduced both new ideology and new policy tools adapted to the demands of the time, and they had important consequences for policy development in the decades that followed—in fact, all the way to the present. The new policies were intended to stop the stream of low-qualified workers from countries from the Global South while at the same time keeping the channels open for qualified workers in demand. This latter category was especially important for Norway, which in the early 1970s had made the first discoveries of oil in the North Sea and was on its way into the strongest period of growth in the country's history, with significant need for foreign expertise.

When the legal channels for labor immigration were tightened, a new immigration pattern materialized in large parts of Europe, including Scandinavia. Guest workers not only settled in the recipient country rather than returning "home" but also were allowed a considerable degree of family reunification from the country of origin in accordance with international agreements. Thus the strong increase in immigration to Scandinavia after the 1970s entailed refugees and asylum seekers as well as family members of already established immigrants. Denmark (with certain fluctuations) had almost as many immigrants as Sweden up to the turn of the century. Since this time, immigration to Denmark has stabilized, whereas it has doubled in both Norway and Sweden (Vatne Pettersen and Østby 2013). Before 1970 Sweden had significantly higher immigration (especially from Finland) and, early in the 1990s and after 2005, a greater acceptance of refugees than the two other countries. In the whole region, immigrants accepted for humanitarian reasons from non-OECD countries dominated, up to the expansion of the EU to the east in 2004, when labor immigration again increased. Over time, the variation between the countries has created a situation in which today Sweden has a significantly higher share of immigrants in society than Denmark and Norway.[8]

Regulation of Nordic immigration from the beginning of the 1970s came about by way of three conditions, with slightly different emphases in the respective countries: economic competition, welfare state concern, and lessons learned from other European immigration countries. The sustainability concerns of welfare states interacted with news coming from the continent:

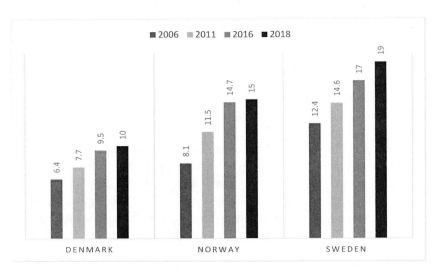

FIGURE 1. Stock of foreign-born immigrants, 2006–2018, percent of population
Source: OECD stat.

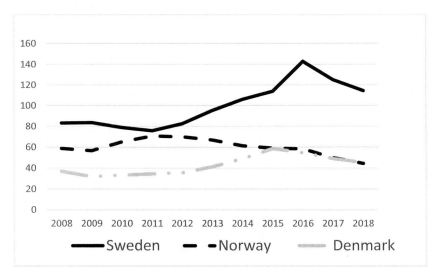

FIGURE 2. Migration inflow, 2008–2018, in thousands
Source: OECD Migration Outlook 2020.

Immigration to Scandinavian Welfare States in the Time of Pluralism 37

unemployment, social problems, poor living conditions, and occasional cultural conflicts, inducing a sense of caution—that is, a conclusion that the safest approach was to follow the European tendency to introduce restrictions. It was believed that increasing economic internationalization would also lead to the different recipient countries becoming a function of each other's policies: one country's restrictions could quickly have spillover effects elsewhere.

THE NORDIC MODEL: INSTITUTIONAL PREREQUISITES

The new immigration increased in Scandinavia at approximately the same time that the fundamentals of the Nordic Model, the central organization of the welfare states, fell into place. Gøsta Esping-Andersen and Walter Korpi (1987) have characterized this model as comprehensive, institutionalized, and universal: comprehensive regarding the kinds of social needs it tries to satisfy; institutionalized via social rights that give all citizens—in practice, all those legally domiciled—a right to a decent standard of living; and solidaristic and universal—that is, welfare policy has been intended for the entire population and not just particularly exposed groups.[9] The state plays the main role in handling risks and relieving the family institution from obligations of care (Sejersted 2005). This means that welfare *services* play an important role in the model, giving the local levels of government a central position in welfare service. Welfare policies have also contributed to high levels of employment among women, even though the labor market remains divided by gender, and many women work part-time. The Nordic Model is financed mainly by taxes, and social expenditure is high compared to other countries.

An important characteristic in the Nordic Model is its structural connections with the organization of working life. Regulation of the labor market through collective agreements, three-party cooperation, and welfare assurance for life have contributed to productive economies with good adaptability and high human capital. Working life and welfare have represented mutual buffer functions with high rate of employment as the economic mainstay: employment must both finance welfare and reduce public expenditures.

The composition of the Nordic Model is an important premise for the development of immigration policies in Scandinavia. Initially it was established without immigration in mind; immigration was not a politicized topic, and none of the governments could have known the degree to which it would increase in the years to come. The Nordic Model assumed the character of *bounded universalism* (Benhabib 2002), that is, "universalism in one country."

First, controlling the inflow was seen as a prerequisite for sustaining the system as such. As the scope of social rights was extensive and therefore also expensive, inflow control had to be a chief concern. Ideally, only labor in demand was to be let in. Second, the Nordic Model, with its finely balanced welfare/labor nexus, required equal treatment of newcomers. This element was argued by the labor unions in particular, which were afraid of low wage competition and the undermining of their hard-won labor standards. Good welfare states could not systemically accept substantial numbers of residents who were not being productively absorbed in the labor market, disturbing the regulated world of work and burdening social budgets. This reflects a recognition that a society cannot function properly if a large part of its population is marginalized and socially excluded. *Integration* policy—beyond labor market inclusion—added to this logic: to have newcomers become full members of their new home countries, states had to make an active effort to facilitate well-functioning citizenship for new residents. What later would be called the *work line* was central here. In order to maintain the expensive welfare state, people had to be integrated into productive work to the greatest extent possible, as the work line was a constitutive element in the Nordic Model as such. The expectation of self-sufficiency among immigrants was underlined in the first Swedish document on the topic as well (Borevi 2014).

Immigration policy can be divided into two main spheres: an "outer" and an "inner." In the outer sphere it is a matter of *access*, that is, who will have the opportunity to enter a country. The inner sphere has to do with *rights* and, ideally, *integration*, that is, what conditions are offered to the newcomer. The Scandinavian states built up a somewhat fragile legitimacy after the 1970s by means of a dual approach: a tough front and a softer interior. Strict and selective arrival control was combined with an inclusive distribution of rights for those allowed in. After new regulations in the 1970s, the Nordic authorities in principle wanted only specially requested workers, but other groups came as well, especially through family unification and asylum.[10] And when new immigrants first legally live in a country, the logic has been that they should be integrated as well as possible, both for their own sake and for that of society, along the lines of the welfare state model.

Even though there are important links between the inner and the outer spheres, politically and legally they are usually handled separately. Regulation of access to the country is closely connected with the nation-state's historically based right to territorial control. Border control is an important part of the *sovereignty principle*, recognized as a theory for legitimate government and

Immigration to Scandinavian Welfare States in the Time of Pluralism 39

confirmed in international law (Østerud 1991). As regards the inner sphere, the civil, social, and political rights for foreigners who settle in the country have been closely associated with the historical development of the country's rule of law. Modern states are obligated by international agreements to treat legally established immigrants and native citizens equally with regard to most civil and social rights. Gradually, the Scandinavian countries have also extended voting rights to immigrants in local elections.

Beyond this, modern welfare states have developed extensive policies to promote *integration*, that is, actual inclusion in society beyond what is legally required. Integration policies entail initiatives directed at legally established immigrants to give them support in their adjustment process.[11] To various degrees the Scandinavian states have also worked to influence resistant attitudes of the *majority* in order to buttress the integration project. Sweden has clearly gone farthest in placing demands on the *majority* to accommodate cultural diversity.

NATION BUILDING AND HUMAN RIGHTS: NORMATIVE PREREQUISITES

In his book *Philosophies of Integration* (1998), sociologist Adrian Favell argues for the existence of relatively stable national approaches to the multicultural project in European immigrant-receiving countries. He argues that approaches to integration by nation-states are formed by deeply anchored societal conditions in which the interplay between ideas and institutions forms leeway for the actors. In other words, existing institutions create a *rationality* that various actors can relate to in their context-dependent behavior. Favell's (1998, 19) argument refers to new (sociological) institutional theory in which ideas and policy objectives are seen as institutional structures that form interest-driven political actors in their work toward different goals. These idea-based mechanisms do not mean that questions of integration are depoliticized in different national contexts but that the conditions for acting—what is possible to do within a national context—are formed by inherited common frames of reference. In other words, there exists a historically created national, political, social, and cultural grounding that forms a common framework for what grants legitimacy and what functions as effective arguments in public discourse. Sociologist Ann Swidler (1986) calls this grounding "cultural repertoires," that is, often nonexplicit norms for action in a society. This type of definition breaks down the difference between institution and culture: culture becomes an institution in itself (Hall and Taylor 1996). Thus one might ask, Which cultural repertoires were central to the actors in Scandinavia when the new immigration era began? We must look to Sweden to find the "sources of the cultural authority," as Peter Hall and Rosemary Taylor call it (1996, 16).

Sweden had a head start in many ways. It had already had significant immigration for a long time and had therefore gained experience with cultural diversity (even if the majority of immigrants were Finns and thus not drastically "different," in majority opinion), and it had established itself internationally in the postwar period as a "humanitarian superpower."[12] Sweden could therefore work out an understanding of immigrant policy earlier than Denmark or Norway. Already in the 1960s Sweden had promulgated the first political documents to sketch new ideas about immigration and "integration" in Sweden. The main principle should be a solid entry control (i.e., the number let in should be in tune with the capacity for integration into society) in combination with equal treatment in terms of public welfare. An important public report came out in 1974 in which Swedish authorities adopted the principles for an Immigration and Minorities Policy with the slogans "equality, freedom of choice, and cooperation" (SOU 1974). (The Swedish parliament passed the policy in 1975.) This policy meant a two-sided approach in which new members of society should be able to achieve the same socioeconomic standard as the majority population while also getting to choose their cultural association. New immigrants should be given lessons in Swedish, but they should not be expected to "become Swedish" in a cultural sense. In addition, they should get state support for "cultural maintenance" pertaining to norms and values they bring with them (Borevi 2010). The cultural rights of immigrants were even protected by a new formulation in the Swedish constitution. Equality and cooperation were well-known concepts in the normal repertoire of the welfare state, but freedom of choice stood out as an anomaly in heavily equalizing Sweden.

In the process of modernization and nation building that took place in postwar Sweden, assimilation, in both the economic and cultural understandings, had been viewed as natural and necessary. To be assimilated in Sweden meant to become modern, to live in a progressive and (paradoxically) antinationalistic country. Many of the progressive assimilationists were in fact well-integrated immigrants. Assimilation was viewed as more humane than, for example, the German guest worker policy (Wickström 2013, 119), in which immigrants were expected to maintain the culture they brought with them on the assumption that they would return after a guest stay in Germany. Social engineering was given a central place in the development of Swedish welfare, and a significant part of this political orientation involved the molding of attitudes and values (Hirdman 2000; Sejersted 2005). The state could go far in efforts to influence the upbringing of children, the relationship between spouses, the formation of taste, and the general way of life.

When the new immigrants arrived in the 1970s, however, and cultural molding was explicitly exempted from their introduction to life in Sweden, it had ambiguous effects for inclusion and cooperation. It is interesting that Sweden, the Scandinavian country in which social engineering had been elaborated furthest, also became the pioneer in multicultural *liberality* (Gür 1996), declaring that immigrants should get to have their everyday culture in peace, so to speak. Sweden actually made this diversity approach part of its continuous nation-building process after the 1970s.

After this approach was in place, the Swedish state went to work with a heavy hand on the attitude of the majority in order to get them to accept the new ideology (Wickström 2013). The new multicultural ideology was made a part of wider nation building to a greater degree than in neighboring countries. Traditional Swedish culture was toned down, to the advantage of a collection of values associated more broadly with democracy and human rights. The multicultural ideological frame was predominant in the following years and was still going strong a good decade into the twenty-first century.

In Norway, Swedish ideological developments were closely followed, and this same multicultural thinking was adopted without much reservation for a long time. Swedish slogans were translated, and many public documents were strongly affected by predecessors in Sweden, as were adjustments to those policies over time. But in Denmark this approach was considerably modified. From the beginning there was a more national approach to ideology in Denmark. Danish language and culture were expected to have an advantage in accommodating new members of society, and making demands on immigrants had become a norm earlier. The Danish approach to equality meant an absence of special treatment. Even so, Denmark also introduced many of the Swedish novelties, such as voting rights in local elections, mother-tongue education, economic support for immigrant cultural organizations, and so forth.[13]

JUSTICE AND WELFARE IN MULTICULTURAL STATES

The interaction of norms and institutions explains much of the original formation of Scandinavian immigrant policies. The new human rights regimes in the postwar period, combined with welfare state preconditions, created a new context for political action. Central actors were also influenced by new ideas on value diversity and cultural tolerance. Radical bureaucrats, interest groups, researchers, and some elite immigrants had a strong influence. In Sweden this very positive approach to immigration was also due to the fact that previous immigration had consisted of Finns, whose presence was largely favorable for the Swedish economy. This group had achieved breakthroughs in many social and cultural demands, and these breakthroughs continued when new groups began to arrive (Borevi 2010).

The early development of ideas in Sweden can be spelled out as the relative autonomy of ideology. Sociologist Yasemin Soysal (1994) argues that the integration policy introduced in many Western countries in the 1970s was not "functional" for the states; that is, they were not directed by national interests. Because a human rights regime had been established internationally, a more normative, value-based approach to immigrants was imposed on the states. But it can also be argued, in line with historian Mats Wickström (2013), that immigration and minority policy was a new twist on "social engineering," a Swedish attempt to create a well-functioning plural society. He claims that the foreigners from the South were viewed as being so different from Swedes and at the same time seen as so "vulnerable and dangerous" that they would have to be treated in a different way. Special considerations would have to be made so that they would not disturb the basic structure of *folkhemmet* (the people's home).[14] One could even see the approach as a variation on traditional Swedish corporatism. The authorities encouraged immigrant groups to form organizations that could represent them to the authorities, who, on their side, got "someone to communicate with" (Borevi 2010).

In any case, the ideology of integration had a strong impact, probably because it combined the radical zeitgeist at the end of the 1960s with established institutional prerequisites. At the same time, the Scandinavian approach revealed a tacit unease between different measures for justice and welfare. American philosopher Nancy Fraser (1995) has formulated this as the tension between the *politics of recognition* and the *politics of redistribution*. The ambitious social policy of the three Scandinavian countries has traditionally aimed at using the tax system and services, as well as various kinds of social engineering, to level out class differences in society. This redistribution was supposed to be done in a color-blind way: equal treatment regardless of cultural or social background. The recognition policy, however, appreciates that injustice has a cultural and symbolic dimension. Some groups' values and identities render them invisible and subjugated when they are not specifically recognized beyond equal treatment. The integration policies of Scandinavia ideally were to do both: on the one hand, secure newcomers access to equal rights and the possibilities of social mobility; on the other, create room for conservation and cultivation of their original cultural or religious tradition. Increasingly (although to different degrees), these two agendas have been in conflict in the three countries since the initiation of the integration policy. In practice, cultural and religious affiliations have more frequently been seen as obstacles to equal rights (i.e., equality in terms of social and livelihood performance) as well as to social mobility over time. Women's rights are most commonly addressed as an issue within this schism (see, e.g., Eisenberg and Spinner-Halev 2005; Okin 1999; Siim and Skjeie 2008).

IMMIGRANT POLICY

The immigration and immigrant policy that was formulated in the 1970s presumed that immigration could be guided in step with the needs of the labor market and the capacity of the welfare state. Rather quickly, the receiving states encountered a changed migration reality in which the people who came to Scandinavian countries no longer fit into the pattern of mobile labor that had been the basis of the policy in the first place. In part this reflected changed conditions internationally, with more refugee-producing conflicts, but the new migration pattern was also a result of changes in the immigration policies proper in the recipient countries. After chances to seek work elsewhere in Europe were strongly curtailed, people sought other possibilities. The desire for a family life and flight from war and persecution became important criteria for residence in the new immigration regime. Thus some of the bottom fell out of the newly established immigration policy. The immigration that occurred after the "stops" could not be regulated with the tools that were then in place. Both international obligations and genuine wishes for a humanitarian immigration practice meant that new arrivals could not easily be dismissed merely with reference to the capacity of the national welfare state or demand in the labor market. Asylum and family immigration policies ought to be controlled not by national interests but by humanitarian norms.

Sweden continued to be the first to experience changed patterns of international migration in Scandinavia. The country already accepted a greater number of refugees in the 1970s, and the scope of this immigration continued to be larger compared to Denmark and Norway. While the refugees of the 1970s came to a great extent via organized transfers, so-called quota refugees or transfer refugees, the refugees in the 1980s came as asylum seekers. They arrived unannounced at the border and sought asylum on their own initiative. The asylum-seeker category would to a great degree dominate the stream of refugees in the decades after 1970, even if quota refugees still existed as a category.

The number of asylum seekers grew quickly. In Denmark the number of arrivals rose from around 300 in 1983 to 8,700 in 1985. Norway experienced a corresponding increase in the period from 1985 to 1987, from 830 to 8,600. Sweden was already at a far higher level, with about 14,500 in 1985 and over 30,000 in 1989; it reached a temporary peak of 84,000 asylum seekers in 1992.

Secondary immigration of family members has also been significant in all three countries since the 1970s. Family members represented an exception to the immigrant stops, giving the migrant in question the chance to reunify with spouses and children under twenty years of age. Since the great majority of labor migrants from the 1970s were married men immigrating alone, the potential for this so-called secondary immigration was significant. Family reunion could, however, mean two different things. It could be actual reunion of a family divided because the husband had migrated to Scandinavia, or it could be a matter of establishing a new family, in which the migrant imported a partner after he or she was established in the receiving country. In the period after the immigration stop, it was, by and large, a question of actual reunions, since, like other countries in Europe, the Scandinavian countries had accepted many married men coming to improve the family's income, imagining short-term stays or commuting between the work and home countries. After the stop the possibilities for labor immigrants to travel back and forth were more limited, making the motivation for reuniting the family much stronger. However, the possibility of establishing new marriages by fetching spouses from the home country made family reunification an important channel of immigration well beyond the policy regarding preexisting nuclear families. This form of reunion attracted increased attention after the 1990s.

As we have seen, when it comes to the interplay between access policy and welfare state integration policy, all three countries have the same basic structure: restrictions on access from the outside and, once inside, an inclusive and equal-rights orientation. Until the turn of the twenty-first century, their integration policies were also roughly similar, though with national specificities. The problems of unforeseen consequences in the wake of the control policy were also almost alike. Seen from a position of clear-cut economic interest, few immigrants would have entered Scandinavia after the immigration stops.

At the same time, however, the countries' relatively liberal humanitarian principles meant that many came anyway for legitimate human rights reasons. This created self-reinforcing mechanisms that steadily led to more and more immigrants.

It was not, however, until the end of the 1980s that the three countries (again to varying degrees) began to discuss how humanitarian-based immigration could be reduced in scope. The question of asylum-seeker legitimacy became a tool in this connection. Since not everyone who came could appeal to a need for protection under the UN refugee convention, it was possible to establish principles for delimitation that way. Treatment of asylum seekers has since been a touchy nexus of strife and conflict in all three countries. It is difficult to assess how effective the asylum policy approach has been in reducing illegitimate applicants. There are many unpredictable forces in play, and the fluctuations in asylum application have been considerable over the decades. There is also much to indicate a certain degree of regime competition between the Scandinavian countries: when one has introduced a restriction, the flow tends to increase in the other two countries. Nonetheless, there is no doubt that Sweden has been, and still is, the region's great magnet for asylum immigration.[15]

In looking at the control policy for asylum seekers, the 1990s was the decade when the governments put more weight on limiting the flow at the same time that preconditions for actually having control became more limited through the international human rights regime and the borderless EU. Containing immigration of families thus gradually became a goal of control policy, foremost in the sense of new family establishment rather than of actual reunions. In the wake of the right to import a spouse from the country of origin, forced marriage, arranged marriage, and family-related violence became highly focused issues in the Scandinavian context. The problem revealed a complicated and charged interaction between immigration control, integration, human rights, and family relations.

Denmark has been a leading country, also in a European context, in introducing restrictions on family immigration. When Fogh Rasmussen's Center-Right government took over in 2001, heavy restrictions were put in place on many fronts at once. One of the most important of the Danish reforms was removal of the category "de facto refugees," so that protection should only be extended to refugees meeting the definition of the UN Geneva Convention of 1951. In addition, in order to achieve residence in Denmark for establishment of a new family, both partners must be at least twenty-four years old, and their common attachment to Denmark must be stronger than to any other country. Couples must have a "decent place to live," an annual income over a certain amount, and a bank guarantee to cover expenses of the foreign spouse. Neither Sweden nor Norway introduced restrictions of this kind, even though they gradually introduced some limitations with a similar motivation. Both Norway and Sweden have also gradually introduced maintenance requirements (with a considerable number of exceptions in Sweden), and in Norway the government introduced the requirement that applicants for family establishment should have at least four years of training or local work experience before permission is granted.[16]

For a short period up to the financial crisis in 2008, the public debate on immigration changed its character. Worries about the strain on the welfare state were replaced by attention to features of demographic change (an aging population) that foresaw increasing need for labor from abroad. "Norway will come to a halt without immigration" was a popular political slogan in the Norwegian election campaign at the turn of the twenty-first century. Trained labor from abroad was viewed in all three countries as a necessary addition to maintain the accustomed level of welfare in society. The public image of the immigrant shifted from consumers to producers in record time. In reality, one spoke of different groups of immigrants. The Indian IT engineer became the symbol of what was wanted, while humanitarian-based immigration continued to cause worry under the surface. The result was a two-sided policy. The Nordic governments expanded their restriction policies toward asylum seekers and family immigrants at the same time that they tried to stimulate increased immigration of qualified labor. Sweden was alone in introducing demand-controlled liberalization of labor migration from third countries (outside the EU) in 2008.[17] Denmark and Norway estimated that the new and comprehensive flow from the new EU countries after 2004 was sufficient to cover their demand. Immigration from the EU/EEA was especially high in Norway, but Denmark and Sweden also received essential contributions of labor from the EU. This labor had the right to free mobility within the area of the EU/EEA, which meant, in effect, that immigration control within the EU/EEA region was abandoned.

Integration Policy

Sweden was, as we have seen, the pioneer country in Scandinavia to develop new ideas on multicultural societies, that is, access to rights, equal treatment, and freedom of choice regarding cultural accommodation. Sweden also came

Immigration to Scandinavian Welfare States in the Time of Pluralism

out early with revisions to some of this thinking. The authorities realized during the 1980s that the multicultural approach had created an unforeseen consequence of group thinking—an "us-and-them" perspective (Borevi 2014). The ideology was revised, first quietly in 1986 and then more explicitly in 1997, and the political ambitions from the 1970s about preserving minority culture were scaled down considerably. The state's responsibility to safeguard the needs of the individual was emphasized over the needs of ethnic minority groups, and the minority policy was changed to the immigrant policy. Diversity (based on a plurality of individuals rather than groups) was the new slogan, and the concept of minorities was reserved for groups with a long history in the country. Without any grand gestures, freedom of cultural choice was reduced—it would now be impossible to resign from Swedish society, ignore learning Swedish, or dissent from central societal norms and rules (Borevi 2010). There was no comparable revision in Denmark and Norway, where the governments had never introduced group thinking to the same degree as Sweden. Instead, after the shift in Swedish policies the ideological basis of its integration policy was brought into line with the basic ruling principles in Norway and Denmark: integration through equal rights and equal opportunities, realized with the help of the general welfare state system, incorporating respect for minority culture in an overall goal of a common and overarching citizenship.

But what did all these ideological gymnastics mean in practice? Were the immigrants received officially and socially in new ways? As reflected in public documents and in the climate of debate, of the three countries Sweden has had the most continuity in basic attitudes to immigration as a phenomenon. In Denmark and to a certain degree in Norway attitudes have changed during the past twenty years in the direction of a more critical public largely stimulated by parties critical to immigration, which again have played on sentiments in the population. "Making demands on immigrants" has had a different resonance in Danish and Norwegian society than in Swedish. "Misplaced kindness" was invented as a concept in Norway at the beginning of the 1990s, alluding to the concern that the state did portions of the population a disservice by placing too few participation requirements on newcomers, especially in working life. The politics of rights received criticism in new ways, but it took a decade before this criticism had tangible political consequences. This topic has been controversial in public debate from the beginning. The somewhat ambivalent question, "Is the welfare state too kind or not kind enough?" basically sums up the variations in attitude in public opinions and political approaches to integration within and between the three countries, ever since revisions of the multicultural policy were introduced in the 1990s (Brochmann 2014, 290).

All three countries meanwhile have tried to create equal possibilities for newcomers with regard to all important areas of society, such as work, health care, and education, and all three countries have employed measures central to the welfare state to achieve this. Behind all the ideological noise was a pragmatic, day-to-day endeavor to get new members of society functionally integrated in work and in the broader society. Activation (the work line) has been given greater emphasis both in general welfare policies and in connection with integration of newcomers. All countries have carried out changes in their immigrant reception and qualification systems, most clearly for refugees, but other groups have become subject to integration measures as well.

An important twist in policy approach in the wake of the Swedish changes was the idea that special treatment should be used primarily for new refugee arrivals, while other immigrants should mostly be included in the same welfare apparatus as the rest of the population. This was realized toward the end of the 1990s in a comprehensive new orientation to integration by means of the so-called introduction policy. This new creation was motivated by concerns that a disproportionately large part of the immigrant population (refugees and family immigrants) was dependent on social assistance from day one, and, more seriously, this dependence seemed to continue for years afterward. A pattern appeared in all three countries in which immigrants (with considerable variation between groups) had a markedly lower degree of employment than the majority population. To turn this pattern around, Sweden first (1993, updated in 2010), then Denmark (1999), and finally Norway (2004) introduced this altered approach to new arrivals.[18] The aim of the programs was to provide a targeted introduction, including language training, information about society and polity, and—not least—"work-oriented" training. The participants were given a salary (the scale varied among the three countries); in Norway it was at a higher level than the social assistance rates. The introductory program, which municipalities were obligated to provide, was mandatory in Denmark and Norway for new arrivals. It entailed both a right and an obligation for the immigrants, as wages were withdrawn from participants in cases of unapproved absence. In Sweden the program was voluntary both for the municipalities and for potential participants. In Sweden and Norway the introduction program was implemented to parallel the principle of equal treatment in other welfare services. In Denmark, on the other

Immigration to Scandinavian Welfare States in the Time of Pluralism 49

hand, the Fogh Rasmussen government introduced so-called start help in 2002, which was financial aid at an essentially lower level than the social assistance rates.[19]

Debate on the costs of immigration to the welfare state took place earlier and more forcefully in Denmark than in Norway and Sweden. In Denmark economists had a more central role as integration policy experts in the 1990s, which probably explains some of the early preoccupation with the sustainability of the welfare state there (Vad Jønsson and Petersen 2012). Economists emphasized the significance of incentive structures for integrating immigrants into the labor market. Because non-Western immigrants by and large find themselves in the low-wage segment of the labor market, the relatively high welfare benefits contributed to making such work less attractive for them. With the start help Denmark broke with the equal-treatment policy of the universal welfare model, with the objective of raising incentives for immigrants to promptly enter working life. The Thorning-Schmidt government of 2011 tried to reverse the differential treatment, but when the Løkke Rasmussen government took over in 2015, start help was again introduced.

One area where Sweden's policy on freedom of choice was very significant is its system for so-called self-settlement of asylum seekers. With self-settlement newly arrived asylum seekers can determine for themselves where they want to settle, even prior to a decision on permanent acceptance. This policy has resulted in a much more segregated settlement pattern and greater accumulation of social problems in Sweden than correspondingly in Denmark and Norway, where immigration authorities guide settlement, first at the level of reception and later in municipalities. This freedom to make individual choices of residence, language acquisition, and labor market qualification is perhaps one of the most striking elements of the integration policy of the Swedish welfare state. Another important deviation on the Swedish side was established in 2008 by the Reinfeldt government when asylum seekers were permitted to "change tracks" and apply for residence permits if they obtained jobs after their applications for asylum had been denied. This is a sharp contrast to the long-dominant principle in Scandinavia that refugee status and immigration status should not be mixed together (Borevi 2010).

The rhetoric of public integration has continued to be different in the three countries at least up to 2015. In Denmark and Norway there is more open talk about immigrant obligations than in Sweden. What is called "obligation" in Denmark is generally called "rights," "motivation," or "facilitation" in Sweden. Obligations and rights are more merged in Norway. The backgrounds of these different approaches include different analyses of integration problems in the three countries. Swedish authorities have targeted the structural discrimination and resistant attitudes of the majority population. Danish authorities have pointed to weak labor incentives due to the (over)generous welfare provisions, while Norway has stressed more the quality of public regulation and deficient follow-up (Brochmann and Hagelund 2010).

After 2004 a new reality overtook integration policies in Scandinavia. With the considerable EU labor immigration that ensued after the EU extension eastward, a split immigration regime materialized in Scandinavia: one applies to immigration based on humanitarian principles, and the other applies to EU/EEA immigrants. Labor immigrants have free access in line with a market-based regime and should in principle not receive assistance to integrate, whereas the others have limited access yet are exposed to extensive programs for improving their competence and integration.

Naturalization: Becoming a Citizen

Increasing worry about development of a parallel society in the wake of multicultural immigration has put new discussions on the agenda in Scandinavia. Questions associated with social cohesion—the connecting forces or "glue" in society—were not among the first topics discussed by the Scandinavian public when the new immigration started. More functional goals, such as integration in working life, education, and health care, dominated public discourse at first, and it was some decades before challenges of the value basis for welfare citizenship came up for discussion. How can relatively homogeneous welfare states, with very high ambitions in terms of material security and social redistribution, handle the challenges associated with cultural diversity? How do such states reproduce societal loyalty and solidarity under new circumstances? In other words, how can one recognize cultural difference without at the same time weakening the ties that hold the society together— a community with shared basic values?

Toward the end of the twentieth century these questions had surfaced, influenced by international discussions on the challenges and dilemmas of diversity. Immigration indirectly contributed to directing the spotlight at the receiving countries themselves—their history, political values, self-reflection, and identity. But the discussions hit the different countries with unequal force and direction.

Citizenship legislation was revised in all three countries after the turn of the twenty-first century. The region has in common that their reforms of the naturalization process relate explicitly to the process of integration (Midt-bøen 2009), but the premises for integration are different. Broadly speaking, the three states disagree on whether extension of citizenship should be a part of the integration process itself or a reward for a completed process. Sweden firmly represents the first position, whereas Denmark is solidly on the reward side. Norway has an intermediate stance, although (after the conservative coalition government took over in 2013) it has been increasingly moving away from the Swedish model and closer to Danish thinking. The underlying national concept, which we have seen differs most between Denmark and Sweden, has important implications for this policy. To merit becoming a Dane one must qualify by learning the language, becoming self-sufficient, and making an effort to learn about Danish history, polity, and culture. Applicants for Danish citizenship must be examined on this knowledge and must declare their allegiance and loyalty to their new home country. In Sweden, on the other hand, very few requirements are imposed beyond five-year residency. Multicultural Sweden is seen as an enrichment, both for democracy and the nation, and naturalization is a desirable statutory right for new, equal members of society. Requiring knowledge and skills for naturalization has been viewed as making citizenship into an elitist institution, which would undermine the feeling of unity in the nation (SOU 1999, 318, cited in Midtbøen 2009). Danish authorities want a process that makes it more attractive, even necessary, for new immigrants to acquire language skills and basic knowledge of their new homeland in order to achieve citizenship. Sweden, which included dual citizenship as part of its reforms, wanted to "modernize" the law, to bring it more in line with a multicultural reality, and to "contribute to increased well-being and faster integration into the new society" (203). In Norway new citizenship legislation took a kind of middle position in which some sections of the law most resembled the Danish solutions (e.g., both Norwegian and Danish law rejected dual citizenship). Norway also introduced a (voluntary) citizenship ceremony with an oath.[20] On the other hand, in closer resemblance to Sweden, Norway strengthened the legal status of foreigners in that those who fulfilled the conditions for naturalization had a *right* to Norwegian citizenship.

The differences in approach to the politics of citizenship reflect differences in the ideological basis of the integration policy, which for many decades has developed in different directions in the three countries. Denmark and Sweden are often analyzed in light of the ethnos/demos dichotomy. In Denmark the nation is in the seat of honor; in Sweden it is liberal democracy. What the content of the "glue" should be (i.e., what is required of community and common understanding of basic societal values in order to maintain the formation of society) is viewed differently. All three countries are, however, solidly anchored in a liberal-democratic polity tradition.

"National" as meaning "Danish" has been given a more central position in Denmark than corresponding "Norwegian" in Norway and, not least, "Swedish" in Sweden. Where the Danish introductory act aims to give foreigners an understanding of the values and norms of Danish society, the Swedes in corresponding documents speak of respect for democratic—not Swedish—values. And while the Norwegian and Swedish authorities say that they are positive to cultural, religious, and value based diversity, this type of formulation has disappeared in the Danish context (Brochmann and Hagelund 2010).

Features of this general picture will most probably be continued in the near future, yet there are signs indicating convergence in some areas of citizenship-making in Scandinavia. Increased focus on terrorism and security, as well as the political shock of the refugee crisis in 2015, has induced more concern in Sweden about being too liberal in the European context. Norway has moved more clearly toward a Danish position by introducing language and knowledge tests, as well as pushing for a longer waiting period. Denmark, perhaps surprisingly, moved to allow dual citizenship in 2015, although it was motivated more by the security and rights of emigrated Danes than by immigrant interests. Lastly, Norway allowed dual citizenship beginning on January 1, 2020.

The countries have had different philosophies of integration in line with Favell's (1998) model. All of the countries wish to have integrated members of society, and all of the countries are liberal-democratic states. But in terms of efforts to achieve integration, responsibility is placed differently by the three respective states. All three states have elements of a quite liberal, if paternalistic, approach but rooted in strikingly different conceptions of who should be the target for disciplining efforts. In Sweden the majority is the target. They are seen as potentially critical or hostile; therefore, they need—in the traditional Swedish way—to be trained and molded into endorsing the multicultural society (see Wickström 2013). Denmark, in contrast, sees the immigrant population as the target: they are required to learn liberal values to be able to function well in a modern *and* plural Denmark. Norway has taken an ambivalent and somewhat unclear position in this terrain.

All three countries draw on their respective historical and cultural repertoire as they encounter a new multicultural era. In Denmark social cohesion has been understood as solidarity, created by a virtue of a homogeneous population. Consequently, multicultural immigration becomes a challenge both culturally and institutionally. In Sweden cohesion has been understood as a product of welfare state guidance, and the challenges have been the capacity of the institutions and the ability of society to readjust.[21] In any case, what in fact creates cohesive forces in any national context will be affected by institutionalized norms and rules (Offe 2006), which is to say, previous processes and previous "upbringing" in the form of historic norm formation in the society. What creates cohesiveness can thus vary from context to context.

CONCLUSION

Close to fifty years have passed since the new immigration began in Scandinavia. Sweden was the pioneer country in the region in the matter of establishing central tools for immigration policy early in the 1970s. Denmark and Norway followed in Swedish footsteps to different degrees during the first years but have followed their own paths increasingly since then.

Sociological theories tend to emphasize the mutual constituting relationship between institutions and human action. Actors act rationally, but what is experienced as "rational" is institutionalized and culturally embedded. Norms and culture also create informal institutions that shape incentives for or inhibitions to action (Thelen 1999, 377). Institutions and cultural repertoire, on the other hand, tend to create durable structures, "path dependence," as it is often called (Pierson 2004): the easiest or most available route is often the one already trampled out.

The three countries we have followed in this chapter in connection with immigration and societal integration policies shared many institutional preconditions at the outset, where the welfare model had a special place. The cultural repertoire had many common features, but it also comprised important differences. These differences contributed over time to an internal dynamic interaction between philosophies of integration politics, public debate, and party politics. Central political actors positioned themselves differently in the three countries in relation to immigration policies and had different strings to play on in their respective majority populations. Immigration-critical parties to the right have been important here. The Danish Progress Party (Fremskridtspartiet) already had a critical stance on immigration in the early 1970s, dampening the otherwise friendly climate toward immigrants. Its successor, the Danish Folk Party (Dansk Folkeparti), played an important role as a supporter of the Fogh Rasmussen government after 2001, which strongly contributed to developing the restrictive Danish policy in the following years. The social democrats in Denmark have also been more split on the question of immigration than their sister parties in neighboring countries.

In Norway the Progress Party (Fremskrittspartiet) began to play a central role in immigration policy after the field became "politicized" at the end of the 1980s. The party managed to capitalize on the strands of population critical of immigration and grew considerably, especially after the turn of the century. The rest of the political scenery was by and large pressed into a more restrictive immigration policy. After 2013 the Progress Party entered government for the first time, together with the Conservative Party (Høyre), and in 2018 also with the Liberal Party (Venstre). The Christian Democratic Party (Kristelig Folkeparti) joined in 2019 whereas the Progress Party left again in 2020.

For many years Sweden had a political party situation lacking any serious populist opposition to immigration. The more ideologically founded immigration policy was therefore hardly challenged by critical voices on the right. This scene changed in 2010, when the Sweden Democrats won 5.7 percent of the votes in the parliamentary elections. This tendency was reinforced later on: the party got 13 percent of the votes in the 2014 election. Since 2014 the political situation in Sweden has changed drastically, caused largely by the refugee crisis in 2015, in which Swedish authorities had to make a U-turn in their immigration policy after the arrival of 160,000 asylum seekers. During the fall of 2015 a more clearly restrictive approach was instituted overnight. These measures were meant to be temporary, yet it is hard to believe that Sweden will return to its former liberalism after the September 2018 election, in which the Sweden Democrats reinforced their influence with 17.6 percent of the vote.

In spite of their political and cultural differences, all three countries face similar challenges in the field of immigration under the current circumstances. Their national welfare models depend on the greatest possible number of inhabitants being employed in order to maintain generous and universal welfare. On the other hand, the generous welfare states and the compressed wage structure (high wages for low qualified work) constitute challenges for a significant part of the immigrant populations to fulfilling this prerequisite due to their low levels of job qualification.

In the years ahead, much will depend on EU policy-making. The refugee crisis caused a literal breakdown of the hard-won EU regulations on immigration, with resurrected border control in major member countries and a more restrictive line on rights for asylum seekers. In Scandinavia 2015 triggered

Immigration to Scandinavian Welfare States in the Time of Pluralism   55

more convergence among the three states on central immigration issues, although Denmark remains the hardliner. Yet inflow control will most likely be seen as crucial in Sweden and Norway also. Through the years all three countries have tried, to different degrees, to control access. At the same time, all three countries have developed new tools in welfare and working life to integrate newcomers more effectively. Through general welfare policy and more targeted means, the Scandinavian governments have trusted that social engineering, equal treatment, and antidiscrimination would do the job of integration.

The past ten to fifteen years have also brought into focus questions of *social cohesion*: what it takes to uphold trust, solidarity, and community feelings in a more multicultural setting. Value conflicts have gained attention in all three countries. Citizenship policies have been addressed to deal with these issues. This is a nebulous field, yet as long as citizenship exists as an institution, the content of naturalization policies will signal what kinds of membership and polity are considered desirable to preserve and to cultivate.

NOTES

This chapter is a translated and revised version of Grete Brochmann, "Innvandring til Skandinavia: Velferdsstater i pluralismens tid," in *Det norske samfunn*, ed. Ivar Frønes and Lise Kjølsrød (Oslo: Gyldendal Akademisk, 2016), 130–55.

1. Sweden, which was not occupied by the German Nazi regime during World War II, had an economic head start over war-torn Denmark and Norway and was in need of foreign workers soon after the war. They were mainly Finns, but workers from farther away also came to Sweden first.

2. In this connection I use "Nordic" and "Scandinavian" as synonyms, even if "Nordic" formally also includes Finland and Iceland. The three Scandinavian countries have the most common features as regards the organization of their societies and historical development relevant to immigration.

3. The following section is based on Brochmann and Hagelund (2010).

4. The refugee crisis in the summer and fall of 2015 caused significant changes in all three countries in order to inhibit further flow. The most pronounced change was in Sweden. After having received a record number of refuges (just over 160,000 by the end of the year), the government was forced to introduce border controls. At the same time, there was comprehensive tightening of the rights of immigrants after asylum had been approved. Also, Denmark and Norway, which accepted far more asylum seekers than normally (approximately thirty thousand in Norway and approximately twenty thousand in Denmark), instituted border controls and tightened immigrants' rights. The crisis of 2015 also triggered a rougher public debate in Sweden.

5. This approach was inspired by Christina Boswell (2007), who in employing new institutional theory uses *interests, ideas,* and *institutions* as a starting point to explain the countries' immigration policies.

6. See Brochmann and Kjeldstadli (2014) for a more detailed treatment of the history of immigration in Norway and Brochmann and Hagelund (2010) regarding the development of immigration politics in the three Scandinavian countries from 1945 to 2010.

7. Sweden quite explicitly followed a different line from guest worker policies and signaled early on that foreign employees were welcome to settle permanently in Sweden.

8. In 2018 Sweden's share of immigrants of the total population was 19 percent. The corresponding figure for Norway was 16 percent and for Denmark 12 percent.

9. *Universalism* in the Nordic model needs to be qualified. The benefit system actually represents a combined model with both universal and earned benefits. The level of compensation also varies with qualification period. But the Nordic model is doubtless *more* universal than other welfare models in most areas.

10. Denmark was opened for labor from the EF (EEC) from the time the country became a member in 1972. The same was true for Sweden and Norway (respectively, EU and EEA) in 1994.

11. These policies cover numerous areas that affect the situation for immigrants in a receiving country, such as the labor market, housing, social services and general welfare, education, language instruction, support for organizational work, and so on.

12. See Borevi (2010) and Wickström (2013) for a more thorough report on the ideological basis of immigration policies in Sweden.

13. See Brochmann and Hagelund (2012) for a comparison of the three countries in this policy field.

14. "The people's home" is a Swedish metaphor for a society that is organized to take care of citizens from the cradle to the grave.

15. The year 2015 was decisive in this way. Sweden signaled an open attitude, especially for Syrians fleeing war. Most other countries (except Germany) in Europe tightened up, and consequently, Sweden received a disproportionately strong flow until the Swedish authorities introduced border control in November of the same year.

16. The four-year requirement means that the immigrant with refugee status, residence status on humanitarian grounds, or residence through the regulations on immigration of a family must have been in full-time work or full-time training in Norway for four years before family establishment can be granted. The four-year requirement is in addition to the support requirement.

17. "Demand-controlled" meant that the need for this labor must be determined specifically by the employer.

Immigration to Scandinavian Welfare States in the Time of Pluralism   57

18. The target groups for these plans are somewhat different in the three countries. In Sweden and Norway only humanitarian-based immigrants are included, whereas Denmark also includes other groups of new arrivals (Breidahl 2012; Brochmann and Djuve 2013).

19. The "start help" should, in principle, treat all who had residence in Denmark for less than the past seven years equally; consequently, it avoided accusations of discrimination.

20. In recent years, both Denmark and Norway have allowed dual citizenship, and Norway has also introduced a language and knowledge test as a requirement for naturalization.

21. See Borevi (2015) for an interesting analysis along these lines.

References

Benhabib, Seyla. 2002. "Transformations of Citizenship: The Case of Contemporary Europe." *Government and Opposition* 37(4): 439–65.

Borevi, Karin. 2010. "Sverige: Mångkulturalismens flaggskepp i Norden." In *Velferdens grenser: Innvandringspolitikk og velferdsstat i Skandinavia 1945–2010*, edited by Grete Brochmann and Anniken Hagelund, 41–131. Oslo: Universitetsforlaget.

Borevi, Karin. 2014. "Multiculturalism and Welfare State Integration: Swedish Model Path Dependency." *Identities: Global Studies in Culture and Power* 21(6): 708–23.

Borevi, Karin. 2015. "Diversity and Solidarity in Denmark and Sweden." *ECPR Warsaw*, March 29–April 2.

Boswell, Christina. 2007. "Theorizing Migration Policy: Is There a Third Way?" *International Migration Review* 41(1): 75–100.

Breidahl, Karen N. 2012. "Når staten lærer: En historisk og komparativ analyse af statslig policy læring og betydningen heraf for udviklingen i den arbejdsmarkedsrettede del af indvandrerpolitikken i Sverige, Norge og Danmark fra 1970 til 2011." PhD diss., Aalborg University.

Brochmann, Grete. 2007. "Til Dovre faller: 'Å bli norsk—å være norsk—troskapsløfte og statsborgerskap i den foranderlige nasjonen" [To become Norwegian—to be Norwegian—pledge of allegiance and citizenship in a changing nation]. In *Migration och tillhörighet: Inklusions- och exklusionsprocesser i Skandinavien*, edited by Gunnar Alsmark, Tina Kallehave, and Bolette Moldenhawer, 99–126. Gothenburg: Makadam Förlag.

Brochmann, Grete. 2014. "Governing Immigration in Advanced Welfare States: The Scandinavian Case." In *Controlling Immigration: A Global Perspective*, edited by Philip Martin and James F. Hollifield, 281–302. Stanford, CA: Stanford University Press.

Brochmann, Grete, and Anne Britt Djuve. 2013. "Multiculturalism or Assimilation? The Norwegian Welfare State Approach." In *Debating Multiculturalism in the Nordic*

Welfare States, edited by Peter Kivisto and Östen Wahlbeck, 219–46. London: Palgrave Macmillan.

Brochmann, Grete, and Anniken Hagelund. 2010. "Sammenlikning: En modell med tre unntak?" In *Velferdens grenser: Innvandringspolitikk og velferdsstat i Skandinavia 1945–2010,* edited by Grete Brochmann and Anniken Hagelund, 307–68. Oslo: Universitetsforlaget.

Brochmann, Grete, and Knut Kjeldstadli. 2014. *Innvandringen til Norge 900–2010.* Oslo: Pax Forlag.

Brochmann, Grete, and Idunn Seland. 2010. "Citizenship Policies and Ideas of Nationhood in Scandinavia." *Citizenship Studies* 14(4): 429–45.

Eisenberg, Avigail, and Jeff Spinner-Halev. 2005. *Minorities within Minorities: Equality, Rights and Diversity.* Cambridge: Cambridge University Press.

Esping-Andersen, Gøsta, and Walter Korpi. 1987. "From Poor Relief to Institutional Welfare States: The Development of Scandinavian Social Policy." In *The Scandinavian Model: Welfare States and Welfare Research,* edited by Robert Erikson, Erik Jørgen Hanson, Stein Ringen, and Hannu Uusitalo, 112–45. New York: M. E. Sharpe.

Favell, Adrian. 1998. *Philosophies of Integration: Immigration and the Idea of Citizenship in France and Britain.* London: Macmillan.

Fraser, Nancy. 1995. "From Redistribution to Recognition? Dilemmas of Justice in a 'Post-Socialist' Age." *New Left Review* 212 (July/August): 68–93.

Gür, Thomas. 1996. *Staten och nykomlingarna: En studie av den svenska invandrarpolitikens ideer.* Stockholm: City University Press.

Hall, Peter A., and Rosemary C. R. Taylor. 1996. "Political Science and the Three New Institutionalisms." *Political Studies* 44(5): 936–57.

Hirdman, Yvonne. 2000. *Att lägga livet til rätta.* Stockholm: Carlssons.

Holm, Lærke Klitgård. 2007. "Folketinget og udlændingepolitikken: Diskurser om naturaliserede, indvandrere og flygtninge 1973–2002." PhD diss., Akademiet for Migrationsstudier i Danmark, Ålborg University.

Joppke, Christian. 2008. "Immigration and the Identity of Citizenship: The Paradox of Universalism." *Citizenship Studies* 12(6): 533–46.

March, James G., and Johan P. Olsen. 1989. *Rediscovering Institutions.* New York: Free Press.

Midtbøen, Arnfinn Haagensen. 2009. "Statsborgerrettslig revisjon og integrasjonspolitisk variasjon i de skandinaviske landene." *Tidsskrift for samfunnsforskning* 50(4): 523–50.

Ministry of Labor and Social Affairs. 2003–4. *Mangfold gjennom inkludering og deltakelse: Ansvar og frihet.* No. 49. Regjeringen.no. Oslo: Kommunal- og Regionaldepartementet.

NOU (Norges offentlige utredninger). 2000. *Lov om erverv og tap av norsk statsborgerskap.* Oslo: Statens Forvaltningstjeneste.

Offe, Claus. 2006. "Is There, or Can There Be a 'European Society'?" In *Civil Society: Berlin Perspectives*, edited by John Keane, 169–88. New York: Berghahn Books.

Okin, Susan Moller. 1999. "Is Multiculturalism Bad for Women?" In *Is Multiculturalism Bad for Women? Susan Mollar Okin with Respondents*, edited by Joshua Cohen et al., 7–24. Princeton, NJ: Princeton University Press.

Østerud, Øyvind. 1991. *Nasjonenes selvbestemmelsesrett*. Oslo: Universitetsforlaget.

Pierson, Paul. 2004. *Politics in Time: History, Institutions, and Social Analysis*. Princeton, NJ: Princeton University Press.

Sejersted, Francis. 2005. *Sosialdemokratiets tidsalder: Norge og Sverige i det 20. århundre*. Oslo: Pax.

Siim, Birte, and Hege Skjeie. 2008. "Tracks, Intersections and Dead Ends: Multicultural Challenges to State Feminism in Denmark and Norway." *Ethnicities* 8(3): 322–44.

SOU (Statens offentliga utredningar). 1974. *Invandrarna och minoriteterna: Huvudbetänkande av invandrarutredningen*.

SOU (Statens offentliga utredningar). 1999. *Svenskt medborgarskap: Slutbetänkande av 1997 års medborgarskapskommitté*.

Soysal, Yasemin. 1994. *Limits of Citizenship*. Chicago: University of Chicago Press.

Swidler, Ann. 1986. "Culture in Action: Symbols and Strategies." *American Sociological Review* 51(2): 273–86.

Thelen, Kathleen. 1999. "Historical Institutionalism in Comparative Politics." *Annual Reviews of Political Science* 2:369–404.

Vad Jønsson, Heid, and Klaus Petersen. 2012. "Denmark: A National Welfare State Meets the World." In *Immigration Policy and the Scandinavian Welfare State 1945–2010*, edited by Grete Brochmann and Anniken Hagelund, 97–149. New York: Palgrave Macmillan.

Vatne Pettersen, Silje, and Lars Østby. 2013. "Innvandrere i Norge, Sverige og Danmark." *Samfunnsspeilet* 5 (December).

Wickström, Mats. 2013. "Conceptual Change in Postwar Sweden: The Marginalization of Assimilation and the Introduction of Integration." In *Debating Multiculturalism in the Nordic Welfare States*, edited by Peter Kivisto and Östen Wahlbeck, 110–40. London: Palgrave Macmillan.

Folkhemmet

"The People's Home" as an Expression of Retrotopian Longing for Sweden before the Arrival of Mass Migration

ANDREAS ÖNNERFORS

To paraphrase Freud, "Immigration to Sweden and Its Discontents" would make a fitting title for a much-needed study of the country's contemporary political climate. It would have the potential to outline a political psychology, even what one might call a political pathology, of Sweden and the Swedes today. Over the last decades, Swedish attitudes toward migration have shifted profoundly. Sweden was once seen as a modern model country with cosmopolitan attitudes and ambitions of solidarity on the world stage, but now parochialism, xenophobia, and "welfare nostalgia" or "white melancholy" prevail, which have led to increasing support for the right-wing populist party Sverigedemokraterna (SD, Sweden Democrats), with historical origins in neo-Nazism (Lundström and Hübinette 2020; Pallas 2011). In the 2018 general elections, the SD received almost 18 percent of the vote, and its impact on the Swedish political landscape cannot be ignored (see Wodak 2015, 204–5, and for the electoral success of European right-wing parties in general, see 29–32).

Part of Sweden's recent political pathology is an irrational longing for "the past as the future," or "retrotopia," in the words of Zygmunt Bauman (2017). As I will argue in this chapter, these sentimental desires for past national homogeneity during the golden "record years" (*rekordåren*) between 1945 and about 1970, and thus before the definite arrival of mass migration, gravitate around the political master concept of *folkhemmet*, "the people's home."[1] Once floated during the interwar era as a vision of the Swedish coercive welfare state, predominantly of social democratic and modernist fashion, its aim was to create a coherent national society with strong redistributive justice and public delivery of political goods with a robust component of statism. But this return to the past is more than simple nostalgia. It informs a vision of the future *as* the past, a presumed golden age of purity undisturbed by "the foreigner," its diverging body, and its mentalities.

In this state, interpreting Sweden's past has become a contested battle ground of politicocultural memory. Since the origins and heydays of *folkhemmet* are placed in the period before the advent of mass migration to Sweden, my claim is that the concept is of exceptionally salient value in contemporary Swedish retrotopian political rhetoric. It suggests social security and cohesion (*trygghet*), exclusively delivered to the native members of the national community of welfare. This partly explains why privileged membership or citizenship is so highly contested, particularly when coupled with ideas of culture. By claiming *folkhemmet*, or at least its welfare agenda, it is possible to argue for exclusion and supremacy against the significant other, who has not yet earned his membership or never will turn "Swedish" enough to deserve it. At the same time, it is possible to create enemy images of those who have contributed to the erosion of *folkhemmet* and thus to point out scapegoats responsible for the collapse of security in an age of "persistent instrumental crises" (Bauman 2017, 153).

The retrotopian desire to reestablish a new home for the Swedish people as a vision for the future harks back to a relatively short time frame in Swedish history when the country was not immediately affected by *any* migration—neither emigration nor immigration. It is therefore also an excellent signifier and place marker for anti-immigration politics without being forced to name immigration (and integration) as societal challenges today. This follows what Ruth Wodak (2015, 52–54) has called a discursive strategy of "calculated ambivalence" in contemporary European right-wing discourses. By referring to *folkhemmet*, it is possible to evoke strongly symbolically charged memories of an uncorrupted golden age and at the same time cloak other ideological positions that more easily could be decoded as outright exclusionary or aggressively xenophobic. In terms of memory politics, this is a deliberatively selective strategy.

As a matter of introduction, I will thus argue that the history of Sweden until 1905, which was informed by experiences of multicultural encounters, dynamic hybridizations, and processes of identification (albeit placed in Scandinavia and the Baltic Sea area), could provide perspectives upon contemporary political imaginaries that are completely different from the short time frame of the "golden years" (intrinsically tied to *folkhemmet*). Thus, the topos of history, so permanently evoked as it is in the populist Right rhetoric, is manipulated to fit into favored fallacies of argumentation. Moreover, since the valuable concept of *folkhemmet* is so closely tied to the history of Svenska Socialdemokratiska Arbetarepartiet (SAP, Swedish Social Democrat Labor Party) and its exceptionally long time in power (between 1932 and 2000; SAP has been the opposition party only nine years), it has recently become a main objective of Swedish right-wing rhetoric to undermine social democracy and its "contaminated history."

The empirical core of my chapter is constituted of a game-changing example illustrating these semantic shifts. In his 2017 speech at the Swedish political event Almedalsveckan, held on the Baltic island of Gotland, SD's leader, Jimmie Åkesson, reclaimed the term *folkhemmet*, to which he referred more than forty times.[2] Simultaneously, he recited the 1899 poem "Medborgarsång" (Citizens' song), written by his favorite author, Verner von Heidenstam (1859–1940), one of the most prominent writers of the national Romantic era. For Åkesson, this combination signaled SD's vision of a fusion of socialism and conservatism into an "idea of the same rights and duties for all citizens" beyond the traditional Left/Right division of politics, which the European New Right (ENR) claims to have left behind (Bar-On 2014). Åkesson made a case that *folkhemmet* can be restored for the benefit of the national community.

It would be useful to engage in inter-Scandinavian comparisons to see what may or may not be unique about this recovery of a central concept in political rhetoric, in particular, the idea of the welfare state as synonymous to the national community. Across the Nordic region, redistributive justice in social democratic fashion was an essential feature of modernization. However, populist right-wing movements and parties in Denmark and Norway originated in antitaxation sentiments and ideas of heterodox libertarianism rather than collectivist ideals of a new nationalism (as in SD) (Bergmann 2020, 147–67). Nonetheless, across the region "excessive" immigration and the related issue of "failed" integration are framed rhetorically as common threats against the values of a "Scandinavian lifestyle," which has placed the countries steadily on the upper right corner of the World Values Survey.[3] In a comparative perspective, an interrogation about received truths and narratives related to the evolution of the different nation-states (and the implications of national community today) would enhance the analysis of managing multiculturalism in the Scandinavian countries since it would reveal several layers of meaning that otherwise might be overlooked.

Folkhemmet   63

A 2020 ad produced by Scandinavian Airlines that challenges essentialist self-definitions is a good example of how contested this level of cultural connotations is.[4] The two-minute, twelve-second film was removed from SAS's social media accounts within twenty-four hours after a massive right-wing protest campaign, boosted by the media outlet Samhällsnytt and the Russian disinformation platform Sputnik, which disseminated the clip together with the message that it represented a self-destructive promotion of multiculturalism in the region (Tronarp 2020). In the film, a female voice-over asks, "What is truly Scandinavian?" together with images of "typical" scenes such as a Swedish camper, a blonde girl wearing a Norwegian *bunad* (folk dress), a birthday party scene, a designer chair, and a Danish seafarer's tattoo. The reply to this question is "absolutely nothing," followed by stunning shots of Scandinavian landscapes and people in different languages also negating the question. The voice-over then explains, "Everything is copied": democracy originated in Greece, parental leave started in Switzerland, "the iconic Scandinavian windmills" were actually invented in Persia, Danish transport bicycles are credited to Germany, Sweden's famous *rugbrød* came from Turkey, and the national dish of *smørrebrød* started in the Netherlands. Not even the iconic Swedish midsummer pole is of Scandinavian origin, and "it gets worse," one of the disillusioned characters in the clip states. The "even-so-Swedish" meatballs are Turkish, Danish pastry is in reality Austrian, and the pride of Norway, the paperclip, was actually invented by an American (the United States is then thanked for female suffrage!). In the second part of the ad, people of non-Scandinavian extraction are portrayed explaining that "we are as good as our Viking ancestors," taking everything we like from our trips abroad and just adjusting it a bit. This bricolage is celebrated as "a unique Scandinavian thing," to go out in the world and to get inspiration: "Every time we go beyond our borders, we add colors, innovation, progress." Scandinavia in this narrative thus was not constituted by and in itself, the ad claims, but by these processes of assemblage: "In a way, Scandinavia was brought here piece by piece." It is the global mobility of the Scandinavians that has created its spirit and meaning, and the ad concludes: "We cannot wait to see what you bring home next." One might think that this seemingly innocent advertisement for an airline company would not stir up strong emotions, but right-wing trolls mobilized and then poured their disgust across the internet, complaining about attitudes of self-harm and self-hate and the corrupting influence of multiculturalism. Moreover, the composition of speakers and actors representing Scandinavians, together with their place in "typical" settings, was as heavily criticized as the practice of non-Scandinavian customs. The SAS ad, together with its negative reception, serves as an illustration of the many subtexts and layers that constitute managing multiculturalism in Scandinavia. In the case of Sweden, the root metaphor of the people's home is embedded in specific cultural and historical contexts, which explains its constitutive significance in political meaning-making (Bauman 2017, 153).

FOLKHEMMET AS A METAPHOR OF NEW RIGHT POLITICAL MYTHOLOGY

The text of the speech delivered by Åkesson offline at Almedalsveckan in July 2017 is now available, as is his performance of it (Åkesson 2017b). The Swedish text manuscript, which constitutes the basis of my analysis, can likewise be consulted online and is briefly summarized in the following paragraph (Sweden Democrats 2017). Its total of 237 lines can be divided into nineteen parts around a core of central concepts, analyzed in detail below.

First, Åkesson attempts to synthesize the communitarian idea of *folkhemmet*, with Heidenstam's national Romantic era poem as a shorthand vision of his politics, fusing and moving beyond Left and Right, socialism and conservatism. On a number of occasions, he points at culprits and scapegoats that consciously have driven Sweden into a polarizing and destructive antagonism between "us" and "them," "them" being the liberal Left establishment in particular. A major part of his speech is devoted to a travel account from which Åkesson deduces the pathology of a broken Swedish society. The political mission of the Sweden Democrats is to (re)establish a balance of rights and liberties against demands and duties in exchange for community, cohesion, security, and solidarity. The second largest part of the speech describes his party as the one guaranteeing social and medical care and true welfare. Highlighting "Medborgarsång," Åkesson extends a very conditional welcome to those who arrive to Sweden from outside predicated on their total assimilation to national norms.

Taken as a whole, Åkesson's speech represents a textbook example of rhetorical elements in what Wodak describes as a "micropolitics of fear": (1) a focus on the people and nativist body politics; (2) a stress on the heartland and constructed (external and internal) threat scenarios; (3) protection of the fatherland and the belief in a common narrative of the past combined with revisionist histories (in Åkesson's case, reclaiming *folkhemmet*); (4) conspiracist narratives, in which scapegoats are identified who malignantly and

Folkhemmet

intentionally aim at the downfall of the nation; (5) traditional and conservative values and morals ("family values," loyalty, the value of "hard work," righteousness); (6) commonsense explanations and solutions; together with (7) the need for a savior and leader "who oscillates between the role of Robin Hood, protecting the social welfare state and helping the 'man and woman on the street,'" and the "strict father," demanding but fair (Wodak 2015, 66–67). To do this, a number of discursive strategies are employed, such as Manichaean divisions, generalizations, blaming, the topoi of history and the savior, the construction of conspiracies coupled with "unreal scenarios," and finally the strategy of calculated ambivalence (68).

Since Heidenstam's poem occupies a significant place in Åkesson's rhetoric, it is presented in full below, together with an English translation.[5]

Medborgarsång

Så sant vi äga ett fädernesland,
vi ärvde det alla lika,
med samma rätt och med samma band
för både arma och rika;
och därför vilja vi rösta fritt
som förr bland sköldar och bågar,
men icke vägas i köpmäns mitt,
likt penningepåsar på vågar.

Vi stridde gemensamt för hem och härd,
då våra kuster förbrändes.
Ej herrarna ensamt grepo till svärd,
när varnande vårdkase tändes.
Ej herrarna ensamt segnade ner
men också herrarnas drängar.
Det är skam, det är fläck på Sveriges banér,
att medborgarrätt heter pengar.

Det är skam att sitta, som vi ha gjort,
och tempel åt andra välva,
men kasta stenar på egen port
och tala ont om oss själva.
Vi tröttnat att blöda för egen dolk,
att hjärtat från huvudet skilja;

vi vilja bliva ett enda folk,
och vi äro och bli det vi vilja.

Citizens' Song

As sure as we have a fatherland,
We are heirs to it one with another,
By common right in an equal band
The rich and his needy brother.
Let each have his voice as we did of old
When a shield was the freeman's measure,
And not all be weighed like sacks of gold
By a merchant counting his treasure.

We fought for our homes together when
Our coast by the foeman was blighted.
It was not alone the gentlemen
Drew sword when the beacons were lighted.
Not only the gentlemen sank to earth
But also the faithful yeomen;
'Tis a blot on our flag that we reckon worth
By wealth, and poor men are no men.

'Tis a shame to do as we oft have done,—
Give strangers the highest places,
But beat our own doors with many a stone
And publish our own disgraces.
We are weary of bleeding by our own knife,
When the heart from the head we sever;
We would be as one folk with a single life,
Which we are and shall be forever.

Detailed Analysis of Åkesson's Speech

The following analysis is based on the written manuscript and live performance of Åkesson's speech at Almedalsveckan referred to previously. Since these can be consulted in the public domain, I have refrained from quoting the Swedish original. I have added very short thematic codes, which introduce each passage and summarize their primary rhetorical function.

Folkhemmet 67

Åkesson, the Uncorrupted Truth Teller (Lines 1–13)

It is obvious that Åkesson in the opening of the speech attempts to distance himself from other politicians and their bickering. He styles himself as a truth teller, expressing what the electorate wants to hear. In outlining his vision for the future, he immediately turns to the past, including a key quote by the *pater patriae*, Per Albin Hansson, about the idea of *folkhemmet*.

Bridging Socialism and Conservatism (Lines 14–25)

Everyone in the Swedish audience recognized Åkesson's quote from Per Albin Hansson as part of the social democratic legacy; therefore, Åkesson hurried to combine it with Heidenstam's conservative "Medborgarsång." This is an interesting second historical reference and worth commenting on at some length, since Åkesson also recited the poem personally at the end of his speech. The poem was first published in 1899 as a part of a cycle with six parts titled *Ett folk* (One people) in the newspaper *Svenska Dagbladet*. It was later inserted in the volume *Nya dikter* (New poems) in 1915. *Ett folk* outlines a grand vision of a nationally united Swedish people within clearly defined boundaries in space who are inspired by Sweden's heroic history and its common will, expressed through universal suffrage. *Ett folk* was set to music in the critical year of 1905 by Wilhelm Stenhammar (1871–1927), a national Romantic composer (see Stenhammar 1997). Thus, there is a direct link to the formative years of modern Swedish nationhood, which, as I argued previously, came into being after the dissolution of the political union with Norway in that year.

But there are also other readings of the song that reach out to the contemporary Swedish extreme Right. A version of "Medborgarsång" was recorded by the Nordic pagan folk band Solblot as recently as 2008. In 2012 it was posted on YouTube with a video that celebrates the supremacy of white Swedishness by the channel Theodiskfolk (4,523 subscribers, almost three million views), which has a clear right-wing, identitarian, and revisionist pro-Nazi edge (see Solblot 2008, 2012). In 2015 the Swedish neo-Nazi organization Nordiska Motståndsrörelsen (NMR, Nordic Resistance Movement, in 2018 outlawed in Finland) recommended Solblot's song to the readers of its website. Thus, when Åkesson cited his favorite author in 2017, he simultaneously (consciously or unconsciously) struck a chord within camps of the Swedish extreme Right. Questioned by journalists about this use of Heidenstam, Åkesson denied any knowledge of connections with NMR (see Åkesson 2017a).[6]

Åkesson combined Hansson and Heidenstam in order to construct a cultural bridge between Swedish conservatism and socialism and thus to present SD's political synthesis beyond the traditional Left/Right division, which is a typical characteristic of the program of the European New Right.[7] At the same time, Åkesson formulated a core element of his recipe for political order: the "idea of rights and obligations for each citizen" (line 20). Class struggles are left behind for the common good, for the benefit of the "community, necessary for each individual" (line 22). Åkesson proposes a great vision of consensus and community.

Traveling the Troubled Heartlands of Sweden (Lines 26–34)

One of the largest parts of his speech is devoted to his travels "in my home, in our home. I have traveled around in Sweden. I have met with thousands of people" (lines 26–27), thus linking the topos of the home with the topos of travel as a form of authentic and empirical generation of knowledge. His combined travel account (lines 26–34 and 53–95) can be read as a symbolic encounter with everyone, a fusion of Jeremy Bentham's *Panopticon* (1791) and Thomas Hobbes's *Leviathan* (1651) in the sense that Åkesson can make the claim to have seen the entirety of Sweden's problems and to embody the whole body politic of the common people, just as the frontispiece of *Leviathan* indicates. The leader of the SD has traveled *to* the people, which suggests a direct and private proximity, a feature of recognition. He has listened to *them*; he has tried to understand how *they* feel, think, and experience *their* real lives. He has attempted to understand *their* worries.

At least three associations can be made here. First, Åkesson is in a sense a political traveler in the Linnaean tradition. Just as Carl von Linné's (1707–78) disciples traveled around the Swedish landscape with the task of empirically mapping the three realms of nature, as well as human culture, Åkesson travels from north (Gällivare) to south (Malmö) and from west (Skövde) to east (Husby). Furthermore, his travels represent a form of *Eriksgata* even before Åkesson represents formal governing power. *Eriksgata* was the name of the traditional travel of a newly elected king in the Swedish Middle Ages, seeking and confirming the local endorsement of the monarch. By having visited his country's heartlands, Åkesson can legitimately claim to articulate the voice of his subjects and to have been empowered by them; he morphs into *their* subject position and thus incarnates Ernst Kantrowicz's (1981) idea of the "two bodies" of the medieval king: the physical and the abstract.[8]

Yet in a more symbolic sense, "Jimmie's wonderful adventures" resemble the travels of Selma Lagerlöf's child-hero Nils Holgersson: Åkesson gauges the human and sociopolitical geography of the nation through the tantalizing testimonies of inhabitants named Tari, Joachim, Linn, Ann-Britt, and Petronella. Appeal to the "common people" and the articulation of their "general will" is an essential feature of populist discourses, presupposing the existence of a homogeneous people (Wodak 2015, 8–9). In combination with Heidenstam, it appears as if 2017 is the reimagined moment just before the Swedish people are reborn as a single unit—and Åkesson styles himself as its savior. We learn from the Nils Holgersson travel story that every hundred years the magic city of Vineta resurfaces from the floor of the Baltic Sea, and Nils visits the magical Vineta together with the Pomeranian stork Herr Ermenrich in one of the rare accounts of fictional geography in Lagerlöf's novel. Åkesson in a later passage reflects upon the fact that it is impossible to travel back in time, but he aims still to rescue *folkhemmet*, drowned as it currently is under the seas of neoliberal clearance sales, new public management fantasies, and earlier social democratic austerity politics. From there *folkhemmet* will rise again, he promises, in a new guise.

Placing Polarizing Blame on the Scapegoats of Sweden's Demise (Lines 35–52)

But before Åkesson could provide his audience with accounts of his travel encounters, it was necessary for him to address alienation and fears, to identify culprits, to launch a Manichaean division between "us" and "them." The creation of scapegoats, argues Wodak (2015, 3–4), is a typical feature of populist right-wing discourses of fear. Sweden cannot be recognized any longer because the present has turned into a foreign country (Bauman 2017, 57). For "some" this is a positive development, deliberately meant to destroy "our" cohesion and community, to remove the foundations of "our" society what "we" in generations have created together. "We" are concerned about segregation, division, polarization, parallel societies, insecurity, and "their" encroachments on state welfare; "we" have an overwhelming sense of deprivation (96). This image has only been reinforced by Åkesson's travel encounters.

Representing the Victims of the Swedish Breakdown (Lines 53–94)

The immigrant "Tari" (from Kurdish Iraq, potentially signifying that he is not Muslim but secular or belonging to a religious minority such as the Yazidis) is styled as an authentic and legitimate witness of the Stockholm suburb of Husby as an emblematic "no-go zone" plagued by physical assault, terrified women, burglary, drug trafficking, and omnipresent organized crime. Åkesson's conclusion is that insecurity negates freedom. His sentence can be interpreted as a variation of a notorious 1997 book by the former social democratic prime minister Göran Persson, *Den som är satt i skuld är icke fri* (He who is indebted is not free), which outlined the matrix and self-justification of his 1990s harsh and sober austerity politics. But exactly twenty years later, political issues are no longer about economy and economic performance but about personal security, something that can be linked indirectly to the entire frame narrative of immigration, integration, law and order, and any punitive regime of securitization. These frames touch the nerve of our times and also reach the international media.

The next example goes in the same direction. "Joachim" from China confirms the breakdown of society in Malmö, another geographic shorthand metaphor of *systemkollapsen*, the alleged "collapse of the system" that dominated the societal discourse in Sweden mainly in 2015 and 2016.[9] On a couple of occasions, Joachim has had his restaurant vandalized "by local gangs" and received repeated death threats, but still the police do nothing: "Society has surrendered" (line 68). Joachim represents a hard-working, entrepreneurial, non-European, and well-integrated immigrant, the quiet and diligent Asian who does not originate from the Middle East or North Africa and is not a Muslim.[10]

Åkesson's first two examples reveal what Wodak (2015) calls a rhetorical strategy of "calculated ambivalence": both Tari and Joachim are obviously "good" immigrants, suffering themselves from the consequences of failed immigration and integration policies. Thus, Åkesson can criticize these failed policies without being accused of xenophobia himself, since the victims of the crime are "useful foreigners" (to paraphrase the term "useful idiots," wrongfully ascribed to Lenin).

Discussion with "Linn" in Linköping but originally from Dalarna (arguably the iconic landscape of true Swedishness) confirms the exposure of the (presumably Swedish) female body to sexual violence by foreigners, which she gives as the reason she joined the SD. "Ann-Britt" in Gällivare illustrates a particular betrayal of the Swedish welfare state turned inhuman by denying personal assistance to her multiply disabled son (a hotly debated topic in Sweden) and thus symbolically undermining her caring motherhood. The burnout of another caring woman, "Petronella" from Skövde, points in the same direction. Her stressful labor situation as an emergency nurse places her at the hazardous limits of her physical capacity and her (psychological) loyalty to her coworkers.

Diagnosing the Health and Disease of the Nation-State (Lines 95–108)

Åkesson states that welfare is backed up by those who are loyal and dutiful, who see their job as a mission. He opposes this attitude to "those who only demand—demand more and more—demand their rights without reflecting upon [the fact] that all these rights rest on mutual duties and obligations" (line 95), thus adding fuel to his division of people into "we" and the indefinitely greedy "others" without exactly naming those dogmatists on the Far Left who speak only in the language of social justice. Åkesson's traveling empiricism allows him to style himself as a truth teller. This is the life reality of "true people of flesh and blood" (line 98), and the SD leader is capable of the diagnosis that "Sweden is ill" (line 99). Finally, he names the pathogen that has to be neutralized, the "Left liberals" who have "disassembled what people in our country have built up in generations" (line 101). Their experiments have to be stopped, their destruction must be accomplished, and *folkhemmet* will be resurrected from their ashes.

Rescuing the Historical Memory of the Golden Age (Lines 109–17)

Speaking about his retrotopian vision, Åkesson is aware that his audience might dislike the idea of returning to bygone history, which, he asserts, is an impossible and undesirable act. However, his recovery of *folkhemmet* can be likened more to a search-and-rescue operation of selective memory along the path of destruction that the Left liberals purportedly have left behind in their fervor to experiment with and reshape the country. Jimmie does a deep dive to search for his version of Lagerlöf's sunken city of past security, Vineta, and hopes it can resurface. As Bauman quotes David Lowenthal, "the past is more admirable as a realm of faith than of facts." Selective memory turns the past into a compelling comfort zone (Bauman 2017, 59, 65). What is still missing from the speech is a proper revision of Swedish history and historiography, which was produced a year later by the SD in its documentary *Ett folk, ett parti* (One party, one people) (Wodak 2015, 21).

Honoring Righteousness in a Tradeoff between Duties and Liberties (Lines 118–27)

In the next passage, Åkesson again highlights the key principle of his societal vision, balancing rights and liberties against duties and obligations. What this exactly implies remains ambiguous but can be explained with what Bauman refers to as "the unending 'security vs freedom' game played by the human condition," contemporarily playing out in the nostalgic wish to again contain freedom and uncertainty within security and stability: back to Hobbes, back to tribes, back to inequality, back to the womb, as the chapters of his book are titled (2017, 9, 141).

Whipping Up the Fear of Division and Death (Lines 125–35)

According to Åkesson, Sweden is existentially threatened by ruptures and divisions. People are concerned and filled with despair; they fear for their future, security, and health. In right-wing populist discourses, Wodak argues, fear is the major fuel: "Almost everything can be constructed as a threat to 'us,' an imagined homogeneous people inside a well-protected territory." Quoting David L. Altheide, Wodak continues: "Fear has emerged as a framework for developing identities and for engaging in social life." Fear is created hand in hand with dichotomies that identify scapegoats, who are held responsible for "real and exaggerated crises as well as related horror and moral narratives." This scapegoating aims to legitimize exclusionary policies (Wodak 2015, x, 2–5).

Promising a Vision of Future Community and Cohesion (Lines 136–45)

Åkesson evokes the topos of fear mainly to vilify the liberal Left establishment, but it serves also as the dramatic overture to the subsequent SD offer of grandiose community and security. These ten lines expound on the SD's concepts of justice, solidarity, societal cohesion, and shared values of righteousness, remedies against all those ills that lie at the heart of retrotopian longing.

Attacking Those Who Sow Discord with a False Agenda (Lines 146–55)

In the next passage, Åkesson once more lashes out against the liberal Left establishment and illustrates what he has tried to say about those who perpetually claim their "rights." In outlining true versus false conflict lines, Åkesson makes clear that typical issues of social justice proponents, such as class, gender, sexual identity, race, and origin, are all constructed to legitimize those proponents' existence. The true conflict revolves around a dualism between forces of destruction and forces of construction, those who "build the cars" (i.e., diligent blue-collar workers) and those who "burn the cars" (i.e., criminal youngsters of immigrant extraction in Swedish suburbs; line 153).

Pushing for Law and Order (Lines 156–63)

In the modern *folkhem*, law and order will be supported by tougher law enforcement. These lines open a section in which Åkesson indulges in a "punitive obsession" with security, as well as law and order (Bauman 2017, 35).

Pledging Public Health as a National Political Good (Lines 164–204)

The second-largest thematic part of his speech (lines 164–204) is devoted to the endemic crisis in health care. Åkesson scourges queues, the lack of hospital beds, understaffing, and threats to the security of patients. The world's highest taxation has not materialized in the delivery of health as a political good, which points at previous political mismanagement. The SD will upgrade the social status of health workers and turn their jobs into attractive workplaces and careers. All patients will receive appropriate health care nationwide, everyone will receive a responsible doctor, and compulsory shift work will be abolished.

The question is, why does Åkesson choose to elaborate a relatively low-key topic as one of his main priorities? Possibly it is because the health crisis is tangible and is examined and discussed daily in the media and among people, and almost everyone can relate to it in one way or the other. As a result, Åkesson can "draw on and mobilize common knowledge" (Wodak 2015, 12). It cannot be denied that austerity politics and naive privatizations over the last decades have eroded the status of Sweden as a leading country of public health and public healthcare. Furthermore, the large number of people working in the sector are prospective voters for the SD, particularly when exalted to the status of heroes. In the SD's *folkhem*, people working in the welfare sector will be rewarded for their heroism (*välfärdens hjältar*, "the heroes of welfare," line 189), and every patient will be guaranteed a speedy treatment everywhere. But the topos of health can also function as a subcategory to the larger frame: the topos of *folkhemmet* and its delivery of welfare as a constitutive feature of societal security. Furthermore, as Wodak argues, the "body as [rhetorical] source domain" is a key component in populist Far Right discourses. The healthy body has to be protected against illness and diseases (internal and external pathogens). This basic metaphor is projected upon the "family" as a rhetorical target domain. Several bodies make up the ideal family living in a home under patriarchal rule and maternal care. And from here the family is united with others in a larger framework, the "nation," the native community of birth in a fatherland (Wodak 2015, 76). When Åkesson proclaimed that Sweden was ill, he attempted to diagnose a national pathology

ANDREAS ÖNNERFORS

that could be fixed once *folkhemmet* was resurrected. To brand his party as the "true party of care" (line 187) has therefore both a concrete and a symbolic meaning: welfare is a national interest for the nativist community in order to cure the country, to make Sweden whole again.

Prescribing Healthy Attitudes of National Pride (Lines 205–10)

Another integrated part of this holistic project is the "citizen's spirit," following the idea of the Roman saying *mens sana in corpore sano*, "a healthy mind in a healthy body," which Åkesson evokes. This spirit is constituted by pride in history, culture, and intergenerational achievements over time, over centuries, which of course begs the question of who can be included in this spirit and its content and who by definition is excluded from it.

Extending a Very Conditional Welcome to National Assimilation (Lines 211–23)

Åkesson subsequently extends a welcome to everyone around the globe, but it soon emerges that this welcome is strongly conditional. There must be a will to assimilate, to adapt, to learn the language and the fabric of society. It is necessary to respect the law as well as societal norms and customs, such as democracy and equality. Respect also encompasses nature, animals, and the inherited soil, children's and women's self-determination, gender equality (in topical areas such as public swimming and bus rides, issues that in 2016 were, and from time to time still are, hotly debated in Sweden). It is obvious that Åkesson here endorses "pseudo-emancipatory gender politics. ... Gender becomes instrumentalized and linked to the rhetoric of exclusion" (Wodak 2015, 6).

Liberties are balanced against obligations, everyone has to work for his or her own provision, and duties are prioritized over rights. These are the rules of the game. Accept them, and you can stay; if you can't, then move elsewhere. Thus, Åkesson in principle does not rule out immigration; however, in the very moment the borders are crossed, integration implies almost total assimilation. Swedish culture and cultural Swedishness are presented as entirely static parameters defined from inside, and they have remained so over time. There is no room for hybridization or cross-fertilization—the alternative of multicultural coexistence is ruled out. No immigrant can expect to be supported passively (presumably with social benefits) with reference to any rights (presumably even rights as outlined in international conventions); he or she thus has the obligation to actively earn membership in the national community through hard labor: *Arbeit macht frei.*

Folkhemmet

Displaying Sympathy for Those Left Behind (Lines 224–29)

In two passages before his recital of Heidenstam, Åkesson pushed for solidarity with the poor and unemployed, support for entrepreneurs and businesses, and aversion to any political and religious extremism.

Reciting a Poetic Vision of National Homogeneity (Lines 230–37)

A last note on the recital of "Medborgarsång" and its function as a rallying cry of political mobilization: the poem represents a piece of political and occasional poetry, a piece of mythopoesis, "a reformulated historical narrative" composed as it was in the immediate run-up to the formation of the modern Swedish national state (Wodak 2015, 6). It is a sign of the contemporary climate of debate that politics are increasingly fictionalized and fiction is politicized (12). For what is the aim of reciting "Medborgarsång" from 1899? How is its meaning constituted in Sweden of 2017? A fatherland inherited by all, "by common right in an equal band," where all shall exercise their equal voting rights, as is imagined to have taken place during an unspecified Germanic past.

But we shall not "be weighed like sacks of gold / By a merchant counting his treasure." To what does this refer in the contemporary context? A reference to a mythical, primordial, and martial (presumably male) community? A rejection of capitalism (or even the "globalist" economy as shorthand for "greedy plutocrats," i.e., Jewish bankers)? The second stanza evokes further images of blood and soil in which gentlemen and yeomen fight and die together in resisting foreign intruders. To measure citizenship rights with money casts shame on the Swedish flag. We have again a warlike community united by its fate and a negative reference to the economy. Perhaps it is the final stanza that holds the key to the true vision of Åkesson's fictionalization of politics: Swedes have come to care more about others than about themselves. They have engaged in destructive self-criticism and separated reason from passion. Now is the time to unite as a people and to take our destiny into our own hands—a battle song for what Bauman has called a "nostalgia for the emotional warmth of belonging" (2017, 55).

CONCLUSION

As part of its 2018 election campaign, the SD produced a documentary titled *Ett folk, ett parti*, denigrating the history of the SAP (Robsahm 2020, 30–33). Whereas much could be said about the film's style, form, and content, it is obvious that a main aim of the film was to undermine the credibility of the critique against the fascist legacy of the SD by placing reverse blame on the SAP (by using the well-established formula of reverse blame: "You are the *real* Nazis") and by criticizing its involvement in highly questionable policies and programs (such as racial biology, eugenics, and sterilization), particularly between 1930 and 1950, as well as its open collaboration with Nazi Germany. On the website of the documentary, it is stated that the SAP "stole the conservative idea of *folkhemmet* but realized it only partly" (Samtiden Dokumentär n.d.).[11]

Thus, the film contributes to an ongoing revision of Swedish history. By accusing the SAP of having stolen and abused the concept of *folkhemmet* in its allegedly pro-Nazi politics in a modern racist mania, it is possible for the SD to reclaim that concept. The significance of whatever the "true" conservative *folkhemmet* represents to any social democratic legacy is thus denied and manipulated. However, it is at the same time recovered as a powerful frame narrative that resonates with the golden age myth of Swedish history during the golden *rekordåren*. By the same token, it is now open to being filled with new meaning, promises of welfare, solidarity, sociocultural cohesion, law and order, and a strong national community. As a strong signifier of an attractive past before the arrival of mass migration, this newly charged *folkhemmet* serves as a shorthand for and a rich rhetorical repertoire to formulate cloaked and subtle discourses of exclusion and inclusion.

The SD's manipulated construction of *folkhemmet* and the romanticized fictionalization of the past through the lens of Heidenstam's poetry represents a historiography open for political abuse. Heidenstam glorified the Swedish bellicose past as a great power (*stormaktstiden*) exactly at the time the modern state of Sweden was shaped. But these visions of the past do not take into account the heterogeneity of Sweden and Swedishness in the age before the dissolution of the union with Norway in 1905. What is suppressed in these attempts of hegemonic readings of Swedish history are centuries in which different varieties of cultural identifications coexisted across the Swedish realm, coupled with phenomena such as intermarriages, multilingualism, and diversity of religious praxis. This blindness toward and general ignorance of a significant Swedish *histoire croisée* and its rich instances of the cultural encounters, hybridizations, and transfers that shaped it inhibits any affirmation of cultural diversity as an asset, especially of immigration and integration in contemporary society. Historical memory is reduced to a selective past of mythologized modernity, which instead is aggrandized as a

Folkhemmet 77

golden age, currently lost but open again for rediscovery and exploitation in political psychology.

NOTES

1. As recently as 1999, the SD proposed that immigrants who arrived to Sweden after 1970 ought to be "repatriated" (Hellquist 2018).

2. This event was organized for the first time in 1968 and has over the five decades of its existence developed into a major political fair, with more and more institutions and organizations participating in the extensive program. See http://www.almedal sveckan.info/om-almedalsveckan. Denmark hosts a similar event on the island of Bornholm called Folkemødet, organized for the first time in 2011. See https://folke moedet.dk/om/tidligere-folkemoeder/.

3. "The Inglehart-Welzel Cultural Map," World Values Survey 7, 2020 (Provisional version), accessed May 24, 2021, https://www.worldvaluessurvey.org/WVS Contents.jsp.

4. A similar negative reaction was caused by Volvo's ad in 2014 featuring Zlatan Ibrahimovic, in which the slogan "Made by Sweden" was launched. The clip has since been watched more than seven million times; see https://youtu.be/cbvdzQ7uVPc.

5. The translation by Charles Wharton Stork is not literal. It is available in the public domain at http://www.babelmatrix.org/works/sv/Heidenstam%2C_Verner_ von-1859/Medborgarsång/en/38377-Fellow-citizens.

6. The dynamic between populist right-wing parties and Far Right extremist groups (which has the populist parties appear in a moderate light) has been observed by Wodak (2015, 58–59). Anyone more overtly expressing right-wing ideas has the SD appear as a more reliable and respectable voice, whereas almost identical political positions only are expressed in a more cloaked fashion. Thus, these positions are mainstreamed due to the existence of a more articulate and extreme Right.

7. "Right-wing populism cuts across the traditional left/right divide and constructs new social divides" (Wodak 2015, 21).

8. On the concept of "heartland," see Wodak (2015, 26).

9. According to the media database Retriever, references to the term *systemkollaps* in the Swedish media increased from 64 in 2013 to 83 in 2014 to 1,050 in 2015 and 1,583 in 2016, followed by 949 in 2017 and 629 by October 2018. Search carried out October 24, 2018. The PDF of these search statistics was downloaded by the author of this chapter.

10. I would like to thank Tobias Hübinette for discussing this trope with me. See also Hübinette (2017).

11. Samtiden Dokumentär also has a YouTube channel with about three thousand subscribers. As of October 26, 2018, *Ett folk, ett parti* had been watched almost 590,000 times; see https://www.youtube.com/channel/UCv-Yp1WBM6Ijgb8YP00 _t_Q/featured.

ANDREAS ÖNNERFORS

REFERENCES

Åkesson, Jimmie. 2017a. "Åkesson (SD) om von Heidenstam som även citeras av nazisterna—Nyheterna (TV4)." July 7. https://www.youtube.com/watch?v=8p StzZZpTxg.

Åkesson, Jimmie. 2017b. "Hela Jimmie Åkessons (SD) tal i Almedalen—Nyheterna (TV4)." July 7. https://www.youtube.com/watch?v=A4IP8°1lYF0.

Bar-On, Tamir. 2014. "The French New Right: Neither Right, nor Left?" *Journal for the Study of Radicalism* 8(1): 1–44.

Bauman, Zygmunt. 2017. *Retrotopia.* Cambridge: Polity.

Bergmann, Eirikur. 2020. *Neo-nationalism: The Rise of Nativist Populism.* London: Palgrave.

Hellquist, Annie. 2018. "SD går tillbaka till sina 90-talsrötter." February 25. https://www.etc.se/ledare/sd-gar-tillbaka-till-sina-90-talsrotter-0.

Hübinette, Tobias. 2017. "Asia as a Topos of Fear and Desire for Nazis and Extreme Rightists: The Case of Asian Studies in Sweden." *Positions: East Asia Cultures Critique* 15(2): 403–28.

Kantrowicz, Ernst. 1981. *The King's Two Bodies: A Study in Mediaeval Political Theology.* Princeton, NJ: Princeton University Press.

Larsson, Petter. 2018. "Med reportaget om godhetsknarkare står SVT återigen med foten i klaveret." August 17. https://www.sydsvenskan.se/2018-08-17/med-report aget-om-godhetsknarkare-star-svt-aterigen-med-foten-i-klaveret.

Lundström, Carin, and Tobias Hübinette. 2020. *Vit melankoli: En analys av en nation i kris.* Stockholm: Makadam.

Nordiska Motståndsrörelsen. 2015. "Veckans låt: Solblot—Medborgarsång." October 9. https://www.nordfront.se/veckans-lat-solblot-medborgarsang.smr.

Pallas, Hynek. 2011. *Vithet i svensk spelfilm 1989–2010.* Gothenburg: Filmkonst.

Persson, Göran. 1997. *Den som är satt i skuld är icke fri.* Stockholm: Atlas.

Robsahm, Maria. 2020. *Sverigedemokraterna och nazismen.* Eskilstuna: Vaktel.

Samtiden Dokumentär. n.d. Accessed October 26, 2018. https://dokumentar.samti den.nu.

SAS (Scandinavian Airlines). 2020. "What Is Truly Scandinavian?" February 11. https://www.adforum.com/creative-work/ad/player/34613729/what-is-truly-scandinav ian/sas-scandinavian-airlines.

Solblot. 2008. "Medborgarsång." Uploaded by Vorphs, November 22. https://www .youtube.com/watch?v=QHQKZZa22Gg.

Solblot. 2012. "Medborgarsång." Uploaded by theodiskfolk, June 18. https://www.you tube.com/watch?v=SKk6lIAiSJk.

Stenhammar, Wilhelm. 1997. "Ett folk" (1905) and "Kantat till allmänna konst- och industriutställningen." Label Sterling. https://www.youtube.com/watch?v=vqE9 KYb8NnM. Uploaded by Gunnar Fredriksson July 25, 2017. "Medborgarsång" at

15'48"–19'00". See also https://musicbrainz.org/release/4a0d28fe-ffdc-4fee-a4ec-158c19d608fa.

Sweden Democrats. 2017. "Manus för Jimmie Åkessons tal i Almedalen." July 7. http://www.mynewsdesk.com/se/sverigedemokraterna/pressreleases/manus-foer-jimmie-aakessons-tal-i-almedalen-2057065.

Tronarp, Gustaf. 2020. "Så kapade högerpopulistiska nätverk SAS nya reklamfilm." February 12. https://www.aftonbladet.se/nyheter/a/OpJrgk/sa-kapade-hogerpopulistiska-natverk-sas-nya-reklamfilm.

Wodak, Ruth. 2015. *The Politics of Fear: What Right-Wing Discourses Mean.* London: SAGE.

Racing Home

Swedish Reception of Black/White Identity Politics in the 2016 US Presidential Election

BENJAMIN R. TEITELBAUM

Race doesn't exist in Sweden, at least not officially. Arguably the birthplace of pseudoscientific race biology in the nineteenth century (Broberg and Tydén 2005; Rastas 2019), the country today joins all its Nordic and some of its Western European neighbors in deeming race a fictitious and sinister social construct, one that, accordingly, has no place in demographic statistics and policy. Informally, too, Swedes tend only to speak of "race" (*ras*) when describing nonhuman animals, in the way English speakers use the term "breed." Reversing that trend would only reify the loathsome designation, the reasoning goes. Race is for most Swedes an anachronism and a lie, one to be resisted through enlightened legislation and language.

Taking this stand brings Swedes into conflict with an outside world that sees race, however. The United Nations and its Committee for the Elimination of Racial Discrimination, as well as the Council of Europe, criticize Swedes for dismissing the concept's social (if not biological) reality and thereby blinding themselves to potential prejudice (McEachrane 2018). If racialized forms of discrimination occur—and indications are that in Sweden they do (Marcińczak et al. 2015; Östh, Clark, and Malmberg 2015)—how can the postracial state identify and respond to them?

Confrontation expands beyond the legalistic and the policy-based, however, and in this chapter, I explore the ways that Sweden's racial ideology brings it into conflict with other societies in less formal domains. Sweden has negotiated powerful cultural influence from the United States throughout most of its post–World War II existence. American film, music, and food, as well as news of its social and political dramas, saturate Swedish society. These cultural impulses often carry with them racial taxonomies and discourses from the United States, discourses that both treat race as an explicit reality and proscribe particular ways to think and talk about it. For Swedes engaging with American culture and society, negotiations of competing racial ontologies beckon. This chapter investigates that process, exploring the ways Swedes embrace, reject, translate, and transform American racial discourses, and it does so by tracing Swedish reception of the 2016 US presidential election. American social movements surrounding the campaign offer prime opportunities for insight, in part because each presidential election prompts extensive coverage and discussion in Sweden, in part because this election featured uncommon amounts of explicit racial mobilization manifest most sharply through the Black Lives Matter movement, which protests police violence against African Americans, and the so-called alt-right, an online movement that gathers white nationalists and anti-immigrant activists. Each movement aligned informally with a presidential candidate, Hillary Clinton and Donald Trump, respectively.

In this chapter, I analyze political and journalistic commentary to better understand Swedish reception of the persons and movements surrounding the US presidential campaign. I deal in particular with Swedish actors most politically and culturally invested in the campaign and its racial discourses, which is to say those on Sweden's Far Left and the Far Right. I show how observing and participating in American racial politics prompted Swedes to reconsider the status of race in their own society. Some took the opportunity to speak of Sweden's social identities in terms of race, too. Others saw American-style racialization as an unsightly potential for Sweden and blamed their domestic political opponents for its threat. Still others—the majority of professional politicians and commentators I surveyed—recognized an equivalency to race in Sweden but decided to label it in other terms, thus striving to preserve the notion that race is, if not fictional, then at least foreign to their society. I conclude by suggesting that such hesitation to acknowledge domestic racialization stems from a confluence of political investments in color blindness, whether those investments are in Sweden's status as an enlightened global beacon of moral authority, a liberalized open society, or a national cultural community that can assimilate outsiders.

My discussion supports claims (e.g., O'Dell 1997) that Americanization in Sweden has not been a story of passive reception; instead, it has been one of adaptation and translation. Oft-noted disinclinations toward nationalism, self-promotion, and individualism in Swedish society have meant that much

American popular culture has been only partially assimilated (Wallengren 2018). Swedes likewise make use of American racial discourses selectively, adopting their terminology only in certain instances and translating it in others. Thus, although Sweden has historically generated racial discourses that gained a global reach, and although Europe is the site of various domestic conceptions of race (Goldberg 2006), my analysis in this chapter recognizes a continued export of Black/White racial taxonomy from the Anglo world in general and the United States in particular (Brännström 2016; Chin and Fehrenbach 2009; Dominguez 1998; Jung 2015) to public political discourse. Before addressing these topics, however, I will first turn to race in Sweden and the ideological milieu anticipating reception of the 2016 presidential election.

Racial Politics in Sweden

Political commitment to color blindness in Sweden, like historic investment in multiculturalism (Ålund and Schierup 1991, 4), remained stable throughout decades of Center-Left and Center-Right leadership. One of the initial salvos in the country's rejection of legal race came during the transformative Social Democrat administration of the 1970s, when Sweden issued a report to the United Nations explaining that legislation geared toward racial discrimination was unnecessary in Sweden due to existing antibias laws (Lappalainen and Lundgren 2005, 115–16). That agenda would grow into a series of efforts to purge Sweden's law books of reference to the concept beginning in 1998. By the 2000s, Center-Right leadership was offering anthropological rather than merely policy-based justifications for excluding the concept from official public life. The 2007 administration of Moderate Party prime minister Fredrik Reinfeldt, for example, prefaced the proposal of legislation to further eradicate references to race in legal documents and procedures with the statement "all people belong to the same race: the human race" (cited in McEachrane 2018; Reinfeldt and Sabuni 2008). Minister of Integration Erik Ullenhag explained ahead of an effort in 2014 to remove previously overlooked references to race in Swedish law: "We know that there really is no such thing as different races of humans. We also know that the foundation of racism is that people believe there is such a thing as different races, that racial identity causes one to behave in a particular way, and that certain races are superior to others" (quoted in Hambraeus 2014).

Official Sweden's stance on race is not uncontroversial. As international organizations like the UN criticized the stance, so too did domestic political actors at the social margins. The Afro-Swedish National Association, building on claims made in a report by the Center for Multiculturalism (Hübinette, Beshir, and Kawesa 2014), called upon Sweden's government to retain and expand references to race in its language and policy. At the core of their appeal was the suspicion—necessarily unverifiable because of prevailing statistical practices—that Afro-Swedes were discriminated against on the basis of race. The protests of groups such as the Afro-Swedish National Association were paralleled by renegade Swedish academics in the field of critical Whiteness studies, most notably, Tobias Hübinette and Catrin Lundström. Inspired by North American scholars and relying on data analyzing the experiences of adopted children in Sweden, they argued that lenses such as ethnicity and national origin were insufficient in grasping the type of discrimination that Swedes of non-European ancestry faced. Adding race to the battery of measures for equality, they argued, would illuminate problems otherwise relegated to speculation (Hübinette et al. 2012; Lundström 2018).

Indeed, the proliferation of terms appearing to approximate race suggests that the concept lives clandestinely in Sweden today. Demographers in the country speak of "visible minorities" (Östh, Clark, and Malmberg 2015). Informally, the term "immigrant" appears to be applied more often to those with non-European ancestry regardless of nationality or place of birth (Loftsdóttir and Jensen 2012). And more recently, the political Left has adopted from American critical race theory the term "racialization" (*rasifiering*), which includes describing someone as being "racified," marking race as a process of construction rather than an entity. It is the term and concept of "ethnicity," however, that most closely represents race in official discourse—ethnicity here regarded as an identity composed of biologically inherited traits along with culturally learned practices emblematic of national or nationalistically aspirational groups. But despite boasting fewer pretensions to scientific objectivity, "ethnicity," too, has been a maligned and inconsistently applied concept in Swedish political discourse and policy (Brännström 2016). On the one hand, governmental agencies seldom collect more statistics on ethnicity than they do on race: Sweden's agency for monitoring crime notably ceased recording national origin of criminals in 2005. On the other hand, ethnicity appears as an intelligible and legally sanctioned concept in the country's constitution, or *grundlagar*. In 2002 the ruling Center-Left government altered the constitution to declare, "Ethnic, linguistic, and religious minorities' ability to preserve and develop their own culture and social life should be promoted." Eight years later, in the fall of 2010, the government altered the concluding statement, "should be promoted," to "shall be promoted" (Ministry of Justice 2018, chap. 1, 2§) with limited public attention or fanfare. Meanwhile, public voices who speak of majority "ethnic Swedes" encounter pushback and challenges to the notion of ethnicity, a process that parallels tendencies in the United States to see race as a flawed concept when it is applied to Whites (Dyer 1997).[1]

Despite claims that consideration of race in Sweden would advance egalitarian ideals, and despite indications that race is experienced but not labeled in mainstream discourses, those agitating for increased recognition of the concept face criticism. Leftist academics in Sweden, especially those operating within a broad Marxist framework of emancipatory, engaged scholarship, challenged what they saw as efforts to adopt Black/White racial categorization while at the same time asserting that racism (though not race) can still be observed and counteracted in Sweden. Professor Paulina de los Reyes criticized Lundström's work in the popular press outlet *Dagens Arena*, arguing that the analytical use of White and Black racial categories in scholarship would only feed their social impact and that colonial Anglo racial taxonomies did not align with the particular forms of discrimination active in Sweden (De los Reyes 2013). Alternately, calls for increased race consciousness attracted the ire of prominent Center-Right columnist Ivar Arpi (2013), who mocked Hübinette's advocacy of race statistics as a frightening example of unhinged left-wing identity politics. Voices like the Afro-Swedish National Association and critical Whiteness scholars have made advances nonetheless. In February 2018 the Left (formerly Communist) Party made a surprise move by adopting an official position advocating the inclusion of ethnicity in census taking and other state statistics, channeling arguments used by Whiteness scholars.

Others espousing domestic racial consciousness in Sweden are to be found at the opposite end of the political spectrum. Organized white nationalist and National Socialist groups in Sweden have since the 1980s produced statements and culture espousing the reality of racial grouping. Their commentary often champions an Aryan, Nordic, or white community, looking beyond the boundaries of the nation-state and with it the concept of Swedish ethnicity. The intellectual and expressive forms they adopt frequently come from the United States. For example, the unofficial creed for late twentieth-century white nationalists in Sweden, as throughout Europe, was the fourteen-word statement "We must secure the existence of our people and a future for white children," penned by the late American activist David Lane (Michael 2009), and when Swedish National Socialist organizations such as the Nordic Resistance Movement spread online material or hold documentary viewings related to race, they often feature the work of American White nationalist icons such as David Duke and Craig Bodeker.

While political parties on the Far Left have shown subtle receptiveness toward critiques of color blindness, the same is not true for parties at the opposite end of the political spectrum. The Far Right in Sweden is represented in parliamentary politics principally by the nationalist Sweden Democrats (Sverigedemokraterna). The party, in turn, relies on a score of officially unaffiliated commentators and media outlets to advance its cause in public, outlets like *Nyheter Idag*, *Fria Tider*, and, previously, *Avpixlat*. After first entering parliament in 2010 with 5.7 percent of the national vote, the Sweden Democrats saw their share of the electorate double in 2014 to 12.9 percent and then rise to nearly 18 percent in 2018. Thereafter, the party emerged as a viable contender to become the largest in the country. Though the Sweden Democrats' growth is unparalleled in modern Swedish history, their formal political inroads have been limited because most other political parties and much of mainstream Swedish society regard them as too extreme to tolerate as partners. That judgment stems not from their policy proposals (which place them on the moderate scale of nationalist/populist parties in Europe) but from their social profile and history. The party was founded in 1988 via the fusion of an antitax populist party and a White nationalist campaign organization. Distancing themselves from roots in the latter organization has been the party's main public undertaking since its founding. Their claim to legitimacy and their appeal for acceptance hinges, from their perspective, on convincing others that they have reformed themselves.

How have they made this case? With reference to race and its derivative, ethnicity. The party declared its ideology "cultural nationalist" to distinguish itself from race or "ethnonationalist" forces (Teitelbaum 2017). With this designation, the Sweden Democrats professed themselves color-blind, asserting that what they fought for was the preservation of particular Swedish traditions, values, and behaviors rather than bodies. In a recent version of their official party platform, they declare that one is Swedish either by native birth or by assimilation: "Native-born Swedes are in our mind those born in Sweden or adopted at an early age to Swedish-speaking parents who identify as Swedes or Nordics. Those assimilated into the Swedish nation are those with a non-Swedish background who speak fluent Swedish, see themselves as Swedes, live in harmony with Swedish culture, see Swedish history as their own, and feel greater loyalty to the Swedish nation than to any other" (Sverigedemokraterna 2011). Their designations strive to disallow a racialized understanding of

Swedishness, rendering skin color and country of origin inessential to being considered both "native" and "assimilated." It is a message that frames the Sweden Democrats both as proper members of a Western liberal political establishment that assumes openness to foreign money and people and as aligned with prevailing racial ideologies in Sweden, particularly by denying meaning to race. It is a message aimed further at telling mainstream Sweden that the party is hardly radical. The counterpart to cultural nationalism—race or ethnonationalism—offers no inclusion of foreign bodies in Swedishness: one can only be born a Swede, never become Swedish throughout a lifetime. That position, espoused in various forms by all organized nationalist, anti-immigrant movements in the country aside from the Sweden Democrats, thus serves as the contrasting example of race consciousness and extremism, allowing the party to claim moderation.[2]

Critics of the Sweden Democrats seldom find the party's vision of a culturally homogeneous nation comforting, nor do they believe that official ideological proclamations reflect the inner yearnings and values of the party faithful. Mirroring the long-established academic criticism of Western declarations of color blindness (e.g., El-Tayeb 2011; Lentin and Titley 2011; Weber 2013), the Sweden Democrats have been accused of using the ostensibly de-racialized concept "culture" as public facade for racism—as a more socially palatable way to, as they do, speak of immutable and irreconcilable differences between people. Elsewhere I have argued that it is perilous to dismiss the party's cultural nationalism as a mere gimmick (Teitelbaum 2016). But as we shall see, the party, like other actors throughout the political spectrum in Sweden, participates in a process of rebranding and relabeling when it references race.

"PRETTY MUCH LIKE SWEDEN":
RACE IN THE 2016 US PRESIDENTIAL CAMPAIGN

The 2016 US presidential election forced the topic of race onto global spectators. While American electoral politics typically expose and implicate racial divides, this election inspired added racial mobilization and demonization (Tatum 2017). That, powered further by the sensational candidacy of Donald Trump, stirred conversation and debate and compelled foreign audiences to position themselves in relation both to American racial political statements and to linguistic and conceptual tropes.

At first glance, what is so remarkable about this commentary on American racial politics in Sweden is the double standard. Swedish authors, journalists, and politicians spoke about race in the United States as though it were real while implicitly or explicitly denying its presence in Sweden. Often, this divide is at its most plain when commentators report on demographic studies done in the United States by American agencies. Given that demographers use race to make sense of social phenomena in the United States, reporting the findings of such studies without reference to the designation becomes a challenge. Some of the only references to "White" and "Black" races one encounters in Swedish media and academic literature report on racial disparities in educational outcomes, life expectancy, or judicial process in the United States. Likewise, some Swedish commentary on the presidential election included channeling of American racial categories. For instance, journalistic outlets from the Center Right (e.g., *Expressen*) to the Far Left (e.g., *ETC*) reported on polling data that identified "white Americans" as being the core demographic supporting Trump's candidacy. Even the Sweden Democrats' nominal party paper, *Samtiden*, followed suit, never describing individuals in Sweden with racial nomenclature (to do so would be more politically compromising for them perhaps than for any other major political party) while freely referring to "Black" and "White" people when analyzing politics in the United States.

But treating race as a foreign, non-Swedish concept becomes more strained when those living in Sweden refer to American racial politics in order to address domestic issues. It is in these instances when we see selective adoption of American racial terminology based on who is commenting and whom they are describing. Specifically, one can see a tendency for nonprofessional politicians and journalists—especially those who do not identify as White—to describe Swedish society in racial terms, while the language of elite commentators avoids racial monikers for domestic analysis. For examples of this we can first turn to Swedish coverage of the Black Lives Matter (BLM) movement in the United States. In the midst of the BLM protests, Gothenburg's leading news daily, *Göteborgsposten*, interviewed BLM supporter and former instructor of the city's opera, Black American Nigel Campbell, about race relations in the United States. His commentary during the interview shifted to Sweden, where, he remarked, "I've learned that racism is a global issue. It's not just the US. I had a really hard time in Sweden. Sweden sees itself as a liberal utopia, but I didn't experience that." He reported having been told by drunk Swedes to go "back to Africa" and added, "People tell me that I'm exaggerating, making things up, or that nobody really means it. 'Nobody in Sweden would do that,' they say. But people need to understand that if you are a white Swedish man, would someone want to send you 'back to Africa'? It's something that I have to deal with because I'm a black immigrant who doesn't speak Swedish" (quoted in Edstam 2016). Nowhere in the article did the author or other voices protest against Campbell's racialized portrayal of Swedish society—nowhere did they question his claim that people in Sweden could be reasonably described as being "Black" and "White."

Campbell could be seen as a national, racial outsider in Sweden, one whose profession had little to do with analyzing and shaping political opinion. Others fitting that profile seem to be given license to break Sweden's code of color blindness, and again, commentary on American politics provided the occasion. During the presidential campaign, on July 28, 2016, roughly five hundred people in central Stockholm organized a public demonstration of solidarity with BLM. Physically and figuratively coalescing around Black/White racial nomenclature and concepts appeared more intuitive for some participants than others, particularly when directing their messages not to the United States but to their own society. Rank-and-file participants seemed more inclined to embrace the term "Black." One attendee, Marie Gaye, said in an interview, "This affects all black people in the world. If I go to the US now I could be shot by a policeman even if I come from Sweden. My skin color determines whether I live or die" (Mulinari 2016). For such voices, the designation "Black" was neither unintelligible nor foreign. However, politicians and journalists tended to avoid such expression. A speaker at the event, Malcolm Momodou Jallow of the Left Party, spoke of "Afro-Swedes," while the most extensive article on the event, written by Felicia Mulinari for the magazine *Feminist Perspective*, described participants as predominantly "young and racialized" and decried racism in Sweden, but it generally reserved the term "Black" for references to American society. Racism could exist anywhere, it seemed, but for the elite voices, race is American.

Voices on the political Right adopted a similar approach. In an *Aftonbladet* op-ed, Sweden Democrat Henrik Vinge criticized BLM for having an allegedly "racist, violent agenda," racist, in his mind, because it encouraged hatred and attacks on "white police officers." Vinge further discussed the demographics of police violence and crime in the United States, adopting racial categories without comment. However, his political objective was not to take sides in American social conflicts; instead, he attempted to leverage the example as criticism against identity politics in Sweden, accusing feminist activists of striving for a similar agenda of infinite segmentation and disintegration, of

Racing Home 89

mobilizing groups against each other rather than fostering unity. His message to Sweden removed the discrete White/Black racial monikers that formed his discussion of the United States: "There is no natural reason why the core divisions in society must be between men and women or people with different skin colors" (Vinge 2016).

While BLM served as a beacon of Black racial consciousness and protest, white mobilization coalesced implicitly in Trump's campaign itself and explicitly in the alt-right. As I argue elsewhere (Teitelbaum 2019), the racial overtones of Trump's candidacy spawned a tortured reception among the Sweden Democrats. The affinities between the American politician's and the party's critique of immigration, political correctness, and a so-called economic and cultural establishment were balanced by Trump's occasional departure from rhetorical and ideological codes central to the Sweden Democrats' claim to legitimacy, notably, commentary on ethnicity and relative receptiveness to autocratic rule.

Nonetheless, marginal party members critical of the leadership's moderation agenda took the US election as an opportunity to racialize their cause in Sweden. One such member is Christoffer Dulny, former head of the Sweden Democrats' Stockholm chapter. Having recently been sidelined because of an exposé tracing him to scandalous insults of Muslims online, he was so energized by what he saw of the Trump campaign that he traveled to New York City and the Trump campaign headquarters to be a spectator on election night. The following week, in a private Facebook post on November 14, 2016, he offered an explanation for his interest:

> This election is ultimately about the quickly declining, marginalized white majority and its protest against a national and global elite that would prefer to see them disappear. It is the countryside versus the big city, affluent whites and minorities against traditional Americans. ... For many years there has been an agenda to flood the United States with people from the Third World, people whom large corporations want to use as cheap labor, whom the [American Democratic Party] wants to use as vote-producing livestock, and whom a political elite that crisscrosses party lines wants to control. Pretty much like Sweden, in other words. ... This elite sees benefits to having a Third World population that doesn't understand its constitutional rights and that won't complain about principles and values as long as money rolls in. Concepts such as democracy, freedom of speech, freedom of choice, and individual rights are, after all, a product of Western civilization.[3]

Statements like this, revealing Dulny's interest in White nationalism extending from the United States to Sweden, prompted his resignation from the Sweden Democrats. He would later emerge as a founding member of the organization Nordic Alt-Right; travel to march alongside white nationalists in the 2017 Charlottesville, Virginia, protest; and produce memes, videos, lectures, music, and podcasts, where one of his key slogans was #svenskarärvita (Swedesarewhite).

Dulny's embrace of racial mobilization via Trump was dramatic, as was his exit from the officially color-blind Sweden Democrats. Other voices in the party, however, discussed the US election and Sweden in ways that suggested, rather than declared blatantly, that American racial divisions might be relevant to their own society. Sweden Democrat Ulf Hansen, drummer for the flagship nationalist punk band Ultima Thule and a writer for the party newspaper, *Samtiden*, provides one example. In an article exploring the election of Trump and the riots in Charlottesville the following year, he wrote the following: "The tensions that led to Charlottesville began due to efforts to remove statues that represented America's history as a continent populated primarily by WASPs. Frustration grew when plans were announced to rename a park bearing the name of Confederate general Robert E. Lee and to tear down his statue. Don't patriots in the United States have the same right to express their disapproval with that in a democracy without being subjected to Far Left violence? Shouldn't the police protect those with a permit to protest?" The article continues: "Don't think that left-wing liberals in Sweden are too good for such an assault on Sweden's history, on our forefathers' struggles and sacrifices. Swedish patriots have every reason to see events in the United States as a dystopic scenario for the future" (Hansen 2017).

Hansen's argumentation is obscure, though he implies that being a patriot involves resisting efforts to erase US history, particularly its history as a country "populated primarily by WASPs," or White Anglo-Saxon Protestants. To say that Swedish history could fall victim to a similar fate, as Hansen claims, is to invite the reader to consider the commonalities between Sweden's "primary" population—whose historic role in constituting the nation might be questioned by left-wing liberals—and WASPs in the United States.

Hansen, because of commentary that dances on the edges of party ideological and rhetorical protocol, has never been a leading spokesperson. However, even the Sweden Democrats party leadership drew parallels—similarly vague and suggestive—between the population they fight for in Sweden and the racial community buttressing Trump in the United States. Party ideologue and former leader Mattias Karlsson seemed to describe a global White revolt when analyzing Trump's victory the day after the election. He responded to a reporter's question about his general impressions of the then president elect: "I haven't been impressed by Trump's personality and character. But in election after election these past years we have seen that the dissatisfaction of the native-born, Western working class with globalism, cultural radicalism, and multiculturalism is larger and deeper than what experts had predicted. . . . The question is when the establishment is going to start listening to its people" (quoted in Svensson and Hagnestad 2016). A population in the United States that is both "native-born" and "Western": it need not necessarily be a race-specific working-class community that Karlsson describes in this instance. Perhaps the concepts he works with here mirror those in the official Sweden Democrats party platform (which he was instrumental in drafting), where designations such as "Western" are described as racially and ethnically un-committed. It is unlikely that he would have seen such characterization in US discourse, however, for American commentators seldom segment their own population based on who is Western and who is not. It is more likely that for Karlsson these are substitute expressions he has applied in place of and in order to qualify and further nuance the label "White." And if race could define that transnational population in one locale, why couldn't it in another?

CONCLUSION

The examples I have explored in this chapter show Swedes drawing parallels between racialized discourses of the United States and social conflict in their own society. In some cases, the political use of reference to the United States takes the shape not of analogy or metaphor but instead of posited equivalency—that the same divisions and prejudices occur in both countries. Why, then, have we seen race discussed in this fashion? Why do certain Swedes, particularly those in formal political or commentator positions, relabel what appears to them as race in another context?

To address those questions, we ought to consider the implications of what seems to be the prevailing observation behind all this, namely, that the social boundaries endemic to archetypical postcolonial societies such as South Africa, Great Britain, and the United States have become relevant in Sweden as well. That prospect surely frightens diverse interests in Swedish politics, and for varying reasons. For the Swedish Left, it seems that the country's allegedly enlightened rejection of race failed to keep the concept from germinating within its borders. Likewise, that prospect suggests that Sweden's relatively minimal participation in European colonization projects did not shield the country from colonialism's aftereffects and the moral depravity that comes with them. Sweden's contemporary and historic status as an exceptional humanitarian superpower and role model dies if it succumbs to race.

For the liberal Center Right, race's reality in Sweden poses an additional hurdle in justifying reforms to the interventionist state. Race constitutes a new arena for potential inequality that must be addressed if the ideal of a liberal, meritocratic open society and free market is to hold legitimacy. And for members of the populist Far Right, race is poised to invalidate both their official visions for Sweden and their own claims to moderation. In the first instance, the prospect that race lives in the country and marks impressions of belonging—of being a "normal" Swede—threatens the agenda of assimilation, for how can one assimilate into a Swedishness defined by a generally involuntary trait such as race? But party members' particular treatment of the topic lends credence to their critics' assertions that monikers such as "real Swedes," "normal people," and "native-born" are in fact placeholders for race and thus that the party's claims to color blindness via the embrace of cultural nationalism conceal a racial agenda.

Across these examples, however, we might also note a broad investment among Swedes to resist the notion that their predominant demographic belongs to a global population of whites. The notion that, to quote alt-rightist Christoffer Dulny, "Swedes are white" would hardly seem controversial to the generation of late nineteenth-century race biologists who grew to regard Swedes as the standard bearers for Whites worldwide. But in a post–World War II context where Whiteness bears the mark of guilt, sharing in or typifying it does damage to the reputation that Sweden has cultivated throughout its post–World War II history: a reputation that it is a nation filled with more modernity, justice, and goodness than any other.

Notes

1. Consider, for example, the controversy surrounding former prime minister Fredrik Reinfeldt after he spoke of inequalities between immigrants and "ethnic Swedes." See TT Nyhetsbyrå (2012).

2. It should be noted, however, that most ethnonationalist organizations mind mainstream Sweden's gentle preference for the concept of "ethnicity" over "race." As Vávra Suk, former leading activist for the National Democrats Party, once explained

Racing Home 93

to me, "In Sweden, 'race' . . . has a strongly negative connotation. It makes you think of skull-measuring and gas chambers" (Vávra Suk, electronic message to author, March 24, 2012).

3. Reprinted from Facebook with permission.

REFERENCES

Ålund, Aleksandra, and Carl-Ulrik Schierup. 1991. *Paradoxes of Multiculturalism.* Aldershot: Avebury.

Arpi, Ivar. 2013. "Vet Ullenhag vad han lånar sig till?" *Svenska Dagbladet,* December 12.

Brännström, Leila. 2016. "'Ras' i efterkrigstidens Sverige: Ett bidrag till en mothistoria." In *Historiens hemvist: II. Etik, politik och historikerns ansvar,* edited by Patricia Lorenzoni and Ulla Manns, 27–55. Gothenburg: Makadam Förlag.

Broberg, Gunnar, and Mattias Tydén. 2005. *Oönskade i folkhemmet: Rashygien och sterilisering i Sverige.* Stockholm: Dialogos.

Chin, Rita, and Heide Fehrenbach. 2009. "Introduction: What's Race Got to Do with It? Postwar German History in Context." In *After the Nazi Racial State: Difference and Democracy in Germany and Europe,* by Rita Chin, Heide Fehrenbach, Geoff Eley, and Atina Grossmann, 1–29. Ann Arbor: University of Michigan Press.

De los Reyes, Paulina. 2013. Vem är antirasismens politiska subjekt?" *Dagens Arena,* November 22.

Dominguez, Virginia R. 1998. "Exporting US Concepts of Race: Are There Limits to the US Model?" *Social Research* 65(2): 369–99.

Dyer, Richard. 1997. *White.* London: Routledge.

Edstam, Fanny. 2016. "Nigel Campbell: Min svarta hud är en måltavla." *Göteborgs Posten,* July 10.

El-Tayeb, Fatima. 2011. *European Others: Queering Ethnicity in Postnational Europe.* Minneapolis: University of Minnesota Press.

Goldberg, David Theo. 2006. "Racial Europeanization." *Ethnic and Racial Studies* 29(2): 331–64.

Hambraeus, Ulf. 2014. "Rasbegreppet ska bort ur lagen." *SVT Nyheter,* July 30.

Hansen, Ulf. 2017. "När historien suddas ut." *Samtiden,* August 29.

Hübinette, Tobias, Samson Beshir, and Victoria Kawesa. 2014. *Afrofobi: En kunskapsöversikt över afrosvenskars situation i dagens Sverige.* Botkyrka: Mångkulturellt Centrum.

Hübinette, Tobias, Helena Hörnfeldt, Fataneh Farahani, and René León Rosales, eds. 2012. *Om ras och vithet i det samtida Sverige.* Botkyrka: Mångkulturellt Centrum.

Jung, Moon-Ki. 2015. *Beneath the Surface of White Supremacy: Denaturalizing U.S. Racisms Past and Present.* Stanford, CA: Stanford University Press.

Lappalainen, Paul, and Marcus Lundgren. 2005. "Det blågula glashuset: Strukturell diskriminering i Sverige." *Statens offentliga utredningar 56.*

Lentin, Alana, and Gavan Titley. 2011. *Crises of Multiculturalism: Racism in the Neoliberal Age*. London: Zed Books.

Loftsdóttir, Kristín, and Lars Jensen, eds. 2012. *Whiteness and Postcolonialism in the Nordic Region: Exceptionalism, Migrant Others, and National Identities*. Farnham, UK: Ashgate.

Lundström, Catrin. 2018. "Icke/vit migration: Reflektioner kring ras, medborgarskap och tillhörighet i en svensk kontext." In *Studier om rasism: Tvärvetenskapliga perspektiv på ras, vithet och diskriminering*, edited by Tobias Hübinette and Andréaz Wasniowski, 273–301. Malmö: Arx Förlag.

Marcińczak, Szymon, Tiit Tammaru, Magnus Strömgren, and Urban Lindgren. 2015. "Changing Patterns of Residential and Workplace Segregation in the Stockholm Metropolitan Area." *Urban Geography* 36(7): 969–92.

McEachrane, Michael. 2018. "Universal Human Rights and the Coloniality of Race in Sweden." *Human Rights Review* 19(4): 471–93.

Michael, George. 2009. "David Lane and the Fourteen Words." *Totalitarian Movements and Political Religions* 10(1): 43–61.

Ministry of Justice. 2018. "Kungörelse (1974:152) om beslutad ny regeringsform." *Sveriges Riksdag*. https://www.riksdagen.se/sv/dokument-lagar/dokument/svensk-forfattningssamling/kungorelse-1974152-om-beslutad-ny-regeringsform_sfs-1974-152.

Mulinari, Felicia. 2016. "Hundratals i demonstration för Black Lives Matters i Stockholm." *Feministiskt perspektiv*, July 29.

O'Dell, Thomas. 1997. "Culture Unbound: Americanization and Everyday Life in Sweden." PhD diss., Lund University.

Östh, Johan, William A. V. Clark, and Bo Malmberg. 2015. "Measuring the Scale of Segregation Using k-Nearest Neighbor Aggregates." *Geographical Analysis* 47(1): 34–49.

Rastas, Anna. 2019. "The Emergence of Race as a Social Category in Northern Europe." In *Relating Worlds of Racism*, edited by Philomena Essed et al., 357–81. New York: Palgrave Macmillan.

Reinfeldt, Fredrik and Nyamko Sabuni. 2008. "Ett starkare skydd mot diskriminering." Proposition to Sweden's Riksdag 2007/2008:95.

Svensson, Niklas, and Rebecca Hagnestad. 2016. "Jimmie Åkesson, SD: 'Det skrämmer mig.'" *Expressen*, November 9.

Sverigedemokraterna. 2011. *Principprogramm*. http://partiprogram.se/sverigedemokraterna#som-infodd-svensk-raknar-vi-den-som.

Tatum, Beverly Daniel. 2017. *Why Are All the Black Kids Sitting Together in the Cafeteria? And Other Conversations about Race*. 2nd ed. New York: Basic Books.

Teitelbaum, Benjamin R. 2016. "Ignorerade band: Politik och ofullständiga ontologier i forskning om Sverigedemokraterna." *Arkiv* 5:93–110.

Teitelbaum, Benjamin R. 2017. *Lions of the North: Sounds of the New Nordic Radical Nationalism*. Oxford: Oxford University Press.

Teitelbaum, Benjamin R. 2019. "Tremors from Afar: Donald Trump and the Sweden Democrats." *Patterns of Prejudice* 53(5): 534–53.

TT Nyhetsbyrå. 2012. "Reaktioner på Reinfeldts uttalande." *Expressen*, May 15, 2012.

Vinge, Henrik. 2016. "Black lives matter vilar på en rasistisk grund." *Aftonbladet*, July 16.

Wallengren, Hans. 2018. "Volvo Trucks and Cowboy Hats: American Trucking Music Replanted in a Swedish Cultural Context." Paper delivered at the Annual Meeting of the Society for the Advancement of Scandinavian Studies, Los Angeles, California.

Weber, Beverly. 2013. *Violence and Gender in the New Europe: Islam in German Culture.* New York: Palgrave Macmillan.

Racist Resurgences

How Neoliberal and Antiracist Lefts Make Space for the Far Right in Sweden and the United States

CARLY ELIZABETH SCHALL

Recent events in the United States and Sweden, as well as elsewhere in Europe and farther afield, have caused researchers and journalists alike to highlight the similarities of Far Right parties across multiple cases in regard to issues of immigration and racism (e.g., Caiani and Parenti 2016; Westlake 2016). At the same time, a stream of research highlights the "death" or "hollowing out" of social democracy and the rise of the neoliberal Left, focusing on the production of inequality (e.g., Evans and Schmidt 2012). Less scholarly attention, however, has been paid to the *racial effects* of the neoliberal Left and the way that this creates opportunities for the Far Right.[1] This is the primary goal of this chapter: to explain how the neoliberal Left's failures to adequately address structural racism created space for resurgences of Far Right racism in both the United States and Sweden and the renegotiation of boundaries of belonging in the nation.

This account uses a pair of events that severely disrupted "politics as usual" in their respective countries as a jumping-off point. These two events are the November 2016 election of Donald Trump as president of the United States and the governmental crisis of 2014 in Sweden. This is not a close analysis of those moments but rather an examination of the background ideological-cultural conditions that allowed these unexpected events to become possible. I use the concept of the *crises of closure*—"acute challenges to the agreed upon boundaries of a membership community" (Schall 2016, 8)—to understand these background conditions. Neoliberalism is an ideology that suggests that unfettered individual freedom and, by extension, a truly free market are the primary paths to successful societies. This ideology, beyond simply providing economic guidance, suggests a set of cultural tools for reconfiguring the boundaries of belonging not, perhaps, for those seeking entry (migrants and minorities) but for those seeking to keep out or welcome in new migrants (e.g., voters and parties).

Neoliberalism provides a similar set of tools but finds a different expression in Sweden compared to the United States, even in the establishment Left. This is reflective of neoliberalism's inherent internal contradictions (on contradictions within neoliberalism, see Campbell and Pedersen 2001). This is particularly true in the case of the neoliberal perspective on race. In Sweden neoliberal racial politics is primarily seen in a shift toward a kind of racial individualism, especially in terms of antiracist action, and away from structural considerations of racial inequality (Schall 2016; Schierup and Ålund 2011). In the United States the neoliberalism of the Left is reflected in a free market ethos that pushes racial concerns out of focus entirely. Yet the two countries have something important in common, which is a tendency toward color-blind rhetoric from the establishment Left that leaves that part of the political spectrum without adequate tools for effectively combatting openly racist rhetoric, which appeals, in particular, to disaffected working-class and unemployed whites in both contexts.

THEORETICAL BACKGROUND: CRISES OF CLOSURE IN A NEOLIBERAL WORLD

The study of immigration and diversity often centers on questions of boundaries, both symbolic and material. Michèle Lamont and Virág Molnár (2002), for instance, focus on the way symbolic boundaries—such as those of race or class—harden into social boundaries that prevent access to the benefits of living in a society. Similarly, Bernadette Nadya Jaworsky (2013) discusses the ways concepts of legal boundaries (such as citizenship) and moral boundaries (such as the sense that a given person or group is "one of us") are deployed to define others as others and us as us. The finding here is that there is an important link between legal boundaries—and Bridget Anderson, Matthew J. Gibney, and Emanuela Paoletti (2011) add physical boundaries to this—and social boundaries. The meanings that become attached to physical and legal boundaries are heavily influenced by the moral (and perhaps cultural) boundaries that inform people's reading of the Other (see also Voyer 2013). In other words, the drawing and hardening of boundaries around a membership group (what Max Weber [1978] and Andreas Wimmer [2007] call "social closure") is dependent on how in-group members perceive and use notions of boundaries in terms of legal and physical borders as well as moral and cultural boundaries.

Mismatches between these two sets of boundaries can sometimes provoke conflict over previously agreed upon boundaries. Sometimes, if the scale of these conflicts is large enough (e.g., in cases of a large influx of refugees or increased economic marginalization of a subgroup within a larger membership group), then crises of closure can occur. Crises of closure (Schall 2016) refer to moments when the agreed-upon boundaries of a membership community, boundaries that can either include within or "close out" potential new members, become troubled. These crises of closure can center on who gets "let in" to a membership community—*closure as entry*, which, in the case of national closure, includes things such as citizenship or residency rules and border security. These crises can also center on questions around who gets access to the material and/or symbolic benefits of membership—*closure as access to goods*, which, in the case of national closure, includes things such as access to welfare provisions, employment, and cultural goods. These types of closure often but not always occur simultaneously and are often deeply entwined. The resolutions of crises can create dramatic changes in the terms on which people are included or excluded, creating shifts in national identity and new cultural-political landscapes (Schall 2016).

Both the election of Donald Trump and the Swedish governmental crisis of 2014 can be seen as emblematic of ongoing crises of closure, as both struggles occurred on terrains of entry. In the US case, the focus is on entry for both Central Americans and Muslims, who are central to an ideological struggle between Left and Right over what it means to be an American (Wong 2017). In Sweden that same struggle has occurred over the entrance of refugee/ asylum seekers. In both cases, access to goods has been contested for citizen "others." This is most strongly seen in the US case of African American claims of unequal access to justice and safety (M. Alexander 2012) and their claims even to Americanness. In Sweden the claims of long-term and Swedish-born Swedes of immigrant background have also been highlighted by recent political crises.

These crises have been colored by the ideological context in which they are set. Ideology is deeply connected to boundaries, in some ways creating the rules for what is an acceptable dividing line in society, what mechanisms are available for inclusion, and what it even means to be "included" (Schall 2014a). While societies contain multiple competing and/or blended ideologies, I focus here on a particular ideological component present in varying degrees in both the United States and Sweden, namely, neoliberalism. Neoliberalism is an ideology that favors the free market and is given concrete form in policies—both proposed and actual—to deregulate many segments of the economy and reduce trade barriers between states. Initially intended to describe a particular type of capitalism ascendant in the late twentieth century, the term has expanded to include a whole host of affiliated ideas. Central to neoliberalism is an underlying belief that the individual is both the prime and proper driver of development (and disorder). For economics, this means a belief that an economic system that leaves individuals as free from government interference in their economic decision making as possible is most likely to produce growth, as well as what those who subscribe to this ideology deem a fair distribution of resources (Mudge 2008). In the sociocultural realm, neoliberalism includes ideas about freedom of choice in cultural contexts and the overwhelming importance of the individual as the causative and explanatory mechanism for much of social life (Springer, Birch, and MacLeavy 2016). Whether these ideas are integral to neoliberalism itself or are an outgrowth of the economic aspects of the ideology is up for debate (see, e.g., Verhaeghe 2014). Initially an ideology espoused by the Right, neoliberalism has increasingly been adopted by parties traditionally thought of as leftist: Labor in the UK, the Social Democrats in Sweden, the Democrats in the United States. While some may argue that the adoption of neoliberalism makes a party/movement inherently "rightist," this argument ignores the fundamental shifts in the political Center that have reconfigured the political spectrum across Western Europe and the United States (Mudge 2018).

Applied to race, neoliberalism often functions as a source for "color-blind racism," a term that has been applied both to individual orientations to race (Bonilla-Silva 2003) and to policy contexts (M. Alexander 2012; Lieberman 1998). Color-blind racism encompasses any ideology that either deemphasizes/denies the role of race in inequalities or relegates racism to a problem of individual, anomalous cases of interpersonal racism. Color-blind racism suggests solutions to racial inequality that involve merely ignoring race in favor of other, especially economic, sources of inequality. This adds up to an approach to racism that focuses entirely on individual racist actions to the exclusion of the racial inequalities inherent in systems (Valdes and Cho 2011). American neoliberalism and Swedish neoliberalism take different forms (the former is more historically anchored and more integral to American identity than to Swedish), but color blindness and color-blind racism have become ascendant among the established neoliberal Left in both places.

Of course, policies intended to deal with difference in various ways have been present in both countries: Sweden's official, constitutionally anchored multiculturalism, dating back to the mid-1970s, was certainly an attempt to deal with difference. However, this official multiculturalism was not at the time and even more recently has not been rooted in understanding of differences as *racial* differences (see, e.g., Brännström 2018 on the omission of the term "race" in Swedish legislation historically). The United States, too, has had a great deal of racially conscious legislation, but there has been a swing away from writing race into legislation since the end of the civil rights movement (for examples from the criminal code, see M. Alexander 2012).

The establishment Left, however, is not the only leftist force in either place. Crucial to the story told here in both cases are the differences, though not necessarily antagonisms, between an establishment Left—by which I mean the Left represented in the political parties and via official politics— and a movement Left—by which I mean the host of formal social movements and informal thought leaders generally on the left side of the political spectrum (see, e.g., McAdam and Tarrow 2010). In the United States the movement Left includes but is not limited to antiracist movements such as Black Lives Matter and anticapitalist movements such as the Occupy movement, which also tend to take radical stances on race and racism. In Sweden we might place movements such as antifa in this category. Race provides a crucial example for teasing out the differences between the movement Left, which tends toward radicalism, and the establishment Left, which tends toward conventionalism.

Case 1: The United States, the Democrats, and Donald Trump

In November 2016 Americans were stunned by the largely unpredicted victory of Republican presidential candidate Donald Trump. Trump had run on a populist campaign colored by nationalist and sometimes blatantly racist rhetoric. When the dust had settled, many Americans on the left were perplexed as to how this could happen. The undertone to much of the conversation was a question: *How could the American Right have gotten so racist?* There has been an explosion of research on the causes of the seeming increase in overt racism among members of the Right both preceding and following the election, with much of the argument focused on the legitimation of racism, which had always been there. Some point to conventional populism (Kivisto 2017), others to cultural exclusion (Hochschild 2018), and still others to partisan political resentment (Cramer 2016). Some, however, paused to consider a different question: *How could the Left have lost the very people they/*

we supposedly fight for, those most vulnerable to the damages caused by economic inequality? The first question is, of course, an interesting one, and the parallels between the Far Right and the moderate Right contexts that enable the extremes are an enticing field for potential analysis. Yet the second question is just as interesting and just as vital for understanding politics going forward.

It should be noted that voting patterns show that Trump voters were, on the whole, more wealthy than those who voted for Hillary Clinton, the Democratic Party candidate. This is not unexpected. Trump is a businessman who made promises of deregulation and the creation of a business-friendly climate. Wealthy Americans, particularly wealthy whites, are the traditional base for the Republican Party. It is worth examining why Trump's antiestablishment profile and extremism did not put off these voters. However, this group of voters did not provide the votes that swung crucial states in Trump's favor. Rather, new voters and voters who switched from President Barack Obama, a Democrat, in 2012 to Trump in 2016 are the part of the polity in need of explanation. Recent research shows that this group in particular is overwhelmingly white, non-Hispanic, and working class (Morgan and Lee 2018).[2]

Since Bill Clinton's administration (1993–2001) especially, the American establishment Left has been distinctly neoliberal, seeking market solutions to problems from welfare (Mink 1998) to health care (Giaimo 2002). Likewise, the Democratic Party has done little to stem the bleeding of labor unions or small-scale businesses, including family farms (see, e.g., Reich 2008; Robinson 2002). The weakening of the social safety net, the decline in taxes, the disinvestment in education, and the loss of small enterprise has meant suffering for most on the lower end of the income scale, including whites. This suffering came to a head in the 2008 economic crash. While Democrats held both houses of Congress until 2011 and the Senate until 2015, a uniquely obstructionist Republican Party limited the policy options available to the Democratic Party. Even without this barrier, however, the modern Democrats had few policy instruments that could have fixed the underlying inequality of the system. The economy recovered, but this recovery was not particularly felt by poor whites in rural areas or in rust belt states. It was downplayed by the conservative state-level politicians who sounded alarm bells about insolvency, greedy public sector unions, and federal overreach. This strategy was largely successful for the Republicans, who came to power in record numbers at the state level during Obama's first term. The neoliberal Left had very little with which to respond in terms of either rhetoric or policy. Without unions, without strong economic policy levers at the state level, and with a recovery that did not correct thirty years of growing inequality, poor whites felt abandoned by Democrats (see, e.g., McQuarrie 2017).

At the same time, poor whites felt that others—African Americans especially but people of color in general—*were* being included in the Democrats' vision of America via "welfare" and other forms of special treatment on bases that were unfair or unearned.[3] In reality, due to unequal distributions of wealth and racism in the housing industry, people of color were hit harder by the initial shock of the Great Recession, and their recovery has been slower (Kochar and Fry 2014). In addition, little race-specific support was actually offered by the Democrats, and even within that party, support for group-specific programs such as affirmative action has waned. In line with our expectations about neoliberalism and the Left, Democrats continued to offer primarily color-blind solutions to problems of racial inequality (see, e.g., Burke 2017). However, whites hearing the race-conscious rhetoric of the movement Left (e.g., antipolice violence and #BlackLivesMatter) likely linked this race consciousness and race-specific remediation to established Democrats. Meanwhile, these outsider groups engaged in a concerted effort to call out color-blind racism in the establishment Left by, for instance, disrupting events held by Democratic candidates, both "insider" candidate Hillary Clinton and "outsider"/"movement" candidate Bernie Sanders. The post-Obama establishment Left had little to offer poor whites left behind by an economic recovery touted by Hillary Clinton but even less to inspire those minority voters who had turned out in droves for Obama.

In sum, the establishment Left has neither the policy tools to conquer economic inequality nor the conceptual tools to counter the explicit racism of Trump's Far Right. Color-blind ideology offers only platitudes about the humanness of humanity. This vocabulary is inadequate for addressing the complex systems of institutional racism that have long characterized the United States (Bonilla-Silva 2003). That ideology is even less well suited to countering rhetoric like Trump's that paints Mexicans, Muslims, and African Americans as violent threats to America. Thus poor whites are excluded from the Democratic Party's vision of America's social and moral boundaries via Democrats' abandonment of them economically and would likely be repelled by a rhetoric explicitly aimed at remediating racial inequality. Republicans, on the other hand, offer white America a vision of Americanness in which if only we could control our borders, physically and socially, then America could become "great again" and, the subtext goes, whites would recover their position of privilege in the "natural order" of American society. Under these conditions, attempts by the movement Left to seek inclusion of migrants and minorities in narratives about Americanness can be dismissed as mere "identity politics"—an attempt to make a claim for special treatment based on belonging in a nonwhite (and, sometimes, nonmale) group. Whites, on the other hand, benefit from the elision of whiteness with Americanness: if they can be made successful again, regardless of the success or failure of Mexican, Muslim, or Black Americans, then America will be made great again.

The United States, then, has experienced a crisis of closure as entry and closure as access to good. This crisis has been mostly manufactured by Trump's campaign rhetoric but has been given space by a neoliberal American Left without a clear plan for healing decades of economic harm to poor whites or a race-conscious strategy for moving forward on racial justice. The result has been an electoral victory that has worked to shift the boundaries of belonging in the United States, such that any claims to belong from minorities are met with an increasingly legitimated racist rhetoric that equates belonging in the American nation with whiteness.

The movement Left in general and #BlackLivesMatter in particular have pushed back stridently on these new boundaries of belonging, and movement-building efforts seem to be gaining some traction. The murders of George Floyd and Breonna Taylor, along with other less well publicized instances of police violence, sparked protests in the summer of 2020 that were larger, more consequential, and whiter than previous actions. There has been some accommodation of antiracist movement Left rhetoric by some mainstream Democrats, including presidential candidate Joe Biden. Yet for most activists this was too little, too late, and the choice of an establishment Democrat disappointing. In fact, Joe Biden's share of the Black vote was smaller than Hillary Clinton's. #BLM's conceptions of belonging are not the kind of individualistic belonging that has, since the late 1980s, come to characterize the neoliberal ideological commitments of the centrist wing of the Democratic Party. Thus, the split still remains.

CASE 2: SWEDEN, THE ANTIRACIST LEFT, AND THE SWEDEN DEMOCRATS

In Sweden there has not been a single electoral moment analogous to the Trump victory; instead, there has been a steadily growing Far Right, making it one of the top three largest parties after the 2018 election, with 17.5 percent of the vote. Nonetheless, the Far Right in Sweden was behind a governmental crisis in early 2014 that highlighted and exacerbated growing divisions in public opinion over immigration. The crisis occurred when, rather than abstaining from a vote on the ruling Center-Left bloc's (the Red-Green bloc) budget proposition, as is the norm for nonaligned parties, the Sweden Democrats voted instead for the opposition's budget. Because the SD had become the third largest parliamentary party in the 2013 election, with an unexpected 13 percent of the vote, this sunk the government's budget. The Red-Green bloc, however, refused to govern under the opposition's budget. Initially, a new and early election was called, something that had happened only once since full suffrage in Sweden. A last-minute compromise prevented new elections from being called, but the underlying problems of the SD's refusal to follow established political norms and its intransigence on issues of immigration were not addressed. Furthermore, this so-called December Compromise has since fallen apart, leaving the SD in a position of power disproportionate to its size.

Behind the crisis was the refusal of the SD to support a budget in which the Green Party—at the time, largely considered to be the most proimmigration party in parliament—would have any influence on migration policy.[4] The SD promised, therefore, to make the unrealized new election a "referendum for or against increased immigration" (Hjärpe 2014). The SD is an anti-immigration party. Members paint migrants—nearly always Muslim in the SD imagination—as uncivilized, backward, and savage. Like Trump's depictions of Mexicans, party members describe Muslim immigrants as criminals and, especially, as rapists (see, e.g., Linus Bylund's statement that "rape is deeply rooted in Islamic culture" and that the Koran says that rape is "a Muslim punishment" [Hjärpe 2014]). In SD rhetoric, Muslims are a cultural threat, deeply destructive to the Swedish way of life. The SD also points to the Islamic subjection of women and Muslims' backward views on same-sex relationships, as well as migrants' welfare dependency, caused by a culturally predicated lack of work ethic or sense of personal integrity.[5] The party adds to these points a mainstream critique of immigration that argues that there is a "structural limit" to the number of migrants that can be admitted and that, in particular, the refugee acceptance system is overtaxed and administratively "broken." Both of these ideas have popular support, but the cultural/crime argument is primarily expressed by the SD, while the structural limitation argument is common across all political parties. It is important to note that anti-immigration/immigrant sentiment does not neatly fit in a Left/Right pattern. Some of the strongest proimmigration sentiments have come from the established, mainstream Center Right. In addition, the visa restrictions and increased border security that followed the 2015 refugee crisis were also spearheaded by the Social Democrats with the support of mainstream, centrist parties.

Much as with Trump's election in the United States, the success of the SD in disrupting politics as usual made the Swedish Left ask where it had gone wrong (Borg and Jansson 2015). The SD's support came from the young, the working class, and the unemployed. Like Trump voters, they were less educated. Unlike Trump supporters, they were overwhelmingly low income. Like the Democrats, the Swedish establishment Left sees itself as the "natural" choice for this group of voters, though that natural support has eroded in the last two decades.[6] The Red-Green bloc was forced to ask many of the same questions as the American Democrats: How did they lose a part of their "natural" base to a party so virulent and objectionable?

In the United States the establishment Left created space for Trump through a combination of ineffective economic neoliberalism, mainstream color-blind racism, and an incorrect perception of race consciousness and other so-called identity politics by poor whites. In Sweden the Left—both the established Red-Green bloc and the antiracist movement Left—set the stage for the Sweden Democrats through an increasingly individualist conception of antiracism that abandoned its prior focus on structural and political incorporation. Some of this looks similar to the mechanisms of the American Left—the abandonment of "strong" social democracy for "soft" neoliberalism, similar to that found in Tony Blair's Labor Party by the Social Democrats, for instance (see, e.g., Evans and Schmidt 2012; Wennström 2016). Additionally the adoption by the antiracist movement Left of a proimmigrant, prodiversity frame that focuses on the individual experiences of racism and the differential treatment of Swedish people of color has shifted the conversation in a culturally neoliberal direction. Consider, for instance, two high-profile instances of distinctly color-conscious, antiracist talk: the 2013 open letter by author Jonas Hassen Khemiri, a Swedish-born citizen with a Tunisian father (taken up also elsewhere in this volume), and the 2014 parliamentary speech by hip hop artist Jason "Timbuktu" Diakité, the Swedish-born son of a Black American civil rights lawyer and a white American mother, both of which follow similar lines.

Khemiri's letter, written to then justice minister Beatrice Ask, became and remains the most shared article of all time in the Swedish media. It asks Ask to consider what it might be like to go through life in Sweden in darker skin. The picture he paints is one of constant outsiderness, and it is a visceral, individualist piece that puts personal experience at the center of one's conception of racism. The letter is distinctly color-conscious, pointing to experiences that are individual, personal, and even bodily. While the letter provoked a longer newspaper exchange on structural racism, the letter itself discussed none of that, focusing on interpersonal racism alone.

Similarly, Diakité pointed to his state of not belonging. Diakité, in a dramatic gesture, held up his Swedish passport and explained that it proved that he was Swedish. Any hatred toward him, therefore, was about his skin color, which made it racism. His legal status as a Swedish citizen did not protect him, in other words, from the personal experience of racism. Diakité's speech reflects concerns that are important to scholars of color-blind racism who see the absence of references to race or color in legal systems as not only unhelpful but also actively harmful in terms of racial inequality (e.g., Lieberman 1998). Diakité's speech, an acceptance speech for an award recognizing his antiracist work, was also shared extensively. Both sets of stories hit home. Both examples are noteworthy because they do not argue that there is no "space" for people like them in the *structure* of Swedish society. Khemiri and Diakité are both wildly successful cultural producers who have traded on their unique experiences as insider/outsiders in Sweden and have benefited from a Swedish system that supports the kind of art they produce. No one is seeking their official exclusion, as in the case of newly arrived refugees. Rather, they argue that they are pushed out of the boundaries of belonging in their day-to-day lives.

On the one hand, one would expect artists in particular to make arguments based on human experience. On the other hand, Khemiri and Diakité have in other places made arguments about the lack of structural "space" for immigrants and Swedes of color. Yet in terms of the public impact of specific interventions in the discourse on race, it is these two personal/individualist arguments that made such a large impact. The argument here is an argument about bad people doing racist things. While this was not the dominant discourse of any political party, there has been an upsurge in political talk specifically about racism—not xenophobia or ignorance but race and racism as seen through the acts of racists and the experiences of distinctly raced individuals. This is paralleled by similar discussions of the experiences of other marginalized groups subject to poor treatment, even outright attack, in the public sphere, such as women and Jews.

The adoption of a more individualist frame by the Swedish antiracist movement Left makes that discourse look similar to the one on the American movement Left. The context and meaning of individualist antiracism in

Sweden is differently nuanced, however. It is a pushback against official color blindness first and foremost. Everyday racism and popular anti-immigration discourses have been present in Sweden since the first immigrants arrived in Sweden. Yet Sweden since the late 1980s has been characterized primarily by a constrained official discourse on immigration that has restricted both anti-immigrant sentiment and race- and ethnicity-conscious discourse (see, e.g., Odmalm and Bale 2015). Indeed, the taboo against mentioning ethnicity or race in a Swedish context has been considerably stronger on the Swedish Left (as well as the Right) than on the American Left, despite adequate documentation that race plays a role in the experience of immigrants in their day-to-day life (Brännström 2018; Hübinette et al. 2012; Voyer 2016). It is both the prior silence and the present increase of attention that creates space for a Far Right resurgence.

This is not to argue that the increase of "race talk" in the Swedish context has created the Sweden Democrats.[7] On the contrary, the attempt to renegotiate boundaries based on cultural individualism instead created that space. For most of recent Swedish history, boundaries of belonging were centered on social democracy with an undercurrent of statist but not cultural individualism (see, e.g., Berggren and Trägårdh 2015; Schall 2016). To be Swedish was to be left alone, perhaps in your little red cottage in the woods, supported by and supporting the state. To belong in the Swedish nation now, according to the antiracist Left, is to participate in a society that has acceptance, recognition, and inclusion as a central Swedish characteristic while neither stigmatizing nor silencing the fact of racial realities (this is Jeffrey Alexander's [2006] definition of multiculturalism; see also Schall [2014b]). SD voters—young, less educated, low income, and unemployed, by and large—find themselves not only on the outside of the new boundaries but also framed as a threat to these boundaries. The irony, of course, is that the SD (and its supporters) see Muslim refugees as the threat to Sweden, both literally in terms of terrorism and crime and figuratively in terms of Swedish culture.[8]

Like poor white Trump voters, these SD voters find themselves unsupported by the current economic and social system and often unmoored from traditional political distinctions. Where the two sets of voters differ is that this system was built up and then dismantled by a small-s social democracy they still largely believe in. Here is where we can see the effect that the abandonment of strong social democracy by the Social Democrats has. Previously, the social democratic welfare state had acted as an engine of incorporation for both migrants and potentially marginalized working-class native Swedes

(Schall 2016). When the Swedish Social Democrats took their neoliberal turn in the late 1980s and early 1990s, that engine for incorporation stalled for both groups, particularly given the Social Democrats' abandonment of full employment as a primary policy goal. Previously loyal working-class Left voters began to understand migrants, particularly the new Muslim nonwhite asylum seekers, as threats to the viability of that mode of incorporation. The response for some was to attack immigration as unsustainable, and the Sweden Democrats provided a vehicle for this kind of attack. Thus, the Sweden Democrats fulfill two vital needs for this set of voters: first, a need to see their views about the worth (and, indeed, superiority) of the traditional white Swedish culture vindicated; and second, a need to see that the remaining economic prosperity of the welfare state is protected from a group they view as unworthy and perhaps incapable of incorporation both economically and culturally.[9]

CONCLUSION: THE TWIN PERILS OF INDIVIDUALISM AND COLOR BLINDNESS

It is no inexplicable accident that Donald Trump mentioned Sweden as a site of a nonexistent terrorist attack, responding as he was to a heavily criticized *Fox News* story about a nonexistent immigrant crime epidemic in the country. Sweden as a place "ruined" by immigration has existed for many years in the imaginary of the international Far Right. Sweden represents a cautionary tale for Americans and for the Far Rights of continental Europe as well—it is a place of fictitious "no go zones" and the supposed "rape capital of the world."[10] It is of course worthwhile to point out that the sites of inclusion that working-class whites in the United States and working-class whites in Sweden imagine are, as a matter of fact, quite different. In the United States the white working class imagines a world where they can succeed by working hard without government interference or assistance. The idea promulgated by the racist Right is that both immigrants and American-born minorities do not "buy into" the American work ethic and make demands for government assistance that undermine the American dream. In Sweden the cradle-to-grave welfare state and the trust that underlies it are a central part of Swedish identity, and it is immigrants' capacity to undermine that trust and "steal" that welfare that forms the threat. In both cases, however, immigrants and nonwhites become the scapegoat for that lost "paradise."

The comparison of these two cases indicates that we ought to be suspicious of overly simple descriptions of either Left or Right voters. It was not merely the fact that the Democrats have for years ignored the so-called economic anxiety of rural white voters in the United States nor the underrepresented social and economic unrest of young white unemployed men in Sweden that created a soil fertile for a virulently racist Far Right in both these places. It was also not only backlash against antiracism or so-called identity politics in either place that sent a wave of racists into the halls of governance. Rather, it is the way that these things have coexisted in both places that creates a political landscape in which Far Right racism becomes legitimized and, indeed, popular. More importantly, there is nothing wrong with calls for cultural inclusion that sometimes get labeled as identity politics. Calls for inclusion that start and end with identity without proffering a critique of the structural conditions that underlie systems of inequality, however, present a stumbling block for native-born whites, people of color, and migrants alike.

In both countries, the key to moving forward is to find compelling ways of resolving crises of closure for both poor whites and minorities, whether the terms of those closures are centered around American-style or Swedish-style individualism or other, more community-based ideas of belonging. In both cases, the establishment mainstream Left, insofar as it continues to follow both economically and culturally neoliberal tenets, seems ill-equipped to offer any notion of belonging. The movement Left provides some clues but does little to bring poor whites into the fold. It should be possible to combine honest and critical conversations on race with honest and critical conversations on economic inequality that include poor whites.

NOTES

1. The popular press has, to a certain extent, picked up on this. See especially Klein (2016). It was the Democrats' embrace of neoliberalism that won it for Trump.

2. Note that another large part of the story is the loss of the population of new Obama voters, largely young and/or nonwhite, who failed to turn out for Clinton. This is discussed below.

3. Hochschild (2016) talks about this as "line jumping," though she is primarily discussing the attitude and dispositions of solidly Republican voters in the South.

4. The title of "most immigrant friendly" party has shifted since. The Greens were a part of the decision to restrict refugee migration heavily amid the 2015 refugee crisis. The Center Party was perhaps more rightly considered "most immigrant friendly" in the run-up to the 2018 election.

5. It should be noted that these problems, particularly problems of gender inequality, do exist within the Islamic community. They are, however, exaggerated by the SD. Most Muslims in Sweden are either secular or non-Fundamentalist.

6. The Swedish Right, initially unwilling to cooperate with the SD, were also left flat-footed by the SD's political disruptions. This is an important point in explaining the electoral victory of the SD, but it is outside the scope of the current argument.

7. Exclusive attention to structural racism previously left certain kinds of real and valid claims about raced experiences unexpressed or invalidated, in fact. The "mentioning of race" here occurs in a context that is very different from that talk in the US case.

8. This kind of struggle—multiculturalism as threat versus multiculturalism as the central uniting concept of a new Swedish identity—can be seen, for instance, in the use of the sarcastic term *kulturberikare* (culture enricher) by Swedish immigrant opponents.

9. It should be noted that while the Sweden Democrats present themselves often as protectors of the welfare state, they do not vote consistently in that manner.

10. Trump has used both of these phrases, but they originate in alt-right internet forums.

References

Alexander, Jeffrey C. 2006. *The Civil Sphere*. Oxford: Oxford University Press.

Alexander, Michelle. 2012. *The New Jim Crow: Mass Incarceration in the Age of Colorblindness*. New York: New Press.

Anderson, Bridget, Matthew J. Gibney, and Emanuela Paoletti. 2011. "Citizenship, Deportation and the Boundaries of Belonging." *Citizenship Studies* 15(5): 547–63.

Berggren, Henrik, and Lars Trägårdh. 2015. *Är svensken människa? Gemenskap och oberoende i det moderna Sverige*. Stockholm: Norstedts.

Bonilla-Silva, Eduardo. 2003. *Racism without Racists: Color-Blind Racism and the Persistence of Racial Inequality in America*. Lanham, MD: Rowman & Littlefield.

Borg, Maja, and Malin Jansson. 2015. "'Här faller en brun skugga över Sverige': En innehållsanalys av *Aftonbladets* och *Expressens* gestaltning av Sverigedemokraterna valet 2014." Mid Sweden University, Division of Media and Communication Studies.

Brännström, Leila. 2018. "The Terms of Ethnoracial Equality: Swedish Courts' Reading of Ethnic Affiliation, Race and Culture." *Social and Legal Studies* 27(5): 616–35.

Burke, Meghan A. 2017. "Colorblind Racism: Identities, Ideologies, and Shifting Subjectivities." *Sociological Perspectives* 60(5): 857–65.

Caiani, Manuela, and Linda Parenti. 2016. *European and American Extreme Right Groups and the Internet*. New York: Routledge.

Campbell, John L., and Ove K. Pedersen, eds. 2001. *The Rise of Neoliberalism and Institutional Analysis*. Princeton, NJ: Princeton University Press.

Cramer, Katherine J. 2016. *The Politics of Resentment: Rural Consciousness in Wisconsin and the Rise of Scott Walker*. Chicago: University of Chicago Press.

Evans, Bryan, and Ingo Schmidt, eds. 2012. *Social Democracy after the Cold War*. Athabasca, AB: Athabasca University Press.

Giaimo, Susan. 2002. *Markets and Medicine: The Politics of Health Care Reform in Britain, Germany, and the United States*. Ann Arbor: University of Michigan Press.

Hjärpe, Jan 2014. "SD-Topp: Våldtäkt en muslimsk straffmetod." *Dagens Nyheter*, January 8. http://www.dn.se.

Hochschild, Arlie Russell. 2018. *Strangers in their Own Land: Anger and Mourning on the American Right*. New York: New Press.

Hübinette, Tobias, Helena Hörnfeldt, Fataneh Farahani, and Rene Leon Rosales. 2012. *Om ras och vithet i det samtida sverige*. Tumba: Mångkulturellt Centrum Tumba.

Jaworsky, Bernadette Nadya. 2013. "Immigrants, Aliens and Americans: Mapping Out the Boundaries of Belonging in a New Immigrant Gateway." *American Journal of Cultural Sociology* 1(2): 221–53.

Kivisto, Peter. 2017. *The Trump Phenomenon: How the Politics of Populism Won in 2016*. Bingley, UK: Emerald Publishing.

Klein, Naomi. 2016. "It Was the Democrats' Embrace of Neoliberalism That Won It for Trump." *The Guardian*, 9.

Kochar, Rajesh, and Richard Fry. 2014. "Wealth Inequality Has Widened along Racial, Ethnic Lines since End of Great Recession." *Pew Research Center* 12(104): 121–45.

Lamont, Michèle, and Virág Molnár. 2002. "The Study of Boundaries in the Social Sciences." *Annual Review of Sociology* 28(1): 167–95.

Lieberman, Robert C. 1998. *Shifting the Color Line: Race and the American Welfare State*. Cambridge, MA: Harvard University Press.

McAdam, Doug, and Sidney Tarrow. 2010. "Ballots and Barricades: On the Reciprocal Relationship between Elections and Social Movements." *Perspectives on Politics* 8(2): 529–42.

McQuarrie, Michael. 2017. "The Revolt of the Rust Belt: Place and Politics in the Age of Anger." *British Journal of Sociology* 68:S120–S152.

Mink, Gwendolyn. 1998. *Welfare's End*. Ithaca, NY: Cornell University Press.

Morgan, Stephen L., and Jiwon Lee. 2018. "Trump Voters and the White Working Class." *Sociological Science* 5:234–45.

Mudge, Stephanie L. 2008. "What Is Neo-liberalism?" *Socio-economic Review* 6(4): 703–31.

Mudge, Stephanie L. 2018. *Leftism Reinvented: Western Parties from Socialism to Neoliberalism*. Cambridge, MA: Harvard University Press.

Odmalm, Pontus, and Tim Bale. 2015. "Immigration into the Mainstream: Conflicting Ideological Streams, Strategic Reasoning and Party Competition." *Acta Politica* 50(4): 365–78.

Reich, Robert B. 2008. *Supercapitalism: The Transformation of Business, Democracy, and Everyday Life*. New York: Vintage.

Robinson, Ian. 2000. "Neoliberal Restructuring and US Unions: Toward Social Movement Unionism?" *Critical Sociology* 26(1–2): 109–38.

Schall, Carly Elizabeth. 2014a. "Ideology, Race and the Social Politics of Belonging in the West." Paper presented at the Social Science History Association meeting, Toronto, ON.

Schall, Carly Elizabeth. 2014b. "Multicultural Iteration: Swedish National Day as Multiculturalism-in-Practice." *Nations and Nationalism* 20(2): 355–75.

Schall, Carly Elizabeth. 2016. *The Rise and Fall of the Miraculous Welfare Machine: Immigration and Social Democracy in Twentieth-Century Sweden.* Ithaca, NY: Cornell University Press.

Schierup, Carl-Ulrik and Aleksandra Ålund. 2011. "The End of Swedish Exceptionalism? Citizenship, Neoliberalism and the Politics of Exclusion." *Race & Class* 53(1): 45–64.

Springer, Simon, Kean Birch, and Julie MacLeavy. 2016. "An Introduction to Neoliberalism." In *Handbook of Neoliberalism*, edited by Simon Springer, Kean Birch, and Julie MacLeavy, 29–42. New York: Routledge.

Treitler, Vilna Bashi. 2016. "Racialization and Its Paradigms: From Ireland to North America." *Current Sociology* 64(2): 213–27.

Valdes, Francisco, and Sumi Cho. 2011. "Critical Race Materialism: Theorizing Justice in the Wake of Global Neoliberalism." *Connecticut Law Review* 43:1532–72.

Verhaeghe, Paul. 2014. "Neoliberalism Has Brought Out the Worst in Us: An Economic System That Rewards Psychopathic Personality Traits Has Changed Our Ethics and Our Personalities." *The Guardian*, September 29.

Voyer, Andrea. 2013. "Notes on a Cultural Sociology of Immigrant Incorporation." *American Journal of Cultural Sociology* 1(1): 26–41.

Voyer, Andrea. 2016. "Betydelsen av etnisk bakgrund." In *Skolframgång i det mångkulturella samhället*, edited by Anna Lund and Stefan Lund, 39–64. Lund: Studentlitteratur.

Weber, Max. 1978. *Economy and Society.* Edited by Guenther Roth and Claus Wittich. Berkeley: University of California Press.

Wennström, Johan. 2016. "A Left/Right Convergence on the New Public Management? The Unintended Power of Diverse Ideas." *Critical Review* 28(3–4): 380–403.

Westlake, Daniel 2016. "Multiculturalism, Political Parties, and the Conflicting Pressures of Ethnic Minorities and Far-Right Parties." *Party Politics* 24(4): 421–33.

Wimmer, Andreas. 2002. *Nationalist Exclusion and Ethnic Conflict: Shadows of Modernity.* Cambridge: Cambridge University Press.

Wong, Tom K. 2017. *The Politics of Immigration: Partisanship, Demographic Change, and American National Identity.* Oxford: Oxford University Press.

ON THE GROUND

Coming to Terms with Belonging

Unemployed Migrants and Sociocultural Incorporation in Norway

KELLY MCKOWEN

A promise—not yet broken—brought Martim to Norway.[1] It was 2013, and Portugal, his home, teetered on the edge of the financial cliff over which the hapless Greeks had tumbled only a few years earlier. Jobs were rare, good jobs were rarer. Amid high unemployment (17.5 percent in 2013), stagnating wages, and uncertain public finances, Martim and other young Portuguese recognized that working abroad had long ceased to be a gamble—the gamble was staying and trying to make a life in Portugal. One day, hoping for much and expecting little, Martim traveled to Lisbon for a job fair. There he met a recruiter from a large, well-known multinational corporation looking to fill an engineering position in Trondheim, Norway. The recruiter seemed to know exactly what Martim and the others in the long queue wanted to hear. "A job for life," Martim remembers the person saying. An "El Dorado," he remembers thinking. He applied. Shortly thereafter, he received word that he had been chosen. He bid *tchau* to his parents and the Mediterranean warmth and sun for a professional opportunity in a "cold, very cold" country he knew little about.

In 2014 the price of Brent crude oil plummeted. At Martim's office, "the bomb hit" in September when the staff was notified that half of them would be laid off. A month later, he learned that he had not made the cut and his contract would be terminated in January. *That* was the broken promise. Still, he was undeterred. Life in Trondheim, both in the office and outside of it, had suited him. He decided to move to Oslo to look for another job, possibly even something in another field. When he and I met there in early 2016 to discuss the experience of being unemployed and foreign in Norway, I asked him why he stayed. After all, it had been a year since his last day on the job—a year of cold calls, unanswered emails, unsuccessful interviews. Moreover, there were certainly opportunities for experienced engineers elsewhere in Europe. Why tough it out in Oslo?

"I still believe in the Norwegian dream," Martim insisted. I asked him to clarify. He continued, "It's if you work, you get rewarded for it—and you can evolve. As I see it in Portugal, in Spain, in Greece, in Italy right now, I think you work to make ends meet. You work to get to the end of the month. . . . Here, you make enough to really establish yourself, settle in, start thinking about a family, start looking for houses. You really evolve in a short period of time. You see your life going forward. *That's* why I want to be here."

For a young person coming from a distressed part of Europe, where work is increasingly precarious and the future uncertain, Norway presented Martim with a contract with clear—and to his mind, fair—terms for building a life. He articulated these terms by alluding to and modifying the trope of an "American dream" to reflect the Norwegian promise of stability and predictability. This was not a dream of riches or even social mobility, as in the American case, but of decent recompense for a reasonable amount of work. In a subsequent conversation, Martim also seemed to appreciate that the chance to "evolve" even extended to periods of joblessness, when comparatively generous unemployment benefits kept him afloat while he participated in a Norwegian-language class that he hoped would improve his prospects. To him, all of this—this Norwegian dream—was something to stay and struggle for.

In an article on foreign au pairs in Norway, Olga Tkach (2016, 231) argues convincingly that migrants are like "amateur anthropologists," whose close contact with the nonmigrant population over an extended period furnishes them with copious amounts of "data" on how local norms, values, beliefs, and taboos govern things such as parenting, gender relations, and social protection. These data provoke critical self-reflection among Tkach's Eastern European interlocutors, who come to see more clearly the particularity—and relative desirability—of their own cultural lenses. Moving "from fear and hostility towards the Other" (231) to fascination and even admiration, the au pairs engage in idiosyncratic processes of appropriative "boundary work" aimed at improving their class positions.

But managing boundaries is rarely simple. Navigating cultural difference and the desire for sameness can be challenging, unpredictable, awkward, and painful for migrants. Newcomers, for instance, may be caught between the radically divergent embodied dispositions—or "habituses"—of their ethnic communities and host society (Engebrigtsen 2011). They may confront irreconcilable conceptualizations of personhood, often leaving their children, who come of age in Scandinavia, struggling to strike a balance (Eriksen 2015). And depending on the color of their skin, they may discover that recognition as a full member of the community or even as a human being worthy of basic respect is impossible (McIntosh 2015) due to the interpersonal and institutional racism (Gullestad 2006) that undergirds a tacit and exclusionary system of "cultural citizenship" (Ong 1996). In sum, migrants in Scandinavia and elsewhere often live on the threshold between "imagined communities" (Anderson 1991), and though they may grapple with expectations—their own or those of others—to weave themselves, at least partially, into the "webs of significance" (Geertz 1973) of the majority, they may find doing so undesirable, unfeasible, or both.

Nevertheless, it is done—or attempted. People like Martim, confronted with the opportunity to live another kind of life, oriented toward a different kind of dream, change their personal and professional priorities and strive toward new horizons—or dreams. But how and why does this happen? How does someone come to conceptualize and believe in something like a "Norwegian dream"? What makes it "Norwegian" and worth believing in? And what does this tell us about the processes through which migrants incorporate themselves—and are incorporated—into increasingly diverse Scandinavian societies?

These questions offer the opportunity to refine scholarly understanding of migrant incorporation as an everyday process with economic, as well as social and cultural, dimensions (McKowen and Borneman 2020; see also Eriksen 2007). Currently, scholarly accounts of these dimensions are inadequate, if only because they typically treat them as separate or separable. In practice, the economic, social, and cultural aspects of incorporation are so interwoven as to be nearly indistinguishable. For instance, for a middle-aged, able-bodied person to be incorporated economically in a country like Norway, it is necessary to have a job. But finding a job often requires one to be incorporated socially as well, with a local network, and incorporated culturally, with a working grasp of certain practices, beliefs, norms, and taboos of the majority population. In this case, it is not clear where each dimension of incorporation begins and ends.

Further, with respect to the Scandinavian case, scholars have only recently begun to explore the role that Scandinavia's unique welfare model plays in shaping the sociocultural and moral conditions under which migrants are incorporated into extant and emergent groups, communities, and institutions (see Olwig 2011; Olwig and Paerregaard 2011). This model, variously called "social democratic" (Esping-Andersen 1990) or "universal" (Rothstein 1998), features comparatively substantial, tax-funded benefits and services administered by a vast public sector. Except for newcomers from certain northern European countries, none of the migrants one encounters in Norway come from places where one can expect the state to provide this kind of long-term material aid during difficult life events such as unemployment. Rather, in most places, jobless people typically turn to immediate family, an extended kin network (Stack 1983), the informal sector, a trade union, or a religious/sectarian organization (Cammett 2015) to make ends meet when formal employment is not an option. For migrants, the material and normative shift from dependency on these actors to the Scandinavian state happens with little fanfare, yet the implications for individuals and families are potentially quite significant. Material exchanges, after all, mark and maintain relations and reciprocal expectations (Zelizer 2010, 2012), which in turn shape identity, opening possibilities for remapping the coordinates of belonging.

In this chapter, I consider the experiences of unemployed migrants in contemporary Norway. I connect their impressions of Norwegian norms of work and welfare with their desires for and aversions to sociocultural incorporation. This latter concept has three critical points. First, incorporation is an active and creative process that typically involves assembling representations of the "culture" of the host society and population. Second, these representations are rooted in firsthand experience, as well as stories, gossip, and other kinds of information circulated in the migrant's social network. The concept of "culture," which has become a common cross-cultural trope (Hannerz 1999; Wikan 1999), serves to tie these otherwise loose fragments together into coherent, intelligible, and transmissible representations. Third, in Norway in particular and Scandinavia in general, these experiential fragments are shaped by the cradle-to-grave, universal welfare state and the various ways it normalizes certain ethical orientations to work and receiving public support.

In what follows, I illustrate these points by examining how unemployed migrants develop and articulate impressions and representations of Norwegian culture based on their experiences as former employees of companies in Norway and current "users" (*brukere*) of the welfare state's main agency, the Norwegian Labor and Welfare Administration (NAV, Arbeids- og velferdsforvaltningen). The discussion begins with their reflections on the Norwegian culture of work and what they perceive to be the local emphasis on the

Coming to Terms with Belonging

paramount significance of having rather than necessarily *doing* work (see also McKowen 2020), as well as the importance of conflict avoidance. The chapter then looks at the experience of becoming a NAV user and how for migrants this typically fosters the impression of dependency as something that is legitimate but socially undesirable in Norway. Finally, building on these previous sections, I look directly at migrants' reflections on being incorporated into what they perceive as Norwegian society and culture, focusing on the obstacles posed by racism and discrimination.

This chapter draws on ethnographic material collected during a year of fieldwork in Oslo, Norway, between August 2015 and August 2016, as well as brief follow-up research in June and July 2017. This material consists primarily of in-depth interviews—all done in English—with fourteen core interlocutors, all current and former jobless individuals who had previously immigrated to Norway.[2] Eight of the non-Norwegian interviewees were women, and six were men. Of the women, two came from Lithuania, and one each came from Serbia, Estonia, Poland, Switzerland, China, and Dubai. Of the men, two came from Chile, and one each came from Poland, Romania, Portugal, and Somalia. I first met most of my core interlocutors during a six-month period (December 2015–May 2016) as a regular participant and nonparticipant observer in state-funded job-seeker courses for the unemployed. My field notes from the job-seeker courses, as well as visits to local NAV branch offices, provide insight into the experiences of other unemployed migrants whom I encountered, as well as into the spaces and relations through which migrants directly interact with the welfare state, thus shaping their incorporative trajectories.

WORKING TO LIVE

Unlike Martim, most migrants do not come to Norway chasing the promise of a permanent job. That is not to say, however, that they are not chasing the promise of something: an education, steady or well-paying work, under-the-table cash, a reunified family, safety from persecution. As of January 2020 roughly 790,500 of Norway's 5.38 million people—or about 14.7 percent—were born abroad (Statistisk sentralbyrå 2020). The vast majority of these came from the EU/EEA countries (approx. 342,500), Asia (approx. 245,300), and Africa (approx. 99,500). They live predominantly in urban areas such as Oslo, where the nonethnic Norwegian population of some eastern boroughs exceeds 50 percent. Their reasons for coming are diverse. Of the 789,000 immigrants who arrived between 1990 and 2016, about 35 percent came under the family reunification scheme, 33 percent as labor migrants, 20 percent as refugees, and 10 percent as students (Statistisk sentralbyrå 2017).

Regardless of what brings them to Norway, however, people soon discover that behind the small Nordic country's popular reputation as generous is a broadly shared commitment to the right—enshrined in §110 of the country's constitution—and obligation to achieve self-sufficiency through formal employment.[3] Employability, in fact, is the philosophical core of state-driven initiatives aimed explicitly or implicitly at the integration of foreigners (Hagelund 2005; Hagelund and Kavli 2009; Rugkåsa 2010). On a webpage for the Introduction Program, for instance, a two-year activation and education scheme for refugees and their family members, the government states that its aim "is to increase the chances for participating in working and social life for immigrants, along with enhancing their economic self-sufficiency" (Regjeringa.no 2016).[4] A similar goal orients the Qualification Program, a one-year activation and education scheme open to nonrefugees, as well as the various state-sponsored "work-oriented measures" (*arbeidsrettedetiltak*) migrants participate in, including formal evaluation schemes (*avklaring*), job-seeker courses, vocational training (*yrkesrettet opplæring*), and education.

In each of these settings, migrants are introduced to the norms, rhythms, values, and meanings ascribed to work—and, by contrast, worklessness—in Norwegian society. They learn that work is a central feature of what is considered a dignified life, as it provides not only the "manifest" benefit of an income but also the "latent" benefits of a structured schedule, performance measurement, regular feedback, and social contact (Jahoda 1981, 1982). Norwegians themselves, however, are often quick to clarify that their relationship to work is quite different from that of other people, particularly Americans. During my fieldwork in Oslo, conversations with Norwegians about work inevitably prompted the sharing of the same distillation of the difference: in the United States, you live to work; in Norway, we work to live.

For my migrant interlocutors who had been employed in Norway, this distinctive ethic was all too familiar. In fact, there was near unanimity among them that Norwegians were not particularly hard workers—at least if effort is measured in time and initiative. A common view is that of Szymon, a Polish engineer who, like Martim, had immigrated to Norway to work for a large multinational corporation in the oil and gas industry. Based on his experience, he felt that Norway possesses a distinctive work culture where it "doesn't matter how much you actually do at work." Further, he shared, "You don't receive any kind of feedback when you work here, and it's not actually very

Coming to Terms with Belonging

well communicated what you actually should do." For Szymon, this lack of structure was maddening. For Martim, however, it was ideal. He told me:

> I love it. . . . The deadlines here are always dynamic, and we don't feel the pressure like we feel in Portugal. For instance, we're used to saying that if you give a big project like this to a Portuguese company, it would be done in a year. People would be completely stressed. That's the other thing—if you compare the professional life with the quality of life outside the work, there's no comparison at all. But at least [in Portugal] the work would be much faster and with a lot less money, of course. I think that's the major difference. But here it's much more relaxed, and people want you to rest. For instance, I had a week that I declared that I worked for fifty-two hours, and my manager said, "You can never do this again. This is impossible. This cannot happen in Norway."

For Diego, a Chilean engineer, it was his company's employing of more Polish engineers—always paid less than their Norwegian counterparts—that shaped his understanding of how Norwegians see work. He shared that "the Polish engineers were more experienced and more hardworking than the Norwegian ones" and that the Norwegians had no interest in competing or trying to outdo them. Rather, they believed theirs was the proper way of doing things. As Diego put it, "They [the Norwegians] are very proud of this job culture and working culture, how they perform"—or to his mind, do not perform.

The other feature of Norway's work culture that recurred in my conversations with unemployed migrants was making actual work secondary to a fixation on avoiding conflict and dissensus. Szymon recalled that his Norwegian coworkers would spend much of their time trying to get everyone in the office on the same page with respect to the problems that needed to be solved. This was made challenging by the fact that the staff was rather diverse and that, as he put it, "Norwegians tend not to see problems at all" or "prefer not to see them." If they are nevertheless confronted with a problem, Szymon said, "they immediately provide any type of solution" in order to make it disappear. This point was echoed by another Portuguese engineer, Christiano, in one of the job-seeker courses I observed. "Never create a conflict in Norway," he told me. "You will be fired!" To illustrate the point, he shared the story of a confrontational Austrian who made his Norwegian colleagues uncomfortable. On the day the Austrian was fired, the Norwegians took sick leave en masse to avoid the office. Juan, who, like Diego, had immigrated to Norway from Chile, shared with me that he was fired due to a workplace conflict with a non-Norwegian coworker. He stressed, however, that conflict itself would never happen with a Norwegian colleague: "With a Norwegian person, you'll never have these kinds of problems. It's impossible."

Despite different experiences and feelings about these experiences, my unemployed migrant interlocutors seemed to draw relatively similar conclusions about the sociocultural significance of work and productivity in Norway. What they came to believe is that most Norwegians appear to value *having* work more than *doing* it, a view my Norwegian interlocutors themselves expressed with the cliché about "working to live." Szymon summarized the approach by comparing it to the Polish and American ones. In Poland "people care much more about the work, they're much more involved, engaged in what they're actually doing." Americans are distinguished by a "can-do attitude," where problems and conflicts are tackled head-on. By contrast, "in Norway ... you have to work, but people are not really much involved in their work. Work is just to support yourself, to have the money to live."

Active Dependency

If the experience of being employed in Norway suggested to my migrant interlocutors that Norwegians value having work that allows them to "live," then the experience of being unemployed made it clear that work—or at least employment—is nevertheless a core feature of Norwegians' shared conceptions of what constitutes a dignified life. After losing their jobs, my interlocutors typically "did as the Norwegians do" and appealed to NAV for material support and advice while looking for work. In turn, depending on certain factors, such as previous work history, they were granted cash transfers in the form of unemployment benefits, social assistance, housing assistance, or course money. To aid their job-search process, many, including all those named thus far in the chapter, were sent to job-seeker courses, four-week endeavors revolving around polishing CVs, sending job applications, building LinkedIn profiles, and other activities associated with navigating the digital and analog terrain of the Norwegian labor market. The experience of unemployment thus stretched across various spaces—the home, the NAV office, the job-seeker course center, the job interview, and so on—all yielding new fragments that migrants would assemble into the broader whole of an intelligible "Norwegian culture" into which they could perhaps be incorporated.

Reflecting on the period when he and many of his nonmigrant Norwegian colleagues were laid off, Diego observed that, comparatively, "they were very concerned about not having a job." The reason, he surmised, had less to do with money than with applying for unemployment benefits and being seen as NAV users: "I have heard in the good times people talking down about ... social clients. I heard several times that as ... small talk at lunch, and I heard [it] all the time from Norwegian people really. . . . 'The social clients, they are so bad. They have so many problems with drugs, and they don't want to work hard,' and that [*sic*] kind of things."

Later, Diego became, unbeknownst to some of his employed friends, a NAV user himself. At that point, he noted a tendency among people to speak of NAV's clients as if they constituted a homogeneous group. After becoming a NAV user and interacting with other NAV users in a job-seeker course, he came to see this view as gravely mistaken. Though grouped by NAV into the same categories and sent for the same kinds of interventions, the unemployed were individuals with different backgrounds, skills, levels of motivation, and aspiration. Behind his Norwegian colleagues' dread of unemployment, he suspected it was not only stigma but also social isolation they feared. "Norwegians are usually not very skilled in social connections," he insisted, "so many in unemployment become fast alone and isolated."

Aside from behavior and statements that suggest that being a NAV user is shameful, the significance of employment is underlined for some by the fact of its ubiquity. Lena, an Estonian architect who had worked in London before she was laid off in the wake of the financial crisis, came to Norway when her husband's employer transferred him there. Though pleasantly surprised that she was eligible for some support from NAV, despite never having worked in Norway, it was not long before she began to feel a strange pressure. "Everyone works," she explained to me over coffee on a pale Oslo winter afternoon. "So if you don't work . . ." She paused and suddenly broke into a mock dialogue between herself and an imagined Norwegian: "'OK, are you home with kids?' 'No, I'm not.' 'OK, are you looking for work?' 'Yes.' 'Fine.'" She concluded, "But if you're not on this strict course, then you're almost not accepted."

Though surprised by the generosity of the benefits and services provided by NAV, some of my interlocutors soon discovered that there was indeed a social cost to becoming a user: they were seen as *navere*. The term "*naver*" is derived from NAV and refers pejoratively to people who exploit their eligibility for benefits and services to avoid work or education. Though *naving* is hardly as widespread as some histrionic politicians have claimed, the *naving* discourse, which imposes reputational costs on receiving NAV benefits, appears to function effectively as an informal means of tabooing involuntary dependency (McKowen 2018). Martim remembered that when he lost his job, for example, "everyone told me, 'You're going to be a *naver*,'" which he learned is "like a bum that gets money from the benefits that other people pay." His impression was that "to be a *naver*—it's really, really bad." Nina, a young Lithuanian woman who came to Norway as a student, recalled, "I don't know many Norwegians who had any business with NAV, but the impression that I have from five years of living in Norway is that it's not something to be proud of." She recalled the well-publicized case of the woman who later became head of Innovation Norway, a prominent state-owned enterprise: "She was in NAV's system for a while, and she was describing it always as a traumatic and teaching experience. It is never something natural, like, 'Yeah, well, I was unemployed, so I got to use a bit of NAV and then came back to the labor market again.' It's not like that. People are a bit, sometimes, ashamed, or sometimes they see it as being down, in a way."

My unemployed migrant interlocutors shared a sense that being jobless in Norway, though rather comfortable materially, is not supposed to be pleasant and should make one feel ashamed. But knowing that one *ought* to feel a certain way and actually feeling it are rather different things. Sometimes, the "right" feeling is provoked by the "wrong" situation or encounter. For Viktoria, another young Lithuanian woman and entrepreneur, it was not so much the fact of being unemployed that she found distasteful as interacting with NAV's employees, who made her feel like she should be ashamed of being out of work. As she explained, "It was at first when I started talking to NAV that I realized the stigma is there. Or I felt a stigma. I had heard about it, but I never experienced it in my own skin before I actually started to work with NAV. So it was NAV itself that sort of injected me with that stigma."

A sense of shame, Viktoria believed, was supposed to spur one to seek employment and thus live in accordance within the parameters of a Norwegian dream that centers formal wage labor. But the time and resources provided by NAV also create the possibility for moving toward other, unsanctioned dreams. For example, Nicolae, a Romanian who had worked as a consultant in Oslo, had long aspired to start his own company. He decided he would use the first year of his eligibility for unemployment benefits to get started, though he understood that this violated the spirit of the policy, which aimed to provide material support only for as long as one was *involuntarily* unemployed: "Usually, I think what I felt is that they look [at] you as unemployed and [that] you might spoil the system. I talked to somebody from NAV, and he was really stressed about my situation as well, and he told me at one point, 'Look, there are many people exploiting the system that go to Gran Canaria and just have money from NAV and live a good life in Gran Canaria.' I tried to keep it as secret as possible . . . [that] I'm *naving*, doing *nav*. . . . I'm exploiting the system. But I cannot work a lot or work [at all] and in the same time develop my business."

Szymon observed that among his unemployed friends there were two approaches to being a NAV user. One was to say nothing about it—a potentially wise move given that, as he put it, "it seems to be perceived as you were just fired from a job, and you are not successful in your job search. So maybe there is something wrong with you. This is, unfortunately, the impression that we get from some of the employers." The other option is to "candidly and openly" proclaim, "I'm a *naver*." But why would someone do that? Szymon suggested that friends and people who know you well would not mistake candor about NAV as a sign of failure or deficiency.

No two unemployment experiences are the same. Yet in Norway these experiences—for both migrants and nonmigrants—are clearly patterned by the comparatively generous benefits and services provided by NAV, as well as encounters with practices and statements that suggest a widespread moral aversion to being able-bodied and jobless. Perhaps confusingly, migrants discover that while they are entitled to significant support, they are supposed to *feel* uneasy until they find formal employment. From their work experiences in Norway, however, they also know that the Norwegian commitment to work has little or nothing to do with the intrinsic rewards of work itself. After all, as Norwegians are fond of repeating, work is not life; they work *to live*. It is only when one loses a job that one begins to understand that by "to live" Norwegians do not just mean materially. Work—or employment—is the avenue to other, more abstract sociocultural goods. Otherwise at a loss to understand why nonmigrants appear highly committed to finding employment despite comparatively weak material incentives, migrants draw on experiences and things they have heard to develop creative—and perceptive—explanations that highlight the specificities of Norwegian society and culture.

THE NORWEGIAN DREAM

There is typically a whirl of desire, aversion, and uncertainty as migrants consider adopting and rejecting what they believe are ways of seeing and doing things characteristic of the majority population. Sometimes the changes that come over a person are imperceptible to anyone but those who remember the person as they were "back home." Nina said that her mother would some-times tell her, "You have become so Norwegian." Nina said that she retorts, "No, I didn't. I just found my place because I see my values being more at home here than in Lithuania actually." When I asked her about these values, she mentioned Norwegians' tolerance for others, particularly refugees and those from the LGBT community. She shared the memory of the first time she encountered a gay pride parade in Oslo. She was with her Norwegian boyfriend, Magnus, who passed the parade as if it were something completely unremarkable. "Why are you so excited?" she remembered him asking. "It's just a pride parade." "Yeah, but you don't understand, Magnus," she remem-bered saying. "That would not be possible in Lithuania." When recounting the story, she interrupted here to explain: "In Lithuania, in the last pride parade, there were two members of parliament that were throwing eggs at people. I mean, seriously, and I was so ashamed." Later in our conversation, she admitted that she's "much more happy in Norway. Mentally I don't see myself [as] a Lithuanian anymore because I would be frustrated every day. I would be in culture shock there, not here. ... It's not that I've become Norwegian. It's just something that—I don't know. I just love it. ... So maybe I'm become [sic] more Norwegian. Maybe." What to Nina's boyfriend was completely ordinary was to her a sign that pointed toward the sociocultural bridge between where she had been and where she wanted to be—or *who* she was and *who* she wanted to be.

For others, however, whether they would like to cross this bridge or not, they find the way obstructed. Chen, a Chinese woman who had worked in Norway's oil and gas industry, told me that while she planned to stay in the country for the next five years or so, she could not imagine growing old there. Part of the reason is indeed cultural: she and her husband, who is also Chinese, are both only-children, and they share the familial obligation to someday care for their aging parents in China. But even if this were not the case, there is the racism, which she has encountered firsthand and which has been related to her by friends and acquaintances. She recounted a number of incidents for me, including two that directly involved her and her family. In one, her NAV caseworker told her that she would need to learn the Nor-wegian language for the kind of work she can reasonably expect to get in Norway, that is, custodial or domestic. Chen believed that the caseworker had seen her CV, which prominently features her impressive educational back-ground, including a PhD from a Norwegian university and experience in the oil and gas industry. She interpreted the caseworker's advice as a racist slight based on a not-uncommon stereotype that East Asians are unskilled labor migrants who come to Norway to work as cleaners or nannies.

Chen's second anecdote, about another welfare space, the *barnehage* (kindergarten), suggests that sometimes other migrants are viewed as the barrier to belonging in Norwegian society. Chen explained that her four-year-old daughter was teased by other children, who said that because she has black hair, she must be a boy. She watched as her radiant child, who delighted in singing and dancing, became sullen and withdrawn. Chen did not blame the children; instead, she blamed the teacher, also a migrant, who failed to intervene. In this case, she was convinced that a nonmigrant teacher would have done more. "They [Norwegians] protect her well," Chen emphasized. "So she got into each group in a very short time."

For people like Chen who do not look the way many nonmigrants and migrants believe Norwegians are supposed to look, racial difference is layered on top of cultural difference, making the imagined boundary between Norwegian and non-Norwegian culture—at least in Chen's case—seem less permeable. Still, others, like Lena, refused to accept that skin color or place of birth could preclude them from sharing the Norwegian dream. Like Chen, Lena had an upsetting run-in with a NAV employee who ignored her stated desire to get help finding a job and treated her as if she were a covetous foreigner looking to sponge off hardworking Norwegians. She could take this in stride, however, perhaps due to the overwhelming sense of gratitude she later felt when NAV provided her with a small benefit for participating in a job-seeker course. Still, the incident reminded of her status in the eyes of many Norwegians as a "stranger," a figure near to the collective "we" without being part of it (Simmel 1950).

For migrants, particularly those who come from outside of Europe, everyday life in Norway is punctuated by pervasive, sometimes unintended or unconscious, forms of racism and racialization that all too often go ignored (Gullestad 2006; McIntosh 2015). At the same time, to many migrants, the recognition and acceptance of the white, nonmigrant population is critical if they are to imagine a majority culture into which they can be incorporated as full members and contributors. This implies that one can largely adopt or appropriate the ethics of work and welfare characteristic of what one perceives to be Norwegian culture without gaining the corresponding acceptance from Norwegians themselves. Or to put it another way, you might believe in the Norwegian dream, as Martim does, but the Norwegian dream may refuse to believe in *you*.

Conclusion

At a time when an unprecedented number of labor migrants, refugees, and others are crossing Scandinavian borders, policymakers and publics will find it necessary, if not particularly easy, to grapple with the miscommunications and disharmonies that arise from cultural difference. The same holds for migrants themselves. Though Scandinavia was never as homogeneous as most people imagine (Brochmann and Kjeldstadli 2008), there is no denying that the region has entered a new era of multidimensional "super-diversity" (Vertovec 2007), particularly in cities such as Oslo, Copenhagen, Stockholm, and Malmö. Adjusting to the ever-changing sociocultural composition of Scandinavian publics is made even more difficult for everyone by the acceleration of the global processes behind that change (Eriksen 2014). In the early twenty-first century, scholars in Norway began to write about *det nye Norge* (the New Norway) (Alghasi, Eide, and Eriksen 2012; Eriksen 2011). At the time, the phrase was identified primarily with Oslo's multiethnic eastern suburbs, popularly maligned as a distressed ethnic ghetto, where it was said that crime was rife, listless teenage dropouts spent their time smoking hash, and kindergarteners spoke an ethnolect called *kebabnorsk* ("kebab Norwegian"). Looking back from the vantage point of 2021, after the horrific xenophobic violence of the July 22, 2011, attack on the Labor Party's youth wing, the entry of the welfare chauvinist far-right Progress Party into government in 2013, and the massive surge of refugee arrivals in 2015–16, one feels compelled to acknowledge that in the space of just a few years, the "New Norway" has become even newer, even more complex, even more unwieldy.

What remains constant, however, at least for now, is that for migrants, the day-to-day navigation of cultural difference in Norway will inevitably unfold on an experiential terrain shaped by the country's universal welfare state. Regardless of their country of origin, gender, age, or reason for migrating, they will have to at some point grapple with that welfare state's enormous influence over the meanings, norms, values, and taboos associated with work, social protection, and the relationship between them. The modest aspiration of this chapter has been to show that this grappling does not make migrants passive. Rather, they are agents in an active and creative process of imagination and sociocultural incorporation. This process is rooted in experiences and relations that yield representations of Norwegians and Norwegian society directly tied to their perceptions of the desirability and possibility of incorporation—a process that is simultaneously economic, social, and cultural; quotidian and interactive; and ultimately contingent on the belief that the "imagined totalities" (Graeber 2001) of Norway and Norwegianness are things that migrants can reasonably expect to be part of.

This is worth highlighting in part because of the long-standing and not uncommon fear, usually fomented by populists on the right, that migrants do not understand and properly value Norway's welfare system. My conversations with unemployed migrants, particularly those who had been "down and out" in another country, suggest that few people in contemporary Norway are better equipped to understand how special and rare this system is. I once asked Martim, for instance, if he felt Norwegians really appreciated what they had. Still unemployed, he had recently moved to a new apartment and was living with two young Norwegian women who offered him, an unwitting "amateur anthropologist," unparalleled perspective into how nonmigrants actually live and think. "No," he said without hesitating. "I think they don't really." He continued: "They have no idea how the job market works outside. They are shocked when you talk about money, for instance, in Portugal. What's the minimum wage? They are shocked. If you have to explain to them that along with that comes days of ten, eleven, twelve hours of work, and if you miss one day, then the person in charge starts to look for a replacement, and they expect you to do the job that two or three people do around here, and more, and more, and more. They can never understand something like that." If Norwegians did not appreciate how bad it could be, Martim believed, they also did not appreciate how good their way of life was. As he put it, "Their system is cool because they want you to have a quality in your life. They want you to have quality *of* life. That's very good, but they don't appreciate it, because they never lived anywhere else. They never worked anywhere else."

As Norway continues to undergo significant economic, political, and demographic shifts, one wonders what will become of the welfare system and ways of life—the dreams—it makes possible. It may come to pass that the system's most ardent supporters and defenders in the future will be the country's newcomers, who bring not only skills, needs, family obligations, stories, and trauma but also the experiences needed to truly measure the value of the security, predictability, and balance that some Norwegians who have known no alternative may take for granted.

Notes

1. All names in this chapter are pseudonyms.

2. Note that because the bulk of fieldwork coincided with the rise in unemployment that followed the so-called oil crash (*ojlesmell*) in 2015 and 2016, many—though

by no means all—of my interlocutors, both those formally interviewed and those informally engaged, were highly educated and/or previously involved with the oil and gas industry.

3. The original text from 1954 reads: "Det paaligger Statens Myndigheder at lægge Forholdene til Rette for at ethvert arbeidsdygtigt Menneske kan skaffe sig Udkomme ved sit Arbeide." In 2014 the language was modernized, and the right to public assistance for those unable to support themselves was added: "Statens myndigheter skal legge forholdene til rette for at ethvert arbeidsdyktig menneske kan tjene til livets opphold ved arbeid eller næring. Den som ikke selv kan sørge for sitt livsopphold, har rett til støtte fra det offentlige."

4. "Er å styrke moglegheitene for deltaking i yrkes- og samfunnsliv for innvandrarar, samt å styrke deira økonomiske sjølvstende."

References

Alghasi, Sharam, Elisabeth Eide, and Thomas Hylland Eriksen, eds. 2012. *Den globale drabantbyen: Groruddalen og det nye Norge.* Oslo: Cappelen Damm Akademisk.

Anderson, Benedict. 1991. *Imagined Communities: Reflections on the Origin and Spread of Nationalism.* New York: Verso.

Brochmann, Grete, and Knut Kjeldstadli. 2008. *A History of Immigration: The Case of Norway 900–2000.* Oslo: Universitetsforlaget.

Cammett, Melani. 2015. "Sectarianism and the Ambiguities of Welfare in Lebanon." *Current Anthropology* 56(S11): S76–S87.

Engebrigtsen, Ada I. 2011. "Ali's Disappearance: The Tension of Moving and Dwelling in the Norwegian Welfare Society." *Journal of Ethnic and Migration Studies* 37(2): 297–313.

Eriksen, Thomas Hylland. 2007. "Complexity in Social and Cultural Integration: Some Analytical Dimensions." *Ethnic and Racial Studies* 30(6): 1055–69.

Eriksen, Thomas Hylland. 2011. "Hva betyr 'vi'?" In *Kulturell kompleksitet i det nye Norge,* edited by Thomas Hylland Eriksen and Hans Erik Næss, 9–41. Oslo: Unipub.

Eriksen, Thomas Hylland. 2014. "Antropologi på en overopphetet klode: En diagnose og et forslag." *Norsk antropologisk tidsskrift* 25(1): 5–22.

Eriksen, Thomas Hylland. 2015. "Rebuilding the Ship at Sea: Super-Diversity, Person and Conduct in Eastern Oslo." *Global Networks* 1(20): 1470–2266.

Esping-Andersen, Gøsta. 1990. *The Three Worlds of Welfare Capitalism.* Princeton, NJ: Princeton University Press.

Geertz, Clifford. 1973. *The Interpretation of Cultures: Selected Essays.* New York: Basic Books.

Graeber, David. 2001. *Toward an Anthropological Theory of Value: The False Coin of Our Own Dreams.* New York: Palgrave.

Gullestad, Marianne. 2006. *Plausible Prejudice: Everyday Experiences and Social Images of Nation, Culture, and Race.* Oslo: Universitetsforlaget.

Hagelund, Anniken. 2005. "Why It Is Bad to Be Kind: Educating Refugees to Life in the Welfare State, a Case Study from Norway." *Social Policy and Administration* 39(6): 669–83.

Hagelund, Anniken, and Hanne Kavli. 2009. "If Work Is out of Sight: Activation and Citizenship for New Refugees." *Journal of European Social Policy* 19(3): 259–70.

Hannerz, Ulf. 1999. "Reflections on Varieties of Culturespeak." *European Journal of Cultural Studies* 2(3): 393–407.

Jahoda, Marie. 1981. "Work, Employment, and Unemployment: Values, Theories, and Approaches in Social Research." *American Psychologist* 36(2): 184–91.

Jahoda, Marie. 1982. *Employment and Unemployment: A Social-Psychological Analysis.* Cambridge: Cambridge University Press.

McIntosh, Laurie. 2015. "Impossible Presence: Race, Nation and the Cultural Politics of 'Being Norwegian.'" *Ethnic and Racial Studies* 38(2): 309–25.

McKowen, Kelly. 2018. "A Welfare 'Regime of Goodness'? Material Self-Interest, Reciprocity, and the Moral Sustainability of the Nordic Model." In *Sustainable Modernity: The Nordic Model and Beyond,* edited by Nina Witoszek and Atle Midttun, 119–38. London: Routledge.

McKowen, Kelly. 2020. "Substantive Commitments: Reconciling Work Ethics and the Welfare State in Norway." *Economic Anthropology* 7(1): 120–33.

McKowen, Kelly, and John Borneman. 2020. "Digesting Difference: Migrants, Refugees, and Incorporation in Europe." In *Digesting Difference: Migrant Incorporation and Mutual Belonging in Europe,* edited by Kelly McKowen and John Borneman, 1–27. Cham, Switzerland: Palgrave Macmillan.

Olwig, Karen Fog. 2011. "'Integration': Migrants and Refugees between Scandinavian Welfare Societies and Family Relations." *Journal of Ethnic and Migration Studies* 37(2): 179–96.

Olwig, Karen Fog, and Karsten Paerregaard, eds. 2011. *The Question of Integration: Immigration, Exclusion and the Danish Welfare State.* Cambridge: Cambridge Scholars Publishing.

Ong, Aihwa. 1996. "Cultural Citizenship as Subject-Making: Immigrants Negotiate Racial and Cultural Boundaries in the United States." *Current Anthropology* 37(5): 737–62.

Regjeringa.no. 2016. "Introduksjonsprogram." https://www.regjeringen.no/no/tema/innvandring/innsikt/Verkemiddel-i-integreringsarbeidet/introduksjonsprogram/id2343472/.

Rothstein, Bo. 1998. *Just Institutions Matter: The Moral and Political Logic of the Universal Welfare State.* Cambridge: Cambridge University Press.

Rugkåsa, Marianne. 2010. *Transformasjon og integrasjon: Kvalifisering av minoritetsetniske kvinner til arbeid og deltakelse i den norske velferdsstaten.* Oslo: Det samfunnsvitenskapelige fakultet, Universitetet i Oslo.

Simmel, Georg. 1950. "The Stranger." In *The Sociology of Georg Simmel*, edited by Kurt H. Wolff, 402–8. New York: Free Press.

Stack, Carol. 1983. *All Our Kin: Strategies of Survival in a Black Community*. New York: Basic Books.

Statistisk sentralbyrå. 2017. "Immigrants by Reason for Immigration." https://www.ssb.no/en/befolkning/statistikker/innvgrunn.

Statistisk sentralbyrå. 2020. "Immigrants and Norwegian-Born to Immigrant Parents." Updated March 9. https://www.ssb.no/en/befolkning/statistikker/innvbef.

Tkach, Olga. 2016. "'Now I Know Norway from Within': Boundary Work and Belonging in Au Pairs' Narratives." *Nordic Journal of Migration Research* 6(4): 224–34.

Vertovec, Steven. 2007. "Super-Diversity and Its Implications." *Ethnic and Racial Studies* 30(6): 1024–54.

Wikan, Unni. 1999. "Culture—a New Concept of Race." *Social Anthropology* 7(1): 57–64.

Zelizer, Viviana. 2010. *Economic Lives: How Culture Shapes the Economy*. Princeton, NJ: Princeton University Press.

Zelizer, Viviana. 2012. "How I Became a Relational Economic Sociologist and What Does That Mean?" *Politics and Society* 40(2): 145–74.

Crisis and Pattern during the 2015–2016 "Refugee Crisis" in Sweden

ADMIR SKODO

Following the entry of 162,877 asylum seekers during the second half of 2015, Sweden introduced border controls in November 2015, followed by new laws that curtailed the possibility of being granted permanent residence, family reunification, and the social rights of asylum seekers (Skodo 2017b). In 2016 a Swedish government commission was formed to investigate the 2015–16 "refugee crisis." Its findings were published in an official government report in 2017 titled "Att ta emot människor på flykt: Sverige hösten 2015" (Receiving refugees: Sweden in the fall of 2015"). The report is part of a series that started in 1922 (Statens offentliga utredningar, or Swedish Government Official Reports) and that perform various functions in Swedish governance. These functions include providing expert and stakeholder preparatory material for legislation and rhetorically framing or "burying" (or both) an issue to which a popular political solution seems unlikely, as is the case with the report studied here. Historian Lars Trägårdh captures well the ambiguous political position of Swedish government commissions when he writes that they "have in fact been seen both as the epitome of deliberative democracy and, more cynically, as a quasi-corrupt and secretive system whereby a cabal of insiders representing privileged organizations have been able to strike favourable deals with agents of the state" (2010, 237). This ambiguity is certainly present in the report discussed in this chapter, since the report presents conflicting viewpoints and challenges and criticizes certain government assumptions and actions; nonetheless, it structures its findings in accordance with a government directive.

This chapter begins by discussing the official narratives used in the report produced by this commission. This discussion shows that the statements

provided to the commission by the government, state agencies, and municipalities imply a major difference between the narrative of the government
and state agencies, on the one hand, and the municipalities, on the other. The
two narratives are similar in that neither is concerned with a crisis of national
identity; instead, they are concerned with sovereignty and bureaucratic functioning. Yet while the government and state agencies saw 2015–16 as an existential threat to sovereignty and the bureaucracy, the municipalities saw it as
a strain on the bureaucracy that was successfully managed but whose lessons
and resources were lost on the government and state agencies precisely at the
moment when new practices were established that could effectively deal with
another mass entry.

The chapter then shifts focus by examining how the crisis unfolded on the
ground, namely, in the responses to the new restrictive measures and laws by
asylum seekers, here exemplified by six Afghans, a Swedish Migration Agency
official, and two workers in a privately run asylum seeker reception center.
Afghans are chosen because they were the second-largest national group
of asylum seekers in 2015–16 and were especially hard hit by the new laws.
All the interviewees interacted with each other, directly or indirectly, in or
through a reception center in a small Scanian town.

The main argument running through this chapter is that there is a discrepancy between the official government narrative, which is clothed in the
language of crisis, and the reality on the ground, which is highly patterned
and reveals the extensive control the state is able to exert over the daily life
of asylum seekers. Two patterns are highlighted. First, the Afghan asylum
seekers' flight was prompted not so much by a premeditated individual
choice, as the Migration Agency stated in the report, but by the combined
effect of worsened security conditions in Afghanistan, increasingly harsher
measures against Afghans in Iran and Pakistan, and hardened border controls in the EU, which, ironically, opened the door to Western Europe for the
migrant-smuggling industry. Second, a successful asylum application depends
on the possession of experiences, narratives, and skills that are recognized
by the Migration Agency as sufficient ground for protected status. Such recognition is shaped by a variety of preferences, assumptions, and policies that
structurally disfavor Afghans.

Finally, the chapter concludes by briefly reflecting on the policy implications of using the language of crisis versus the language of pattern when
responding to refugee episodes such as the one in 2015–16 in Sweden.

Official Narratives of the 2015–2016 "Refugee Crisis"

The Government Narrative: Existential Crisis

The arrival of more than 160,000 asylum seekers to Sweden in 2015 is as unprecedented as it was unexpected by the Swedish government. It dwarfs the previous record from 1992, when more than 84,000 people, mainly from the former Yugoslavia, sought asylum in Sweden (Swedish Migration Agency n.d.).[1] One would think that such a dramatic change would spontaneously give rise to questions of why, when, how, and who. Yet as the government report from 2017 makes clear, the way the government conceptualized the basic facts of this unprecedented situation betrays not only an utter disregard for global socioeconomic and political developments and Sweden's role therein but also the perspective of asylum seekers. Instead, for the government, *the* basic fact of the crisis was a "mass invasion" of asylum seekers existentially undermining the Swedish welfare state. The government thus *exclusively* interpreted these events and responded to them founded on this basic fact.

The first context through which the government interpreted the basic fact of the refugee crisis is Swedish law. Swedish law, the report makes clear, is composed of the following components: Sweden's adherence to international human rights law, the rule of law, EU directives and regulations, and due process (Statens offentliga utredningar 2017, 15, 41). The government found support in both EU regulations and international human rights law, and thereby Swedish law, for a violation by the government of those same regulations and laws because of the basic fact of crisis. For example, in the case of the Geneva Convention and the Declaration on Territorial Asylum, which inform Swedish asylum law, the report states: "In the Declaration on Territorial Asylum (GA Res. 2312 on December 14, 1967) . . . there is a ban on returning or removing a person who has the right of asylum in a country [the non-refoulement principle], to a country where he or she risks persecution (article 3). *Exceptions may only be made on account of pressing national security concerns or to protect the general population. As examples are mentioned 'a mass invasion of refugees'*" (307, emphasis added). In regard to EU regulations, to take another illustrative example, the report cites "European Council decision (EU) 2016/894 of May 12, 2016, which decided that Sweden, for a maximum period of six months, can perform border controls. . . . The decision makes evident that Sweden ought to be allowed to continue performing such controls because 'it is an appropriate method for managing a serious threat against public order and internal security ties to the secondary movements of irregular migrants'" (109).

The Swedish government saw the crisis as an existential threat against Sweden's sovereignty and the bureaucracy that allows it to function as a welfare state and uphold its commitments to human rights. Sweden's sovereignty was threatened, thereby justifying, on the very basis of Swedish and international law, the violation of Sweden's commitments and the imposition of highly restrictionist measures in 2015–16. Paradoxically, although the universal right of asylum does allow for mass entry as an abstract possibility, as an empirical reality mass entry is perceived by the Swedish government as a threat to Sweden's ability to offer international protection to persecuted people. Or, in the words of Elisabeth Abiri in her discussion of Swedish refugee policy during the 1990s, "A generous refugee policy can only be so when its generosity is not put to the test" (2000, 25).

The government abides by universal human rights only as long as the concrete events that trigger them, an influx of asylum seekers in this case, can be regulated by the will and policy of the Swedish state. As long as the possibility of a large number of asylum seekers finding their way to Sweden remained abstract, Sweden remained committed to accepting them. It is as a champion of this abstract universality that we must decipher Swedish prime minister Stefan Löfven's speech of September 2015 during which he famously said, "My Europe accepts people who are fleeing war. My Europe doesn't build walls," and his subsequent statement that there is no ceiling for how many asylum seekers Sweden can accept (Statens offentliga utredningar 2017, 13). But it is in that same context that we must interpret Löfven's speech from November 2015 in which he spoke of the need for "breathing space" (*andrum*) from the large numbers of asylum seekers.

The second context in which the government and state agencies interpreted the basic fact of the refugee crisis is the Swedish bureaucracy. The Swedish migration bureaucracy divides the reception and management of asylum seekers between state agencies (*stat*), municipality (*kommun*), and county (*landsting*). The primary responsibility for receiving asylum seekers falls on the Migration Agency and the municipalities in a way that gives rise to conflicting policy interpretations of who is responsible for what. This shared responsibility means, among other things, that asylum seekers must register with the Migration Agency but that the provision of housing and other basic necessities is provided by municipalities under the general direction of the Migration Agency (Statens offentliga utredningar 2017, 43).

The government and state agencies saw the municipalities as unable to understand the basic fact of a bureaucracy in crisis and manage the crisis

Crisis and Pattern during the 2015–2016 "Refugee Crisis" in Sweden   137

accordingly. Interviews that I conducted with state officials from the time when the report was published (in early 2017) offer a glimpse into state reasoning on this issue. In an interview with a senior officer at the Migration Agency in Scania County, I was told that it has "been a constant problem getting the municipalities to follow [the laws] or to take their responsibility." The officer was referring to a situation in 2015 when finding housing for asylum seekers became a critical issue. Although it is the responsibility of the municipalities to find housing for asylum seekers after they are assigned to a municipality by the Migration Agency, when it became clear that more and more asylum seekers were arriving,

> the municipalities said that we can't accept them. Initially there was a voluntary aspect built into the system where the counties and municipalities would sign these agreements, but they respond, "[We'll take] girls in this age or boys in this," you know. As a result, the housing needs of asylum seekers were not being met. At that point, *the government came in and said, "Now it's compulsory to take on certain numbers based on various parameters."* Whether it has turned out well I don't know, but it got better. However, there are no sanctions in the law. (emphasis added)

Although the municipalities were able to contest the government, it is difficult to assess the extent and efficacy of such a contestation, especially since the compulsion to accept specific numbers of asylum seekers was ratified as a law that states that municipalities cannot appeal the government's decision (*Dagens Juridik* 2016).

The Swedish Civil Contingencies Agency, the police, and the Migration Agency all described the crisis in a way that implies that essential social institutions and functions, such as housing, health care, and schools, were existentially threatened by the mass influx of migrants. In the words of the Migration Agency, the situation was "entirely out of control" (Statens offentliga utredningar 2017, 110).

It is on the basis of this official crisis narrative that the restrictionist measures were introduced. As early as November 11, 2015, the Migration Agency sent a letter to the Ministry of Justice urging the enforcement of border controls. In this letter, the Migration Agency pointed to the importance of maintaining the official Swedish policy of "managed migration and the police authority's responsibility for internal border control." Managed migration had come under threat not least because of a housing crisis, when "people who cannot find their own housing are thrown out on the street." A particularly vexing problem that called for border controls, according to the Migration Agency, was the existence of asylum seekers who did not intend to seek asylum in Sweden and who were in Sweden without a visa or residence permits. The Migration Agency, then, conflated the concept of asylum seeker with the concept of "illegal immigrant" (a term that is becoming common in Swedish policy discourse), a description that further served to justify the necessity of border controls.

The border controls have been extended far beyond the maximum six months allowed by the Schengen Borders Code. At the time of writing, November 2020, they were still in place, now further justified as a necessary response to the coronavirus pandemic. In one extension, from September 2017, Sweden cited the threat of terrorism as justification for continued border controls (Lönnaeus 2017). The extension came not long after the rejected Uzbek asylum seeker Rakhmat Akilov carried out a terrorist attack in Stockholm in April 2017. By extending, justifying, and timing the extension of border controls in this manner, the government has effectively conflated the concept of asylum seeker with the concept of terrorist. Indeed, in response to the Akilov attack, Löfven stated: "We need to improve the ability to deport people" (Habib and Witte 2017).

The Municipality Narrative: Manageable Strain

The government was not the only public authority that produced a narrative of the events that unfolded in 2015–16. Apart from mapping the government's response, the report also emphasized a deep tension between the government, on the one hand, and counties and municipalities, on the other. The municipalities criticized in no uncertain terms what they perceived as a mischaracterization of the situation in 2015 and how it was managed by the state. In one noteworthy critique,

> the city of Mölndal did not want to use the word "crisis" and claims that it is a word used by the state and not by the municipalities. The municipality experienced a strained situation, not a crisis. And everything happened in the municipalities, not, for example, in the Swedish Association of Local Authorities and Regions. The state was all about calculations and assessments, but the municipalities were all about people. The city of Mölndal believes that the state pushed the problems over to the municipalities. The city of Malmö asked why state-owned buildings could not be used for housing. ... The municipality of

Norberg believes that the fact that the military could not make their stored beds available was strange in the eyes of the municipalities. (Statens offentliga utredningar 2017, 265)

Another scathing critique from the municipalities concerned the government's assessment that the situation was entirely out of control:

Several municipalities describe how the situation with a lot of people suddenly ended with the border controls in November. Yet at that point the municipalities had found routines and scaled their operations for a large number of people, who then never came. . . . The municipality of Trelleborg describes how many processes were started during the fall, such as processes of obtaining permits for building houses for unaccompanied minors. When these processes were completed, there were no more minors. The resources of the municipalities had thus been wasted. (Statens offentliga utredningar 2017, 263)

Because the municipalities offered a radically different perspective on the basic facts, they were led to different policy conclusions. Indeed, multiple municipalities stated that the "greatest difficulty was not to come up with practical solutions on short notice but rather to interpret different regulatory frameworks or the fact that these frameworks were contradictory." The choice for local civil servants was to either "follow the regulations or try to solve the problems, and most chose the latter" (Statens offentliga utredningar 2017, 256).

PATTERNS ON THE GROUND: THE CASE OF AFGHAN ASYLUM SEEKERS

Patterned Reasons for Fleeing Afghanistan

Like the other five Afghan interviewees, Ehsanullah told me about his harrowing journey to "Europa" and the maze of events that led to his flight from Afghanistan: "If this [Hungary] is Europa, I'll stay here, what can I do? He [the smuggler] said, 'No, this is not Europa.' They made a group and said, 'Follow this guy [another smuggler].' When he says, 'Here you stay,' then he'll leave you. We traveled by train, car, [we] walk, [we took the] train, car, [we traveled through] good cities [in Austria and Germany]. I came to Malmö by train. Here the guy [the smuggler] said, 'This is your place. See you, bye'" (interview with Ehsanullah).[2] The Migration Agency stated in the report that the asylum seekers who arrived in 2015–16 "moved through different countries and chose the country in which they would seek asylum" (Statens offentliga utredningar 2017, 291). This statement lacks an empirical foundation while it insinuates an image of asylum seekers as having the luxury, information, and intention to pick and choose the "best" country of asylum. Certainly, the Afghan asylum seekers did want to maximize their chances of being granted asylum, but *they* did not choose Sweden, the smugglers did.

Three of the interviewed Afghans learned that Sweden was a country at the time their smuggler told them that they had reached their final destination, while three learned about it haphazardly in one of the transit countries. Ilhan related: "When I came to Turkey, one family told me, 'We're going to Europa, they don't have war, nobody will kill you.' I told the smuggler, 'That's where I want to go.' I knew the name Europa, Europa was one country. Now I know how many countries there are in Europa." Jawid explained: "The smuggler in Iran divided us in two groups. When our group came to Sweden, they said, 'This is Sweden.'" Nadir had learned about Sweden when he met a fellow Afghan at Victoria Square in Athens, which was then known as a gathering place for Afghan asylum seekers (Gaglias and Seferoglou 2015). Mansoor, to take a final example, discovered Sweden by researching potential countries after he arrived in Greece and was able to access the internet. He liked Sweden because he read somewhere that it offered freedom of religion. Mohammad said that he learned about Sweden through a friend who had come before him.

Three of the interviewees stopped their journey in Sweden because they were told to do so by their smuggler. Smuggling networks are a lucrative part of the migration industry—one interviewee that is not included in this chapter told me he paid $5,000, and he reckons that his fellow Afghan asylum seekers paid around the same amount. Smuggling networks exploit the opening created between an effectively managed border control, both nationally and supranationally (Mungianu 2013; Triandafyllidou and Maroukis 2015), on the one hand, and the neoliberal privatization and deregulation of the public sector, on the other (Menz 2013). For example, private detention centers and private service providers for asylum seekers have grown since their inception in the 1980s. Sweden may be a late starter, but it too is moving in this direction, since for-profit companies were, during the 2015–16 episode, for the first time allowed to operate asylum seeker reception centers.

Smuggling networks were essential in determining the routes Afghan asylum seekers took and the countries in which they ended up. Business was good in 2015, since the combined effect of the worst fighting season in Afghanistan since 2009 in terms of casualties (Crews 2015, 289), mass deportations of Afghans from Pakistan and Iran (Human Rights Watch 2017), and diminished legal paths to enter European countries all led to the flight of a large number of Afghans beyond the region even as Europe closed the door to Afghans who were legally exercising their right to seek asylum. Through various techniques employed in the calculus of profit—such as bribing border patrol guards or police officers, knowing about unpatrolled border crossing points, abandoning asylum seekers if they risked exposing a smuggler, knowing about countries with the most "generous" asylum policies, and having an effective payment system—smugglers provided the transnational network that brought the interviewees from Afghanistan or Iran to Sweden.

Ehsanullah explained that there was no personal trust involved between a smuggler and an asylum seeker or whoever was paying for the safe arrival of an asylum seeker. It worked like a contract regulating the provision of a service, but one that guarantees neither the safety of the client asylum seeker nor adherence to the initial terms of the contract. Ehsanullah explained the contract his father made with the smugglers: "This is the way it worked. There was no option. They [the smugglers] say, 'I need this money, and I send your son to Europa. When he arrives to Europa, you give me money.' But they have to see money first. You are smuggler, I am person [paying]. There's a third person. I phone, 'OK, I'm here,' then they give the money to the third person." Nadir described how each smuggler—from the driver to the person selling food and water at resting points along the way—demanded payment upon taking charge of an asylum seeker: "In every place when they change people, they take some money from everyone because of the driving, although they have no right to take money, because my father had already paid." Nadir felt that different smugglers "were selling people to another."

Sociologist Noah Arjomand (2016) has interviewed Afghan smugglers in Turkey, and his description of the smuggling system broadly matches Ehsanullah's and Nadir's accounts. A well-connected chain of smugglers in different countries from Afghanistan to the Balkans would hand groups of asylum seekers to one another at established points along an established route. For additional payments along the route, asylum seekers would agree with the smuggler on a price "and then give or have the money transferred via the *hawala* system [an informal money transfer system] to an Afghan *sarraf* [a money exchanger] at a call shop or other front. The *sarraf* would hold the money and give the migrant a numerical code to memorise. Upon arrival at their destination, the migrant would call [the smuggler] or a subordinate and tell them the code, which would allow them to collect the money from the *sarraf*" (Arjomand 2016).

The Pattern of Constraints for
Being Granted Asylum as an Afghan

Once they arrived in Sweden (at some point between August and September 2015), all six of the interviewed asylum seekers were put up in a hotel in Malmö for a few nights before being moved to a reception center, better known to the asylum seekers in everyday life as a "camp." Some had been in the privately run camp where I interviewed them in 2017 for close to a year, while others had been moved there more recently from other camps.[3] This particular camp in a small Scanian town, together with hundreds of others, closed down during the first half of 2017. These closures were preceded by a drastic drop in the number of asylum seekers as a result of the internal border controls that were introduced in November 2015. When I left them, five of the interviewees were still waiting for a decision on their asylum application, while one, Jawid, had received a negative decision but intended to appeal. Mona told me that roughly 5 percent of those who appeal their rejected asylum application see the initial decision overturned. Afghan asylum seekers are currently seeing the lowest approval rates among all national groups in Sweden (Skodo 2021).

If the interviewees were at the mercy of smugglers when making their way to safety in Sweden, then once they were temporarily settled in the camp, their asylum applications and everyday life came to be patterned through their interactions with officers from the Migration Agency (including Mona), the head of the asylum camp (Martina), and voluntary workers (including Birgitta, the Swedish-language teacher).

Regulated inventiveness or deviation within the bounds of Swedish asylum law and regulations have allowed, after 2012, Syrians to be processed faster than Afghans. It has also meant that Syrians' grounds for asylum have been recognized seemingly without question. Mona sought to explain this state of affairs by pointing to "ministerial rule" (*ministerstyre*), which means that the government has unofficially influenced an administrative branch to apply the law in a certain way, namely, to give Syrians preferential treatment. According to Mona, the government is only interested in seeing results—fast decisions on asylum applications—without regard for human cost: "The Migration Agency has considered this and said, 'OK, this'll mean that many Afghans and Iraqis will have to wait. We'll first take those that are easiest. . . .' All Syrians, or stateless people from Syria, have gone through a simplified asylum investigation, which simplifies making a decision." The Migration Agency has developed practices that do not always cohere with those of the government,

Crisis and Pattern during the 2015–2016 "Refugee Crisis" in Sweden 143

and Mona has in turn expressed personal frustration over seeing asylum seekers sometimes being treated like commodities.

Martina and Birgitta, for their part, voiced stronger critiques of the Migration Agency's differential treatment of Syrians and Afghans: in their eyes, Syrians have sailed through the asylum process, while Afghans have been placed in a protracted asylum limbo and run a high risk of being deported. According to Martina, "As more and more Syrians were being granted asylum, more and more Afghans were being denied. We're talking August to September 2016."

According to Mona, apart from ministerial rule working for them, Syrians seemed better equipped than Afghans to navigate the asylum process. Afghans often do not speak English, and they do not publicize the moral indignity of their situation to attract voluntary associations and journalists that can advocate on their behalf. Syrians do. "I don't think that the volunteer workers do this systematically, I think there's a general shyness among Afghans," Mona suggested. "With volunteer workers, you have to shout and yell, and especially those that speak English have done well here."

Martina entertained the idea of Afghans as passive asylum seekers—as too humble, too shy, too polite—as well. She reflected on the Afghans' moral disposition and self-presentation and the way these traits present them in the eyes of the Migration Agency in negative terms:

> Afghans are grateful, they're kind. Their problem, as I see it, is that they lack language skills. Unless you have an interpreter it's hard, and it's hard to find Dari interpreters. When you come to the Migration Agency for the most important interview of your life, and a lot of Afghans are ignorant in the educational sense, they're very subdued; they're really afraid and uncertain, more uncertain than Syrians. A Syrian comes here, tells me he's a doctor, and is really self-confident. An Afghan wouldn't even tell you he's a doctor. If that person gets a bad interpreter and is too afraid and kind to say he's a bad interpreter, now that's a hell of a problem.

Whatever their differences, Mona, Martina, and Birgitta all implied that the (in their minds) passive Afghan asylum seeker is in a weak position to traverse the asylum landscape and be granted asylum.

Birgitta was acutely aware of the fact that Afghans, under such conditions, need to learn how to properly state their grounds for asylum to increase their chances of being granted protection. She explained that this involved demonstrating knowledge of Swedish, showing that you are employable, and acting strategically in the new restrictionist environment:

> I tell them, "You have a much better chance of staying if you learn Swedish." One of them, he just quit after hearing about the new [restrictionist] laws [of 2016]. And he'd learned so much. I tell him, "It's now you put in the extra work. Because if you get a job, and you can, then you can earn the amount required by the Migration Agency, and then you can stay. Just read on the website—you know how to read Swedish now!" He was granted temporary status for three years. I use this, I tell them [the Migration Agency], he's been diligent, he knows Swedish, he can speak. . . . He's worked hard to get a job, to adapt. He's had an internship.

Birgitta was able to use her knowledge of the most recent asylum laws and her connections in the Migration Agency to help this particular asylum seeker. Birgitta and Martina took pride in being personally familiar with officers from the Migration Agency, as well as being friendly with each other, in their work with Afghan asylum seekers. Although Martina could not directly interfere with an asylum seeker's application, she could, and did, in informal conversations with Birgitta casually mention that one of her asylum seeker students might be having some problems without providing any details. Birgitta could, and did, pick up on this coded message and simply turn to the asylum seeker to find out which problem he or she was experiencing before proceeding to help through her voluntary association or personal engagement.

It is safe to say that the interviewed Afghan asylum seekers were only vaguely aware of what counts as grounds for asylum recognized by the Migration Agency. Moreover, being in Sweden, where they could not rely on pre-established networks and information from their close relatives and friends, the Afghan asylum seekers were forced to rely on the Migration Agency, rumors, risky assumptions based on uncertain knowledge, and in some cases, knowledge provided by voluntary workers for the framing of their asylum claims. And being in a situation where the Migration Agency harbors strong misgivings on whether Afghanistan is even in a condition that causes a well-founded fear of persecution (according to international human rights law) renders Afghan asylum seekers' claims inherently dubious.

The Afghan asylum seekers did not seem to pick up on this misrecognition on the Migration Agency's part. Jawid could hardly understand why his application was rejected because he believed that he had clearly explained how both army officers and the Taliban threatened his life, forcing him to flee: "The Migration Agency told me that they interrogated and found that Hazaras easily can find work in the army. I didn't say that Hazaras don't find work in the army easily, I said that I had a problem with them [the army officers]." It does not seem like the Migration Agency was willing to explore whether Jawid's narrative met conditions for other grounds of protections other than refugee status determination (such as "in alternative need of protection") that would allow him to stay in Sweden. Jawid said that the Migration Agency offered him money to voluntarily return to Afghanistan: "The Migration Agency told me, 'We'll you give you this money, and you go back to Afghanistan.' I said no. I don't have money problems. If I go back, they give me 30,000 Swedish kronor. I don't have a money problem, I have a problem with my life. If I die, what will I do with 30,000 kronor? What will my wife and children do?"

As Christina Johansson (2005, 111–12) has shown, "voluntary" return of asylum seekers, which remains an option even after the granting of asylum in the guise of voluntary repatriation, has been a part of Swedish migration policy since the 1990s. Through informing asylum seekers about their "option" to return and incentivizing them through a one-time financial resettlement contribution, the state hopes to solve an imagined future problem of integration for large numbers of asylum seekers who are not considered to be true asylum seekers. This policy affected groups such as the Somalis and Bosnians in the 1990s and has been affecting the Afghans since the 2010s (Bergman 2010, 23–24). In November 2016 Sweden and Afghanistan signed a bilateral memorandum regulating the return of rejected Afghan asylum seekers, by force if necessary, in a "dignified" and "safe" manner in line with human rights law (Swedish Government 2016, 1). The memorandum states that an individual returnee will receive 30,000 kronor as a resettlement contribution and that Sweden will help with various resettlement projects in Afghanistan (11). This kind of practice follows the policy of "humanitarian development" and "vicinity aid," touted by Sweden and other Western European governments as offering a durable solution to the global refugee problem.

THE LANGUAGE OF CRISIS AND THE LANGUAGE OF PATTERN: CONCLUDING REMARKS

Language matters in the way policy is designed and political responses are shaped. It is because the Swedish government used the language of crisis that it was able to impose unprecedented restrictionist laws and measures. These measures (including limitations to family reunification, decreased financial aid, and unpredictable relocation), as the government report from 2017 makes clear, have had detrimental effects on the mental health and social well-being of asylum seekers (Statens offentliga utredningar 2017, 344, 350–51).

But as sociologist Saskia Sassen (1999) and I (Skodo 2021) have argued, there is another language that we can and should use: the language of pattern, based on empirically verifiable sociological, historical, political, economic, and cultural research. Such language can, in Sassen's words, "re-frame the immigration question today" (1999, x). It can do so by showing that "migrations are patterned, bounded in scale and duration, and conditioned on several particular processes" and that "the regularities and basic features matter because they ought to determine policy" (xiv).

Indeed, even Sweden's crisis narrative follows a long-established pattern. Thus, as I (Skodo 2021, 1080) have argued in a study on Swedish responses to Afghan asylum seekers during the 1980s, refugee crises are to a large extent imagined and constructed and never without historical precedents and continuities. In the 1980s there were no more than 150 Afghans seeking asylum in Sweden per year, nor was there an entry of a number of asylum seekers that remotely compares to 2015–16. Yet the language used by the Swedish government then much resembles that of today.

Equally if not more important are the practical lessons we could learn by looking at 2015–16 from the angle of a patterned forced migration that allows for a patterned response. The municipalities that feature in the 2017 government report did just that. As they were responding to the problems posed by the large number of people, they were in the process of finding new patterns of how to solve them. But precisely when they developed effective patterns, the patterns became useless because the government had significantly halted the entry of asylum seekers: "Several municipalities describe how the situation with a lot of people suddenly ended with the border controls in November. Yet at that point the municipalities had found routines and scaled their operations for a large number of people who then never came" (Statens offentliga utredningar 2017, 263). The lesson here is that more critical, long-term, and systematic thinking on the part of key stakeholders in responding to asylum seekers can be used to build institutional memory to effectively respond to future comparable situations during which asylum seekers are not seen as existential threats to national security, identity, and welfare provisions. After all, the Swedish welfare state did not collapse after 2015–16.

Crisis and Pattern during the 2015–2016 "Refugee Crisis" in Sweden   147

APPENDIX:
BRIEF INTERVIEWEE PROFILES

Ehsanullah is an ethnic Pashtun in his early twenties from Helmand province. Sought protection from persecution by the Taliban.[4]

Ilhan is an ethnic Arab (in Afghanistan, Arabs are a small Dari-speaking group that are ethnically unrelated to the Arabs of the Middle East) in his midtwenties from Balkh province. Sought protection from persecution by the Taliban.

Jawid is an ethnic Hazara in his early thirties from Ghazni province. Sought protection from persecution by fellow Afghan army officers after refusing to partake in corruption.

Mansoor is an ethnic Tajik in his late teens who lived in Iran but whose family originated in Herat province. Sought protection from persecution by an individual of another family with which Mansoor's family had been in conflict.

Mohammad is an ethnic Hazara in his early thirties from Balkh province. Sought protection from societal discrimination on account of his ethnicity.

Nadir is an ethnic Tajik in his early twenties from Kunduz province. Sought protection from persecution by the Taliban.

Martina is the site manager of a privately run camp for asylum seekers in Scania.

Mona is the executive officer at the Swedish Migration Agency's southern region and is responsible for overseeing Martina's camp.

Birgitta volunteered as a Swedish-language teacher in Martina's camp.

NOTES

1. State and government perceptions of the refugee crisis of 1992 were in some ways remarkably similar to perceptions of the 2015–16 crisis. For example, the 1992 crisis was seen as overstretching the capacity of the Swedish bureaucracy, the need to restore order was voiced, and countries such as Poland and Hungary were seen as not sharing the burden of accepting a fair share of the refugees (Abiri 2000).

2. See the appendix at the end of this chapter for information on the interviewees.

3. Ironically, a company owned by Bert Karlsson—a businessman who cofounded Ny Demokrati, the first Far Right anti-immigrant party to be elected into the Swedish parliament in 1991—ran this reception center.

4. The interviews were conducted in Swedish, English, Dari, and Pashto (for the latter two, I used interpreters). The translations from Swedish to English are mine. The translations from Dari and Pashto to English were provided by the interpreters.

The interviews followed a protocol reviewed and approved by the Swedish Ethical Review Authority. To ensure the confidentiality of the interviewees, I have fictionalized all names and chosen not to disclose the location of the camp or the name of the voluntary association in which the interviewed voluntary worker is a member.

References

Abiri, Elisabeth. 2000. "The Changing Praxis of 'Generosity': Swedish Refugee Policy during the 1990s." *Journal of Refugee Studies* 13(1): 11–28.

Arjomand, Noah. 2016. "Afghan Exodus: Smuggling Networks, Migration and Settlement Patterns in Turkey." *Afghanistan Analysts Network*, September 10. https://www.afghanistan-analysts.org/afghan-exodus-smuggling-networks-migration-and-settlement-patterns-in-turkey/.

Bergman, Jonny. 2010. "Seeking Empowerment: Asylum-Seeking Refugees from Afghanistan in Sweden." PhD diss., Umeå University.

Crews, Robert D. 2015. *Afghan Modern: The History of a Global Nation.* Cambridge, MA: Harvard University Press.

Dagens Juridik. 2016. "Staten får tvinga kommuner att ta emot flyktingar—Riksdagen klubbade lagen." January 28, 2016. http://www.dagensjuridik.se/2016/01/staten-far-tvinga-kommuner-att-ta-emot-flyktingar-riksdagen-klubbade-lagen.

Gaglias, Alexis, and Orestes Seferoglou. 2015. "A Day in the Life of Afghan Refugees in Athens' Victoria Square." *Huffington Post*, September 11. http://www.huffingtonpost.com/entry/afghan-refugees-athens_us_55f31708e4b042295e361daa.

Habib, Heba, and Griff Witte. 2017. "Swedish Police Say Stockholm Truck-Attack Suspect Was Failed Uzbek Asylum-Seeker." *Washington Post*, April 9.

Human Rights Watch. 2017. "Pakistan Coercion, UN Complicity: The Mass Forced Return of Afghan Refugees." https://www.hrw.org/report/2017/02/13/pakistan-coercion-un-complicity/mass-forced-return-afghan-refugees.

Johansson, Christina. 2005. "Välkomna till Sverige? Svenska migrationspolitiska diskurser under 1900-talets andra hälft." PhD diss., University of Linköping.

Lönnaeus, Olle. 2017. "EU ger klartecken till Sverige att fortsätta med gränskontroller." *Sydsvenskan*, September 27. https://www.sydsvenskan.se/2017-09-27/eu-ger-klartecken-till-sverige-att-fortsatta-med-granskontroller.

Menz, George. 2013. "The Neoliberalized State and the Growth of the Migration Industry." In *The Migration Industry and the Commercialization of Global Migration*, edited by Thomas Gammeltoft-Hansen and Ninna Nyberg Sørensen, 108–27. New York: Routledge.

Mungianu, Roberta. 2013. "Frontex: Towards a Common Policy on External Border Control." *European Journal of Migration and Law* 15(4): 359–85.

Sassen, Saskia. 1999. *Guests and Aliens.* New York: New Press.

Skodo, Admir. 2017a. "How Afghans Became Second-Class Asylum Seekers." *The Conversation*, February 20. https://theconversation.com/how-afghans-became-second-class-asylum-seekers-72437.

Skodo, Admir. 2017b. "Swedish Immigration Is Not out of Control—It's Actually Getting More Restrictive." *The Conversation*, February 28. https://theconversation.com/profiles/admir-skodo-335289/dashboard#.

Skodo, Admir. 2021. "The Long and Short Arms of the State: Swedish Multidirectional Controls of Afghan Asylum Seekers during the Cold War." *Journal of Refugee Studies* 34(1): 1060–82.

Statens offentliga utredningar (Swedish Government Official Reports). 2017. "Att ta emot människor på flykt: Sverige hösten 2015." https://www.regeringen.se/493a12/contentassets/e8c195d35dea4c05a1c952f9b0b45f38/att-ta-emot-manniskor-pa-flykt-sou-201712-hela.

Swedish Government. 2016. "Samförståndsavtal mellan Sveriges regering och Islamiska republiken Afghanistans regering om samarbete på migrationsområdet." http://www.regeringen.se/4ab5e0/contentassets/da1ae2805f5d41bd9782c1779d916e92/avtal-mellan-sverige-och-afghanistan.pdf.

Swedish Migration Agency. n.d. "Asylsökande till Sverige 1984–1999." Accessed May 22, 2017. https://www.migrationsverket.se/download/18.2d998ffc151ac3871598171/148555607.

Trägårdh, Lars. 2010. "Rethinking the Nordic Welfare State through a Neo-Hegelian Theory of State and Civil Society." *Journal of Political Ideologies* 15(3): 227–39.

Triandafyllidou, Anna, and Thanos Maroukis. 2015. *Migrant Smuggling: Irregular Migration from Asia and Africa to Europe.* New York: Palgrave Macmillan.

Contesting National Identity as a Racial Signifier

Mixed-Race Identity in Norway and Sweden

SAYAKA OSANAMI TÖRNGREN and TONY SANDSET

Increased international mobility and globalization have brought about a significant increase in intimate interracial relationships, including in Norway and Sweden. As a consequence, the children of these unions—that is, multiethnic and multiracial persons—are undeniably part of contemporary society (see, e.g., Osanami Törngren, Irastorza, and Song 2016; Rodríguez-García 2015). Sweden and Norway are not alone in this global trend.

The racial and ethnic composition of Sweden and Norway has changed dramatically in a relatively short period of time through immigration. In both countries, the majority of ethnic and racial minorities have a Middle Eastern and Muslim background. In 2018 18 percent of the ten million residents of Sweden were born abroad; 5 percent of people born in Sweden had two foreign-born parents; and 7 percent were the children of binational marriages, the offspring of one Sweden-born and one foreign-born parent. When it comes to the population under the age of eighteen in three major cities (Stockholm, Gothenburg, and Malmö), native Swedes with two Sweden-born parents are a numerical minority: more than 50 percent have a foreign background (i.e., either themselves or one or both of their parents were born abroad). Around 17 percent of the population have one parent born in and one parent born outside Sweden in the three biggest cities, potentially representing a multiracial and multiethnic population (Statistics Sweden 2018). In Norway 14 percent of the total population were born abroad; that is, they are categorized as "immigrants" by Statistics Norway (SSB, Statistisk sentralbyrå; see Statistics Norway 2018). Some 3.2 percent of the population are so-called Norwegian-born with immigrant background; that is, both parents were born outside

Norway. Of these, the majority—10 percent—are of Pakistani background, followed by those of Somali and then Polish background (Statistics Norway 2018). Norwegian "binationals," defined by the SSB as the "Norwegian-born with 1 foreign-born parent and 2 foreign-born grandparents," accounted in 2019 for 4 percent of the population. Statistics show that there has been a steady increase in this segment of the population since 2004, when the figure was 3 percent of the total population (Statistics Norway 2018). We can observe a clear trend, based on which we can expect that this segment of the population will gradually become more visible within the Norwegian population.

Most studies on mixed-race identities are conducted in English-speaking countries, although there has been a significant increase in the amount of literature produced on mixedness outside this context (e.g., Childs 2018; Edwards et al. 2012; King-O'Riain et al. 2014; Rocha and Fozdar 2017; Rocha et al. 2019). Despite the increasing number of mixed populations in Nordic countries, the field of mixed-race studies has not taken off there (exceptions are Appel and Singla 2016; Sandset 2014, 2018; Skadegård and Jensen 2018). Mixed populations, therefore, are "overlooked" (Appel and Singla 2016), and their stories are rendered invisible as yet another immigrant story (Sandset 2018, 4). Research on mixed populations in Sweden and Norway is very limited.

This chapter, based on twenty-two interviews with mixed-race Norwegians and sixteen interviews with mixed-race Swedes, explores how they are ascribed with the dialectic categories based on the visibility of mixedness, such as phenotype or name, and how they respond and contest these ascribed identities by challenging the notion of national identity as a racial category. We discuss how mixed-race Norwegians and Swedes are claiming national identity as Norwegian or Swedish as an overarching identity category that goes beyond the dichotomy and embraces their mixedness. This is one of the first articles that addresses mixed identity in a comparative Nordic perspective and contributes to the growing literature of global mixed-race studies.

THE NORDIC CONTEXT

Color blindness, "a mode of thinking about race organized around an effort to not 'see' or, at any rate, not to acknowledge, race differences" (Frankenberg 1993, 142), is prominent in Sweden and Norway (see Gullestad 2004; Hübinette et al. 2012; Osanami Törngren 2019). Tobias Hübinette and Charlotte Hylten-Cavallius write that "color-blindness in the Swedish contemporary context means that for many Swedes it is even difficult to utter the word 'race' in everyday speech, and it is equally uncomfortable to talk about white and non-white Swedes" (2014, 30). The idea of color blindness is officially applied, to such an extent that there were efforts in 2001 to abolish the word "race" (*ras*) from the official language; this was followed in 2009 by the removal of "race" as a basis for discrimination (Hübinette and Hylten-Cavallius 2014). In 2014 the Swedish government announced that the word "race" should be erased from all existing legislation in the country and be replaced with another word (SVT Nyheter 2014). The very same year, the word "racialized" (*rasifierad*) was officially recognized as a new Swedish word, referring to a person who is categorized as belonging to a certain racial group because of his or her visible differences. While the acknowledgment of the word should be marked as the first step toward recognizing racial problems in Sweden, the color-blind idea is still dominant. In academia, opinions are polarized between those who advocate talking about race and those who deny that it exists (e.g., Demker and Heinö 2013; Jebari and Magnusson 2013).

In Norway many of the same mechanisms seem to prevail when it comes to the discourse around race. As in the Swedish context, the word "race" has no official hold in the discourse; instead, "ethnicity" is the dominant referent when discussing racialized identities. Akin to the Swedish declaration that race should be erased from all official legislation, so it was in Norway. However, although the Norwegian state did not make a decree in the same way as the Swedish state did, we can discern something similar in the way in which the drafting of the so-called Immigration Act (Innvadringsloven) occurred: it was suggested that the term "race" (*rase*) be replaced by the word "ethnic" (*etnisk*) or "ethnicity" (*etnisitet*) (Sandset 2018, 126). The rationale was that the state recognized that race was "a social construct" and that the terms "ethnicity" and "ethnic" represented concepts that were more in line with "current understandings of identity." The same rationale was seen in the law on ethnic discrimination, in which the word "race" was substituted with the words "ethnic" and "ethnicity." However, contrary to the Swedish case, where the word "race" was replaced with the concept of "racialized," the Norwegian state replaced it with the term "ethnicity." In the definition of ethnicity, the term "race" was still used, as can be seen in the following definition by the Ministry of Justice: "Ethnic identity is attached to such variables as culture and identity, such as 'race,' skin color, descent, religion, and so on, but does in addition to this connote the relations between different groups and identities" (Regjeringen.no. 2000, my translation). As a result, the Norwegian state never discarded the term "race" in the same way that the Swedish state did. Nor did the Norwegian state replace the term with a concept that could be used to see the links between race and ethnicity through the usage of racialization. Instead, the Norwegian state continued to highlight ethnicity as the preferred category while at the same time allowing race to be confused or entangled with that of ethnicity.

Due to this color-blind approach to both countries' populations, information on an individual's race and ethnicity on self-reported or assigned forms does not exist in Sweden and Norway. Both the Swedish Statistical Office (SCB, Statistiska centralbyrån) and the SSB only collect administrative data, which include information on place of birth, country of origin, citizenship, and parental country of birth. As such, the SCB and the SSB have introduced dichotomized categories such as "Swedish-born / Swedish background," "foreign-born / foreign background," "immigrant," and "Norwegian-born with immigrant parents" (Statistics Norway 2021). A person of "Swedish background" is defined as someone who was born in Sweden and has one or both parents born in Sweden, while a person of "foreign background" would have been born either outside Sweden or in Sweden with two foreign-born parents (Statistics Sweden 2018). In Norway a greatly contested and debated issue has been how and when "Norwegian-born with immigrant parents" *become* "Norwegian"; that is, when does this genealogical way of thinking about belonging and ancestry end (Gullestad 2004; Sandset 2018)?

As well as the difficulty of statistically identifying a multiracial and multiethnic population, the terms and awareness equivalent to "multiracial," "multiethnic," and "mixed" do not exist in either Swedish and Norwegian society or the language, which may limit people's abilities to identify themselves in neither/nor or both/and terms (for more details, see Arbouz 2012, 2017; Sandset 2018). Self-identifying as mixed does not necessarily mean that a person will be identified as such but that the identity can be invalidated (Lou and Lalonde 2015).

Based on these categorizations, those who were born in Sweden or Norway who have one parent born in Sweden and who are potentially "first-generation multiracial" (Daniel et al. 2014) are incorporated into the category of those with a Swedish or Norwegian background. Recently, statistics separating persons with one foreign-born and one Swedish-born parent from those having two foreign-born parents of different countries of origin are also available, and further divisions based on the geographical location can be seen in official reports. Statistics Norway does not allow for or enable the collection of data on "mixed-racial" or mixed-ethnic individuals either, nor does it allow for or enable a tactic of "mark as many as you want" in the collection of data on ethnic and racial backgrounds. Rather, country of origin or of parental origin is used as a proxy. Therefore, identifying "mixed individuals" based on such statistics is still a challenge in Sweden and Norway. Moreover, the ethnic and racial belonging of the individual is often inferred through information on country of birth and origin or citizenship. This *genealogical logics of identity* practice risks the essentialization and fixation of culture, race, and ethnicity of the person to the country of origin (Jebari and Magnusson 2013).

While the administrative statistics create a dichotomized categorization of the population, the "mixed population" may also be perceived in a dichotomized way depending on how visible their mixedness is. Research in Sweden shows that whiteness and visible phenotypical differences (i.e., whether one "looks Swedish") shape the definition of Swedishness and non-Swedishness (e.g., Gokieli 2017; Hübinette and Lundström 2011; Lundström 2017; Mattsson 2005; Runfors 2016). Different researchers illustrate how "immigrant" identities in Sweden develop through interaction and contact with the majority society, through which they become aware of not being white (see, e.g., Kalonaityte, Kwesa, and Tedros 2007; Khosravi 2006; Lundström 2007, 2017). In the public imaginary and in daily conversation, the word "Swedish" as a result connotes whiteness and functions as a white racial category, while "immigrant background" is linked with nonwhiteness and becomes a category that lumps all nonwhite Swedes together. Similarly, in Norway the conflation of "Norwegian" with "white" has been documented by researchers working in the fields of anthropology and sociology (e.g., Andersson 2007; Berg 2004; Berg and Kristiansen 2010; Gullestad 2002, 2004; Sandset 2018) and has brought attention to the ways in which, as in the Swedish context, people with an "immigrant background" are, more often than not, racialized through connotations of nonwhite phenotype and thus are often lumped together through the concept of "immigrant" or "nonethnic Norwegian."

Mixed populations are increasingly becoming visible in Swedish society without being recognized as such. Exceptions are to be found in the literary work of, for example, Jason Timbuktu Diakite (African American Swedish), Johannes Anyuru (Ugandan Swedish), and Jonas Hassen Khemiri (Tunisian Swedish), whose backgrounds as multiracial persons are well known and who publicly engage with their personal experiences of racialization (e.g., Anyuru 2013; Diakite 2016; Khemiri 2013). They are also ascribed with male immigrant images by the public (Gokieli 2017). Recently, comedian David Batra (Indian Swedish) ventured into his Indian roots in a TV show called *The World's Worst Indian* (Sveriges Television AB 2018). In Norway the visibility of "mixed people" has also increased; however, this visibility is often clustered within entertainment and sports. A case in point would be the now-retired soccer player John Carew, who has a Norwegian mother and a father from the Gambia, or Mira Craig, a Norwegian singer who has a mother from Norway and a father who is African American. Another example would be celebrity fitness trainer and TV personality Yngvar Anderse, who is of Norwegian and Moroccan background. However, the discourse around being mixed is, as in academic scholarship in Norway generally, all but invisible, and the thematic seems to be relegated to sporadic and often short-lived discussions about belonging and racism.

Theoretical Framework and Literature Review

In this chapter, we examine mixed identity through the concept of race. Race should be understood as socially constructed ideas evoked by visible phenotypical differences (e.g., Daynes and Lee 2008). Race as a social construct implies that the meanings and categories of race are constructed in a specific context and vary according to place, society, and time; therefore, race is something that exists not as a biological but as a social reality. Although a social construction, race is socially real for some groups of people and "affect[s] their social life whether individual members of the races want it or not" (Bonilla-Silva 1997, 473). The social reality of race is obvious for the everyday lives of people who are categorized as "Swedish" or "Norwegian" or as "foreign background" according to their visible phenotypical differences.

Identity is not a static thing but, rather, a two-way dialectic process (Jenkins 2005, 20). An individual may identify herself or himself and others through relational modes such as kinship or friendship but may also do so through a categorical attribute such as race, ethnicity, language, nationality, or gender (Brubaker and Cooper 2000). Identity can also emerge from experiences and can be influenced by the attitudes of and pressures from others (Deaux 2018). In the process, the distinction needs to be made between self-identification (acquired identity) and identification by others (ascribed identity) (Brubaker and Cooper 2000; Jenkins 2005).

The knowledge of this dialectic of identification among mixed populations is well advanced and explored. Previous studies show that there are different ways in which "mixed people" identify and redefine their identity (e.g., Aspinall and Song 2013; DaCosta 2007; Harris and Sim 2002; Houston and Hogan 2009; Song and Aspinall 2012). A mismatch in identification may occur, since a person's self-identification is not always affirmed by others, and their ethnic options—their ability to choose their ethnic identity—can be constrained. Here, the conceptual difference between race and ethnicity becomes important: racial appraisals are based on visible phenotype, whereas ethnicity is not always visible (Daynes and Lee 2008; Song 2003). "Mixed persons" may experience a gap between their racial identity and their "reflected race" (Morning 2018; Roth 2018)—how you believe others assume you to be based on phenotype (Song 2003; Waters 1990). When racial phenotypical difference is not visible, individuals may have the option to identify and present themselves as being of a different race (Goffman 1990). This practice of racial categorizing as a member of the majority or minority population for multiracial and multiethnic individuals should be conceptualized as an ethnic option over which they may or may not have control (Brubaker 2016; Song 2003). The important questions to ask are what identity labels people choose for themselves and why (Deaux 2018).

As mentioned earlier, research on mixed-race Swedes and Norwegians is almost nonexistent in Sweden, discernible by the lack of scholarly engagement with the topic and field. Some quantitative studies indicate that persons of mixed origin may experience different kinds of discrimination and disadvantages in Sweden (see, e.g., Behtoui 2006; Kalmijn 2015; Smith, Helgertz, and Scott 2019). Qualitative studies exploring how mixed Swedes identify and how they maneuver white racial norms are emerging yet scarce still (Adeniji 2014; Arbouz 2017; Hübinette and Arbouz 2019; Romero 2012; Osanami Törngren 2020). After a thorough search of the literature, we found only three academic works that discuss different aspects of being mixed in Norway (Aiwerioba 2007; Hallvik 2008; Sandset 2014, 2018). Clearly, there is a lack of engagement with the topic in Sweden and Norway. This may be due to the fact that the group is perceived as numerically small, as well as to the various ways in which the history of immigration has unfolded in the two countries, where, in recent years, research has focused on refugees and immigrants with Muslim background. This chapter will fill in the gap in the literature on mixed identity in the Nordic context.

METHOD AND DATA

Our Swedish interview data consist of sixteen semistructured interviews with mixed Swedes (eleven females and five males) conducted between August 2018 and January 2019.[1] Interviewees were recruited through social media and university networks based on their identifying with the description "has one Swedish parent and one parent with a foreign background or is not a Swedish citizen" and with their upbringing being predominantly in Sweden. The interviews lasted between thirty minutes and an hour. Two of them were conducted in person, with the rest via Skype or FaceTime. The average age of the Swedish interviewees was twenty-six. Fourteen of the interviewees grew up in one of the three biggest cities in Sweden. Eight of the interviewees visited their non-Swedish parent's home country regularly; however, none spent a significant portion of their upbringing in their non-Swedish parent's home country. Six interviewees were of Latin American and Swedish mix, eight were of Asian and Swedish, one was of Middle Eastern and Swedish, and one was of African and Swedish. The research attracted many interviewees of Japanese and Swedish origin, an interest that might be linked to Osanami Törngren's own ethnoracial background.

The Norwegian interview data consist of material collected in 2013 on twenty-two people of mixed background and reinterviews with four of them in order to clear up and add to the original interviews. The sample pool consisted of ten men and twelve women, ranging in age from twenty to thirty-five. All were living in Oslo and therefore shared a certain commonality as far as geographical location is concerned. When it comes to the racial makeup of their parents, they were diverse but had one common characteristic: one of their parents was an ethnic Norwegian, meaning in this context that the parent was white. The other parent's native countries varied, from Asia to Africa to the Caribbean. What is of note is the fact that seventeen of the twenty-two interviewees had grown up within a household with only one parent present. Furthermore, of these seventeen, the parent raising them was the one with an ethnic Norwegian background. The interviews were conducted in public places, such as in cafés or at the University of Oslo. They were built on a semistructured interview guide divided into topical sections, and they lasted between fifty and ninety minutes.

All the Swedish and Norwegian interviewees gave both oral and written consent to participate in the study. All the interviews were recorded, and the transcriptions were forwarded to the interviewees for them to review. All interview materials were treated anonymously and confidentially. The transcriptions have been translated from Swedish or Norwegian to English, and the names that appear in this chapter are pseudonyms.

ANALYSIS

Swedish Mixed-Race Identification

Among the sixteen Swedish mixed-race interviewees, only four self-identified as solely "Swedish," while the others identified themselves in multiple terms and as mixed in different ways. How they self-identify reflects the emergence of different ways of identification in Sweden, which includes the identification of compound nationalities and specific terms imported from the English language, such as being "half" (*halvis*), "mixed" (*mixad* or *blandad*), or half-and-half (*halv-halv*). Moreover, two interviewees identified themselves completely outside racial, ethnic, and national belongings. Despite an emerging flexibility in self-identification, the majority of the mixed-race Swedes in our sample had found that they are ascribed with the traditional dichotomy of Swedish or non-Swedish and other specific words that imply nonwhiteness. There was a clear gap between their self-identification and their ascribed identification. Some had experienced scrutiny of their claim to be "Swedish," while some passed as Swedish despite their claim to mixedness.

As previous studies indicate, there are different responses to these gaps (e.g., Aspinall and Song 2013). For example, two members of our sample, Adam (Argentinian and Swedish) and Agnes (Latin American and Swedish), shared their experience of the complex feelings they have about being excluded from the category "Latino" since they can pass as Swedish. However, they responded differently. Adam said, "I do not identify with the Swedish category," and strongly identified himself as Sephardi, Jewish, and Latino. Contrary to Adam, Agnes did not stress her Latin American identity: "Appearance-wise, I pass easily as white, and that is exactly what has led to me having a complex feeling." She explained how being in a predominantly white middle-class environment also limits her claim to being Latino. Edvin (French and Korean adoptee) and Felicia (Cuban and Finnish) both stated that they cannot pass as Swedish and are seen as nonwhites. They both identified themselves completely in other than ethnoracial terms as a way of resisting the idea of Swedish being white and other types of ethnoracial identification.

A feeling of being misrecognized and having one's identity scrutinized due to phenotype was manifested in many of the interviewees' experiences. For example, Elise (Ethiopian and Swedish) said that she is Swedish but explained that her physical appearance contradicted her "cultural background," which made her claim to be Swedish constantly questionable:

> It is quite confusing because it is such a contradiction that one sees oneself in one way and then it is pointed out that you are not [that way]. So it gets a little bit, it gets hard to handle, . . . because despite it all, it feels like it is not possible [to be accepted as Swedish]. I know that if I say so [that I am Swedish], they [people] will say the contrary [that I am not]. . . . At the same time, if I can't say that, what else am I?

Her claim to being Swedish is based on her national and cultural belonging; however, as the idea that being Swedish means being white is strongly embedded in society, her claim to be Swedish is not validated. Many of the interviewed mixed-race Swedes actively used the term "Swedish" as a national and cultural identification rather than a white racial category. Tova also shared the same experience as Elise in having her claim to be Swedish questioned. When asked how she identified herself in ethnic and racial terms, she answered very clearly "Swedish" and admitted that it was an easy answer and choice for her, although it was difficult to have to defend it all the time. Her parents are adoptees from Finland and India who grew up as Swedes; Tova therefore is a person of mixed race who grew up as a monocultural Swede. However, she is always seen as an "Indian" because of her physical appearance:

> Swedish is my native language. I have not been able to speak any other language. I was born here. Neither of my parents speaks any languages other than Swedish, although neither of them was born in Sweden. There are different definitions [of what it means to be Swedish]. Some think that one must be born in Sweden, some think that your parents must be born in Sweden, some think that one must be able to speak the language, and some say that it is just to have a passport. I feel that I can tick the majority [of these things] but not all. Some think that you have to look Swedish, which I may not do. But *I* think I look Swedish—in my definition of Swedish.

Lucia (Spanish, Swedish, and Chilean) also articulated her identification as Swedish in a similar way to Tova. Lucia has found that she cannot pass as Swedish. She constantly gets asked, "Where are you from?" and when she answers, "From Sweden," people insist, "But where are you *really* from?" She explains her identity through national belonging and contests the idea of Swedish identity as being only for whites: "I want people to see me as a person who is a mixture of different things and, like, having different interests and not really box [categorize] me—'You are a foreigner' or 'You are typically Swedish.'"

Mina (Japanese and Swedish) said that she does not feel comfortable saying that she is Japanese in front of a white Swedish person due to the stereotype of "being Japanese" and almost always say that she is "Swedish." Like Lucia, Mina experienced questioning and interrogation of her Swedish identity and was asked all the time, "Are you more Japanese or more Swedish?" Mina's words clearly depicted the existing idea of Swedish as a white racial category:

"It is so tense. In Sweden it is so clear that I am Japanese because I do not fit in and because I am not white. But then, personally and absolutely, I myself think I am more Swedish than Japanese."

Similarly, Eman also described how he was reminded by others that he is "not Swedish." Eman identified himself based on his parental origins— a "Swedish mother and Moroccan father." He said that he cannot pass as Swedish and is seen as an "Arab": "I think it is others who help me, other people and not me, who help me to clarify, other people who emphasize national identity more than I do myself. That is why I think of my national identity, because it is obvious that this is what people think of."

Even in cases where interviewees can pass as phenotypically Swedish, other visible markers, such as name, function as a policing mechanism for Swedish identification. For example, Adam, quoted earlier, said that his last name evokes ideas of him being "different." Another interviewee, Ines, also found that as soon as people noticed that her name was not "Swedish," they would not accept her as being "completely Swedish" despite the fact that she can pass as Swedish phenotypically: "[My name] comes up directly, and then I am not given a chance to say how people should treat me before they realize that I have Latin American ancestry."

Norwegian Mixed-Race Identity

While the Norwegian interview guide did not specifically ask for self-perceived ethnoracial identity or sense of belonging in a way that is easy to quantify, we can get a sense of the multitude of contextual ways of identifying that emerged in the material. As in the case of the Swedish interlocutors, many of the persons interviewed often found themselves in settings in which they were seen as immigrants or "not fully Norwegian," which often ran contrary to self-identified markers of belonging. This emerged mostly in relation to what Jin Haritaworn has called the "Where are you really from?" encounter (2009b, 121–22). One case in point is the following excerpt from the interview with Stine (Indian and Norwegian):

> STINE: I have to say that I've been very aware about showing that I'm Norwegian, let's say at least the last five years or so. . . . When people see me they often raise the question of "Where are you from?" and then I say, "Norway." Then they just ask in turn, "No, where are you *really* from?" and then I answer, "Halden." I try to take an attitude like that, but it doesn't make any

Contesting National Identity as a Racial Signifier   161

sense . . . since I already know what they want. And I understand why they're asking. They're curious, they are interested, and, as I become older, I'm more understanding as to why they wonder, because I, too, wonder when I meet people who are dark-skinned.

INTERVIEWER: And yet you have this attitude where you want to underline their Norwegianness?

STINE: Yes, I do. I think I had a real need to do that because, like I said earlier, I used to be so afraid to be identified with a multicultural background.

INTERVIEWER: Can you remember why that was so scary?

STINE: I'm not sure. I guess it's because they're a bit looked down upon in our society, and I didn't want to be a part of that . . . and it's that thing about when somebody asks you that question they also question who you are or doubt who you are, and that's very frustrating.

Stine's encounter with the "Where are you *really* from?" question prompted both an identification that connects her to Halden—that is, Norway—and an acknowledgment that the question is posed to discern her identity through her skin color. Stine stated that this is frustrating because it casts doubt on who she *is* and implicitly on her connection to Halden and Norway.

Another version of this encounter but with a slightly different analytical take can be seen in an interview with Mike, who has a Norwegian mother and a father from the Ivory Coast:

On all public forms I write that I'm Norwegian, and if people I don't know ask where I am from, I answer that I'm Norwegian and add that I have a father who is non-Norwegian, because most people can see that I'm not white. But if I'm with friends, for instance, whom I have grown up with, who aren't Norwegian, then I might define myself as African or as a mulatto or something else like that. It really depends on the circumstances. The reason why I do that is really because it's a way of fitting in. And the same when I call myself Norwegian—it has to do with how I feel about belonging to that particular group I'm with at that particular time.

In Mike's narrative, we can see the multitude of identifications at play that are highly contextual and contingent upon the setting. In encounters with the "state" or the state apparatus, such as administrative forms, Mike identifies as Norwegian, but he identifies as a Norwegian with a non-Norwegian father when he encounters people who do not know him. What is interesting in Mike's narrative is that this latter way of identifying is connected to his statement that "most people can see that I am not white"—an indirect connection between whiteness and Norwegian as an identity category. Finally, Mike also explained that the ways in which he identifies as "African" are predicated upon whether he is with friends or family who themselves are not "Norwegian." What is of interest here is that while "Norwegian" as an identity category is both flexible and contested, as in the case of Mike, "Norwegian" is a category on which he plays depending on the context in which he finds himself.

A final example that is telling of the ways in which the categories of immigrant and Norwegian come into play in the lives of the people interviewed in Norway can be seen through the words of Obi, who has a mother from Norway and a father from Nigeria. When asked why he did not identify solely as Norwegian, Obi replied: "They view you as a foreigner and then you become a foreigner. Then you start behaving accordingly. And that can have something to say. . . . Had everybody treated me as if I was completely Norwegian, then maybe I would have thought right away that I *was* completely Norwegian." This excerpt shows the ways in which the notions of "feeling Norwegian" and "being seen as a Norwegian" are powerfully played out in the interactions that Obi has with others who have *not seen him* as Norwegian. The above excerpt represents a site where being "hailed" into a subject position of "Norwegian" is supported by the silence of *not* being called a "Norwegian."

Being "almost" Norwegian is premised on being in that zone that is outside the norm of what a Norwegian looks like or is taken to be (Sandset 2018, 183). As such, for all mixed-race Norwegians, skin color and phenotypical appearance did play a role in the degree of contextual and fluid ways of claiming to be Norwegian or having a mixed and racialized identity. Conversely, this also prompted questions about belonging and Norwegian identity by others that the mixed Norwegian interviewees had to deal with.

CONCLUDING REMARKS: BEING MIXED-RACE IN SWEDEN, NORWAY, AND BEYOND

A final point that is perhaps of note and to which we alluded in the introduction to this chapter pertains to the question of what, if any, commonalities people of mixed-racial background have across and even within national borders but across various constellations of "mixedness." Most Swedish mixed-race interviewees identified themselves as mixed in different ways; however, as earlier studies in a variety of contexts show, their mixed identity is not validated, and others may not accept mixed status as a meaningful category. Moreover, it is also very clear that many identify themselves as Swedish not as a white racial category but as a reference to cultural and national belonging. However, depending on their phenotype and in some cases their name, the identification as Swedish is not validated.

In the Norwegian case, phenotypical appearance was often key to being perceived as Norwegian and, conversely, to being placed "outside" the category of Norwegian. As such, skin color and phenotypical appearance came to dominate many of the interviews. This reveals a theme running across both the Norwegian and the Swedish settings in that phenotype seems to be deeply connected to ideas about what "Norwegian" and "Swedish" can be said to be. However, as in the Swedish case, the Norwegian interlocutors were also able to navigate and claim a Norwegian identity that was outside a hegemonic and stereotypical idea of "white Norwegianness." Here, culture and nationality seem to come into play as ways to craft a flexible identity that, although it often included contestations about and obstacles to identifying as "Norwegian," allowed interlocutors to make a claim to Norwegian identity.

Since this chapter is set within a framework that involves material collected in both Sweden and Norway, the issue of crafting a flexible identity that allows for multiple modes of identification also presses up against the "political economy of race" in the Nordic and Scandinavian settings. While the chapter's main focus has not been to evaluate or track the commonalities that we can discern from the material between people of mixed-racial background in Sweden and in Norway, it is worth noting some commonalities. First, in both the Swedish and the Norwegian contexts, the people we interviewed were able, in some way or form, to relate to the notion of being perceived as an "immigrant." The tension between being perceived as being an immigrant and the self-defined feeling of belonging was a clear commonality among the mixed-race Swedes and Norwegians who were interviewed. Phenotypical appearance was a factor in enabling or foreclosing identification in certain situations where they were perceived as "immigrants" or as "Swedish" or "Norwegian." This points to the connection between a normative idea of Swedish and Norwegian as being deeply rooted in the body politic of these nations as white and the individual white bodies that are coded as being Swedish and Norwegian. The normative enactment of white being associated with Swedish and Norwegian became telling in the narratives of those interviewees who made claims to be Swedish and Norwegian and to belong to Sweden and Norway. The experiences of misrecognition and of feeling a gap between one's self-identification and the ascribed identification play on well-known tropes from the literature within critical mixed-race studies (e.g., Aspinall and Song 2013; Rockquemore and Brunsma 2002; Song and Aspinall 2012; Osanami Törngren 2016).

As different identity theories suggest, the interviewees' words clearly show how identification as "either/or" is often more a case of flexibility and fluidity in terms of situational engagements with self and others (Brubaker 2016; Jenkins 2005). This, we remark, also reveals that while there is a tension-filled space between self-identification and the assigned identification, the overarching markers of "Swedish" and "Norwegian" are, by and large, transformed into a "flexible" identity marker that our respondents use to expand the existing association between the image of "Swedish" and "Norwegian" with whiteness. What is interesting is that for many mixed-race interviewees, their identification based on parental country of origin weighs less than their being Swedish or Norwegian. Embracing their mixed heritage, they redefine what it means to be Swedish or Norwegian through national and cultural belonging. This identification as a race-neutral term, independent of whether or not the interviewees can pass as Swedes, resonates with previous research showing how mixed persons identify through national belonging (Song and Aspinall 2012). It also resonates with prior research that has highlighted the ways in which people of mixed-racial background define their identity in complex yet multiple ways according to the situation in which they find themselves (Haritaworn 2009a, 2009b; Sandset 2018).

This chapter, based on twenty-two interviews with mixed-race Norwegians and sixteen with mixed-race Swedes, has explored how they are ascribed with dialectic categories based on the visibility of mixedness, such as phenotype and name, and how they respond and contest these ascribed identities by challenging the notion of national identity as a racial category. This flexibility of identity should not, however, lead us to think that the identity markers of "Swedish" or "Norwegian" as *markers of national belonging* become dissolved into a relativistic notion of "nonbelonging." Rather, we have argued that the mixed-race Swedes and Norwegians whom we interviewed navigate these markers of belonging by expanding and playing on them through the situational "foregrounding" of various markers of identity, in particular on the importance accorded to phenotypical appearance.

NOTE

1. These interviews were conducted within the project "Half, Double or Mixed," during which twenty-three interviews with multiethnic and multiracial Swedes were conducted. This chapter only analyzes the interviews with the fifteen mixed-race participants.

REFERENCES

Adeniji, A. 2014. "Searching for Words: Becoming Mixed Race, Black and Swedish." In *Afro-Nordic Landscapes,* edited by M. McEachrane, 169–81. New York: Routledge.

Aiwerioba, N. P. 2007. "Identity Development for Mixed Race Persons in Western Norway." Master's thesis, University of Oslo.

Andersson, Mette. 2007. "The Relevance of the Black Atlantic in Contemporary Sport: Racial Imaginaries in Norway." *International Review for the Sociology of Sport* 42(1): 65–81.

Anyuru, Johannes. 2013. *En storm kom från paradiset.* Stockholm: Norstedts.

Appel, Helene Bang, and Rashmi Singla. 2016. "Mixed Parentage: Negotiating Identity in Denmark." In *Contested Childhoods: Growing Up in Migrancy,* edited by Marie Louise Seeberg and Elżbieta M. Goździak, 139–57. Cham, Germany: Springer.

Arbouz, Daphne. 2012. "Vad betyder det att inte känna sig hemma där man är född och uppvuxen? Om mellanförskap i dagens Sverige." In *Om ras och vithet i det samtida Sverige,* edited by Tobias Hübinette, Helena Hörnfeldt, Fataneh Farahani, and René León Rosales, 37–42. Tumba: Mångkulturellt Centrum.

Arbouz, Daphne. 2017. "Multirasial identitet på tvärs med den svenska vithetens rasiala inramning." In *Ras och vithet: Svenska rasrelationer i går och i dag,* edited by Tobias Hübinette, 201–14. Lund: Studentliteratur.

Aspinall, Peter, and Miri Song. 2013. *Mixed Race Identities.* Basingstoke: Palgrave Macmillan.

Behtoui, Alireza. 2006. *Unequal Opportunities: The Impact of Social Capital and Recruitment Methods on Immigrants and Their Children in the Swedish Labour Market.* Linköping: Department of Social and Welfare Studies, Linköping University. http://urn.kb.se/resolve?urn=urn:nbn:se:liu:diva-7789.

Berg, Anne-Jorunn. 2004. "Taus forlegenhet? Rasialisering, hvithet og minnearbeid." *Kvinneforskning* 28(2): 68–83.

Berg, Anne-Jorunn, and Tone Gunn Stene Kristiansen. 2010. "Synlig forskjell: Om 'nyankomne innvandrere'—kjønn og rasialisering." In *Likestilte norskheter: Om kjønn og etnisitet,* edited by Berit Gullikstad, Anne-Britt Flemmen, and Anne-Jorunn Berg, 225–59. Trondheim, Norway: Tapir Forlag.

Bonilla-Silva, Eduardo. 1997. "Rethinking Racism: Toward a Structural Interpretation." *American Sociological Review* 62(3): 465–80.

Brubaker, Rogers. 2016. *Trans: Gender and Race in an Age of Unsettled Identities.* Princeton, NJ: Princeton University Press.

Brubaker, Rogers, and Frederick Cooper. 2000. "Beyond 'Identity.'" *Theory and Society* 29(1): 1–47.

Childs, Erica Chito. 2018. "Critical Mixed Race in Global Perspective: An Introduction." *Journal of Intercultural Studies* 39(4): 379–81.

DaCosta, Kimberly McClain. 2007. *Making Multiracials: State, Family, and Market in the Redrawing of the Color Line*. Redwood City, CA: Stanford University Press.

Daniel, G. Reginald, Laura Kina, Wei Ming Dariotis, and Camilla Fojas. 2014. "Emerging Paradigms in Critical Mixed Race Studies." *Journal of Critical Mixed Race Studies* 1(1): 6–65.

Daynes, Sarah, and Orville Lee. 2008. *Desire for Race*. Cambridge: Cambridge University Press.

Deaux, Kay. 2018. "Ethnic/Racial Identity: Fuzzy Categories and Shifting Positions." *Annals of the American Academy of Political and Social Science* 677(1): 39–47.

Demker, Marie, and Andreas Johansson Heinö. 2013. "Slopa kollektiva identiteter i den officiella statistiken." *Dagens Nyheter*, July 26. https://www.dn.se/debatt/slopa-kollektiva-identiteter-i-den-officiella-statistiken/.

Diakite, Jason Timbuktu. 2016. *En droppe midnatt*. Stockholm: Albert Bonniers Förlag.

Edwards, Rosalind, Suki Ali, Chamion Caballero, and Miri Song, eds. 2012. *International Perspectives on Racial and Ethnic Mixedness and Mixing*. New York: Routledge.

Frankenberg, Ruth. 1993. *White Women, Race Matters: The Social Construction of Whiteness*. London: Routledge.

Goffman, Erving. 1990. *Stigma: Notes on the Management of Spoiled Identity*. Harmondsworth: Penguin Books.

Gokieli, Natia. 2017. "'I Want Us to Trade Our Skins and Our Experiences': Swedish Whiteness and 'Immigrant Literature.'" *Scandinavian Studies* 89(2): 266–86.

Gullestad, Marianne. 2002. "Invisible Fences: Egalitarianism, Nationalism and Racism." *Journal of the Royal Anthropological Institute* 8(1): 45–63.

Gullestad, Marianne. 2004. "Blind Slaves of Our Prejudices: Debating 'Culture' and 'Race' in Norway." *Ethnos* 69(2): 177–203.

Hallvik, Jørgen. 2008. "Skoleprestasjoner i grunnskolen blant 2.5 generasjonselever: En kvantitativ studie av elever med en ikke-vestlig utenlandsfødt og en norskfødt forelder." Master's thesis, University of Oslo. https://www.duo.uio.no/bitstream/handle/10852/15814/Hallvik.pdf?sequence=1.

Haritaworn, Jin. 2009a. "'Caucasian and Thai Make a Good Mix': Gender, Ambivalence and the 'Mixed-Race' Body." *European Journal of Cultural Studies* 12(1): 59–78.

Haritaworn, Jin. 2009b. "Hybrid Border-Crossers? Towards a Radical Socialisation of 'Mixed Race.'" *Journal of Ethnic and Migration Studies* 35(1): 115–32.

Harris, David R., and Jeremiah Joseph Sim. 2002. "Who Is Multiracial? Assessing the Complexity of Lived Race." *American Sociological Review* 67(4): 614–27.

Houston, H. Rika, and Mikel Hogan. 2009. "Edge Dancers: Mixed Heritage Identity, Transculturalization, and Public Policy and Practice in Health and Human Services." *Applied Anthropologist* 29(2): 143–70.

Hübinette, Tobias, and Daphne Arbouz. 2019. "Introducing Mixed Race Sweden: A Study of the (Im)possibilities of Being a Mixed-Race Swede." *Culture and Empathy: International Journal of Sociology, Psychology, and Cultural Studies* 2(3): 138–63.

Hübinette, Tobias, Helena Hörnfeldt, Fataneh Farahani, and René León Rosales. 2012. *Om ras och vithet i det samtida Sverige.* Tumba: Mångkulturellt Centrum.

Hübinette, Tobias, and Charlotte Hylten-Cavallius. 2014. "White Working-Class Communities in Stockholm." Open Society Foundations. https://www.opensociety foundations.org/uploads/d353046d-006a-48b4-bda9-eabed21c7eb1/white-working -class-stockholm-20140828.pdf.

Hübinette, Tobias, and Catrin Lundström. 2011. "Sweden after the Recent Election: The Double-Binding Power of Swedish Whiteness through the Mourning of the Loss of 'Old Sweden' and the Passing of 'Good Sweden.'" *Nordic Journal of Feminist and Gender Research* 19(1): 42–52.

Jebari, Karim, and Måns Magnusson. 2013. "En färgblind stat missar rasismens nyanser." *Tidskrift för politisk filosofi* 17(2): 2–18.

Jenkins, Richard. 2005. *Social Identity.* Enskede: Tpb.

Kalmijn, Matthijs. 2015. "The Children of Intermarriage in Four European Countries: Implications for School Achievement, Social Contacts, and Cultural Values." *Annals of the American Academy of Political and Social Science* 662(1): 246–65.

Kalonaityte, Viktorija, Victoria Kwesa, and Adiam Tedros. 2007. "Att färgas av Sverige: Upplevelser av diskriminering och rasism bland ungdomar med afrikansk bakgrund i Sverige." Ombudsmannen mot etnisk diskriminering. https://www .do.se/globalassets/publikationer/rapport-att-fargas-av-sverige.pdf.

Khemiri, Jonas Hassen. 2013. "Sweden's Closet Racists." *New York Times,* April 20.

Khosravi, Shahram. 2006. "Manlighet i exil: Maskulinitet och etnicitet hos iranska män i Sverige." In *Orienten i Sverige: Samtida möten och gränssnitt,* edited by Simon Ekström and Lena Gerhlm, 77–104. Lund: Studentlitteratur.

King-O'Riain, Rebecca Chiyoko, Stephen Small, Minelle Mahtani, Miri Song, and Paul Spickard, eds. 2014. *Global Mixed Race.* New York: New York University Press.

Lou, Evelina, and Richard N. Lalonde. 2015. "Signs of Transcendence? A Changing Landscape of Multiraciality in the Twenty-First Century." *International Journal of Intercultural Relations* 45:85–95.

Lundström, Catrin. 2007. *Svenska Latinas: Ras, klass och kön i svenskhetens geografi.* Stockholm: Makadam.

Lundström, Catrin. 2017. "The White Side of Migration: Reflections on Race, Citizenship and Belonging in Sweden." *Nordic Journal of Migration Research* 7(2): 79–87.

Mattsson, Katarina. 2005. "Diskrimineringens andra ansikte: Svenskhet och 'det vita västerländska.'" In *Bortom vi och dom: Teoretisk reflektioner om makt, integration och strukturell diskriminering,* edited by Stadens offentliga utredningar, 139–257. Stockholm: Regeringskansliet.

Morning, Ann. 2018. "Kaleidoscope: Contested Identities and New Forms of Race Membership." *Ethnic and Racial Studies* 41(6): 1055–73.

Osanami Törngren, Sayaka. 2016. "Attitudes toward Interracial Marriages and the Role of Interracial Contacts in Sweden." *Ethnicities* 16(4): 568–88.

Osanami Törngren, Sayaka. 2019. "Talking Color-Blind: Justifying and Rationalizing Attitudes toward Interracial Marriages in Sweden." In *Racialization, Racism, and Anti-racism in the Nordic Countries*, edited by Peter Hervik, 137–62. London: Palgrave Macmillan.

Osanami Törngren, Sayaka. 2020. "Challenging the 'Swedish' and 'Immigrant' Dichotomy: How Do Multiracial and Multi-ethnic Swedes Identify Themselves?" *Journal of Intercultural Studies* 41(4): 457–73.

Osanami Törngren, Sayaka, Nahikari Irastorza, and Miri Song. 2016. "Toward Building a Conceptual Framework on Intermarriage." *Ethnicities* 16(4): 497–520.

Regjeringen.no. 2000. "NOU 2002: 12: Rettslig vern mot etnisk diskriminering." March 3. https://www.regjeringen.no/no/dokumenter/nou-2002-12/id145418/.

Rocha, Zarine L., and Farida Fozdar. 2017. *Mixed Race in Asia: Past, Present and Future*. London: Routledge.

Rocha, Zarine L., Farida Fozdar, Kristel Anne Acedera, and Brenda S. A. Yeoh. 2019. "Mixing Race, Nation, and Ethnicity in Asia and Australasia." *Social Identities* 25(3): 289–93.

Rockquemore, Kerry Ann, and David L. Brunsma. 2002. "Socially Embedded Identities: Theories, Typologies, and Processes of Racial Identity among Black/White Biracials." *Sociological Quarterly* 43(3): 335–56.

Rodríguez-García, Dan. 2015. "Intermarriage and Integration Revisited." *Annals of the American Academy of Political and Social Science* 66(1): 8–36.

Romero, Madeleine. 2012. "Bastard eller exotisk cocktail?" In *Om ras och vithet i det samtida Sverige*, edited by Tobias Hübinette, Helena Hörnfeldt, Fataneh Farahani, and René León Rosales, 187–88. Tumba: Mångkulturellt Centrum.

Roth, Wendy D. 2018. "Unsettled Identities amid Settled Classifications? Toward a Sociology of Racial Appraisals." *Ethnic and Racial Studies* 41(6): 1093–112.

Runfors, Ann. 2016. "What an Ethnic Lens Can Conceal: The Emergence of a Shared Racialised Identity Position among Young Descendants of Migrants in Sweden." *Journal of Ethnic and Migration Studies* 42(11): 1846–63.

Sandset, Tony. 2014. "Color as Matter: A Different Deployment of Color." *Ethnologia Scandinavica* 44:7–22.

Sandset, Tony. 2018. *Color That Matters: A Comparative Approach to Mixed Race Identity and Nordic Exceptionalism*. Abingdon: Routledge.

Skadegård, Mira C., and Iben Jensen. 2018. "'There Is Nothing Wrong with Being a Mulatto': Structural Discrimination and Racialised Belonging in Denmark." *Journal of Intercultural Studies* 39(4): 451–65.

Smith, Christopher D., Jonas Helgertz, and Kirk Scott. 2019. "Time and Generation: Parents' Integration and Children's School Performance in Sweden, 1989–2011." *European Journal of Population* 35:719–50.

Song, Miri. 2003. *Choosing Ethnic Identity.* Cambridge: Polity Press.

Song, Miri, and Peter Aspinall. 2012. "Is Racial Mismatch a Problem for Young 'Mixed Race' People in Britain? The Findings of Qualitative Research." *Ethnicities* 12(6): 730–53.

Statistics Norway. 2018. "14 prosent av befolkningen er innvandrere." March 5. https://www.ssb.no/befolkning/artikler-og-publikasjoner/14-prosent-av-befolkningen-er-innvandrere.

Statistics Norway. 2021. "Innvandrere og norskfødte med innvandrerforeldre." March 9. https://www.ssb.no/befolkning/statistikker/innvbef.

Statistics Sweden. 2018. "Antal personer med utländsk eller svensk bakgrund (fin indelning) efter region, ålder och kön, år 2002–2018." http://www.statistikdatabasen.scb.se/pxweb/sv/ssd/START__BE__BE0101__BE0101Q/UtlSvBakgFin/.

Sveriges Television AB. 2018. "Världens sämsta indier." October 3. https://www.svtplay.se/varldens-samsta-indier.

SVT Nyheter. 2014. "Rasbegreppet ska bort ur lagen." https://www.svt.se/nyheter/inrikes/rasbegreppet-ska-bort-ur-lagen.

Waters, Mary C. 1990. *Ethnic Options: Choosing Identities in America.* Berkeley: University of California Press.

Managing Multicultural Tenants

Rental Agreements and Feminist Qualms in Auður Jónsdóttir's *Deposit* and Vigdis Hjorth's *A House in Norway*

ELISABETH OXFELDT

Å arve eller ikke arve, det er spørsmålet (To inherit or not to inherit, that is the question).

> —VIGDIS HJORTH, *Et norsk hus* (*A House in Norway*)

Since the first World Happiness Report was published by the United Nations in 2012, the Nordic countries have consistently ranked among the top ten countries on the list, as they are relatively wealthy, egalitarian, safe, and experienced as offering their inhabitants lifelong opportunities to realize their potential and ambitions.[1] The so-called Nordic Model is often hailed internationally as exemplary and is a source of pride to many Scandinavians. Nevertheless, as Shakespeare would have it, something is rotten in the state of Denmark (or the Nordic countries at large). The point of departure for this article is that the well-being, happiness, and privilege of inhabitants of the Nordic countries entail their share of moral scruples and discomfort. In films, TV series, educational materials, political speeches, and literature in the new millennium, we find various us-versus-them narratives that question the moral integrity of the privileged Nordic Self as he or she is confronted with the less privileged Other—an Other who often contributes to the well-being of the Nordic Self. These may be narratives about child laborers, trafficking victims, beggars, au pairs, and refugees.[2]

In what follows, I will turn to Vigdis Hjorth's *Et norsk hus* (2014; *A House in Norway*, 2017) and Auður Jónsdóttir's *Tryggðarpantur* (Deposit, 2006). (On her official English website, Jónsdóttir refers to the novel as *Deposit*, which I will also do throughout the rest of the chapter, but it has not yet been

Managing Multicultural Tenants

translated into English. I have read and will cite a Danish translation of the novel.) I consider both novels to be postfeminist, that is, feminist while also critical of, especially, the second-wave feminism of the 1960s and 1970s. Both novels are about white privileged Nordic women who are able to sustain a life of creativity and leisure by renting out part of their property to precariat immigrant tenants.[3] The Nordic woman protagonists have inherited their homes and are part of the propertied classes, allowing them to work freelance, engaging—somewhat hypocritically, it would seem—in issues of social justice, solidarity, and compassion. In *A House in Norway*, the protagonist is allowed by an inheritance to buy her own house close to that of her ex-husband after their divorce. In *Deposit*, the protagonist inherits vast sums from her grandmother; in addition, she is granted her childhood apartment by her parents when they move abroad. The tales are thus replete with metapoetic reflections that pose a series of aesthetic and political questions about inspiration and representation.[4] In addition to being artist tales, the novels function on a second level as (post)national allegories.[5] They allow us to explore ambivalent national attitudes vis-à-vis the immigrant Other who becomes a source of nuisance as well as a source of income.[6] The notion of the house and home as a stand-in for the nation is particularly well established in the case of Hjorth's novel, which includes the word "Norwegian" or "Norway" in the title. Not only does the notion of national belonging figure prominently in the title, but the expression of building *det norske hus* (the Norwegian house) was also coined by former Norwegian prime minister Thorbjørn Jagland when he took office in 1996. It was, in sociologist Marianne Gullestad's words, "a new way of visualizing the social democratic notion of the integrated Norwegian nation-state" (2006, 94–95). The metaphor, as Gullestad furthermore points out, was subsequently "amply criticized and ridiculed, while at the same time being referred to often" (94). Hjorth's novel may be considered yet another comment on this metaphor, situating "the Norwegian house" within a postnational era. Jónsdóttir's *Deposit*, too, functions as this type of allegory, in this case because it is carefully *not* situated within a particular nation. Rather, it reflects on northern European countries more broadly, emphasizing again postnational conditions.

In the following, I will explore the discomfort depicted in these novels first and foremost in terms of postfeminism, situating the identities of the protagonists at the intersection of art, nation, and gender. The novels are written by women about women in the roles of capitalists, owners, landladies, immigrants, and tenants. They evoke Sianne Ngai's (2005) "ugly feelings" as they reveal the dark sides of privilege, altruism, capitalism, feminism, and creative ambition. They are postfeminist in the sense that they reflect critically not only on patriarchal structures but also on past and present phases of feminism (Brooks 1997). In their particular focus on the protagonists' ignorance of a contemporary feminist agenda concerning the privilege of majority women versus underprivileged minority women, they can also more specifically be considered indicative of intersectional feminism (i.e., third- and fourth-wave feminism), which is attuned to overlapping systems of oppression to which women are subject due to ethnicity, sexuality, and economic background, often tied to an immigrant background (Crenshaw 1991). The novels illustrate that the haves may have capitalism, laws, and regulations on their side, but these do not safeguard them emotionally and ethically. With multicultural cohabitation comes both comfort and discomfort. As the novels show, however, discomfort and antagonism offer opportunities for personal and political growth—if not for the novels' protagonists, then at least for their readers. Overall, I will argue that the novels leave us with hope for what Nancy Fraser discusses as a reinvention of the "project of feminism for a globalizing world" (2005a, 295).[7]

UGLY FEMINISM

A House in Norway and *Deposit* both revolve around the following sets of tension: owner/renter, wealth/poverty, majority/minority, individualism/ solidarity, with the protagonists inhabiting all the primary positions in these binaries. At the heart of these binaries lies feminist unease. One could, of course, regard the problems as universal (transcending gender), as Lilie Chouliaraki does in *The Ironic Spectator* (2013). Here Chouliaraki (2013, 5) discusses a change in public morality and humanitarianism from 1970 to 2010 linked to changes in capitalism that have ended up blurring the boundaries between what were previously considered separate spheres—a public, economic sphere and a private, sentimental sphere. In Chouliaraki's terminology, this change has led to the "ironic spectator" of vulnerable, suffering Others, "an impure or ambivalent figure that stands, at once, as skeptical towards any moral appeal to solidary action and, yet, open to doing something about those who suffer" (2). In *A House in Norway* and *Deposit*, we have particularly clear cases of economic and emotional concerns merging, as the landlady/ tenant relationships are also relationships between neighbors living in or on the same property.

Ngai coined the term "ugly feelings" to describe such an ironic emotional state: "Ugly feelings" are "negative emotions" experienced by people in "ambivalent situations of suspended agency" (2005, 1). They produce a sense of emotional confusion and disorientation characteristic of our late capitalist times (5). They are also noncathartic, "offering no satisfactions of virtue . . . nor any therapeutic or purifying release" (69). Focusing on art instead of humanitarian campaigns (cf. Chouliaraki 2013), she further explains that ugly feelings are captured in aesthetic works that draw the reader into a universe characterized by irony, ambivalence, and an apparent lack of morals. These works express a sense of impotence in a neocapitalist era where individuals are uncertain of how and if they can change the world. They also capture a shift in focus from the suffering of the Other to the discomfort of the Self in his or her meeting with the Other. In accordance with Chouliaraki's findings, the focus shifts from a contemplation of a distant suffering Other evoking pity "towards a subjective representation of suffering as something inseparable from our own 'truths' that invites contemplation on our own condition" (2013, 3). In short, an "ethics of pity" is replaced by an "ethics of irony" (3). In the novels, as we shall see, the authors nevertheless put the stance of irony and ugly feelings into perspective by depicting immigrant girls who inhabit emotional positions of purity—from pure joy to pure fear.

While Chouliaraki and Ngai both regard a contemporary position of ambivalence, hesitation, and irony as connected to (neoliberal) capitalism, Fraser further emphasizes how feminism fits into this development. Fraser (2013) maintains that second-wave feminism became capitalism's handmaiden: "A movement that once prioritised social solidarity now celebrates female entrepreneurs." The novels' protagonists are presented as such entrepreneurs, lacking in solidarity with their less privileged "sisters." Fraser (2013), as mentioned above, ties this change in feminism to a change in capitalism: "The state-managed capitalism of the postwar era has given way to a new form of capitalism—'disorganized,' globalizing, neoliberal. Second-wave feminism emerged as a critique of the first but has become the handmaiden of the second." This sense that feminism has gone awry can be seen as creating an underlying sense of discomfort in the two novels, as they more or less directly reflect upon various phases of feminism.

In *A House in Norway*, reflections around the historical development of feminism are captured through the thought processes of the protagonist, Alma, as she creates large tapestries (based on her research into the connections between democracy, feminism, and women's right to vote) as well as through her more mundane reflections upon the unease she feels in encountering her Polish tenants. "Was it because she owned what they rented?" she asks herself. "Because the power balance was unequal" (Hjorth 2017, 22).[8] A feminist issue is connected to the question of power relations as she furthermore wonders whether the Polish woman, when they meet, might be ashamed of her dependency on her husband, while Alma is an independent woman. While Alma is in her fifties, the protagonist in *Deposit* is in her thirties, and her personal reflections embody fewer historical overviews. Nevertheless, Jónsdóttir, as we shall see, constructs a story that encourages the reader to compare various stages of activism, especially that of the 1960s and 1970s with that of a neoliberal era. In addition, reflections around feminism and capitalism are captured by the prominent image of the pig, basically insinuating that Alma is a pig—and/or is trapped in a system upheld by pigs that is characterized by greed, capitalism, and supporters of the status quo. Significantly, the novel's greedy capitalists are presented as women; hence, capitalism becomes a feminist issue.

At this point we are back to Fraser's argument. As she puts it, also using the image of the pig, "neoliberalism turns a sow's ear into a silk purse by elaborating a narrative of female empowerment." Neoliberalism seeks to frame individualistic greed as appealing in a feminist manner: it justifies exploitation by harnessing "the dream of women's emancipation to the engine of capital accumulation" (Fraser 2013). So whereas the image of the pig was used avidly in the second-wave women's liberation movement to connote male chauvinism, in these postfeminist novels we find it applied to the protagonist women. These are the capitalists seeking to maintain their power and privilege within an oppressive system, maintaining, among other things, that the law is on their side. Keeping this backdrop of interconnections between capitalism, feminism, irony, and ugly feelings in mind, we shall now look more closely at how the novels depict the discomfort of their protagonists as they seek to "manage" their immigrant tenants (and themselves) emotionally, economically, and legally.

A HOUSE IN NORWAY

Hjorth's *A House in Norway* is a third-person narrative about the unequal power relationship between Alma and the Polish work immigrant Slawomira, to whose family Alma has to rent out part of her house in order to survive as a freelance textile artist. The first part covers the seven years of their cohabitation, providing us also at the very beginning with an almost twenty-year-long history of Alma living as a divorcée and renting out her annex to make ends meet. As the narrator puts it, "She would be happy to take multicultural tenants, or whatever the current term was, but being able to speak to them would be an advantage" (Hjorth 2017, 15).[9] Thus, before the Polish tenants, Alma has had Finnish and Danish tenants on her property but has avoided non-European refugees. She is loath to admit it, but she feels anxious at the thought of "veiled women, unemployed men, large numbers of children and clothes hanging on washing lines between the trees" (16); a Polish couple, on the other hand, leaves her with a sense of relief.[10] The second part takes place about a year after Slawomira has moved out. It covers a couple of months during which Alma renovates her rental, reflects upon her antagonistic relation to Slawomira, advertises for new tenants, and finally decides on two Polish employees working for the company that has renovated her apartment.[11] The story is told by a narrator who is close to Alma, using both direct and free indirect discourse to render Alma's thoughts while also maintaining an ironic distance to her protagonist. This ironic distance indicates a critical stance toward both Alma and the narrating self, who apparently identifies with Alma's predicament and expects the reader to do so as well.

If we look at the artist aspect of the novel, we find Alma working with an art form typically attributed to women. She prefers being left in peace by her tenants so that she can concentrate on her tapestries. She does so with lofty ideas of changing the world through her art: "In her work she strove to address big issues," and she wants to "promote good causes," yet she wonders whether this is "pretentious self-delusion" (Hjorth 2017, 32–33).[12] During the course of the novel, she is commissioned to design and embroider two large tapestries for public buildings.[13] One is for her old high school, where she wishes to encourage the students to nourish what she thinks of as the flame of engagement they harbor within their youthful hearts. The second is for an exhibit that will tour the nation in 2014 on the occasion of the bicentennial of the Norwegian constitution. The tapestry is to focus on the evolvement of democracy and women's rights. Here we encounter the novel's persistent focus on and historicizing of the feminist movement in a national context.

The climax of the story occurs when Alma realizes how she is able to treat such topics aesthetically, through her art, while she fails on all accounts vis-à-vis her real-life Other, her neighbor. Alma does all she can to avoid contact with Slawomira—even when Alma discovers that Slawomira is a victim of domestic abuse. The satire turns especially grotesque because Alma reflects so thoroughly on the role of activism and the extent to which she has been engaged in movements for women's rights and world peace and the extent to which she is able to inspire others to become similarly engaged through her art. The novel, however, suggests that it is particularly difficult to be politically engaged in this corner of the world: "Norway was a peaceful and wealthy country; it was hard to feel outraged by or passionately committed to the causes that had featured on the political agenda at the time [of her youth]" (Hjorth 2017, 31).[14] Still, she had made tapestries back then that were "highly radical in their themes, women's liberation and peace work, but the time for that seemed to have passed" (31).[15] Through indirect free style, we gain insight into Alma's ugly and confused thoughts and emotions. In Ngai's words, we recognize that Alma is experiencing "an unpleasurable feeling *about* [her] feeling" (2005, 10). She is ashamed of her lack of grand emotions vis-à-vis the greater problems in life, whereas she has no problems feeling rage at smaller issues. The irony, however, remains that while Alma associates her youth with radical feminist themes that "*had* featured on the political agenda" (my emphasis), she seems ignorant of a contemporary feminist issue pertaining, for instance, to minority women suffering a higher rate of domestic violence due to their dependence on their husbands, to poverty and underemployment, and to language barriers (Crenshaw 1991, 1245–55; Salimi 2014). Hence, Alma's postfeminist engagement is limited to reflections upon the history of feminism. She herself is stuck in a position of what Fraser depicts as the tragic results of second-wave feminism, while she seems blind to and detached from subsequent waves of engagement.

The novel's first part ends with Slawomira resenting Alma for continually raising Slawomira's rent with no regard for her life situation. It is a matter of law versus justice: Alma has the law on her side, but her harsh treatment of Slawomira seems unjust as well as lacking in the above-mentioned intersectional feminist perspective. Slawomira's departure leaves Alma shameful and guilt-ridden, especially as Alma realizes how she must come across from the perspective of Slawomira's little daughter, Izabela. The perspective of the child, as indicated above, puts that of the "ironic spectator" in perspective. Here is a girl who grows up fearing a powerful, white, Norwegian-majority woman touting women's liberation while showing no sense of solidarity with her Polish tenant and victim of abuse. Izabela is "terrified" that her family will be evicted (Hjorth 2017, 41), and "her eyes [are] frantic with fear" when she witnesses confrontations between Alma and her mother (156).[16] In Fraser's terms, this is an image of "the mainstream feminism of our time," encouraging women who "lean on" other women "by offloading their own care work and housework onto low-waged, precarious workers, typically racialized and/or immigrant women" (Gutting and Fraser 2015). Alma does not use Slawomira for care work and housework, but Alma's subsistence in Norway pertains to Slawomira working as a cleaner.

Alma does, however, feel that she has gained important new insight from her neighborly failures. In the brief second part of the novel, she fixes up her house and gets ready to rent out her apartment again. Interviewing applicants, she tries "to be an advocate for the ordinary and see the big picture in the little things, but it was hard going" (Hjorth 2017, 174).[17] She rejects those who are farthest down on the social ladder, the precariat, the unemployed and sick. Finally, she accepts when the aforementioned Norwegian company contacts her on behalf of two of its employees. Alma is relieved to sign a contract with a well-established Norwegian company. Then two smiling Poles become her new neighbors. Alma resigns herself to life's unpredictability. It is somewhat ironic that her annex is occupied by Poles once more. This time, however, they appear to be two men, and Alma, we may conclude, will no longer have to worry about everyday cross-cultural female solidarity.

In terms of national identity, the ending emphasizes today's globalization, multiculturalism, and that in these postnational times, a "Norwegian" company and a "Norwegian" house are made up of people from various ethnicities and backgrounds, with Poles being the largest immigrant group in Norway (Blaker 2016). Fraser writes about the problem of framing issues of social injustice in terms of the nation-state and national citizenry: above and beyond first-order questions of substance, "arguments about justice today also concern second-order, meta-level questions. What is the proper frame within which to consider first-order questions of justice? Who are the relevant subjects entitled to a just distribution or reciprocal recognition in the given case? Thus, it is not only the substance of justice, but also the frame, which is in dispute" (Fraser 2005b). To what extent should Slawomira figure within the frame?

This issue of the frame ends up figuring prominently in Alma's final tapestry. The artist's insight into her double standards (revealed by her cynical treatment of Slawomira) leads her to cut up and burn the tapestry she had embroidered for the bicentennial of the Norwegian constitution. She momentarily feels deeply ashamed. At the last minute, she submits a frame she had sewn but discarded for the high-school tapestry, leaving it for viewers to fill in the missing picture themselves.[18] The frame, it turns out, becomes a great success. With Fraser we can view it as a feminist project questioning the way in which we frame issues: "Misframing . . . is emerging as a central target of feminist politics in its transnational phase" (2005a, 305). Alma's frame, we know, was made on a journey to Tunisia, as she has traveled abroad to gain a distant perspective on Norway (and to attain peace and quiet in pleasantly warm countries). Subsequent options for the content of her frame have been, on the one hand, her boyfriend's suggestion of a focus on class equality as it appeared in Eidsvoll, where the Norwegian constitution was signed in 1814 (Hjorth 2017, 96; 2014, 104). This, in Alma's opinion, constitutes a smug national perspective that disregards a global understanding of Norway's position in the world that would take into consideration what one country's freedom and independence cost other countries. On the other hand, Alma also finds the juxtaposition of rich and peaceful versus poor and warring countries trite. Too many artists have already depicted this without it leading to any change (84; 91). The picture that Alma finally burns up consists of people she had seen in Trieste, Italy, apathetically watching a few demonstrators who were protesting against the financial crisis and unemployment (87; 94). Alma identifies entirely—and identifies other privileged Norwegians—with these passive bystanders, sensing as a vague emotion only their fear that the world's poor would ever rise up against them (103; 112). The burning of this scene suggests a desire for a move beyond such a state of fear and apathy, and while Alma may not realize what type of intersectional feminist activism this could lead to, the story about the beaten and battered Slawomira suggests a contemporary feminist issue pertaining to minority violence. As Pakistani-born Norwegian human rights activist Fakhra Salimi (2014) has pointed out (the year Hjorth's novel was published), violence against minority women who have recently arrived in Norway was on the rise.[19]

In the end, Alma's framework constitutes a border around empty, constantly changing, and contingent space. Alma does not know how to fill it, and the implied author only suggests that this gaping hole could contain Slawomira's untold story. A spectator within the fictional universe could fill it with any story relevant to his or her perspective. As Chantal Mouffe puts it, also emphasizing the importance of framing, critical art "is constituted by a manifold of artistic practices aiming at giving voice to all those who are silenced within the framework of the existing hegemony" (2007, 4–5). At the same time, the frame is not neutral. It is made of Alma's hand-embroidered cloth, and the reader is well aware of how it captures her journey through ugly feelings,

Managing Multicultural Tenants   179

shame, and embarrassment, not least because Alma, through her (partial) resignation, once more ends up on top in a position of privilege—as artist, landlady, and representative of the (postnational) "Norwegian house."

DEPOSIT

Like Hjorth's novel, Auður Jónsdóttir's *Deposit* (2006) criticizes the privileged Nordic woman who, in order to finance a leisurely creative-class lifestyle, has to rent out part of her property to immigrant women—without this resulting in any kind of global sisterhood or sense of solidarity. The opening has a strong narrative hook, showing three weary women sitting around Gísella, hoping she will rent out her rooms to them at a price they can afford. Gísella has thought the situation through and carefully goes through her "Gísella rules" of cohabitation, which involve the tenants having to take turns cleaning and cooking and not having male visitors; finally, there is Gísella's right to make further rules if necessary as well as her right as the owner to have the last word in case of disputes.[20] Attempting to be friendly, Gísella explains that she has lived alone for a long time and is used to having things her way. The newcomers will have to be flexible and adapt. It is not difficult to see how this attitude would pertain to a political stance in a national context as well. The assimilationist stance is further reinforced, as Gísella is presented as thinking of herself as the pioneer and founding family of the city in which she lives, a place where "strangers" are welcome if they obtain a resident permit, learn to speak the language perfectly, work and study assiduously, and honor the city's extant values (Jónsdóttir 2009, 10). Gísella announces that the three women and the one woman's daughter can move in the very next day and concludes that she has done the right thing. In the following chapter, we are presented with her background story and subsequently how things evolve in her apartment over a couple of summer months, from when the tenants move in until they leave. Whether Gísella has done the right thing—and if so, for whom and how—remains an open question. This novel is also told by a third-person ironic narrator with full access to the protagonist's thoughts.

Gísella, we learn, is a freelance journalist, writing primarily for glossy magazines, who decides to rent out rooms in her large apartment to immigrant women. Her motivation is part economic, part professional, part social, and part political. She has used up her inheritance and figures she can earn some money by writing an article about the poor and homeless, whom she can invite into her home on a rental agreement, assuring her a sizable income.

It's win-win. Gísella in many ways embodies a posthumanitarian "egoistic altruism" that, according to Chouliaraki, builds less on "notions of common humanity" because it "explicitly situates the pleasures of the self at the heart of moral action" (2013, 4). Further emphasizing this stance, Gísella figures she will also make new and exotic acquaintances, something that will elevate her social status because she will have something exciting to tell her friends, and she may even overcome a bit of existential boredom.

In this novel, too, Gísella's "activism" is historicized, because the person who inspires her to carry out research on homeless women, especially mothers, and write about it is the publisher of *The Fist: A Magazine for the Children of the Earth*, which is full of "radical" articles on the environment, capitalism, war, equality, and inequality.[21] The man and the magazine hark back to an older phase of activism, with the man being old and white haired and the symbol of the magazine being a red fist soaked in black blood, a symbol of revolutionary fights for solidarity and equality among all people on the earth. Gísella, as opposed to Alma in *A House in Norway*, has no previous experience with the activism of the 1960s and 1970s that these images evoke, yet they figure once again as a backdrop provided by an implicit author who sheds a light on how activism, including feminism, has evolved over time.

Gísella suffers from ennui but has learned to live with the dark side of privilege: "Owning everything and longing for nothing was bearable, time slugged along into emptiness, while her fingers floundered for comfort, yet comfort never manifested. Her fingers gripped the empty air. . . . She had learned to turn a bad day into a bearable one."[22] As an image of the capitalist owner, Gísella illustrates that being wealthy and living the life captured by glossy women's magazines is far from fulfilling but that the haves are disinclined to give up their inherited wealth and power. The haves know how to live with their privileges—they "hold out" (*holde ud*). Hence, as in the case of Alma, we understand that it is the nonprivileged who will have to initiate a radical revolution.

While Alma aimed to avoid her tenant, Gísella sets out to befriend, study, and rule over hers all at once. She ends up with three woman tenants representing, perhaps, various Western apprehensions of immigrants. There is exotic and bubbly Dasíma; there is timid Marta; and there is the more skeptical Anna, who struggles to make ends meet so her ten-year-old daughter can go to school. While Dasíma is from an unnamed African nation, Marta and Anna come from unspecified places in what might be Central and Eastern Europe and/or South America. As we have seen, Gísella, as the property owner, feels completely justified in dictating and amending all rules. From requiring the initial deposit to demanding that the women do all the housework and finally adopt her taste (Jónsdóttir 2009, 223), she rules with an iron fist. In her mind, this is a matter of benevolent dictatorship; her norms and values are universal—they provide a framework that no immigrant may contest.

Cohabitation does start out pleasantly, and Gísella strategically maintains her distance and position: "She enjoyed cohabitating without transgressing the boundary that separated tenant and landlady."[23] Within a couple of months, however, the boundaries crumble, and the owner-tenant relationship turns ugly.[24] So do Gísella's emotions. While she initially felt good—even saintly— about her social actions and engagement, she begins to doubt herself: "Maybe she herself was comical. At least naive. A woman who thoughtlessly wasted her livelihood and then invited strangers to live with her in order to save herself. Who was she? The question was overwhelming."[25]

As her tenants begin to contest what they see as the injustices of the rental agreement, the relations between the women become challenging. Marta is the most acquiescent. She eagerly adapts Gísella's norms and taste. Yet this act of emulation and mimicry eventually causes discomfort on Gísella's part. Marta shows up not only wearing Gísella's hand-me-downs but also copying her hairstyle and hair color and wearing contact lenses as green as Gísella's eyes. With Ngai, we could view this as a case of envy, but at a stage where it is admiration not yet turned into antagonism.[26] It could also be discussed in terms of postcolonial mimicry, which Homi Bhabha explores as threatening in its nature. The Other is to become "almost the same but not quite," as his well-known dictum goes (Bhabha [1994] 2003, 89).

Dasíma becomes threatening in a less uncanny and more overt way as she turns into the African rebel who is finally so provoked by Gísella's methods that she attacks her physically (Jónsdóttir 2009, 276). Hence, one could say that Dasíma ends up embodying the Black person's physicality as it is feared by the white person through a logic of racial imagery, described, for instance, by Frantz Fanon ([1952] 2008). Gísella, in turn, has Dasíma arrested for having participated in illegal demonstrations for the homeless; she thus rids herself of her. Again, the law is used against an (illegal) immigrant without this seeming just.[27] Most difficult is the third situation—that with Anna, who consistently acts suspicious, cold, and spiteful toward her landlady. It would be advantageous to get rid of her if it were not for Anna's daughter, who ends up evoking Gísella's maternal instincts and bringing her much joy, the pure joy that she as a child represents.

182   ELISABETH OXFELDT

In the end, the novel holds on to a perspective on neoliberal capitalism in which those with capital always come out on top. Gísella ends up wealthier than ever before. She has squandered her entire inheritance, yet as a deus ex machina, a friend arrives and reminds her that she had once given him a small sum of money to invest in an advertising agency. This agency has developed the perfect politically correct advertisement product. The ads are all over the city, covering the facades of apartment buildings, including Gísella's own. In a manner evoking the Italian clothing company United Colors of Benetton, they show happy fashionable children of all colors. The advertisements are designed to stir social debate—just like Luciano Benetton sought "to develop citizen consciousness."[28] The advertisers, in turn, have to meet requirements pertaining to environmentalism and human rights. Thus, they promote guilt-free consumption: "The consumer is guaranteed that he or she has done something good by purchasing the advertised product."[29] Gísella's tenants complain that the advertisements covering their windows darken their rooms and make life prison-like for them (Jónsdóttir 2009, 208, 241). Evidently these bright and colorful advertisements, carrying a happy message of global co-habitation on the front, leave people in the dark on the back—especially the precariat who are not on the profiting end of consumerism. This particular type of advertisement illustrates the entanglement of present-day capitalism, aesthetics, activism, and global politics. It is this entanglement that makes it more difficult to attack power in particular locations and sets off a post-feminist understanding of women's problems today, leading to the so-called ugly feelings.[30] It is an example of what Fraser refers to as "an especially preda-tory, winner-take-all form of capitalism, fattening investors by cannibalizing the living standards of everyone else" (Gutting and Fraser 2015). And while Gísella is depicted as not transgressing this deplorable state of inactivism, the novel nudges its readers beyond it, as *A House in Norway* does, by pointing in the direction of intersectional feminism, concerned with the oppression of marginalized groups of women.

Significantly in the context of the novels, the advertisement scheme is also related to the activism of the 1960s and 1970s, as the first great client of the advertising agency is a producer of children's clothing (the Benetton-like advertisements) who has chosen the theme "lack of housing" (*bolignød*) and homeless children for his campaign. The logic is that the clothing is produced in cooperatives worldwide, saving families abroad from homelessness. Thus, on neocapitalist premises, the company "succeeds" in fighting homelessness, whereas Gísella never succeeds in completing her radical article for *The Fist* on the same topic. Once he hears about this, her friend reassures Gísella of the incompatibility of such thinking of the past with that of the present. Had she written such an article for an anarchistic "propaganda magazine," he admonishes her, she would have lost her good reputation as a freelance journalist (Jónsdóttir 2009, 300, 302). Overall, Gísella's attraction to the radical magazine can be seen as capturing what Fraser (2013) argues has been the ambivalence of second-wave feminism, which was "susceptible to two different historical elaborations." "In a cruel twist of fate," second-wave feminism became the handmaiden of neoliberalism instead of letting gender emancipation promote "participatory democracy and social solidarity." Gísella convinces herself that her fight for the homeless is better won on neoliberal terms: "It clearly paid off to conduct the good deeds within a familiar framework."[31] Hence, whereas Alma intuitively contests "injustices of misframing" (Fraser 2005b), Gísella reverts to a traditional, evidently outdated framework. Still, the implied author suggests that Gísella and today's feminists may have more to learn from the other direction in which second-wave feminism moved. Fraser (2013) laments that "feminism's ambivalence has been resolved in favour of (neo)liberal individualism" but maintains that "the other solidaristic scenario may still be alive." It is this hope that the reader can garner from the novel, too.

Seen from Gísella's perspective, she has earned millions on the investment and experiences "a wild sense of bliss."[32] Finally, she can leave her recent dilemmas behind, and the novel ends on a happy but also ironic note: "Undisturbed, she could think of herself; it was certainly about time."[33] At this point, Gísella foresees being "undisturbed." The reader, however, is rather disturbed by Gísella's fate and final choice. Homelessness is still a problem in her city. The idea of a consumer frenzy being upheld with advertisements making up ever more of the cityscape is also disheartening. Yet, ultimately, the realization that the protagonist (in whose life we as readers have invested) is choosing the wrong kind of happiness is disturbing. The choice is nicely captured in terms of her choosing between two kinds of smiles. On the one hand, there is the smile of Anna's child. It is a smile that "lit everything up," "evoked an unknown sense of happiness," "could heal wounds," "comforted," and "made Gísella live and die simultaneously."[34] It has imbued Gísella's life with meaning and seemingly filled her existential void. It is a smile pertaining to what sociologists call *bridging* capital within the community, or, in other words, the building of relations between people who are different (Helliwell, Layard, and Sachs 2012, 70). Giving up on her tenants, Gísella instead returns to the memory of her grandmother's smile: "Then she was better off thinking about a smile which since the beginning of time had carved itself into her memories and become an unchangeable part of herself. Her grandmother's smile."[35] Gísella turns her attention to the history of her ancestors, the pioneers of her city, and thus contributes to increasing the *bonding* capital of the community (i.e., relations between people who are similar to each other). Yet the smile of the grandmother is the smile of financial exploitation. Grandmother Gísella was a ruthless, vengeful adventuress, we find out, who made her fortune on a chemical plant that eventually was closed down due to chemical waste *and* on loans that her tenants eventually could not pay back.

Gísella's new fortune likewise comes across as rotten. The haves are able to invest inherited money and eventually win on the stock market. Meanwhile, the have-nots have nothing to gain from these increases in wealth. To make the postfeminist position particularly clear, the evil capitalists in *Deposit* are the world's Gísellas. These are capitalist pigs wearing a pig's mask. As mentioned above, the pig figures as an important symbol in the novel. Gísella, who assumes a maternal role vis-à-vis Anna's little girl, buys her a pig's mask, telling her to keep it a secret from her mother (Jónsdóttir 2009, 154).[36] Later, however, she finds that the girl has crumpled up and rejected the mask—just as she seems to be rejecting Gísella, too (250). The connection between Gísella and the pig is furthermore made quite explicit, as Anna reassures Gísella that her daughter does not need the pig's mask, she needs only look at "Gí . . ." (258). Anna does not complete her sentence, but she does not have to, either.

It is this pig's mask, too, that figures on the front cover of the Danish translation: a smiling, feminized pig, wearing red lipstick and smudged, black mascara, capturing the ugly combination of happiness and distress. It is a pig's mask that captures the saying that you can't put lipstick on a pig, a saying that is more or less synonymous with Fraser's claim that neoliberalism seeks to make a silk purse out of a sow's ear. Toward the end of the novel, Gísella is repeatedly accused of being "a disgusting pig."[37] More concretely, she is accused of being greedy (Jónsdóttir 2009, 264), a trait she has evidently inherited from her grandmother: "She wanted to give you her view on life. . . . She actually had to imprint her understanding of life on you: greed, misanthropy, and distrust."[38] The values are passed on between generations, and Gísella has furthermore attempted to pass them on to the little girl—fortunately, the novel implies, without succeeding. There is still hope for a new type of feminism. In Fraser's (2013) terms, "The current crisis affords the chance to pick up its thread once more, reconnecting the dream of women's liberation with the vision of a solidary society." In *Deposit* it is the immigrant minority women and the next generation, exemplified by the little girl, who leave us with hope for a nonironic perspective on suffering and global inequity and for a better future overall.

CONCLUSION

A House in Norway and *Deposit* are postfeminist novels that question the happiness of the Nordic woman by confronting her—in her own home—with her less privileged minority sisters. At the same time, the novels serve as postnational allegories illustrating how the nation rests on a foundation that is ethically questionable. The metaphorical Nordic "home" is built on the structural economic and historic oppression of Others and is a haunted house that leaves its inhabitants feeling uncomfortable and guilty, even if they are exonerated by the law. Finally, as metapoetic artist novels, they indicate discomfort with aestheticization, captured by the figure of Alma, who thinks she makes ethical, social, and politically valuable art about human rights and equality yet in her everyday life is bigoted and ignores the suffering and hardship of her own tenant. Alma is hypocritical and realizes this herself. In the case of Gísella, she is ridiculed for her more muddled and ugly motives and feelings as she decides to rent out rooms to homeless immigrant women. Immigrant women are a source not only of income but also of inspiration, supporting Gísella's writing ambitions. Gísella, in other words, seeks to take advantage of the less privileged Other in nearly all aspects of her life. For that reason, it seems, her downfall has more dire consequences, as she ultimately withdraws entirely from the position of cohabitation.

At the crux of the capitalist criticism we find the idea of the rental agreement and deposits, two sources of power that allow (at least in principle) the owners to include and exclude the immigrant Other in their home as they please. The capital and power of privileged Nordic women are never at stake within a social structure that systematically privileges them. Yet their integrity is challenged as they live lives fraught with feelings of guilt and shame. Finally, the reader is left pondering the Nordic nations as homes. The novels ultimately uphold a feminist ethics that claims that the law is unethical but also come down hard on women whose lives and art forms are portrayed as fundamentally complicit in global structures of inequality. Both novels can be considered postfeminist, as they express disappointment with the historical development of feminism and the ability of Nordic women to recognize and uphold ideals of intersectional feminism. Yet at the same time, they express hope in a presumed attempt to affect the reader morally, socially, and politically. They remain invitations to reflect upon and not just dismiss contemporary conditions of multiculturalism and oppressed minority women. As Fraser puts it, "Important currents of feminism are challenging the state-territorial framing of political claims-making" (2005a, 304). Hjorth's and Jónsdóttir's novels underpin this challenge, the former mainly by illustrating that the Norwegian house is now a multicultural site of immigration (with its set of feminist causes to attend to) and the latter by consistently undermining a traditional national framing by not even suggesting that the figures of her novels belong to particular nations. Both novels question a taken-for-granted, inherited position of identity, ownership, superiority, and privilege, framing it as a postnational, as well as a postfeminist, issue.

NOTES

1. Specifically, respondents are asked: "Please imagine a ladder, with steps numbered from 0 at the bottom to 10 at the top. The top of the ladder represents the best possible life for you and the bottom of the ladder represents the worst possible life for you. On which step of the ladder would you say you personally feel you stand at this time?" (Helliwell, Layard, and Sachs 2016, 9).

2. For examples and analyses of such narratives, see various publications within the "ScanGuilt" project (Scandinavian Narratives of Guilt and Privilege in an Age of Globalization): Bakken and Oxfeldt (2017); Oxfeldt (2016); Oxfeldt, Nestingen, and Simonsen (2017); and Oxfeldt and Sharma (2018). While I refer to such narratives as Scandinavian, Sharma situates them more broadly in a European context, referring to them as examples of "hyprocrite fiction," read as a response to a specific historical situation in which the European middle class senses that they live at the expense of others (Sharma 2016, 272).

3. I will explain the term "postfeminist" further below. The term "precariat" is originally a portmanteau made up of "precarious" and "proletariat" and depicts a social class living without security and predictability arising with the advent of neo-liberal capitalism. It is often associated with British economist Guy Standing.

4. Strictly speaking, metapoetry is poetry about poetry. Here I use the term more broadly to describe a situation in which the endeavors of an artist figure or writer in the fictional universe of the novel reflect back the novel and its author.

5. I use the term "postnational" to indicate a situation of globalization in which nation-states and national identities lose their importance relative to transnational and global entities. The prefix indicates that our understanding of the national—while still meaningful—is under pressure and is being renegotiated.

Managing Multicultural Tenants

6. Another recent example of this conflict is Jan Vardøen's immigrant film comedy *Det norske hus* (The house of Norway), from 2017.

7. Fraser does not use the terms "postfeminism" and "postnational"; instead, she refers to "feminism for a globalizing world" (2005a, 295) and "a third phase of feminist politics" (303) and to a "Keynesian-Westphalian frame" related to national publics and national states being replaced by a "post-Westphalian human-rights regime" (2005b, 1). She also speaks of a "transnational phase" (2005a, 305). In this chapter, I will use postnational and postfeminist to refer to the same periods and conditions pertaining to globalization and the development of feminism, respectively. Hence, under the term "postfeminism" I collapse aspects of third- and fourth-wave feminism as they pertain to intersectionality and solidarity between white, majority women and women who are underprivileged due to their skin color (WOC feminism), ethnicity, and status as national minorities, as in the case of the novels' immigrant women.

8. "Fordi hun eide, de leide? Fordi maktbalansen var skjev" (Hjorth 2014, 24).

9. "Det måtte gjerne bo fremmedkulturelle eller hva det het for øyeblikket i leiligheten, men det var en fordel om hun forsto hva de sa" (Hjorth 2014, 16).

10. "tildekkede kvinner, arbeidsledige menn, barneflokker og tøy til tørk mellom trærne" (Hjorth 2014, 16).

11. Part 1 is 188 pages long, while part 2 is only 3 pages. In the English translation, part 1 covers 164 pages and part 2 covers 3 pages.

12. "At hun i arbeidene sine søkte seg mot det store og ville virke i verden for de gode sakene . . . en pretensiøs livsløgn?" (Hjorth 2014, 34).

13. At the very onset we also hear about a tapestry she makes for the foyer of the town hall in her hometown, a tapestry in which she successfully depicts a forest (Hjorth 2014, 18).

14. "Norge var et fredelig og rikt land, det var vanskelig å kjenne seg opprørt og brennende engasjert i de sakene som for tiden sto på den politiske dagsorden" (Hjorth 2014, 33).

15. "svært radikale i tematikken, kvinnekamp og fredsarbeid, men tiden var liksom over for det" (Hjorth 2014, 33).

16. "hun er redd du skal kaste henne ut" (Hjorth 2014, 44); "med blikket vilt av redsel" (171).

17. "å være prest for det alminnelige og se det store i det ordinære, men det holdt hardt" (Hjorth 2014, 190).

18. She initially makes a frame for the tapestry for her old high school but decides at the last minute that the theme of "Uforløst brann" (latent fire) cannot be framed (in the sense of being contained).

19. Salimi is founder and executive director of the MiRA Resource Center for Black, Immigrant, and Refugee Women.

20. As in *A House in Norway*, we see an example of the type of mainstream current feminism that Fraser criticizes, claiming that certain women benefit by leaning on

188 ELISABETH OXFELDT

others and by offloading care work and housework onto "precarious workers, typically racialized and/or immigrant women" (Gutting and Fraser 2015).

21. "Næven—et blad til jordens børn" (Jónsdóttir 2009, 23). All translations of Jónsdóttir's novel into English are my own and are based on Clausen's Danish translation.

22. "Det var udholdeligt at eje alt og længes efter intet, minutterne sneglede sig ind i tomheden, mens fingrene famlede efter trøst, men trøsten indfandt sig ikke; fingrene greb i den tomme luft. . . . Hun havde lært sig at lave en dårlig dag om til en, der var til at holde ud" (Jónsdóttir 2009, 12).

23. "Hun nød samlivet uden at overskride den grænse, der skilte husejer og lejere" (Jónsdóttir 2009, 93).

24. Toward the end of the story, the narrator/Gísella ascertains that "grænsen var forsvundet" (the border had disappeared) (Jónsdóttir 2009, 280).

25. "Måske var hun selv komisk. I hvert fald naiv. En kvinde, der tankeløst klattede sit livsgrundlag væk og derefter inviterede fremmede mennesker til at bo hos sig for at redde sig selv. Hvem var hun? Spørgsmålet var overvældende" (Jónsdóttir 2009, 103).

26. The situation is reminiscent of the film *Single White Female* (1992), which Ngai analyzes in terms of envy (cf. Ngai's discussion of Kierkegaard [Ngai 2005, 130]).

27. Reinforcing the notion that Gísella operates with the law on her side—against the immigrants—the narrator informs us that "en venlig politimand viste stor forståelse for Gísellas problemer og roste hende for at have gjort sin borgerpligt" (a friendly policeman showed great understanding of Gísella's problems and lauded her for having carried out her duty as a citizen) (Jónsdóttir 2009, 305).

28. "We did not create our advertisements in order to provoke, but to make people talk, to develop citizen consciousness," Luciano Benetton has explained (http://top 10buzz.com/top-ten-controversial-united-colors-of-benetton-ads/).

29. "Brugeren får en garanti for at have gjort noget godt ved at købe det produkt, der reklameres for" (Jónsdóttir 2009, 290).

30. It is also a final solution (in the novel) that captures Mouffe's point of departure in her above-mentioned article on art and politics: "Can artistic practices still play a critical role in a society where the difference between art and advertizing have become blurred and where artists and cultural workers have become a necessary part of capitalist production?"—a society in which "artistic critique has become an important element of capitalist productivity" (2007, 1). (Mouffe's answer is yes.)

31. "Det kunne tydeligvis betale sig at foretage de gode gerninger inden for kendte rammer" (Jónsdóttir 2009, 302).

32. "en vild lykkerus" (Jónsdóttir 2009, 291).

33. "Uforstyrret kunne hun tænke på sig selv; det var sandelig også på høje tid" (Jónsdóttir 2009, 320).

34. "kastede stråleglans over alt," "vakte en ukendt glæde," "kunne hele sår," "trøstede," and "fik Gísella til at ville leve og dø på én gang" (Jónsdóttir 2009, 42, 316).

Managing Multicultural Tenants   189

35. "Så var det bedre at tænke på et smil, der i tidernes morgen havde mejslet sig i hendes erindring og var blevet en uforanderlig del af hende selv. Farmorens smil" (Jónsdóttir 2009, 317). The image of Gísella being caught between the smile of the matriarch (her grandmother) and the smile of the immigrant child aptly captures the novel's two main concerns—that of maternal relations and that of immigration. As Dagny Kristjánsdóttir (2014) sums up the author's oeuvre: "The relationship to the family, the mother, and to womanhood constitute[s] the first of two main themes in the works of Auður Jónsdóttir (b. 1973). The second theme is the relationship between the Western master races and the emerging international working classes in the new millennium. While seemingly unrelated, these two themes have much more in common than one may initially think."

36. The little girl remains anonymous until the very last chapter, when we find out that her name is Katrín Annasdatter. The anonymity may be part of the novel's strategy of leaving it ambiguous and open where people come from and where they are currently located in terms of nationality. It also opens up an understanding of the "little girl" as a type more than a specific girl. It could, however, also reflect Gísella's view of the girl as "little girl" rather than as her mother's daughter, a girl who is up for grabs and can become *her* little girl.

37. "Dit modbydelige svin!" (Jónsdóttir 2009, 277).

38. "Hun ville give dig sit livssyn . . . Hun var faktisk nødt til at indpode dig sin livsanskuelse: grådighed, menneskeforagt og mistillid" (Jónsdóttir 2009, 311).

References

Bakken, Jonas, and Elisabeth Oxfeldt, eds. 2017. *Åpne dører mot verden: Norske ungdommers møte med fortellinger om skyld og privilegier.* Oslo: Universitetsforlaget. https://www.idunn.no/apne-dorer-mot-verden.

Bhabha, Homi. (1994) 2003. *The Location of Culture.* New York: Routledge.

Blaker, Magnus. 2016. "Norge skiller seg klart ut i Europa på innvandring." *Side3*, October 15. http://www.side3.no/norge-skiller-seg-klart-ut-i-europa-pa-innvandring/3423271468.html.

Brooks, Ann. 1997. *Postfeminisms: Feminism, Cultural Theory and Cultural Forms.* London: Routledge.

Chouliaraki, Lilie. 2013. *The Ironic Spectator: Solidarity in the Age of Posthumanitarianism.* Cambridge: Polity Press.

Crenshaw, Kimberlé. 1991. "Mapping the Margins: Intersectionality, Identity Politics, and Violence against Women of Color." *Stanford Law Review* 43(6): 1241–99.

Fanon, Frantz. (1952) 2008. *Black Skin, White Masks.* Translated by Richard Philcox. New York: Grove.

Fraser, Nancy. 2005a. "Mapping the Feminist Imagination: From Redistribution to Recognition to Representation." *Constellations* 12(3): 295–307.

Fraser, Nancy. 2005b. "Reframing Justice in a Globalizing World." *New Left Review* 36 (November–December). https://newleftreview.org/II/36/nancy-fraser-reframing -justice-in-a-globalizing-world.

Fraser, Nancy. 2013. "How Feminism Became Capitalism's Handmaiden—and How to Reclaim It." *The Guardian*, October 14.

Gullestad, Marianne. 2006. *Plausible Prejudice.* Oslo: Universitetsforlaget.

Gutting, Gary, and Nancy Fraser. 2015. "A Feminism Where 'Lean in' Means Leaning on Others." *New York Times*, October 15.

Helliwell, John, Richard Layard, and Jeffrey Sachs, eds. 2012. *World Happiness Report.* New York: Earth Institute, Columbia University.

Helliwell, John, Richard Layard, and Jeffrey Sachs, eds. 2016. *World Happiness Report 2016, Update.* Vol. 1. New York: Sustainable Development Solutions Network.

Hjorth, Vigdis. 2014. *Et norsk hus.* Oslo: Cappelen Damm.

Hjorth, Vigdis. 2017. *A House in Norway.* Translated by Charlotte Barslund. London: Norvik Press.

Jónsdóttir, Auður. 2009. *Depositum.* Danish translation by Claus Clausen. Copenhagen: Tiderne skifter.

Kristjánsdóttir, Dagny. 2014. "I—or Mother: Mother-Daughter Conflicts in the Works of Auður Jónsdóttir." *The History of Nordic Women's Literature.* https://nordic womensliterature.net/2014/11/28/i-or-mother-mother-daughter-conflicts-in-the -works-of-audur-jonsdottir/.

Mouffe, Chantal. 2007. "Artistic Activism and Agonistic Spaces." *Art and Research: A Journal of Ideas, Contexts and Methods* 1(2): 1–5.

Ngai, Sianne. 2005. *Ugly Feelings.* Cambridge, MA: Harvard University Press.

Oxfeldt, Elisabeth, ed. 2016. *Skandinaviske fortellinger om skyld og privilegier i en globaliseringstid.* Oslo: Universitetsforlaget. https://www.idunn.no/skandinaviske -fortellinger.

Oxfeldt, Elisabeth, Andrew Nestingen, and Peter Simonsen, eds. 2017. "The Happiest People on Earth? Scandinavian Narratives of Guilt and Discontent." Special issue, *Scandinavian Studies* 89(4).

Oxfeldt, Elisabeth, and Devika Sharma, eds. 2018. "Skyld og skam i Skandinavien." Special issue, *Kultur og klasse* 46(125). https://tidsskrift.dk/kok/issue/view/7450.

Salimi, Fakhra. 2014. "Vold mot minoritetskvinner øker!" *Dagsavisen*, August 12. https://www.dagsavisen.no/kultur/2014/08/12/vold-mot-minoritetskvinner -oker/.

Sharma, Devika. 2016. "Kritik på delagtighedens betingelser: Om at være et problem." *Kultur og klasse* 44(122): 263–91.

Swedish Identity and the Literary Imaginary

PETER LEONARD

Discourses of multiculturalism in Scandinavian literature are less clear-cut than debates over immigration policy and more difficult to quantify than demographic change. But literary imagination nevertheless offers a perspective just as rich as sociology and political science in presenting the complicated conditions for multiculturalism in Scandinavia. The first decade of the twenty-first century saw the rise of several young Swedish authors who put national identity under a new lens, one in which multiculturalism was the norm, not the exception.

In past confrontations with transformative societal change, Scandinavians have treated literature as a universally accessible discursive space for debate and intellectual contention. The Modern Breakthrough of the 1870s to the 1890s represented a break from Romanticism spurred in part by literary critic Georg Brandes's 1871 admonition that writers must "put problems under debate" (1872, 5).[1] Writers such as Ibsen and Strindberg responded, ushering in a contentious and productive period that resulted in some of the most renowned literature and drama Scandinavia has ever produced. The subject of much of this work was the rights and responsibilities of women in the new, rapidly urbanizing and industrializing societies of Sweden, Denmark, and Norway. The rights of women to own property, manage their own finances, and define their own identities are the subjects of plays such as August Strindberg's *The Father* and Henrik Ibsen's *Hedda Gabler*, among others.

Although it's too soon to know if the works from the first decade of the twenty-first century will have as great an impact as those from the end of the nineteenth century, Scandinavian authors were just as engaged in the 2000s as they were during the morality debates of the Modern Breakthrough. Beginning around 2005, young authors in Sweden began publishing works that explored the boundaries and limits of national belonging. Four young Swedish writers constituted a starting point for what we might consider a "postethnic" turn in Swedish literature: Jonas Khemiri, Marjaneh Bakhtiari, Alejandro Leiva Wenger, and Johannes Anyuru. Though diverse in genre and style, the work of these authors imagined a Sweden where ethnicity and citizenship were more flexibly coupled and dynamically combined than in the assumed homogeneity and stasis of the past. Although it is reductive to consider these authors in terms of their personal biographies, some characteristics of their personal lives are nonetheless significant. They were either born in Sweden or moved there when young and thus have Swedish as either a first or a coprimary language. More interestingly, their writing depicts a multiethnic society as the *normal* state of affairs, a default rather than a condition that is new or unusual.

This expectation of multiethnicity did not mean that these writers were oblivious to its literary potential; indeed, they reveled in its possibilities. A line from Johannes Anyuru's first collection of poetry, *Det är bara gudarna som är nya* (Only the gods are new), conjures a scene outside a housing project:

You hear no Swedish words here
even the Arabs have learned
to yell
Mira! Mira!
when they rush after a perfectly kicked pass
along the edge of the bike path. (Anyuru 2003, 14)[2]

As this excerpt suggests, texts that take multiethnic society as theme and/or setting evoke geographic spaces and social classes at the margins of the normative Swedish experience. They derive some of their artistic energy from the resulting unexpected and hitherto-undescribed combinations. For better or worse (and despite the intentions of individual authors), the novelty of multicultural themes in "high" literary forms such as poetry and novels triggered market forces that sought out and rewarded "the new" in contexts such as bookstores, newspaper reviews, and television interviews.

The works examined here differed in how they engaged with the new reality of a multicultural Sweden. The cover of Jonas Khemiri's first novel, *Ett öga rött* (One eye red), featured an explosion of golden arabesques against a deep red background. Lotta Kühlhorn's prize-winning cover design replicated the fictional journal in which the narrator constructed his life. As the teenage protagonist begins on the first page to chronicle his life as an Arab Swede, the reader holds in their hands an aesthetic challenge to twentieth-century functionalist rationalism at the same time that the teenager's journal crafts a challenge to modern notions of the bounded nation-state.

While the cover of Khemiri's bildungsroman signaled to readers the urgency of Sweden's current multicultural condition, the novel's content presented the notion of ethnicity itself as unstable—the product of an individual's choices in a strange market economy of identities overlapping and contradictory. In doing so, it stands as an exemplar of postethnic imagination more broadly. The writing of Anyuru, Bakhtiari, Leiva Wenger, and Khemiri employs a relatively cohesive set of strategies and approaches to multiculturalism that can be summarized as follows.

First, these authors have expanded the definition of Swedish literature to be more inclusive and less homogeneous. They have done this by pushing the language itself to represent new and more complex modes of social identification, typified by the idea of *having an accent on purpose*.[3]

Second, their texts consciously examine the tension between identity politics and egalitarianism. In their critique of an outdated (and always fanciful) ideal of Scandinavian ethnic homogeneity, they show interest in what postcolonial theorist Gayatri Chakravorty Spivak ([1985] 2006) has termed *strategic essentialism*, the idea of a monolithic identity for all nonwhite Swedes. This imagined community of native-born citizens who nevertheless don't quite "pass" in their own nation-state is central to their protagonists' lived experience as minorities in Sweden, and the authors devote attention to both positive and destructive aspects of the concept.

Third, these authors have placed the *irrational*—specifically, imagination and fantasy—in explicit opposition to a society that, since the 1930s, has imagined itself as guided by progressive, utilitarian, and logical underpinnings.

Fourth, they have positioned the way in which their characters *performed* their own identities as wholly constitutive of that identity. In other words, they figure identity as performance rather than essence. The way their characters talk, dress, and present themselves to a broader public is more important to them than place of birth or skin color.

These strategies find expression, often alongside and intermixed with one another, in the literary works of Anyuru, Bakhtiari, Leiva Wenger, and Khemiri examined here. Though many other authors would come after them, the first decade of the 2000s was a breakthrough moment for articulating the literary imaginary that would depict multiethnicity and multiculturalism.

In discussing the first strategy (expanding the definition of Swedish literature), there is reason to reflect on the ways that a "national" writing is weighted in a Scandinavian context. Danish literary theorist Hans Hauge, in his 2003 work *Post-Danmark: Politik og æstetik hinsides det nationale* (Post-Denmark: Politics and aesthetics beyond the national), looked across the Sound separating Denmark and Sweden and declared: "The nation-state blurred the difference between state and society, as did the postwar Labor state or welfare state. . . . Many Scandinavians—especially those who belong to Labor parties—don't distinguish between state and society or between nation and state. . . . Sweden in particular represents a country that still does not differentiate between state and society" (2003, 17–21).[4] Hauge's focus on a side effect of the highly successful experiments in social democracy in twentieth-century Scandinavia—the tight linkage between political state and imagined community—casts light more broadly on other unexamined assumptions underlying Nordic societies. Regardless of the actual state of affairs (the Roma peoples, Jewish communities, thousands of years of contact between Germanic, Finnic, and Sámi communities), it had been possible until quite recently for majority populations to pretend that in Scandinavia the concepts of ethnicity, language, and citizenship were one and the same. Indeed, the last great moral panic of national belonging—the pseudoscience of race biology in the 1930s—was at least in part due to a particularly insidious threat to this triangle. Herman Lundborg's photographs of Finns had a practical goal of "racial hygiene," to educate Swedes to what Finns looked like so that they would not mistakenly marry somebody who was blond, who was born in Swedish territory, and who might have spoken Swedish from birth but who had Finno-Ugric genes (Hagerman 2015).

By the 1970s Olof Palme's concept of "moral migration" (an open-door policy to the global Left, with a focus on nations such as Chile, where right-wing oppression posed a threat) would ensure that eventually the tight linkage between ethnicity, state, and citizen was set on the long path toward dissolution. The imagined homogeneity of the nation would be replaced, slowly but surely, with a heterogeneity that some feared—and others celebrated.

It is a celebration of this difference that begins Khemiri's novel *Ett öga rött*: "I dag det var sista sommarlovsdagen och därför jag hjälpte pappa i affären" (Today it was the last day of summer vacation, so I helped Dad in the store). Lost in the English translation is the grammatical error in the first four words: normally, word order is inverted after an adverb of time or place ("I dag var det"). This is only one of hundreds of such deviations from Standard Swedish throughout the book. After opening the first chapter with this syntactical deviance, Khemiri closes the first chapter with the "wrong" gender of a word (using common gender instead of neuter). There are a number of other stylistic characteristics in the book that garnered immediate attention from lay readers and critics alike. The latter sought to describe the book's tone as "suburban slang" (in the American context, "inner city"), containing words borrowed from Turkish, Arabic, and other sources. But it is the syntactic differences that continue to stand out, even as the slang terms age from their initial freshness of a decade ago.

The most important reason why this variant syntax deserves attention is that the protagonist of *Ett öga rött*, Halim, was born in Sweden. Befitting this fact, his journal, which the book presents itself as being, shows that Halim can write perfectly grammatical Standard Swedish when he wishes to. We know this because he transcribes Arabic conversations using precisely the Standard Swedish that he otherwise refuses to use for his own thoughts in the journal. His performance of syntax is thus a cultural and stylistic choice—a self-conscious linguistic construction to express his identity. Khemiri's first novel thus pushes the boundaries of Swedish literature through its conscious rule-breaking, its compulsion to perform an "accent" on purpose.

What is the meaning of this performance of ethnic identity through language, particularly in Sweden, with its tradition of social democracy? Magnus Nilsson, in his comprehensive analysis of this moment in Swedish literature, is wary of how the "strong focus on ethnicity generated by the notion of the multicultural society leads to us often losing sight of class injustice" (2010, 157). Nilsson sees this as Sweden's "postsocialist" moment, where class is redefined through ethnicity. His critique is aimed mainly at the reception of these texts, specifically those (mis)readings that attribute documentary rather than imaginative force to identity performance in the works.

Yet acknowledging materialist criticism of this writing and its reception should not prevent us from exploring the new and interesting contributions it made to Swedish literature. A useful contrast here is the work (as well as the lived experience) of Theodore Kallifatides, perhaps the most eminent first-generation immigrant author of Sweden's postwar period. An economic migrant from Greece who started out peeling potatoes in restaurant kitchens, Kallifatides did not inherit the Swedish tongue as his birthright but rather acquired it through the study of literary classics. "I experienced the beauty and richness of the [Swedish] language through Strindberg," he would say in later interviews (Karlsson 2003).[5] Kallifatides's originary fiction, told over and over in newspaper interviews and autobiographical writing, is thus that of an immigrant's encounter with the world's most famous Swedish author, August Strindberg.

In contrast, Halim's fictive accent in his fictional journal is an exponent of what the real author, Jonas Khemiri, himself asked: "What happens if you deliberately break down language? I began to explore the power shift that entails" (Hjorth 2004).[6] As a native speaker, the protagonist, Halim, did not feel the same pressure to demonstrate mastery of Swedish by invoking Strindberg—no doubt a mandatory part of any high schooler's assigned reading. At the level of syntax, Halim's journal pushes at the borders of the Swedish language, making it more responsive to his own complex identity as he appropriates grammatical errors and nonstandard syntax to express himself. At the level of national identity and assimilation, Khemiri's novel complicates our understanding of the pathway of language acquisition. In a time of language tests for citizenship, *Ett öga rött* questions whether linguistic mastery of Swedish by new citizens is the ultimate exponent of cultural assimilation and explores what can be communicated via conscious rejection of the perfection of the national tongue.

Indeed, many characters in these works take rejection of normative homogeneity to a variety of creative extremes. The pattern is distinctive enough to constitute the second of the four strategies enumerated above: the promise and peril of "strategic essentialism." Halim intersperses his teenage angst with a glimmer of something genuinely new: a kind of postethnic Swedish imaginary, a sense of belonging that somehow exceeds the bounds of Swedishness:

The *blattar* at school aren't so many but still come in two versions. Number one is the ordinary *blatte*: fuckup, sneak, shoplifter, gangster. . . .[7] *Blatte* type number two is the wannabe who studies for tests and uses big words and never jumps the turnstile or tags walls. For example . . . all the Iranians who kiss up to teachers and want to be dentists and engineers. They think they're respected, but really all the teachers laugh at them because, you know, they're lost.

But today I philosophized that there's also a third kind of *blatte* who stands completely free and is the kind the *svennar* [literally "svens," a slang term for white Swedes] hate the most: the revolutionary *blatte*, the thought sultan. Who sees through all the lies and never lets himself get fooled. Sort of like al-Kindi,

Swedish Identity and the Literary Imaginary

who broke all the codes and wrote thousands of tight books about astronomy and philosophy but also about music and math. Last semester I was probably mostly a troublemaker, but from now on I swear I'm going to be a thought sultan. (Khemiri 2003, 38)[8]

That sense of postethnic belonging struggles to emerge throughout *Ett öga rött* mainly because the writer of the journal, Halim, is possessed of an extremely deficient understanding of geopolitics. His shining view of the Arab world is unsullied by empirical observation, a fact not lost on his emigrant father, who views his son's idealism with bemusement. Halim's project is one of *strategic essentialism*, to use Spivak's term: in his daydreams inside the golden-red cover of his journal, he collapses all nonwhite Swedes into an imagined community of native-born citizens who nevertheless don't quite belong. Yet just as Spivak found in her work on lower-caste, subaltern subjects in India, creating minority subjects inadvertently exposes the inner workings of a peculiar phenomenon: the subject effect. This confusion of cause for effect is present throughout Halim's journal, not least in the invented immigrant syntactic creole that characterizes the writing itself.

As Khemiri's writing evolved in his second novel, *Montecore: En unik tiger* (*Montecore: The Silence of the Tiger*), so did his ability to play with the complex and contradictory notions of identity creation. Not a direct sequel to *Ett öga rött*, *Montecore* continues and expands upon the same themes, with a shift in focus to a first-generation immigrant perspective hinted at but rarely directly addressed in Halim's journal. A chronicle of growing up as a nonwhite Swede in 1990s Stockholm, *Montecore* has at its center the fractured relationship between a Tunisian immigrant to Sweden and his teenage son. If Halim in *Ett öga rött* swore that "I'm always gonna stand against Swedification. I'm never gonna eat herring and schnaps at Skansen or dance in clogs around the lamest maypole. I'm never gonna let the politicians ban Buffalo shoes or tight shirts or raise the price of hairwax" (Khemiri 2005, 55–56),[9] *Montecore*'s split focus on the father-son relationship allows the older generation to ask, "Do you see now, as an adult, that you acted with the logic of racism? That you and the racists exploited the same terminology, where you praised everything brown and they everything Swedish?" (Khemiri 2006, 296–97).[10] In posing the question, *Montecore*'s fictional father evokes the thesis of Magnus Nilsson's reception study quoted above: that class distinctions have been "culturalized" by market demand for "imagined diversity."

198   PETER LEONARD

This very market desirability of nonwhite Swedish identity crops up as a literary subject in and of itself. In Marjaneh Bakhtiari's chronicle of life in the southern Swedish city of Malmö, *Kalla det vad fan du vill* (Call it whatever the hell you want), such imagined belongings inspire longing in a schoolteacher who wishes her students would bring the authentic ethnic foods, musical instruments, and folktales they must assuredly enjoy at home into the classroom: *"Please, you sweet, colorful, exotic, warm children. WOULD IT KILL YOU TO SHARE?* Carina screamed at the children. In her thoughts. . . . Oh, how she wished it was possible to bring out their warmth and lively cultures! If only there was a way to squeeze it out of them" (2005, 24–25).[11] Bakhtiari's depiction of one of the objects of Carina's desire, Soroush, suggests that he may have much in common with Halim:

> Souroush had it all: the look, the flag on the wall and a gold-plated Iran around his neck. He had lived in Iran for exactly 415 days. Something that he compensated for with posters of Ebi (a singer and exiled Iranian), the Azadi Tower in Tehran, and religious symbols from the pre-Islamic period. . . . He had painstakingly built up a homeland in twenty square meters. A nation that he felt he belonged to more and more each time somebody wondered where he originally came from. His loyalty increased every time he answered Iran. Soroush had succeeded in constructing a closeness to something distant and foreign and created for himself an identity completely of his own. (2005, 255)[12]

The attraction of constructing an ethnic otherness was not restricted to fictional characters; it reigned as well in certain literary circles. Across the Sound in Denmark, journalist Jakob Høyer wrote in *Berlingske Tidende* in 2006:

> In the big picture of Danish literature, there is a total shortage of novels from immigrant authors, a review in today's paper shows. Because of this, Danes— and Danish literature—are missing out on the voices that, in neighboring lands such as Sweden, Germany, and England, are there to create greater cultural breadth and diversity in literature. Here authors such as Salman Rushdie, Hanif Kureishi, Monica Ali in England or the best-seller Jonas Hassen Khemiri in Sweden tell stories that all ethnic groups in the two countries profit from reading. The ethnic minorities can suddenly see themselves in literature in Swedish or English, and the ethnic British or Swedes can get acquainted with new cultures in the world of the novels.[13]

Høyer was in fact instrumental in producing the edited volume *Nye Stemmer* (New voices), which gathered together a group of authors to produce exactly the kind of ethnic literature that Denmark had hitherto lacked (Aidt et al. 2007). Multicultural Scandinavia, it would seem, badly needed to be managed.

The notion of a specific kind of "ethnic voice"—whether it be the mannered syntax and slang of Halim's journal, the posters and gold chains of Soroush, or the depictions of the concrete housing project in Anyuru's poetry—serves as a bridge from the second strategy (exploring strategic essentialism) to the third: inserting the irrational and impossible into rationalist discourses of assimilation. This third strategy finds striking expression in a short story by Leiva Wenger in his 2001 collection *Till vår ära* (In our honor). "Elixir" follows a group of young Latino teenagers in Stockholm after they drink from a mysterious bottle that arrived one day in the mail. At first nothing happens, and the boys are disappointed that their daring came to naught. But slowly some changes occur: "when we talk, he talks diff rent. i said what the hell you talkin like that for fatso??? and i said you talk just like a swede. cause he did. you couldn't hear that he was brown and he said words that swedes know" (Leiva Wenger 2001, 35–36).[14] The boys' realization of the transformative power of the elixir stirs their imagination, drawing attention to how they perform their Latino identity. The changes are not merely linguistic: suddenly, the ones who have drunk the potion start performing better on literature tests in high school, showing that mastery of Strindberg that was Kallifatides's explicit goal. As their hair begins to lighten and their brown eyes become bluer, they begin to achieve the Kafkaesque metamorphosis into fully assimilated Swedish citizens. Yet the very changeability of that identity is what frightens them, as the elixir's power to transform the body is matched by its ability to transubstantiate the soul. The boys' decision that they must stop drinking the elixir "before it was too late," however, cannot prevent the shocking dénouement: "but i think it already was too late cause when i was goin home from vårberg to Fittja i didnt dare jump the turnstile. i stood there and sed to myself come on but i didnt dare thru the gate. so i walked home the whole way and thought is it cuz ive begun to be in my heart??" (39).[15]

Having provided the boys with blond hair and blue eyes, the elixir completes its work by exerting its pull on the behavior of the teenagers in the public sphere of the municipal subway. Here, in this zone of transportation intricately linked with the development of the postwar concrete suburbs, the narrator comes face-to-face with a frightening change in his interaction with the state infrastructure: no longer able to jump the turnstile and avoid paying the fare, he has begun to act like a Swede.

As a short story, "Elixir" works its own magic as both nightmare and dark satire. Underlying both modes (horror and comedy) is the text's insistence on inserting irrationality into the debate, ongoing even in 2001, over ethnic integration and social assimilation. By making corporeal the ideological assumptions of the Integration Ministry, Leiva Wenger imagines a world where the implicit goals of assimilation become manifest in the real world, creating, at least for his protagonists, bodies that betray the souls trapped inside them.

This tension between body and soul powers the last of the four strategies employed by these texts: an emphasis on the performance of identity—and identity's dependence on this performance. Examples of personal style constituting identity in books from this period are numerous: Bakhtiari's main character, Bahar, decides one day to wear a headscarf, to the consternation of her secular family. Halim, the main character in *Ett öga rött*, can usually be found carrying his journal with the red-and-gold arabesque cover as well as an ersatz Turkish fez of dubious authenticity. In "Elixir," it's less the clothes than the skin and hair of the teenagers themselves that bear witness to changing identities and belongings.

These aspects of personal style are mirrored by the inventive, even idiosyncratic approach to language that many of these authors take. Halim's invented immigrant dialect, which occasioned so much discussion in the press, now finds a multiplicity of complements and opposites in Marjaneh Bakhtiari's novel about the southern city of Malmö. *Kalla det vad fan du vill* is unrelenting in its depiction of all sorts of nonstandard linguistic performance. In addition to representing the exact phonemes immigrants from various parts of the Middle East cannot master when they speak Swedish, Bakhtiari's spelling in the original also captures the heavy southern Scanian drawl of Bahar's boyfriend's slightly racist grandfather: "How was it to come to a developed country like Sweden?" (Höur va de åo komma till ett utvecklat land som Svarje?) (2005, 78), as well as the Swenglish of her boyfriend's father: "Thank jo. Vi sej dat den. Havv it good" (129). In Khemiri's second book, *Montecore*, the protagonist's father, a first-generation immigrant from Francophone North Africa, narrates most events with a bracing admixture of improbable French loanwords—some no doubt last heard in the eighteenth-century court of Gustav III—and Arabic portmanteaus. Khemiri himself seemed fascinated by the potential of this purely artificial voice as antithesis—and antidote—to credulous readings of the language of Halim in his first novel as documentary:

"Halim of course chooses to speak 'wrong,' while Kadir is a person who does his best to embellish language ad absurdum. I wanted a voice that was obviously artificial precisely because many had praised the language in *Ett öga rött* for its authenticity. And I wanted to show that there are billions and billions of ways to have an accent" (Nelson 2006).[16]

Khemiri's explorations of authenticity and artifice in the Swedish language crystalize what is most significant about this generation of writers who imagined a postethnic future. The works of Khemiri, Anyuru, Leiva Wenger, and Bakhtiari proposed new and more flexible constructions of national belonging: stories for a Sweden yet to be. If their engagement with identity politics contrasts with the materialist tradition of class consciousness, this may serve to remind us of the imperative of individual performance in an era of transnational forces. In *Publics and Counterpublics*, literary theorist Michael Warner noted that "in modernity ... an extraordinary burden of world-making comes to be borne above all by style" (2002, 129). What else is Bahar's voluntary head scarf or Halim's affected accent but the individual impulse to imagine other possible worlds? The literary imaginaries active in these texts try to answer Warner's question of "how, by what rhetoric, one might bring a public into being when extant modes of address and intelligibility seem themselves to be a problem" (130).

Swedish postethnic literature in the early 2000s existed in this context of just such a crisis of extant modes of address and intelligibility. This afforded certain openings for a new imagination of national identity, beyond race or skin color, through the four strategies discussed here: expanding the boundaries of the literary language, exploring strategic essentialism, celebrating the irrational, and positioning identity as contingent on performance and style. The imaginaries expressed in these texts are concerned with the public sphere and the rights and responsibilities of participation in it. In the vacuum left by the decline of the rationalist, modernist project of the nation-state, the imaginary space of literary fiction became a fertile field for new possibilities of belonging.

NOTES

1. "Det, at en Literatur i vore Dage lever, viser sig i, at den sætter Problemer under Debat." All translations are mine.

2. "Man hör inga svenska ord här / till och med araberna har lärt sig / att skrika / *Mira! Mira!* / när de rusar efter en perfekt slagen passning / längs cykelvägens kant." "*Mira! Mira!*" means "Look! Look!" in Spanish; it is an exhortation to be passed the ball.

3. Khemiri's phrasing "att bryta med flit" (to have an accent on purpose) or "med flit bryter ner språket" (deliberately breaks down the language) occurs in a number of interviews following from the success of his first book, including Hjorth (2004).

4. "Nationalstaten udviskede forskellen mellem stat og samfund, og det samme gjorde efterkrigstidens arbejderpartistat eller velfærdsstat. . . . Mange skandinaver skelner slet ikke mellem stat og samfund—især ikke arbejderpartiernes tilhængere— eller mellem nation og stat. . . . Især Sverige repræsenterer et land, der stadigvæk ikke skelner mellem stat og samfund."

5. "Jag upplevde skönheten och rikedomen i språket genom Strindberg."

6. "Vad händer om man med flit bryter ner språket? Jag började spana på den maktförskjutning det innebär."

7. *Blattar* is the plural term (singular: *blatte*) for Swedes of nonwhite origin, usually derogatory except when used by members of a visible ethnic minority appropriating the term for their own use or in certain contexts where the term is self-consciously reclaimed as symbol of an identity. The *Swedish Academy Dictionary* defines the word as "a dark-skinned person of foreign origin" and dates the term to at least 1991 (although like most slang it almost certainly was in use orally before this time). No clear American English parallel exists.

8. "Blattarna på skolan är inte så många men kommer ändå i två versioner. Nummer ett är den vanliga blatten: knasaren, snikaren, snattaren, ligisten. . . . Blattesort nummer två är duktighetskillen som pluggar prov och använder finord och aldrig plankar tunnelbanan eller taggish. Som exempel . . . alla iranier som smörar lärare och vill bli tandläkare och ingenjörer. Dom tror dom får respekt men egentligen alla lärare skrattar åt dom för man fattar dom är vilsna.

"Men i dag jag har filosoferat fram det finns också en tredje blattesort som står helt fri och är den som svennarna hatar mest: revolutionsblatten, tankesultanen. Den som ser igenom alla lögner och som aldrig låter sig luras. Ungefär som al-Kindi som knäckte alla koder och skrev flera tusen grymma böcker om astronomi och filosofi men också om musik och matte. Förra terminen jag var nog mest knasaren men från nu jag svär jag ska bli tankesultan."

9. "jag svor jag kommer för alltid stå tvärtemot svenniefieringen. Aldrig jag kommer äta sur strömming med sillnubbe på Skansen eller dansa smågrodor i träskor runt töntigaste midsommarstång. Aldrig jag kommer låta politikerna förbjuda buffalos eller spänniströjor eller höja hårvaxpriser."

10. "Inser du nu som vuxen att du handlade med rasistens logik? Att du och rasisterna exponerade samma terminologi där du hyllade allt blattiskt och dom allt svenskt."

11. "*Snälla rara, färgade, exotiska, varma barn. SKULLE DET DÖDA ER ATT DELA MED ER?* skrek Carina åt barnen. I sina tankar. . . . Åååh, vad hon önskade att det var möjligt att dra fram deras varma och livliga kulturer! Om det bara hade funnits ett sätt att klämma det ur dom."

Swedish Identity and the Literary Imaginary

12. "Soroush hade allt: utseendet, flaggan på väggen och ett guldifierat Iran runt halsen. Han hade bott i Iran i exakt 415 dagar. Något som kompenserades av planscher på Ebi (sångare och exiliranier), Azaditoronet i Tehran och religiösa symboler från den förislamska tiden. ... Han hade mödosamt byggt upp ett hemland på tjugo kvadratmeter. En nation som han upplevde sig tillhöra mer och mer för varje gång någon undrade var han ursprungligen kom ifrån. Lojaliteten ökade för var gång han svarade Iran. Soroush hade lyckats konstruera en närhet till något avlägset och främmande och skapat sig en alldeles egen identitet."

13. "I dansk litteraturs store spejl er der total mangel på romaner fra indvandrerforfattere, viser en gennemgang i dagens avis. Dermed går danskerne—og dansk litteratur glip af de stemmer, der i nabolande som Sverige, Tyskland og England er med til at skabe større kulturel bredde og mangfoldighed i litteraturen. Her fortæller forfattere som Salman Rushdie, Hanif Kureishi, Monica Ali i England eller den storsælgende Jonas Hassen Khemiri i Sverige historier, som alle etniske grupper i de to lande har gevinst af at læse. De etniske minoriteter kan pludselig se sig selv i litteratur på svensk eller engelsk, og de etniske englændere og svenskere kan lære nye kulturer at kende i romanernes verden."

14. "när vi snacka så snacka han lite anor lunda. jag sa va fan pratar du så där för tjockis. han sa hur??? och jag sa du snackar fett som en svenne. för han jorde det. man hörde inte att han var svarting och han sa ord som svenskar kan."

15. "men jag tror dEt var redan för sent för när jag skulle åka hem från vårberg hit till Fittja så våga jag inte planka. jag stog där och sa till mej själv kom igen men jag vågade inte gå förbi spärren. så jag gick hem hela vägen och tänkte är det för att jag har burjat bli i järtat??"

16. "Halim väljer ju att tala 'fel,' medan Kadir är en person som gör sitt yttersta för att brodera språket in absurdum. Jag ville ha en röst som var uppenbart artificiell just för att många hyllat språket i *Ett öga rött* för dess autenticitet. Och så ville jag visa att det finns miljarders miljarder sätt att bryta på."

REFERENCES

Aidt, Naja Marie, Jens Andersen, Rushy Rashid, and Janne Breinholt Bak, eds. 2007. *Nye stemmer.* Copenhagen: Gyldendal, Berlingske.

Anyuru, Johannes. 2003. *Det är bara gudarna som är nya: Dikter.* Stockholm: Wahlström & Widstrand.

Bakhtiari, Marjaneh. 2005. *Kalla det vad fan du vill.* Stockholm: Ordfront.

Brandes, Georg. 1872. *Hovedstrømninger i det 19de Aarhundredes Litteratur.* Copenhagen: Gyldendal.

Hagerman, Maja. 2015. *Käraste Herman: Rasbiologen Herman Lundborgs gåta.* Stockholm: Norstedts.

Hauge, Hans. 2003. *Post-Danmark: Politik og æstetik hinsides det nationale.* Copenhagen: Lindhardt og Ringhof.

PETER LEONARD

Hjorth, Elizabeth. 2004. "Oslipat." *Trots Allt* 2 (February).

Høyer, Jakob. 2006. "Dansk litteratur savner indvandrere: Forlæggere og forfatterforeninger bør sikre langt større mangfoldighed i litteraturen." *Berlingske Tidende,* February 18.

Karlsson, Suzanne. 2003. "Kallifatides vägrade vara tråkig." Ledarna. http://web.archive.org/web/20070813012358/http://www.ledarna.se/portal/main.nsf/pages/chefsprofil_kallifatides.

Khemiri, Jonas Hassen. 2003. *Ett öga rött.* Stockholm: Norstedts.

Khemiri, Jonas Hassen. 2006. *Montecore: En unik tiger.* Stockholm: Norstedts.

Khemiri, Jonas Hassen. 2011. *Montecore: The Silence of the Tiger.* Translated by Rachel Willson-Broyles. New York: Alfred A. Knopf.

Leiva Wenger, Alejandro. 2001. *Till vår ära.* Stockholm: A. Bonnier.

Nelson, Cecilia. 2006. "Han närmar sig ämnet som en haj." *Göteborgs Posten,* February 15.

Nilsson, Magnus. 2010. *Den föreställda mångkulturen: Klass och etnicitet i Svensk samtidsprosa.* Hedemora: Gidlund.

Nilsson, Magnus. 2013. "Literature in Multicultural and Multilingual Sweden: The Birth and Death of the Immigrant Writer." In *Literature, Language, and Multiculturalism in Scandinavia and the Low Countries,* edited by Wolfgang Behschnitt, Sarah De Mul, and Liesbeth Minnaard, 39–61. Leiden: Rodopi.

Spivak, Gayatri Chakravorty. (1985) 2006. "Subaltern Studies: Deconstructing Historiography." In *Other Worlds: Essays in Cultural Politics,* 197–221. New York: Routledge.

Warner, Michael. 2002. *Publics and Counterpublics.* New York: Zone Books.

The Issue of Land Rights in Contemporary Sámi Literature, Art, and Music

ANNE HEITH

Already before the rise of the international movement of indigenous peoples and postcolonial studies in the 1970s, there was awareness among the Sámi of the colonization of Sápmi, the transnational region traditionally home to Sámi cultures. Sámi literature scholar Harald Gaski (1987) points out that colonization was seen by the Sámi as theft of land, which was expressed in the traditional Sámi form of chanting, called *yoik*, long before anticolonialism became a framework for expressing protest against land loss. The nomadic reindeer herders were not recognized as the owners of the lands they used (Jebens 2010), but there are also other groups of Sámi who were not nomads. John Trygve Solbakk points out that in addition to reindeer herding and fishing, important Sámi industries today include "agriculture, outfield harvesting (hunting etc.), trade, small-scale industry, service industries and the public sector" (2006, 16). Sápmi traverses four countries: Norway, Sweden, Finland, and Russia. According to Vuokko Hirvonen (2008, 15), there are approximately one hundred thousand Sámi or people of Sámi descent. Hirvonen points out that the definition of who is considered to be a Sámi varies: "In Norway and Sweden, Sáminess is based on a language criterion, while the 1995 Act on the Sámi Parliament in Finland contains wider criteria for who is considered to be a Sámi" (15). Language is one criterion, but a person can also be considered a Sámi if he or she is a descendant of a person who has been registered in the land, tax, or parish register as a "Fell, Forest or Fishing Sámi" (15). Following Hirvonen, there is no official definition in Russia of who is considered a Sámi. It is estimated that there are forty to sixty thousand Sámi in Norway, twenty to twenty-five thousand in Sweden, seven thousand in Finland, and two to four thousand in Russia (15).[1]

The theme of historical anticolonial sentiments among the Sámi is emphasized in Gaski's (1998, 24) discussion of the first book in Sámi written by a Sámi, Johan Turi's (1854–1936) *Muitalus sámiid birra* from 1910, published in English translation as *Turi's Book of Lapland* in 1966.[2] However, it was not until the 1970s that the issue of land rights was highlighted in the media in the Scandinavian countries against the backdrop of the international push for the rights of indigenous peoples. In 1975 the World Council of Indigenous Peoples (WCIP) was founded in Port Alberni, Canada, and among the founders were Sámi from Norway, Sweden, and Finland (Solbakk 2006, 248). The WCIP was a pioneering organization for establishing cooperation among indigenous peoples, and it held several conferences, one of which took place in Kiruna in northern Sweden in 1977. Eventually, its role was taken over within the UN by the Permanent Forum on Indigenous Issues, whose first leader, Sámi Ole Henrik Magga, was strongly engaged in the issue of land rights in the 1980s (see Magga 1985). Like the influential author and artist Nils-Aslak Valkeapää (1943–2001), whose Sámi name is Áillohaš, Magga criticized laws that have not recognized the reindeer-herding, nomadic North Sámi as the owners of the lands they have inhabited since ancient times.

Because the idea of ownership had its basis in settlement, the nomadic Sámi were not considered owners of the lands they used (Jebens 2010; Markussen 2013, 1), a view that prevailed during the nineteenth and twentieth centuries. However, that view has been challenged by the 1989 ILO Convention, whose article 14 declares that attention must be paid to the situation of nomadic peoples and that governments must identify the lands that nomadic peoples traditionally occupy in order to guarantee protection of their rights of ownership and possession (International Labor Organization 1989). While Norway ratified the convention in 1990, the Swedish government has so far refrained from doing so, a circumstance that underlies present-day critiques from Sámi authors and artists protesting against the exploitation of traditional Sámi lands. Nonetheless, the situation of the Sámi in Sweden improved when Sweden ratified the European Charter for Regional or Minority Languages and the Council of Europe Framework Convention for the Protection of National Minorities in 2000. Today all versions of the Sámi language are recognized as national minority languages in Sweden. While the dominant North Sámi language has a quite substantial infrastructure for the preservation of the language in the shape of publishers with a focus on Sámi literature, many of the smaller Sámi languages still struggle for survival. There are researchers who claim that because of assimilationist policies, "all minority and indigenous languages in the North Calotte are presently endangered" (Pietikäinen et al. 2010, 2).

One event of major importance that made the situation of the Sámi visible in media was the Alta dispute, which evolved in Norway in 1979–81 as a protest against the project to dam the Alta-Kautokeino River. The conflict, which attracted worldwide attention, is considered to mark the turning point in the Norwegian government's Sámi policy. Despite protests, the dam was built between 1982 and 1986. However, a Sámi resistance movement, led by a group of Sámi professionals who were able to work with the media and the public, was formed around the issue. Irja Seurujärvi-Kari has pointed out that until then, demands from the Sámi had generally been seen from the vantage point of the Norwegian welfare state either as the problems of a peripheral region or as those of an economy based on the exploitation of natural resources. In the Alta-Kautokeino case, new issues came to the fore, namely, concerns about the protection of nature and environment put forth by an international movement and a clash between the Sámi and the Norwegian government connected with an increasing awareness among the Sámi of their rights as defined in the collective rights of indigenous peoples. According to Seurujärvi-Kari (2005, 11), the dispute resulted in a new definition of a collective identity in a manifesto adopted at the 1980 Tromsø Sámi conference, which named the Sámi as a separate ethnic group with its own territory, culture, and social structure.

The themes of assimilationist policies and land loss are addressed in contemporary Sámi literature and art by those struggling for decolonization. The notion of a Sámi collective identity is of major importance in Nils-Aslak Valkeapää's photo and poetry book *Beaivi áhčážan* (1988), published in English as *The Sun, My Father* (1997), which he called a Sámi family album. The original, written in North Sámi, was published by the Sámi publishing house DAT in Kautokeino. Valkeapää depicts Sápmi as the land of the Sámi, of which they were deprived when newcomers claimed the lands. One difference between *Beaivi áhčážan* and the translations of the lyrical text into various languages is that the translations lack the large number of photographs included in the Sámi original. The fact that several of these are from the collections of museums and scientific institutions worldwide has contributed to othering and exoticizing the Sámi people (Heith 2010, 2014, 2017). While newcomers to Sápmi saw the land as terra nullius (see Smith 2008, 50–53),

Valkeapää challenges this idea of space by using ancient Sámi place-names and photographs of holy rocks and sites that have been part of the Sámi cultural landscape since ancient times, contradicting the colonizers' assumption that this was empty land free to exploit. Valkeapää's use of Sámi place-names and images of holy sites and places of cultural significance function as an anticolonial strategy, showing that there was a Sámi culture that has left traces in the lands, myths, and names. The phrase "beaivi áhčážan" (the sun, my father) refers to an ancient myth, according to which the Sámi are the children of the sun.

Protests in Gállok/Kallak and Girjas Sámi Village: Prosecuting the Swedish State

During recent decades, land loss has also become a major theme in art, music, and literature by a number of other Sámi visual artists, musical artists, and authors of Sámi descent who are similarly preoccupied with decolonization and anticolonial protest in Sweden. The plans of the British company Beowulf Mining to start an iron mine in Gállok (Kallak in Swedish) were widely discussed in the media during the years preceding the county administrative board's rejection of the plan in 2014. During the year before, there was intense discussion between those in favor of establishing an iron mine, represented officially by Jokkmokk Iron Mines, a daughter company of Beowulf Mining, and the reindeer herders from local Sámi villages and others critical of the extensive transformation of the natural environment caused by mining.[3] Among the protesters in Gállok were Sámi activists such as the painter Anders Sunna (b. 1985) and the actors and musicians Mimie (b. 1991) and Maxida Märak (b. 1988). Together with other members of the Sámi activist network Suohpanterror, Sunna and the Märak sisters protested against the mining project. They were inspired by indigenous ecocriticism, which fights against abuses of the natural environment and disruption of the lifestyle of reindeer-herding Sámi villages. The Sámi protests in Gállok/Kallak functioned as an inspiration for subsequent actions among Sámi in northern Scandinavia (Andersson 2018).[4]

The theme of land rights is addressed in the present-day Sámi cultural scene by artists and activists critical of assimilationist policies and the concomitant language loss resulting from marginalization of Sámi culture.[5] Sofia Jannok (b. 1982), a successful singer and songwriter on the Sámi cultural scene as well as in the international arena as an indigenous artist, combines yoik, rap, pop, and electronica music on her album *ORDA—This Is My Land*, released in 2016. The Sámi word *orda* means "tree line," but Sofia Jannok has

Land Rights in Sámi Literature, Art, and Music 209

extended the meaning to refer to the meeting place of diverse landscapes, which have the same right to exist.

The lyrics are performed in three languages: North Sámi, Swedish, and English. The album contains fifteen tracks interspersed with recordings from the court case between Girjas Sámi village and the Swedish state in 2015, in which Girjas Sámi village prosecuted the state over its right to administer small-game hunting and fishing permits in the mountain areas of the Sámi village, traditionally used as pastures. From Jannok's vantage point the court case represented a righteous protest against the state's colonial oppression of the Sámi people, and she places it in a lyric narrative about colonialism, racism, discrimination, and silencing. A theme of several of the album's tracks is challenging the majority's and elite's power to define, manifest in the resistance and reluctance on the part of the Swedish state to acknowledge the Sami as a colonized people. In this respect the lyrics correspond with those of popular protest songs that give voice to disempowered and marginalized groups, and in a radio interview Jannok mentioned the American indigenous artist Buffy Sainte-Marie as an influence (Wicklin 2017). In *ORDA—This Is My Land* there are echoes of Sainte-Marie's hit "Yes, This Is My Country," the title track of the movie *Soldier Blue* from 1970, whose main theme is the massacre of Cree Indians at Sand Creek in 1864.

Jannok's anticolonial, indigenous perspective is reflected in several titles on the album. The phrase "this is my land" in the album's title explicitly declares land rights as the album's major theme, underlined by recordings from the court proceedings in which a Swedish state representative questions the Sámis' rights to the lands. Songs like "We Are Still Here" and "Colonizer" function as a counternarrative, highlighting Sweden's colonial history. While the state spokesperson denies any historical Sámi presence in the disputed area, Jannok claims that Sápmi is ancient Sámi territory, which the Sámi ought to control. The notion that the Sámi were there first is expressed in lines such as "fine that we were first, but we are still here" ("At the Back of My *Kolt*"); "I was here first, not last," and "from us you stole the land once upon a time" ("Snow Lioness"); "steal our mother, thieves are not to blame / that's when laws are written by the same" ("We Are Still Here / Mii leat dás ain").[6]

Jannok's lyrics and performances aim at creating a "Sáminess" that challenges and undermines a colonizing discourse. The album title, *We Are Still Here*, signals that the Sámi are a resilient people who do not accept being oppressed. The themes of resistance and resilience are emphasized in the music video with the same title, made before the album was released, in cooperation with the artist Anders Sunna, who uses portraits of the Sámi pioneer Elsa Laula Renberg (1877–1931) and Anne Karen Sara, a Sámi debater engaged in the youth organization Noereh. The portraits were projected onto a translucent screen with the text "WE ARE STILL HERE." Today, Renberg has attained an iconic status as a pioneering political activist struggling to improve the conditions of the Sámi people, representing a cultural heritage that shows a history of Sámi resistance, resilience, and struggle for self-determination. It was awarded the best music video prize at ImagineNative Canada, the world's largest indigenous film festival.

An Epic Poem about Land Loss, Displacement, and Resilience: Linnea Axelsson's *Aednan*

In the current activist scene in Sweden, the case of Beowulf Mining functions as a catalyst, inspiring protest from Sámi and environmentalists against the establishment of mines in lands used as pastures. Land loss is a central theme of Linnea Axelsson's (b. 1980) epic poem *Aednan*, published in 2018 by the prestigious publisher Bonniers in Stockholm and winner of the August Prize in the fiction category, annually awarded by the Swedish Publishers' Association. Axelsson made her debut with the novel *Tvillingsmycket* (The twin jewel) in 2010. She was born in Porjus, a small place in the municipality of Jokkmokk in the county of Norrbotten in northern Sweden. Porjus, which is a significant place in *Aednan*, grew when a power plant was built there. The oldest plant, which today is a museum, was built between 1910 and 1915. Later a new plant was constructed between 1971 and 1982. Like *Tvillingsmycket, Aednan* is published in Swedish, although it contains Sámi place-names, some Sámi personal names, and an occasional phrase in Sámi.

Aednan is a North Sámi word meaning "the land, the ground, the earth." The book is about three generations of Sámi, starting with a section about the reindeer herder Ber-Joná and his wife, Risten. The opening of the poem consists of a monologue by Ber-Joná in the spring winter of 1913 at Gobmejávri, a lake in Kiruna municipality where the nomadic Sámi used to stay overnight when moving their herds.[7] Ber-Joná and his wife are at home in this land, which has been used by their kin since ancient times. They experience the lands as a living, sentient being, a pluriverse without borders between humans and nature (see Adamson 2001, 9; Adamson and Monani 2017). In this place, at this time, they hear heartbeats in the ground and the wind speaking with the cloth of the tent (Axelsson 2018, 30–31). However, the connection between humans, nature, and different species is disrupted when Ber-Joná and

Risten are compulsorily transferred from their settlement after the river they live by is dammed. Indeed, Ber-Joná and Risten have to decamp several times because of lands being flooded in connection with the damming of rivers. This section of the book depicts a break in continuity, their loss of a sense of belonging, as their traditional way of life is severely affected by dislocation from lands that are part of their identity. After the displacement, they listen quietly to the silence of the tormented river (Axelsson 2018, 179).[8]

Transfers of Sámi are related to the closure of borders as well as the damming of rivers. In the early twentieth century, the number of settled farmers was increasing, which caused conflicts with Sámi who seasonally brought their herds to the coastland. In Sweden the Crown encouraged land reclamation and claimed rights to the areas north of the county of Hälsingland in the fourteenth century. In the nineteenth century, the number of farmers in northern Sweden increased, as there was an excess of births over deaths. When the population grew there was insufficient farmland, which motivated migration to places where farmland was available.[9] The settler-farmers saw the Sámi as competitors for land use. In adjacent Norway, nationalism was strong during this period, which led to demands that "Swedish" Sámi should stay on their side of the border; the result was a new convention restricting their use of lands in Norway. As a consequence, many Swedish Sámi were left without summer pastures for their herds. The Swedish authorities' response to this problem was to force a large number of families to move south from the Karesuando area.[10]

In an interview, Linnea Axelsson mentioned that her maternal grandmother's family was one of the Sámi families transferred from Karesuando to Porjus (Heikki 2018). In her epic poem, the summer pastures on the coast of northern Norway are part of *aednan*, the lands traditionally used by Sámi such as Ber-Joná and Risten who have their winter settlements in Sweden. The consequences of land loss related to the damming of rivers and closure of borders are depicted in *Aednan*'s section about the next generation.

The setting of the beginning of the second part of the poem is a flat in Porjus in the winter of 1977. The lyrical "I" is a woman of Sámi descent, Lise, who has married a Swedish man, with whom she has two children. Lise represents a Sámi who has become assimilated. Her daughter, Sandra, on the other hand, represents the present-day Sámi who are reclaiming the lost language and culture of their ancestors. While Sandra is depicted as an activist fighting for Sámi rights, her brother is portrayed as ambivalent and lost. Thus they represent two dispositions often portrayed in present-day Sámi literature, namely, resilience and resistance, on the one hand, and identity loss, on the other. In Lise's monologue, her daughter's feelings about Sámi culture and territory are described as love:

This land
she loves

Which she and her
friends wanted to defend
against a foreign
mining company. (Axelsson 2018, 278)[11]

Through the depiction of three generations, the poem presents a narrative of belonging and connectedness with *aednan,* dislocation and loss, and present-day activism reclaiming the land and culture, which is conveyed through Sandra's story. Sandra learns the lost Sámi language, and she sews a traditional costume, a *kolt.* The Girjas case is explicitly mentioned in a section in which Sandra is the lyrical "I." The section is preceded by the time reference: "The second day of the legal proceedings. May 2015" (Axelsson 2018, 449).[12]

Concluding Comments

Partly through the engagement of the International Movement of Indigenous Peoples in issues related to land rights and cultural heritage and partly through postcolonial frames of interpretation, the prerogative of the majority and domineering social group to interpret land rights for the Sámi is being challenged. Valkeapää, Jannok, and Axelsson contribute to creating a Sámi collective with a land it has inhabited and used since ancient times.[13] They question the legitimacy of colonizing processes in the ways they construct indigeneity in their artwork, drawing attention to the issue of control over land and self-determination (cf. Maaka and Fleras 2000, 95). When Jannok claims in the title of her album from 2016 that "this is my land," she gives voice to resilience and resistance, like the pioneer Elsa Laula-Renberg in the early twentieth century and the pioneer in the making of modern Sámi literature Nils-Aslak Valkeapää from the 1980s and onward. Valkeapää's trilogy *Ruokto Váimmus* alludes to a nomadic concept of home and place. The title means "the home in the heart," meaning that the nomadic North Sámi did not conceive of a specific, limited place of permanent settlement as "home." The English

Land Rights in Sámi Literature, Art, and Music 213

translation, *Trekways of the Wind*, from 1994, is the first major lyrical work by Valkeapää published in English.[14]

Axelsson's *Aednan*, finally, is a recent example of a poem by an author of Sámi descent that focuses on colonization; loss of land, culture, and identity; and resilience and resistance. While the Alta dispute is a backdrop of Valkeapää's engagement in the issue of compulsory transfers of Sámi and land loss, the conflict between Beowulf Mining and activists and reindeer herders in Gállok/Kallak in the Jokkmokk area, as well as Girjas Sámi village's prosecution of the Swedish state, form a backdrop for Jannok's, Sunna's, and Axelsson's performances of critical Sámi challenges to colonialism, marginalization, and disempowerment in the shape of popular music, visual art, and literature.

NOTES

This chapter is an outcome of the project "Making Place in Literature: Meänmaa in Contemporary Tornedalian Texts," funded by the Swedish Research Council, project number 2015-01164, and the project "Other Places in the Teaching of Literature: Sápmi, Meänmaa, and Migrant Cartographies," funded by Umeå School of Education.

1. Figures concerning the number of Sámi differ. In *The Sámi People: A Handbook* (2006), John Trygve Solbakk mentions that the total number of Sámi is estimated to be sixty to seventy thousand. He mentions that around forty thousand reside in Norway. According to a survey, approximately twenty-five thousand of these use the Sámi language. The figure given for Sweden is an estimate of twenty thousand Sámi, of which twenty-seven hundred are employed in the reindeer-herding industry. An estimated seventy-five hundred live in Finland, and approximately two thousand live in Russia (Solbakk 2006, 16).

2. According to the Sámi literature scholar Vuokko Hirvonen (2005, 200), Turi wrote the book in cooperation with the Danish artist and ethnographer Emilie Demant Hatt. Gaski (1998, 24), on the other hand, mentions that Demant Hatt translated the book into Danish and encouraged Turi to write it.

3. The conflict is the theme of the Swedish documentary *Gállok—kampen i Sameland*, broadcast on August 16, 2018 (SVT2). Another theme highlighted is the issue of Sámi identity: Who has the right to call himself or herself a Sámi? One of the protesters against the mining project, photographer Tor Lundberg, has decided to cherish his Sámi ancestry and to retrieve his Sámi family name, which had been lost in the process of assimilation. His former friend, a miner, questions Lundberg's Sámi identity, claiming that he is not a Sámi. The miner is in favor of creating job opportunities through the establishment of a mine, while the protesters highlight the short-sightedness of

mining projects, known to leave large amounts of toxic waste not handled sustainably by the mining companies. Another problem emphasized is that of loss of lands for the reindeer herders.

4. *Suohpan* is a North Sámi word meaning "throwing a lasso." The network produces a large number of posters, which can be seen on its Facebook group. In connection with the protests in Gállok, Anders Sunna made a couple of posters directed against the plans of Beowulf Mining.

5. There are multiple studies of assimilationist policies affecting the Sámi. One example is Lennart Lundmark's *Stulet land: Svensk makt på samiskt land* (2008), and another is Daniel Lindmark and Olle Sundström's edited collection, *De historiska relationerna mellan Svenska kyrkan och samerna* (2016).

6. The quotes and titles in Swedish are my translations: "fine att vi var först, men vi finns kvar" ("I ryggen på min kolt"), "jag var här först inte sist," "av oss stal du landet en gång" ("Snölejoninna"). The last quote is in English in the original, and the title is in English and North Sámi. *Kolt* is the name of the traditional Sámi costume. Today this costume functions as a positive identity marker, while historically, Sámi who wore it were stigmatized. It is significant that the Sámi girl Elle Marja in the 2016 movie *Sámi Blood* (Swedish title *Sameblod*, written and directed by Amanda Kernell) gets rid of her *kolt*, which singles her out as a Sámi when she goes south. A main theme of the movie is Elle Marja's attempts to become assimilated into the Swedish majority society.

7. "Spring winter" is a direct translation of one of the eight Sámi seasons.

8. "Sen låg vi stilla / och lyssnade // till den plågade / älvens tystnad."

9. See "Sveriges koloniala historia," website of the Sámi Parliament (Sametinget), https://www.sametinget.se/62102.

10. The closure of borders and the subsequent transfer south of Sámi families from Karesuando are the themes of an unsigned article on http://www.samer.se. The title of the article is "Stängda gränser och okända marker" (Closed borders and unknown lands), accessed August 17, 2018. The website is administered by Samiskt informationscentrum (Sámi Information Center) by direction of Sametinget, which in its turn was directed by the government to create a platform for disseminating information about the Sámi in Sweden.

11. "Den här marken / hon älskar // Som hon och hennes / vänner ville försvara / mot ett utländskt / gruvföretag."

12. "Rättegångens andra dag. Maj 2015."

13. Anders Sunna also evokes a Sámi "we," but he highlights conflicts among Sámi people, not least in works related to his family's struggle to preserve their reindeer mark. This is the case, for example, with the painting *Area Infected*, Sunna's contribution to the exhibition *Eight Sámi Artists* at Bildmuseet, Umeå, when Umeå was a European Capital of Culture in 2014 (see Heith 2015).

14. The three books are *Giđa ija čuovgadat* (White spring nights, published in 1974), *Lávllo vizar biellocizáš* (Bluethroat, twitter, sing, 1976), and *Ádjaga silbasuonat* (Streams' silver veins, 1981). The English translation is by Lars Nordström, Harald Gaski, and Ralph Salisbury.

REFERENCES

Adamson, Joni. 2001. *American Indian Literature, Environmental Justice, and Ecocriticism: The Middle Place.* Tucson: University of Arizona Press.

Adamson, Joni, and Salma Monani. 2017. "Introduction: Cosmovisions, Ecocriticism, and Indigenous Studies." In *Ecocriticism and Indigenous Studies: Conversations from Earth to Cosmos*, edited by Salma Monani and Joni Adamson, 1–19. New York: Routledge.

Andersson, Camilla. 2018. "Suohpanterror vill förändra." February 18. www.samer.se.

Axelsson, Linnea. 2018. *Aednan.* Stockholm: Bonniers.

Gaski, Harald. 1987. *Med ord ska tyvene fordrives: Om samenes episk poetiske diktning.* Karasjok: Davvi Media.

Gaski, Harald. 1998. *Skriftbilder: Samisk litteraturhistorie.* Karasjok: Davvi Girji OS.

Heikki, Jörgen. 2018. "Samiskt släktepos på vers—om tvångsförflyttningar och kolonialism." Sameradion and SVT Sápmi, February 26. https://sverigesradio.se/sida/artikel.aspx?programid=4416&artikel=6894466.

Heith, Anne. 2010. "Särskiljandets logik i en kolonial och en antikolonial diskurs: Nils-Aslak Valkeapääs *Beaivi áhčážan.*" *Edda: Nordisk tidskrift for litteraturforskning* 97(4): 335–50.

Heith, Anne. 2014. "Valkeapää's Use of Photographs in *Beaivi áhčážan*: Indigenous Counter-History versus Documentation in the Age of Photography." *Acta Borealia: A Nordic Journal of Circumpolar Societies* 31(1): 41–58.

Heith, Anne. 2015. "Enacting Colonised Space: Katarina Pirak Sikku and Anders Sunna." In "Rethinking Sámi Cultures in Museums," special issue, *Nordisk Museologi / The Journal Nordic Museology* 2:69–83.

Heith, Anne. 2017. "Tradition och förnyelse i Nils-Aslak Valkeapääs bidrag till samisk kulturell mobilisering." In *Sápmi i ord och bild II*, edited by Kajsa Andersson, 575–85. Stockholm: Förlag AB.

Hirvonen, Vuokko. 2005. "Literature." In *The Saami: A Cultural Encyclopaedia*, edited by Ulla-Maija Kulonen, Irja Seurujärvi-Kari, and Risto Pulkkinen, 199–203. Vammala: Suomalaisen Kirjallisuuden Seura.

Hirvonen, Vuokko. 2008. *Voices from Sápmi: Sámi Women's Path to Authorship.* Kautokeino: DAT.

International Labor Organization. 1989. "Convention C169—Indigenous and Tribal Peoples Convention, 1989 (No. 169)." ilo.org/dyn/normlex/en/f?p=NORMLEXPUB:12100:0::NO::P12100_ILO_CODE:C169#A14.

Jannok, Sofia. 2016. *ORDA—This Is My Land.* Gamlestans Grammofonbolag.

Jebens, Otto. 2010. *Det rettshistoriske og folkrettslige grunnlag for eiendomsretten til grunnen i indre Finnmark*. Kautokeino: Sámi Dutkaninstituhtta.

Lindmark, Daniel, and Olle Sundström, eds. 2016. *De historiska relationerna mellan Svenska kyrkan och samerna*. 2 vols. Skellefteå: Artos & Norma Bokförlag.

Lundmark, Lennart. 2008. *Stulet land: Svensk makt på samisk mark*. Stockholm: Ordfront.

Maaka, Roger, and Augie Fleras. 2000. "Engaging with Indigeneity: Tino Rangatiratanga in Aotearoa." In *Political Theory and the Rights of Indigenous Peoples*, edited by Duncan Ivison, Paul Patton, and Will Sanders, 89–111. Cambridge: Cambridge University Press.

Magga, Ole Henrik. 1985. "Are We Finally to Get Our Rights?" In *Native Power: The Quest for Autonomy and Nationhood of Indigenous Peoples*, edited by Jens Brøsted et al., 15–22. Bergen: Universitetsforlaget.

Markussen, Bjarne. 2013. "Law and Multimodal Aesthetics: Nils-Aslak Valkeapää's *Trekways of the Wind*." *Journal of Illustration Studies*, December.

Pietikäinen, Sari, Leena Huss, Sirkka Laihiala-Kankainen, Ulla Aikio-Puoskari, and Pia Lane. 2010. "Regulating Multilingualism in the North Calotte: The Case of Kven, Meänkieli and Sámi Languages." *Acta Borealia* 27(1): 1–23.

Seurujärvi-Kari, Irja. 2005. "Alta Dispute." In *The Saami: A Cultural Encyclopaedia*, edited by Ulla-Maija Kulonen, Irja Seurujärvi-Kari, and Risto Pulkkinen, 11–12. Helsinki: Suomalaisen Kirjallisuuden Seura.

Smith, Linda Tuhiwai. 2008. *Decolonizing Methodologies: Research and Indigenous Peoples*. London: Zed Books.

Solbakk, John Trygve. 2006. *The Sámi People: A Handbook*. Karasjok: Davvi Girji OS.

Valkeapää, Nils-Aslak. 1985. *Ruoktu Váimmus*. Kautokeino: DAT.

Valkeapää, Nils-Aslak. 1988. *Beaivi áhčážan*. Kautokeino: DAT.

Valkeapää, Nils-Aslak. 1994. *Trekways of the Wind*. 2nd ed. Translated by Lars Nordström, Harald Gaski, and Ralph Salisbury. Kautokeino: DAT.

Valkeapää, Nils-Aslak. 1997. *The Sun, My Father*. Translated by Lars Nordström, Harald Gaski, and Ralph Salisbury. Kautokeino: DAT.

Wicklin, Martin. 2017. "Sofia Jannok—om identitet, musik och Sápmis vidder." Sverige Radio, November 19. https://sverigesradio.se/avsnitt/992988.

Afro-Swedish Renaissance

R YAN T HOMAS S KINNER

In this chapter, I trace the contours and explore the substance of an emergent and currently effervescent Afro-Swedish public culture as manifested in the literary, performing, and visual arts.[1] My discussion focuses on the lives and labor of several prominent Black artists working in (and sometimes against) the institutions and markets of Sweden's public and private culture sector. These artists, their audiences, and the communities of which they are a part significantly contribute to Sweden's "cultural life" (*kulturliv*) while confronting endemic racism, actively promote social pluralism against the hardening boundaries of cultural difference, and increasingly captivate the public imagination while resisting assumptions of exoticism and foreignness. By examining the diversity and vitality of this diasporic art world, I claim that what we are witnessing is nothing short of an Afro-Swedish social and cultural "renaissance"—a conjunctural moment of diasporic consciousness, creativity, and critique manifested in a florescence of artistic production, commentary, and interpretation.

To support this claim, this chapter will proceed in three steps by (1) locating an elusive "Afro-Swedish" subject position within the ostensibly "color-blind" public sphere of contemporary Sweden; (2) thickly describing five recent examples of creative practice that give empirical substance to the notion of an "Afro-Swedish public culture"; and (3) reflecting on the conceptual implications of qualifying this public culture and the community it constitutes with the term "renaissance"—implications relevant, I believe, to current Scandinavian and Black studies alike.

WHO ARE THE AFRO-SWEDES?

The term "Afro-Swedish" is relatively new to the Swedish lexicon. It entered the public sphere with the founding of the National Union of Afro-Swedes

(Afrosvenskarnas riksförbund) in 1990 but has gained currency as a term of identification only in the past decade. Today, Afro-Swedish voices are central to ongoing and frequently contentious debates about the possibilities and constraints of social diversity and multiculturalism, as well as a growing critical interest in the history, ideology, and practice of race and racism in Swedish society. Formal definitions of "Afro-Swedish" are typically broad (see, e.g., McEachrane 2012), referring to any inhabitant of Sweden with some form of African background. This may include recent migrants from the African continent; children with African parentage; people who trace their heritage within the broader African diaspora, including the Caribbean, North and South America, and elsewhere in Europe; and individuals who are adopted from Africa or its diaspora. Such definitions suggest multiple subject positions within a diffuse diasporic community. Thus, while some Afro-Swedes may emphasize an intrinsic sense of racial solidarity—embracing a "Black" or "Brown" identity, for example—others might privilege more geographic, historical, and/or filial ties to Africa and its diaspora.[2] Most, however, will acknowledge the extrinsic racism that subjects people of African descent in Sweden to everyday exoticism, exclusion, insult, and injury.[3]

Calculating the size of this community is difficult. A 2014 report on "Afrophobia" in Sweden estimated the Afro-Swedish population to be upward of 180,000 individuals (Hübinette, Beshir, and Kawesa 2014). More recent data from Statistics Sweden (a state-sponsored institute that tracks national demography) indicate that there are approximately 200,000 Swedish residents born in sub-Saharan Africa alone. If one includes children born in Sweden to one or two parents from sub-Saharan Africa, this number rises to more than 300,000 individuals.[4] But national statistics do not tell us the size of the *next* generation of Afro-Swedes, that is, people of African descent whose parents are native-born Swedes. A fixation on "country of birth" (*födelseland*) obscures their demographic presence entirely. Nor do the current statistics allow us to pinpoint the number of Swedes with roots in the broader African diaspora (e.g., from the Americas, the Caribbean, or elsewhere in Europe), given the demographic heterogeneity of many of these countries. The actual number of Afro-Swedes may be in the range of 400,000 to 500,000 people, but that is hard to know for sure.[5] This is because acknowledging the presence of such a broad population of people of African descent posits a more generalized Afro-diasporic identity, which contravenes an official statistical model that emphasizes national origin and obfuscates transnational ties. Further, and perhaps most controversially, acknowledging such an inclusive African-descended population suggests the demographic relevance, if not the reality, of *race*.

The idea that "race matters" (to paraphrase Cornel West) is, simply put, anathema to reigning notions of Swedish being and belonging. From this perspective, to think in terms of race risks reproducing discredited notions of biological and genetic difference. On these grounds, the Swedish state has recently sought to remove the word "race" altogether from legislative and juridical documents (Hambraeus 2014; McEachrane 2014b; see also Brännström 2016). More generally, registering "race" disrupts and disturbs progressive notions of a distinctively Swedish antiracism predicated on decades of anticolonial advocacy, antiapartheid struggle, and Third World solidarity (Hübinette 2013). In this way, Olof Palme, the twentieth-century wunderkind of Swedish social democracy, could assert in 1965 that "foul racial theories have never gained purchase" in Sweden. This statement was made a mere seven years after the dissolution of the state-sponsored Institute for Race Biology in Uppsala, which advanced the theory and practice of eugenics.[6] As a result of such social, political, and historical myopia, current analytic terms such as *rasifierad*—indicating the structural, ideological, and practical production of racial difference—are frequently dismissed in the public sphere as signs of an imported and illegitimate "identity politics" (see, e.g., Lundberg 2016), and official statistics routinely elide racially marked modes of identification such as "Afro-Swedish" (Westerlund 2015).

This color-blind antiracism has had the perplexing effect of making it difficult—sometimes even impossible—to "talk about race" in the Swedish public sphere, which includes interrogations of "whiteness" as a normative, historically deep, and hegemonic ontology (Hübinette et al. 2012; see also Miller 2017).[7] Further, the discourse of color blindness and assumptions of antiracism obscure routine institutional acts of racial profiling and efface collective narratives of everyday racism. As a host of public testimonies, literary narratives, and sociological studies show, many Swedes who are phenotypically non-European—that is, *not white*—share the experience of being labeled foreign, even interlopers in their own country, or, in polite company, not "ethnically Swedish" (see, e.g., Diakité 2016; Hübinette and Tigervall 2009; Khemiri 2013; Norrby 2015). And if you are *Black* in Sweden today, you are not only *not Swedish* but also more likely to encounter disproportionate discrimination in the housing and labor markets (Wolgast, Molina, and Gardell 2018) and face a heightened risk of being victimized by xenophobic and racist hate crime (Djärv, Westerberg, and Frenzel 2015, 39; see also Wigerfelt and Wigerfelt 2017). The issue, in other words, involves not just individual prejudice but also widespread and systemic racism.[8] Creatively circumventing the state's narrowly defined demographic discourse and actively responding to the reality of anti-Black discrimination and abuse, a new generation of people of African descent in Sweden has taken an increasingly public stance in asserting the terms of its racialized status and identity and confronting the structural and everyday hindrances to its agency and well-being as a minority public. These are the "Afro-Swedes."[9]

In what follows, I focus on the ways in which current works of literature, theater, film, music, and visual art serve to foster a coherent but no less complex Afro-diasporic public culture in Sweden today. By highlighting the figures, forms, and features of an "African presence" in the Swedish culture sector (to paraphrase the late Alioune Diop), I hope to elucidate (in the spirit of W. E. B. Du Bois) the particular double, or, as the following narratives suggest, the *multiple* consciousness born of being Black in Sweden today. I will tell five stories about five Afro-Swedish artists and their recent work, each an individually coherent piece of what I have come to understand as a broader sociocultural project. I pay attention to the way these artists—coming from various walks of life and with wide-ranging expressive means at their disposal—critically and creatively address the reality of being marked by their Blackness in a society that overwhelmingly promotes a color-blind and anti-racist outlook. In concluding, I will argue that a specifically Afro-diasporic concept of "renaissance" usefully illuminates and clarifies the conjuncture of these modes of expression and identification in Sweden today.

A Swedish Shore on the Black Atlantic

It is 2003, and I am standing in Stortorget, a large public square in downtown Malmö. Joining me amid the lingering light of a late afternoon in early summer are a few thousand others, all waiting to hear a hip-hop artist named Timbuktu. When the stage lights come on and the beat drops to the tune of "The Botten Is Nådd," the crowd erupts with a cheer. I lift my wife's ten-year-old cousin onto my shoulders so that she can see the show better. Jason "Timbuktu" Diakité is her *favorite* musician. Eleven years later, I am standing on a grassy field at the Uppsala Botanical Gardens, once again waiting in a large crowd for Timbuktu to take the stage. It's a generationally mixed group, but most of those around me are in their early twenties, college students in this university town. A few songs into the show, I turn my gaze from the

Afro-Swedish Renaissance

performance to the audience. Everyone around me is rapping and singing along. They know every word. At that moment, I realize that an entire generation of Swedish youth has grown up with Diakité's music. And as I dance, sing, and rap with this throng of fans, I think, What could be more "Swedish" than *Timbuktu*?

The question is rhetorical, but the answer, once the lights go off and the crowd goes home, is complicated. The name Timbuktu is a tribute to Diakité's paternal heritage. A reference to the storied urban center of Islamic thought on the Saharan frontier, it is a name Diakité shares with his great-great-grandmother Myla Miller, an enslaved woman with origins in what is today Mali in West Africa, where the modern city of Timbuktu still lies (Diakité 2016, 163). Diakité grew up in the small city of Lund in the south of Sweden, another historic university town. There, as a person of color in a place where pale complexions predominate, Diakité's father would always remind his son that Diakité is *Black* and a son of Harlem, though his mother was a white woman from Scranton, Pennsylvania. For most of his life, Diakité struggled to understand, value, and claim this mixed heritage. "Up until just recently," he tells me, "I felt this *hälftenskap*, that I was only *half* of everything." Growing up, he felt condemned to a "no-man's-land" populated by fraught and persistent questions: "Who am I? Am I African or American? Am I Swedish or American? Am I Black or white? Who are my people?"[10]

Published in the fall of 2016, *En droppe midnatt* (A drop of midnight) is Diakité's soulful and frequently poetic reflection on these thorny questions of identity, posed at the contemporary and historic intersection of Africa, Europe, and America. It tells the story of his remarkable upbringing, growing up as an African American boy with a southern Swedish accent and an ear for hip-hop in the waning years of the welfare state. More broadly, it relates the nuances of a particular but by no means unique diasporic experience, bearing witness to an increasingly diverse but still provincial Sweden that Diakité calls "home" and a distant but ever-present America, Diakité's "home away from home," where burdens born of slavery and Jim Crow endure and echo across the Atlantic. Race is at the center of this story. "We are a few telling the nonwhite story [in Sweden today]," Diakité said of his book in a recent interview with *Kupé* magazine, placing himself in the company of "authors like Johannes Anyuru, Jonas Hassen Khemiri, Fanna Ndow Norrby, and a handful of others" (quoted in Hübinette 2016). By calling this literary field "nonwhite" (*icke-vit*), Diakité aligns himself with a critically conscious and culturally prolific community of Swedes whose collective voice has argued—through a variety of media and from different perspectives but no less coherently—that race matters (see, e.g., Diaz et al. 2015).

"The uninitiated might wonder why I emphasize [race] so much," Diakité stated in another recent interview in the Swedish press (Nordström 2016). "But it's because it has had such a strong impact on my life." Then, in a direct address to the reporter interviewing him and the imagined community this exponent of the Swedish media represents, Diakité said, "You'll have to excuse me for saying this, but it's only white people who have this kind of objection [to talking about race]. They haven't had to grapple with it every day of their lives." These particular experiences of struggle have also led Diakité to a sense of solidarity. "The Black Swedish history has not been written down in book form so many times," Diakité told the reporter. "There is value in telling these stories." With me, Diakité speaks of an emergent sense of what he calls *dubbelskap* (doubleness) and, echoing Du Bois, *tvåsamhet* (twoness), the feeling that his Swedish upbringing and African American cultural heritage are not irreconcilable, that being Black in Sweden should be not cause for shame but a source of pride: "Instead of this constant, 'I'm half-this, half-that,' just that semantic change led to some door opening up for me."[11]

Diasporic Dialogues down in the Valley

When one speaks with Josette Bushell-Mingo, sparks fly. The actor, director, cultural advocate, and social activist is a person whose charisma, intellect, and passion refract in all directions. Like lightning bolts, words and gestures chart circuitous paths through topics that are also emotions and relationships, topics that are also the subjects of art. In the presence of this British-born, Caribbean-rooted, and Swedish-resident renaissance woman, the boundary between art and life disappears at the same time that the African diaspora comes into sharp focus. Onstage or offstage, she embodies and exudes her creative practice, which cannot be divorced from her concerns for and engagement with social justice and the struggle to support and sustain Black lives in particular.

On April 18, 2016, we meet at a hole-in-the-wall sushi shop in the trendy Hornstull neighborhood in Stockholm, where she lives. Accompanied by cups of miso soup and hot green tea, we are there to talk about her current theatrical project, *En druva i solen*, a Swedish adaptation of Lorraine Hansberry's classic African American Broadway show, *A Raisin in the Sun*. Directed by Bushell-Mingo, the critically acclaimed play has been on tour in Sweden for the past three months with the National Theater Company and has just wrapped up a series of encore performances in Stockholm, one of which I was able to attend. Remarkably, Hansberry's landmark play had never been staged in Sweden before. Further, its predominantly Black cast and crew represent another first for a culture sector that has long struggled to acknowledge and remediate an endemic lack of social and cultural diversity both onstage and behind the scenes (see Kushkush 2016).

But for Bushell-Mingo, this play is not primarily about the failings of a normatively white Swedish art world. As she puts it, "This is not about the education of whites, this is about the education of Blacks."[12] As she sees it, *En druva i solen*, like *A Raisin in the Sun* before it, is first and foremost about the Black experience and, more specifically, how a story rooted in African American history might translate and signify to a contemporary Afro-Swedish audience. "I'm interested to know what happens when the diaspora meets and they share their experiences," she explains. "Not because I want to observe but because I want to be part of it. . . . I want to create a room where people can talk like this." Bushell-Mingo's intent is not to exclude white audiences, still by far the majority public for this and other national productions in Sweden, but she is interested in, as she puts it, "creating a room" for diasporic encounters. In her view, "the process of [staging] *A Raisin in the Sun* was historic not just because the play was being here for the first time but [because] you were watching actors transform, claiming a space as Black people."

This has meant making space for dialogue and debate among Black performers, audiences, and culture brokers, allowing them to constructively and critically explore their identities together around stories told from the Afro-diasporic archive. In support of this dialogue, Bushell-Mingo invited members of the Afro-Swedish association Black Coffee to attend a preview of *En druva i solen* and insisted that the postshow conversation privilege their voices. This caused some private consternation among white audience members in attendance who cringed at this manifestation of apparent racial separatism in what they view to be a free and open (and, ideally, color-blind and antiracist) society. In the face of such critiques, Bushell-Mingo is undeterred: "Our Afro-Swedish community does not have a home." While her vision is ultimately to create a permanent physical space for the Afro-diasporic arts in Sweden, her current efforts are focused more on repertoire, telling stories that foreground Black lives told from Black perspectives.[13] "*En druva i solen* is not going to change racism," she says, "but it [does] give us a place to rest. It gives us a place to gain courage, and it gives us the insight into argument and what is possible if we lose" (see also Kronlund 2017).

For Bushell-Mingo, the very real prospect of still more loss in the Black community (of status, integrity, dignity, and, indeed, *life*) demands a rigorous and often onerous curatorial method. She calls this, invoking one of her mother's household refrains, "staying in the valley."[14] Speaking of her Afrodiasporic audiences, she says: "I know you want to get to the top, but you need to stay in this bit. . . . Stay in the darkness. Stay in the shit. Stay in the difficult stuff. Face it. Call it out." In her view, it is no less important for her white audiences to "go down" and cohabit these spaces too, but their presence demands a particular ethics of listening with a deference that goes against the grain of privilege. She stresses, on the one hand, the learning that is possible from simply bearing witness and, on the other, the growth that is possible from simply being present. "You go through that experience together, and you walk out of the theater together, and you say, 'I have seen, I have learned, I have witnessed. I understand something else about myself'" and, one might infer, about each other.

At Home in the African World

On December 11, 2016, I sit down with writer and director Dani Kouyaté in a cozy French pastry shop on New York's Upper West Side to discuss his fifth feature film, *Medan vi lever* (*While We Live*). Officially released in Stockholm earlier that fall, the film is Kouyaté's first Swedish production and had just debuted in the United States at the African Diaspora International Film Festival. *While We Live* stages a modern family's transnational experience in which geographic and generational distances spanning two societies—Swedish and Gambian—shape the divergent though not irreconcilable worldviews of a single mother and her adolescent son. It is a diasporic life the filmmaker knows well. Raised in a renowned family of Mande bards and storytellers in Burkina Faso, trained in the cinematic arts in France, and currently settled with his family in Sweden, Dani Kouyaté embodies the existential tensions of living with multiple roots along expansive, though at times restrictive, routes (see Frithiof 2017).

A work of cinematic fiction, *While We Live* is, in many ways, an autobiographical meditation on Kouyaté's experience of movement back and forth between Africa and Europe. At a key moment in the film, Ibbe, an aspiring hip-hop artist who has traveled to the Gambia to join his mother, makes a strong musical connection with Ismael, a young Gambian musician (and the fiancé of Ibbe's cousin). Ismael plays the *kora*, a twenty-one-stringed harp, and in this scene he performs a classic piece from the Mande repertoire, "Miniyamba."

The song relates the mythical origins of the tenth-century kingdom of Ghana. In it, we hear the refrain, "tunga ma lambe lon" (exile knows no dignity).[15] I ask Kouyaté about this notion of *tunga*, a Mande concept that variously signifies travel abroad or migration but also exile, and its resonances with his own life and work.[16] His response is telling: "*Tunga*, for me, is a way of life. I have the feeling of belonging to all places. When I try to position myself as a traveler, I ask myself, in what sense? Am I an African traveler who has arrived in Europe and must return to Africa? Or am I a European traveler who must return to Africa and then come back to Europe?"[17]

There is a fugitive quality to Kouyaté's diasporic sense of self and place. It is simultaneously both *in the world* and *out of place*, at once cosmopolitan and deterritorialized.[18] Or, as Kouyaté himself puts it, "*Chez moi*, in the proper sense of the term, has become a complicated thing!" In his everyday life, "home" is the confluent result of fate, serendipity, opportunity, and often-difficult negotiation. Parentage rooted him in Burkina Faso. Studies took him to France. Love brought him to Sweden. And work has taken Kouyaté to the coffee shop in New York where I sit with him on a cold December morning. Again, there is more than a little of Kouyaté's story and sentiments in the fictional lives he traces in *While We Live*.

"I need to understand who I am in order to know what I want," Kandia (played by Josette Bushell-Mingo) tells her friend Eva over dinner after another long day at work. After two decades in Sweden, with her son, Ibbe, now asserting his independence and an estranged relationship with the family of his father, Kandia feels increasingly alone: "Like an elephant without a herd," she says. Kandia's decision to return to the Gambia, perhaps permanently, is, for her, an act of self-care, but it is hard for those around her to fathom her choice. Ibbe, her son, is incredulous and angry. "This is not about you," she tells him. "It's about me." The questions Kandia confronts echo Kouyaté's own subjective queries: Is she Gambian, returning home from Sweden? Or is she a Swede, reconnecting with her Gambian roots? These questions are not mutually exclusive, nor are the answers Kandia (much like Kouyaté) finds en route.

And then there is Ibbe's journey. At the insistence of his uncle Sekou and in the midst of a debilitating depression, Ibbe follows his mother to the Gambia. According to Kouyaté, "there is something transcendent" about Ibbe's trip. "Symbolically, he returns *chez lui*. It's not a physical return. It's a symbolic return. Because there is a part of him that is over there." Gambia is not Ibbe's home in the same way that it is his mother's home. "Sweden is your country, not mine," she tells him in an earlier scene. Africa, for Ibbe, becomes a site of cultural discovery and a space of personal renewal. While Kouyaté typically loathes explaining the meaning behind events in his films, he does gesture toward an analysis in this case: "If we would want to analyze [Ibbe's situation] in a metaphysical manner, [Kandia] leaves [Sweden] to create the possibility of her son's return." If Kandia travels to Africa to return balance to her life, destiny seems to have brought Ibbe "home." These two travel stories are as different as they are intimately bound up with each other, and both are suggestive of Kouyaté's "complicated" Afro-European mode of being-in-the-world, both physical and metaphysical, in which people make choices and fate is made manifest.

The Swedish Soul of Black Feminism

At one o'clock on Saturday, August 15, 2015, I turn on the radio and tune in to P1, Sweden's national station. A familiar orchestral waltz announces the "summer chat" (*sommarprat*), hosted this week by soul singer Seinabo Sey.[19] It is a much-anticipated edition of this popular program. Following the chart-topping success of her single "Younger" in 2014, Sey is now a household name in much of Sweden. Critics rave about her distinctive "soul pop" style, a mix, perhaps, of the young singer's studious attention to the vocal currents of the Black Atlantic and the remarkable pop alchemy perfected by Swedish musicophiles like Magnus Lidehäll, who produces much of her work.[20] Earlier that year, many watched as Sey won a Swedish Grammy for best new artist. And now, many lean in to hear the artist tell her story, addressed to an imagined community of Swedish listeners, who, for the time being, share in the sounds and sentiments of her voice.

Sey begins with a caveat: "The idea was to talk about music, my friends, philosophy, and those things that I think make my life worth living, but I can't continue my summer chat without naming this." She pauses, takes a breath, and then says: "Everywhere, all across the world, Black people are suffering [from] poverty, segregation, marginalization, war, starvation, and murder." She repeats the word "everywhere" (*överallt*) multiple times, reminding her audience that the global scope of this gruesome reality encompasses their society—Sweden—as well. "Everywhere on earth," she continues, "people whose skin is darker than white continue to be oppressed." She concludes this preface with a question: "Why is this so?" In lieu of an answer, she plays the track "Super Magic" by Mos Def (aka Yassin Bey), which opens with a call to arms echoing from the voice of Malcolm X: "You're living at a time of extremism, a time of revolution, and I for one will join in with anyone, I don't care what color you are, as long as you want to change this miserable condition that exists on this earth."

Born to a Gambian father and a Swedish mother, Sey grew up in two distinct locations of culture: the quiet middle-class town of Halmstad, on Sweden's west coast, and the bustling capital of the Gambia, Banjul, on Africa's west coast. "Gambia is mine, just like Sweden is mine," she tells us. But in the latter case, it has not always been clear that the opposite is true, that she belongs to Sweden. If urban Africa taught Sey of the virtues of what Kwame Anthony Appiah (1997) has termed a "rooted cosmopolitanism"—that she could be a child of the Gambia and a citizen of the world at the same time— small-town Sweden put her in contact with a distinctively European provinciality, the realization that her Black body signals difference, setting her apart from her peers, and, in the eyes of some, that it poses a problem of being ugly and unwelcome.

At this point, Sey's summer chat embarks on a sustained interrogation of this logic of racial difference, exclusion, and abuse with an emphasis on how its practice specifically impacts Black women. Her narrative is as didactic and critical as it is supportive and caring. Addressing the women of color among her listeners, she offers a "guide for a solitary Black girl in Sweden," providing self-care tips about beauty products and advice on how to negotiate and confront everyday racism.[21] She asks the rest of us to get a cup of coffee or just listen respectfully. Then, turning back to the general audience, Sey voices her Black feminist critique of Sweden's provincial racialism in deeply personal terms: "I have never felt beautiful in Sweden. I have seen so few images of people who look like me here that I often wonder if I am simply someone's fetish." She punctuates this statement with more music, carefully chosen to amplify her argument: a strident hip-hop track from Swedish rapper Jaqe and DJ Marcus Price titled "Malcolm," invoking, once again, the martyred African American icon of the Black radical tradition.

The program culminates with an emphatic thesis statement: because Black bodies are so rarely encountered in Swedish media, they are made to seem "more exotic," "unusual and different from the norm," and they become "something obscure, vulgar, and bizarre."[22] She compares this condition to the violent objectification of Sarah Baartman, whose body was made into a spectacle of sexualized exoticism in early nineteenth-century Europe. Invoking a sense of Black feminist solidarity, Sey turns to the voice of Nina Simone to imagine a place beyond the terror and confinement of this gaze: "I'll tell you what freedom is to me: *no fear*! I mean, really, *no fear.*" The program ends, leaving me (like many others, I imagine) silent and pensive for a long moment in its wake. Now fast-forward six months to the 2016 Swedish Grammy Awards, where Seinabo Sey has just taken home the prize for the year's best pop artist. Let Nina Simone's words of fearless defiance ring in your ears. Watch as 130 Black women take the stage with Sey on national television, standing stoic and proud, as she sings, "Hard Time," her anthem to personal struggle and resilience. "I basically just want[ed] to show that we exist," she says.

SWEDEN IN BLACKFACE

On January 30, 2016, I attend the opening of visual artist Makode Linde's eponymous exhibit at Kulturhuset, a vast publicly sponsored arts complex located in downtown Stockholm. The exhibit has for months been the subject of much controversy in the Swedish media, social and otherwise, with discussions and debates revolving around the exhibit's original (and, for the artist, preferred) title: *Negerkungens Återkomst*. We might translate this as "the return of the Negro king," though the N-word in Swedish indexes the more vulgar variant in English as well. This explains Kulturhuset's decision to change the title of the exhibit, against the artist's wishes and to the horror of "freedom of speech" proponents, citing their nondiscriminatory responsibility as a public cultural institution. Linde's designation refers to Astrid Lindgren's term for Pippi Longstocking's estranged father, whom Pippi describes as a "Negro king" (rendered as "king of the natives" in current English translations).[23] Lindgren's (and Linde's) word choice is part of a broader lexicon of racial difference in modern Swedish popular culture in which the N-word figures prominently, appearing in the name of a popular confection, lyrics of children's songs and nursery rhymes, content of primary school textbooks, narratives of cartoons and comic strips, and the common tongue of an everyday vernacular.[24]

The "king" in question is also a reference to Makode Linde himself. "Under all these layers," he says, "my art always points back to me" (as quoted in Pérez Borjas 2016). Linde gained international notoriety for his 2012 work of performance art, *Painful Cake*. Presented at a social gathering of Swedish cultural elites, the cake was in the shape of the Venus of Willendorf, colored in black. Makode Linde, whose body was hidden from view beneath the serving table, appeared as the Venus's head, painted in blackface. As guests cut into the figure's flesh-colored marzipan body, Linde (or the Venus) howled in pain (convincingly, according to those in attendance). In a now-infamous gesture, the then minister of culture, Lena Adehlsohn-Liljeroth, fed the Venus a bite of its own body to quiet the screams, eliciting a cheerful response from the gathered crowd, all of them white except for Linde. This scene resulted in an iconic image of modern racialized spectacle—capturing the delight of a white gaze upon a mutilated Black body—which rapidly spread on social media and around the world. The so-called cake incident led the National Union of Afro-Swedes to call for Liljeroth's resignation and created a firestorm of debate about Linde's artistic intentions and the consequences of reproducing caustic racial stereotypes in the public sphere.[25] Four years later, Linde returned, with controversy following close in his wake.

The 2016 exhibit was composed of old and new works, most of which belong to a series Linde calls Afromantics, in which keepsakes, knickknacks, ornaments, portraits, dolls, and other everyday objects are transformed into gollywogs—painted jet black, with bloated red lips, disjointed teeth, and big white eyes. Many of the figures have limbs cut off, represented with a circle of red flesh surrounding a white bone—evoking, much like the *Painful Cake*, an aesthetic that is at once cartoonish and gory, a visual mix of minstrelsy, kitsch, Looney Tunes, and slasher films. The exhibit carefully stages these playful, if horrifying and grossly stereotyped, figures in scenes that evoke traditional fairytale environments: a magical underwater world, a cabin in the woods, a graveyard, an exotic jungle, a pirate's ship, and a throne room. In an interview with *Vice* magazine, Linde explained that "from the beginning I've wanted to do a show that is related to the world of fairytales," which he strongly associates with the children's books, plays, and films he read and watched at Kulturhuset while growing up. With the exhibit now occupying one of the building's principal halls, one can read Linde's "return" as a nostalgic, satirical, and, in its own way, critical appraisal of the storied sights and sounds of his Swedish youth, populated by stereotypes that loom large for those, like Linde, who are racialized as Black.[26]

But Linde is also a provocateur. If his works suggest an autobiographical reading rooted in a deeply personal response to racism in Swedish society, for many they are also, first and foremost, ugly and offensive. Such critics have accused Linde of willfully and irresponsibly reproducing anti-Black iconography and language, showing more concern for those—civil libertarians and outright racists alike—who affirm their right to use the N-word in public, decrying the apparent excesses of "political correctness" in Sweden today, than for people of African descent who are the unwilling recipients of such anti-Black insult and injury (see, e.g., Järvi 2016; Kyeyune Backström 2016).

"I'm just doing what I am expected to do," Linde told *Vice*. "It's quite surprising that it's such a shock to everyone." Maybe. What *is* clear is that Linde excels at amplifying an already polarized public discourse. This is why Kulturhuset's decision to change the name of his exhibit from *Negerkungens Återkomst* to *Makode Linde* still worked, despite the institution's good intentions and the artist's own protests. Linde's name has become synonymous with controversy and polemic.

Afro-Swedish Renaissance

In sum: a book that relates the burdens of prejudice and champions the virtue of dignity to make an existential case for the possibility of "doubleness" in the world today; a play that is at once foreign and familiar, translated and staged to make space for a minority community so that its members might confront their societal demons and affirm their collective presence; a film that tells a story intimate to those whose lives have been shaped by movement and migration, for whom homelands exist alongside myriad elsewheres as locations of aspiration, pride, rejuvenation, sorrow, and regret; a song that is sung in the company of dozens by a singer who is standing before hundreds, that is broadcast to an audience of many thousands, and that says, in words that need no lyrics to carry them, "We're here. We're strong. We're beautiful. And we aren't going anywhere"; and an exhibition that shocks and gives pause, transmuting commonplace artifacts of everyday life into a spectacle of cruel and macabre fantasy that, for many, is all too real.

These works, seen, heard, and read in relation to the artists who made them and the communities they call upon, illuminate and resound a varied and contested but no less vital and concerted Afro-Swedish *life world*, privileging as they foreground the manifold lives and labors of people of African descent in Sweden today. This collection of literary, dramatic, cinematic, musical, and visual culture also testifies to an increasingly salient, though stylistically irreducible, Afro-Swedish *art world* that is born of a growing community of artists, aficionados, activists, scholars, and culture brokers; exemplified by a range of expressive, interpretative, curatorial, and interventionist practices; attentive to variously African, Afro-diasporic, Black, Brown, and creole modes of identification; and critically focused on "race" as an ontological, epistemological, and always intersectional category of interest, debate, and concern—all against the grain of an ostensibly antiracist and color-blind society. Afro-Swedish artists are demonstrating—with increasing frequency and in some of the most prominent cultural venues in Sweden—how their complex identities may be artfully, thoughtfully, and respectfully represented, performed, embodied, and engendered through both creation and critique. It is precisely at the interface of these worlds of Black lives and Black art that the idea of "renaissance" appears salient as a heuristic of an Afro-Swedish contemporary.

If we center the concept on its Africana genealogy and *not* on the Europeanist historical, philosophical, and aesthetic discourse to which it is more commonly applied, the word "renaissance" refers to moments of effervescent *conjuncture* in the modern African world, to moments when the diaspora becomes constructively and critically conscious of itself, for which cultural production in the literary, performing, and visual arts is both focal and fundamental to the making of diasporic meaning.[27] We can locate such instances of Afro-diasporic awareness, criticism, and cultural florescence in the metonymic significance of place-names like Harlem and Chicago, literary traditions like *négritude* and *negrismo*, political imperatives like Pan-Africanism and Black Power, and so many arts movements qualified as "Black" and "African." Renaissance is understood, within these various Afro-diasporic contexts and configurations, not as a literal "rebirth" of culture and society but rather as a periodic instantiation of what Hannah Arendt terms "natality"—the capacity of human populations to form and fashion themselves anew, to recalibrate human life according to shifting environmental, social, economic, and political conditions ([1958] 1998, 8–9). I read the cultural products we have observed as evidence of Afro-Swedish natality, of a critical, creative, and generative self-awareness that emphatically locates Sweden within various Afro-diasporic cartographies and histories and thereby challenges normative notions of what it means—*and how it looks*—to be "Swedish" in the world today.

As such, this renaissance also marks a significant shift in the terms of debate about how to qualify—and thereby understand—Sweden's increasingly diverse population. In no uncertain terms, Afro-Swedes are explicitly refusing to be marked as foreign others in their own society, as illegitimate outcasts and unwanted "immigrants."[28] Their message is clear: *we can be simultaneously and without contradiction both African-descended and Swedish!* At the same time, Afro-Swedish public works shed critical light on the racialization of identity in Sweden by drawing attention to the ways "Blackness" operates, discursively and symbolically, as both a capacious sign of difference and an urgent locus of solidarity in which a common experience of anti-Black prejudice and abuse and collective affirmations of Afro-diasporic history and culture appear in tandem. Afro-Swedes resist the politics of erasure that normative color blindness prescribes by affirming a multiply conscious Afro-diasporic *and* Swedish being-in-the-world. This is an Afro-Swedish renaissance that insists that it is Sweden that can—*and must*—be reborn in order to embrace and cultivate a social and cultural heterogeneity that is always and already present.

NOTES

1. My first attempt to synthesize this material appeared in a short opinion article written for *Upsala Nya Tidning* titled "Afrosvensk Renässans" (Skinner 2016). This piece accompanied a broader public discussion sponsored by the Forum for Africa Studies at Uppsala University on Afro-Swedish history and the legacy of the transatlantic slave trade in Sweden. The article highlights the mobilization of artistic, intellectual, and political agency and production that is spearheaded by a new generation of Swedes of African descent who are engaged in a broad-based movement of critical and creative identity formation. The current chapter represents a more detailed elaboration of this work and is based on fieldwork conducted in 2015–16. For a broader, dialogic survey of this research, see Buggenhagen and Skinner (2017).

2. For broader transnational and comparative accounts of the African and Black diaspora in the Nordic region, see McEachrane (2014a); see also Sawyer and Habel (2014).

3. For an anthropological account of the varied "routes" that inform the representation and construction of African and Black identities in contemporary Sweden, see Sawyer (2002). My reference to "intrinsic" modes of racial identification and identities shaped by "extrinsically" racist practices is informed by ideas and arguments proposed in Appiah (1992).

4. These population figures are current as of December 31, 2019. Demographic statistics are archived and made available on the Statistics Sweden website (http://www.scb.se).

5. Afro-Swedish political philosopher and Black studies scholar Michael McEachrane also wrestled with Statistics Sweden's dataset, together with those of other Nordic countries in 2011–12, and came to similar conclusions: "Giving an estimate of how many people of African descent in the Nordic countries is difficult as they do not keep racial or ethnic statistics, but only statistics of country of origin" (2014a, 6). He added in a note: "The statistics on African descendants are merely preliminary estimates based on country of origin" (11n12). Such results remain stubbornly "preliminary" in 2020–21 as well.

6. To be sure, Palme's vocal disavowal of racialism in Sweden appears in the context of a nuanced speech, delivered as a national radio broadcast on Christmas Day 1965, in response to an increasingly public xenophobia in a rapidly diversifying post–World War II Swedish society. The full text and audio of this speech is available online on various platforms.

7. For an overview of the recent emergence of a critical "whiteness studies" in the Nordic region, see Lundström and Teitelbaum (2017).

8. On the cultural geography of systemic racism in contemporary Sweden, see Molina (1997) and Pred (2000). For an ethnographic study of anti-Black racism and racialized public culture in the (sub)urban social spaces of Stockholm, see Skinner (2019).

9. For recent collections of Afro-Swedish voices and social criticism, see Gärding (2010); Habel (2015); Norrby (2015); and Stephens (2009).

10. Jason "Timbuktu" Diakité, interview with the author, Stockholm, Sweden, May 30, 2016. Diakité's questions are echoed in Arbouz (2012); cf. Tasin and Landehag (2015).

11. Diakité, interview. On W. E. B. Du Bois's notion of "twoness" and the related concept of "double consciousness," see Du Bois ([1903] 2007, 8).

12. Josette Bushell-Mingo, interview with the author, Stockholm, Sweden, April 18, 2016.

13. In November 2018, Bushell-Mingo spearheaded the launch of the National Black Theatre in Sweden (NTBS), with a permanent location at Kulturhust Stadsteatern in Vällingby, Stockholm, establishing a cultural "home" for the Black and African community in Sweden. In the fall of 2019 the NTBS staged its first production, the South African antiapartheid drama *Woza Albert.*

14. Josette Bushell-Mingo, interview with the author, Stockholm, Sweden, June 22, 2017.

15. For a related meditation on this proverbial theme in West Africa, see Whitehouse (2012).

16. For my own account of the meaning and significance of *tunga* as a social and aesthetic concept in the contemporary Mande world, see Skinner (2015, esp. chap. 2, "Artistiya").

17. Dani Kouyaté, interview with the author, New York, December 11, 2016.

18. Or, in other words, and with an emphasis on the centrality of Africa and its diaspora(s) to Kouyaté's worldly peregrinations, "Afropolitan" (see Skinner 2017).

19. This program can be heard in its entirety on the website for Sweden's Radio: "Seinabo Sey," Sveriges Radio, August 15, 20215, http://sverigesradio.se/sida/avsnitt/592389?programid=2071.

20. For an example of the term "soul pop," see Sey's artist bio on the "Scandinavian Soul" website: https://scandinaviansoul.com/artists/seinabo-sey/.

21. Sey's tips on life, fashion, and beauty as a Black woman in a normatively white Sweden are echoed and elaborated in Jallow (2016).

22. For a critical reflection on "racialized desire" in the Swedish context, see Lundström (2012). For a broader historical and theoretical account of the representation of Black bodies as "primitive," "sexualized," and uniquely "athletic" in European public culture, see Hall (1997).

23. Since 2015, the term *Söderhavskung* (king of the South Seas) has been used in Swedish editions.

24. For a critical commentary on the presence and significance of racist iconography in contemporary Swedish children's literature and film, see Rubin Dranger (2012). On recent debates surrounding the use of the N-word and other racist pejoratives in the Swedish public sphere, see Hübinette (2011). For perspectives on the fraught boundary between racial hate crime and freedom of speech in such debates, see Hübinette (2014); see also Pripp and Öhlander (2012).

25. For a multivocal account of this public spectacle and the criticism that followed in its wake, see McEachrane et al. (2014).

26. As Swedish culture critic and blogger Johan Palme (2016) notes in a review of Linde's exhibition: "Those who look are forced into Makode Linde's own position, constantly observed and judged; into the clown costume forced upon him; inside his feelings of betrayal and wavering self-image, his anger at society's racism and homophobia."

27. In a recent historical survey of the idea of a "Black Renaissance" in America, Ernest Julius Mitchell invokes the thought and spirit of African American philosopher Alain Locke to describe what he calls a "long-term, trans-generational, and interracial cultural shift" (2010, 650), outlining a creative, critical, stylized, and syncretic tradition in the African-descended world. I draw on the spirit of this argument in mobilizing the idea of an Afro-Swedish renaissance in this essay. By invoking the idea of "conjuncture," I echo Stuart Hall's genealogical analysis of the postwar Black diasporic art in Britain. Regarding his method, Hall writes (in words that readily apply to the cases presented in this chapter as well): "Thinking conjuncturally involves 'clustering' or assembling elements into a formation. However, there is no simple unity, no single 'movement' here, evolving teleologically, to which, say, all the artists of any moment can be said to belong" (2006, 3). As Brent Hayes Edwards reminds us, diasporic meaning elusively shifts as it changes tongues, transformed and refracted through processes of translation to engender a multilinguistic plurality. Writing about the discursive migrations of "Black renaissance" in the 1920s, for example, Edwards writes: "The discourse of diaspora that emerges in the print culture of the period is practiced through the complex and diverse attempts to understand the race problem as a world problem, to carry blackness over the boundaries that would contain it. In this sense, in the Renaissance, *diaspora is translation*" (2001, 308; my emphasis).

28. To be an "immigrant" (*invandrare*) in Sweden is both a legal status and identity and a profound social stigma (Eastmond 2011)—a pejorative term for those who do not belong and, given the persistent optics of difference in Sweden society, who are not white (Pred 2000).

References

Appiah, Kwame Anthony. 1992. *In My Father's House: Africa in the Philosophy of Culture.* New York: Oxford University Press.

Appiah, Kwame Anthony. 1997. "Cosmopolitan Patriots." *Critical Inquiry* 23(3): 617–39.

Arbouz, Daphne. 2012. "Vad betyder det att inte känna sig hemma där man är född och uppvuxen? Om mellanförskap i dagens Sverige." In *Om ras och vithet I det samtida Sverige*, edited by Tobias Hübinette, Helena Hörnfeldt, Fataneh Farahani, and René León Rosales, 37–42. Botkyrka: Mångkulturellt Centrum.

Arendt, Hannah. (1958) 1998. *The Human Condition.* Chicago: University of Chicago Press.

Brännström, Leila. 2016. "'Ras' I efterkrigstidens Sverige: Ett bidrag till en mothistoria." In *Historiens hemvist*, vol. 2, *Etik, politik, och historikerns ansvar*, edited by Patricia Lorenzoni and Ulla Manns, 27–55. Gothenburg: Makadam Förlag.

Buggenhagen, Beth, and Ryan Skinner. 2017. "Afro-Swedish Artistic Practices and Discourses in and out of Sweden: A Conversation with Ethnomusicologist Ryan T. Skinner." *Africa Today* 64(2): 92–107.

Diakité, Jason. 2016. *En droppe midnatt.* Stockholm: Albert Bonniers Förlag.

Diaz, Camilla Astorga, Mireya Echeverría Quezada, Valerie Kyeyune Backström, and Judith Kiros. 2015. *Rummet.* Stockholm: Ordfront Förlag.

Djärv, Carina, Sara Westerberg, and Anna Frenzel. 2015. *Hatbrott 2014: Statistik över polisanmälningar med identifierade hatbrottsmotiv och självrapporterad utsatthet för hatbrott.* Stockholm: Brottsförebyggande Rådet.

Du Bois, W. E. B. (1903) 2007. *The Souls of Black Folk.* Oxford: Oxford University Press.

Eastmond, Marita. 2011. "Egalitarian Ambitions, Constructions of Difference: The Paradoxes of Refugee Integration in Sweden." *Journal of Ethnic and Migration Studies* 37(2): 277–95.

Edwards, Brent Hayes. 2001. "Three Ways to Translate the Harlem Renaissance." In *Temples for Tomorrow: Looking Back at the Harlem Renaissance*, edited by Genevieve Fabre and Michel Feith, 288–313. Bloomington: Indiana University Press.

Frithiof, Lotta. 2017. "Vi skapar själva våra identiteter." *Uppsala nya tidning*, April 3.

Gärding, Cecilia. 2010. *Afrosvensk i det nya Sverige.* Stockholm: Notis Förlag.

Habel, Ylva, ed. 2015. "Svensk rapsodi i svart." Special issue, *Ord & bild*, no. 1–2.

Hall, Stuart. 1997. "The Spectacle of the 'Other.'" In *Representation: Cultural Representations and Signifying Practices*, edited by Stuart Hall, 225–79. London: SAGE.

Hall, Stuart. 2006. "Black Diaspora Artists in Britain: Three 'Moments' in Postwar History." *History Workshop Journal* 61(1): 1–24.

Hambraeus, Ulf. 2014. "Rasbegreppet ska bort ur lagen." *SVT Nyheter*, July 30.

Hübinette, Tobias. 2011. "Ord som sårar." *Invandrare & minoriteter* 38(1): 25–27.

Hübinette, Tobias. 2013. "Swedish Antiracism and White Melancholia: Racial Words in a Post-racial Society." *Ethnicity and Race in a Changing World* 4(1): 24–33.

Hübinette, Tobias. 2014. "Race Performativity and Melancholic Whiteness in Contemporary Sweden." *Social Identities* 20(6): 501–14.

Hübinette, Tobias. 2016. "Jason Diakité och det nya icke-vita Sverige." tobiashubin ette.wordpress.com. December 7.

Hübinette, Tobias, Samson Beshir, and Victoria Kawesa. 2014. *Afrofobi: Ett kunskapsöversikt över afrosvenskars situation i dagens Sverige*. Botkyrka: Mångkulturellt Centrum.

Hübinette, Tobias, Helena Hörnfeldt, Fataneh Farahani, and René León Rosales, eds. 2012. *Om ras och vithet i det samtida Sverige*. Botkyrka: Mångkulturellt Centrum.

Hübinette, Tobias, and Carina Tigervall. 2009. "To Be Non-white in a Colour-Blind Society: Conversations with Adoptees and Adoptive Parents in Sweden on Everyday Racism." *Journal of Intercultural Studies* 30(4): 335–53.

Jallow, Lovette. 2016. *Black Vogue: Skönhetens nyanser*. Stockholm: Rabén & Sjögren.

Järvi, Mattis. 2016. "Som afrosvensk ses man som lättkränkt vad man än säger." *Nyheter 24*, January 28.

Khemiri, Jonas Hassan. 2013. "Bästa Beatrice Ask." *Dagens Nyheter*, March 13.

Kronlund, Andrea Davis. 2017. "Josette Bushell-Mingo: A Story about Blackness and Kick-Ass Theatre." *Krull Magazine*, March 16.

Kushkush, Isma'il. 2016. "'A Raisin in the Sun' through the Eyes of Afro-Swedes." *New York Times*, February 2.

Kyeyune Backström, Valerie. 2016. "Makode Linde: 'Mina hatare är resister.'" *Expressen*, January 22.

Lundberg, Johan. 2016. *Det sista museet*. Stockholm: Timbro.

Lundström, Catrin. 2012. "Rasifierat begär: De Andra som exotiska." In *Om ras och vithet i samtida sverige*, edited by Tobias Hübinette, Helena Hörnfeldt, Fataneh Farahani, and René León Rosales, 189–213. Botkyrka: Mångkulturellt Centrum.

Lundström Catrin, and Benjamin R. Teitelbaum. 2017. "Nordic Whiteness: An Introduction." *Scandinavian Studies* 89(2): 151–58.

McEachrane, Michael. 2012. "Afro-Swedes." In *Encyclopedia of Afroeuropean Studies*. Accessed April 19, 2017. http://www.encyclopediaofafroeuropeanstudies.eu.

McEachrane, Michael. 2014a. Introduction to *Afro-Nordic Landscapes: Equality and Race in Northern Europe*, edited by Michael McEachrane, 1–13. New York: Routledge.

McEachrane, Michael. 2014b. "There's a White Elephant in the Room: Equality and Race in (Northern) Europe." In *Afro-Nordic Landscapes: Equality and Race in Northern Europe*, edited by Michael McEachrane, 87–119. New York: Routledge.

McEachrane, Michael, et al. 2014. "Racism Is No Joke: A Swedish Minister and a Hottentot Venus Cake—an Email Conversation." In *Afro-Nordic Landscapes: Equality and Race in Northern Europe*, edited by Michael McEachrane, 149–61. New York: Routledge.

Miller, Monica L. 2017. "Figuring Blackness in a Place without Race: Sweden, Recently." *ELH* 84(2): 377–97.

Mitchell, Ernest Julius. 2010. "'Black Renaissance': A Brief History of the Concept." *Amerikastudien / American Studies* 55(4): 641–65.

Molina, Irene. 1997. "Stadens rasifiering: Etnisk boendesegregation i folkhemmet." PhD diss., Uppsala University.

Nordström, Andreas. 2016. "En identitetsresa med Jason Diakité." *Sydsvenskan*, November 3.

Norrby, Fanna Ndow, ed. 2015. *Svart kvinna*. Stockholm: Natur & Kultur.

Palme, Johan. 2016. "Varför skriver ingen om Makode Lindes konst?" *Kultwatch*, February 9.

Pérez Borjas, Weronika. 2016. "Shock, Race, and Fairytales: A Conversation with Swedish Artist Makode Linde." *Vice*, January 29.

Pred, Alan. 2000. *Even in Sweden: Racisms, Radicalized Spaces, and the Popular Geographical Imagination*. Berkeley: University of California Press.

Pripp, Oscar, and Magnus Öhlander. 2012. "Att uppfatta rasism i Sverige." In *Om ras och vithet i samtida sverige*, edited by Tobias Hübinette, Helena Hörnfeldt, Fataneh Farahani, and René León Rosales, 85–108. Botkyrka: Mångkulturellt Centrum.

Rubin Dranger, Joanna. 2012. "Den rasistiska ikonens logik." *Expressen*, October 30.

Sawyer, Lena. 2002. "Routings: 'Race,' African Diasporas, and Swedish Belonging." *Transforming Anthropology* 11(1): 13–35.

Sawyer, Lena, and Ylva Habel. 2014. "Refracting African and Black Diaspora through the Nordic Region." *African and Black Diaspora* 7(1): 1–6.

Skinner, Ryan. 2015. *Bamako Sounds: The Afropolitan Ethics of Malian Music*. Minneapolis: University of Minnesota Press.

Skinner, Ryan. 2016. "Afrosvensk Renässans." *Upsala Nya Tidning*, January 16, 2016.

Skinner, Ryan. 2017. "Why Afropolitanism Matters." *Africa Today* 64(2): 2–21.

Skinner, Ryan. 2019. "Walking, Talking, Remembering: An Afro-Swedish Critique of Being-in-the-World." *African and Black Diaspora: An International Journal* 12(1): 1–19.

Stephens, Kolade, ed. 2009. *Afrikansksvenska röster*. Malmö: Notis.

Tasin, Lewend, and Anton Landehag. 2015. *Kreol: Ett spoke går runt i orten*. Stockholm: Arena Idé.

Westerlund, Hanna. 2015. "Däför vill de samla in data om hudfärg." *Stockholms Fria*, December 11.

Whithouse, Bruce. 2012. *Migrants and Strangers in an African City: Exile, Dignity, Belonging*. Bloomington: Indiana University Press.

Wigerfelt, Berit, and Anders S. Wigerfelt. 2017. *Hatbrott med främlingsfientliga och rasistiska motiv: En kunskapsöversikt*. Stockholm: Delmi Rapport.

Wolgast, Sima, Irene Molina, and Mattias Gardell. 2018. *Antisvart rasism och diskriminering på arbetsmarknaden*. Stockholm: Länsstyrelsen Stockholm.

INHERITANCE

Within Our Borders

Sámi Mobilization, the Scandinavian Response, and World War II

ELLEN A. AHLNESS

The Sámi are often considered a more successful story in indigenous political mobilization. National Sámi parliaments represent domestic issues at the national level, and a pan-Nordic Sámi Council represents Sámi in international institutions. Over the past four decades, the Sámi have seen great gains in linguistic, livelihood, and land rights in the four countries in which they have traditionally lived: Norway, Sweden, Finland, and Russia. These gains developed from mobilization movements beginning in the 1920s, progressing domestically through the 1960s, and engaging the international community in the 1970s. The 1920s Sámi domestic mobilization and association-forming efforts act as a precursor to contemporary solidarity-building efforts of immigrant minorities within Scandinavia.

The Sámi, often framed as forming a broad, transboundary nation, can point to multiple cases of securing cultural rights and land management claims (Ravna 2015), and their indigeneity is recognized through special legal status in ways unseen in other regions of the globe (Josefsen 2010). This is not to say that the Sámi do not face contemporary barriers and shutdowns from states. Ongoing resource and land-use controversies include hydroelectric power and copper-mining projects that disrupt herding and distribute venture profits away from northern residents (Lawrence and Larsen 2017; Mustonen et al. 2010) and increasing legal, social, and economic disincentives to herding among younger generations (Fouche and Doyle 2018). Instead, to say the Sámi have experienced comparative success is to look at an established history of mobilizing—domestically and with their transboundary counterparts—to establish a trajectory of meaningful social, political, and economic gains since the 1960s in the face of obstinate states.

Internationally, the Sámi are portrayed as an ethnic nation, yet they are not homogeneous in terms of their communities, livelihoods, or languages, nor do they experience rights gains, recognition, or even classification consistently across the four states in which they reside. As Russia is an outlier in Sámi policy, it is not examined here, given its distinct sociocultural trends, smaller Sámi population, and distinct indigenous classification system. Scandinavian resistance to Sámi mobilization varies across borders and over time, with the basis for much of the policy differences emerging from World War II repression.

During World War II, the Scandinavian states experienced varying degrees of internal conflict. Sweden was neutral, Norway was occupied, and Finland experienced two distinct wars, the Winter War and the Continuation War. Differences in each state's experience made it more difficult for the international community (composed of both states and international organizations) to collect reliable information on Scandinavian domestic policies affecting indigenous populations during wartime. Escalation of internal conflicts coincided with a decline in international monitoring capability, as Axis powers restricted communication, while Scandinavian policymaking prioritized wartime strategy.

Examining the cases by increasing degrees of internal conflict—Sweden, Norway, then Finland—illustrates a trend in wartime Sámi policy. Severe internal conflict coincides with the state's level of restrictive Sámi policy, including evacuation and forced conscription. These wartime developments obscured Sámi policies from other countries during a time when human rights violations were rampant in Europe. This chapter proceeds as a narrative and analysis of the Sámi wartime experience. The history of the Sámi in World War II is not easily accessible, given the disruptive effect of war on the states and information-collecting capabilities. The Sámi are a heterogeneous group with distinct languages and livelihoods, and mobilization studies run the risk of falsely homogenizing minorities and their interests to international audiences. The chapter begins with an overview of Sámi mobilization from the 1920s to the start of World War II, highlighting policy relationships among the Scandinavian states and Sámi-pan-European connections of the era. It progresses into the Nordic states' entrance into the war, chronologically by engagement. Finally, it concludes with an analysis of the long-term implications of wartime policy and restrictions for Sámi-state relations.

The postwar years were a crucial point for Sámi self-determination, but Sámi were unable to take full advantage of Europe's ideological changes and less restrictive state policies. War had weakened the Nordic states' bureaucracies, even while awareness of the Holocaust's abuses challenged dominant attitudes toward minorities. Ultimately, the variation in wartime experiences created a legacy of unequal levels of Sámi organizational preparedness to engage the new Europe. Moreover, as the Scandinavian states began to experience an influx of immigrants from distant countries in the current era, concerns about assimilations and traditional practices resurfaced in both contexts.

Setting the Stage

In the 1920s Scandinavia shared colonial attitudes, policies, and histories. Nation-states governed their territories and populations, including Sámi, Greenlandic, and Faeroese minorities. Domestic minority communities were considered subjects of the state, which had complete discretion over policy and enforcement. Politics developed from centuries of assimilation policies (Gaski 1997; Kent 2014). Sámi communities did not have a right to self-determination and relied on the "benevolence" of the state to permit them rights (Kulchyski 2011), while state governments had significant discretion in granting or rejecting policy appeals. Any effort among the Sámi to practice traditional livelihoods, speak their native languages, live in traditional *sameby* (Sámi villages) or *reinbeitesdistrikt* (reindeer pasturing district communities), or use their historical lands required state approval (Lehtola 2005). For indigenous populations, the state's colonial position meant a state of perpetual permission-seeking. Consequently, the mood was rich in incentives to mobilize and strengthen Sámi political power.

The first period of contemporary Sámi political organization, from the early twentieth century to the outbreak of World War II, was considered largely successful. In Norway the Social Democratic Labour Party addressed Sámi issues in its platform. Sámi Isak Saba was elected to the Norwegian parliament for two terms through a program hosted by the Labour Party (Gaski 1997, 74). On February 6, 1917, the first Sámi congress convened in Trondheim, in which Sámi from Norway and Sweden came together across borders to establish a common, comprehensive political platform in the first example of organized transboundary political mobilization. These political events were the result of vocal communities and the efforts of political associations. Political representation was gained through a notably domestic process, wherein Sámi individuals and groups used political channels (e.g., voting and campaigning) and negotiation with state representatives to gain political representation. Such processes can be effective but leave few paths of recourse for minority groups if the state rejects their concerns (Keck and Sikkink 1998).

The Sámi were framed as physically and intellectually distinct from both the white Scandinavians and other ethnic minorities, yet it was presumed to be the state's responsibility to bring them into the fold of European religion and society; consequently, the assimilation policies of the states resembled one another. Assimilation policies tended to focus on visible facets of culture, such as language, dress, and livelihood. The first two components were often addressed through similar education policies. From the mid-nineteenth century well into the 1960s, youth were required to attend state boarding schools, which sought to erase traditional practices among younger generations. The comprehensive schooling restrictions discouraged the use of Sámi languages and separated children from their families, often for years at a time, all while providing a low quality of instruction (Kent 2014). The 1936 Education Act affirmed use of Sámi as a "helping language" allowed in schools, a shift from the linguistic assimilation state schools demanded during earlier years. Despite these gains, the policy norm was assimilation.

The social Darwinist policies of the 1920s in Norway, Sweden, and Finland were also influenced by the vogue "science" of eugenics. Eugenics took root in Sweden's social interest in racial biology and manifested in state policy in the early part of the twentieth century. In 1922 the state founded the Swedish Institute for Racial Biology in Uppsala, creating the first national eugenics agency. The institute established a scale of human superiority based on assumed physical and mental traits. "Pure Swedes" were at the top of the hierarchy. Below were non-Nordic ethnic minorities. At the bottom were Sámi, Jews, and Roma; intermixing was considered detrimental to the "Swedish race" (Drouard 1999). Similar Norwegian eugenics programs existed, focusing on the sterilization of mental and physical "undesirables," but were not expanded in scope or funding until occupation by Germany during the war (exemplified through eugenic breeding programs such as *Lebensborn*) (Ericsson and Simonsen 2008).[1]

While eugenics did not catch on as strongly in Finland as it did in Norway and Sweden, prevailing medical and anthropological opinion still held that there were physical distinctions among "the races," an opinion that affected the course of national research programs (Kent 2014, 104). It was an "inevitable and right" process for the dominant cultures to overtake the minority Sámi culture (Osherenko and Young 1989, 88). Policy trends and social behaviors toward Sámi (alongside Jewish and Roma minorities) suppressed visible aspects of ethnic identity while constraining recourse options. As indigenous groups were considered wards of the state, it was the responsibility of the

Sámi to appeal to the government, but there were no paths for recourse if the state denied these appeals.

Domestic perceptions of Sámi translated in novel ways onto the international stage. While outside Scandinavia there was little basic knowledge on the Sámi at all, much less of their ongoing cultural and political struggles, those in the European community who learned of the Sámi saw them as cultural curiosities. Their livelihoods and culture were largely represented through the humanities, particularly in the arts and linguistics studies. One of the earliest cases of international exposure to Sámi culture came from Emily Demant Hatt (2013), an art student in Copenhagen who photographed, sketched, and painted Sámi from 1907 to 1979. In the 1920s Sámi John Andreas Savio studied art in Oslo, later exhibiting works in Paris and traveling throughout Western Europe from 1933 to 1934. *A Lapp Dictionary* (1932–38) contained studies on three North Sámi languages (referred to as dialects) (Kent 2014, 197). In Europe the Sámi were perceived as subjects, whether of art or research, not as autonomous communities. This framed international perceptions of the Sámi up to World War II.

Transitioning into War

The following chronological case study of state-level Sámi experiences across Scandinavia in World War II illustrates how conflict in one social dimension resulted in the states becoming more vigilant about perceived challenges to their overall security (Henne and Klocek 2017). During times of war, governments adopt organizational forms and behaviors that control the population and protect the state more efficiently. Given the different nature of each country's involvement in World War II, the Nordic governments adopted varying policies governing Sámi, resulting in different degrees of restriction and victimization. Furthermore, World War II was the first time in history that Sámi were conscripted by the Soviet Union, Norway, and Finland to be soldiers. During the six years of conflict, they fully experienced war, an irony, given the lack of any recorded intra-Sámi conflicts (Lehtola 2005).

Sweden

Viewing the increased militarization of mainland Europe, Sweden began to heighten its own military preparedness in 1936. Technically declaring itself "nonbelligerent" rather than neutral in September 1939, Sweden's domestic events remained more transparent to both Allied and Axis powers.

Threat-prioritization patterns emerged early on in Sweden's wartime government. While the prewar environment drew distinctions between Sámi and Swedish society, the threat of occupation hardened attitudes toward minority issues. Parliament refused to increase resources for Sámi during herding crises and livestock deaths, forcing many to search for alternatives. Through the 1938 Reindeer Herding Law, which identified Sámi through reindeer herding, those no longer able to herd were not allowed to speak on behalf of their communities, as they were not engaged in what the state considered to be the basic requirement for Sámi identity. Those able to herd became consumed with the migratory requirements of herding, becoming further isolated during the war, and hindering their ability to congregate or pursue collective Sámi interests.

Unlike its neighbors, Sweden exited the war with a relatively unscathed infrastructure. Given Sweden's neutrality, Swedish Sámi were the only members of the pan-Scandinavian region to avoid forced conscription, yet their prewar political momentum had been stalled. The primary way through which the Sámi had addressed repressive policy—by forming associations—was not sustainable during the war (Kent 2014). The relationship between the state and the Sámi, which up to this point had been defined by the state's assertion of power, mandatory assimilation, and control of land and natural resources, was disrupted. The state, quite simply, had greater concerns. At the dawn of the postwar era, Sámi organizations were primed for activity.

Finland

Finland's war experience was one not only of occupation but also of three stages of open conflict. On November 30, 1939, the Winter War broke out when the Soviet Union invaded Finland three months after the outbreak of World War II. The Winter War ended with the signing of the Moscow Peace Treaty in March 1940. The Continuation War, also between the Soviet Union and Finland, began when Germany invaded the Soviet Union in June 1941 and lasted until September 19, 1944. While Finns and Germans fought the Soviet Union together during the Continuation War, Finnish leadership negotiated an individual peace agreement with the Soviets that required Finland to break ties with Germany and expel any German soldiers left in Finland after September 15, 1944. When German soldiers refused to withdraw from Finland, the Lapland War began, ending in April 1945 with the expulsion of the remaining German forces.

Unlike in Sweden, Finnish ethnology never widely adopted Nazi racial theories, though its interwar policies were also assimilatory in nature. The outbreak of war resulted in a rapid response from the government that further brought Sámi under the purview of the state. Wartime mobilization was so encompassing that communities previously neglected by the state became crucial resources of the wartime strategy through conscription. Conscripted Sámi engaged in the war fronts for both the Winter and Continuation Wars, participating in direct combat against the Soviet Union as part of the northern theater. Military commanders led Finnish and Sámi soldiers in battle against Russian troops, which had also conscripted Russian-based Sámi. One year later, Finnish Sámi supported German troops in driving out the Soviet Union. In theory, Sámi from the two states opposed each other at the Petsamo Front.

Through Finland's multiple war fronts, borders previously flexible for Sámi were transformed into enforced divisions that rejected indigenous unity. The resulting restrictions on Sámi association, communication, and movement created a traumatizing isolation of Sámi from their kindred on different sides of the border. While defined by statehood, borders had always been at least semipermeable for Sámi. The unprecedented barriers to association became an incentive for later mobilization.

Nonconscripted Sámi were also subject to paternalistic policies. In 1939 all the inhabitants of the northern Petsamo province were required to evacuate as Russian troops moved southwest into Finland from the Kola Peninsula. While the inhabitants could return a year later, in the spring of 1940, many no longer had homes to which they could return. Only the Suonikylä village in Petsami remained; all other Sámi villages had been destroyed. Concurrently, much of the northern infrastructure was destroyed by bombing. The Continuation War's southward spread required inhabitants to once again flee in 1941. Nearly all residents, from Petsami to northeastern Murmansk in the Kola Peninsula, were included in the mass evacuation (Kent 2014, 174). Finnish Sámi living in the northern end of the country were evacuated to the southern Sápmi region (as the transnational region of traditional Sámi culture is called) and Narvik, Norway, to escape the violence.

In general, the farther north the war front expanded in Finland, the greater the destruction of land and infrastructure it suffered. Russian troops bombed the land, while German troops left scorched earth behind as they withdrew from Finnish and Norwegian Sápmi. In the Eanodat and Aanaar municipalities, up to 90 percent of the infrastructure was destroyed, and the postwar years were defined by lengthy reconstruction, mass displacement, and the degradation of viable pasturing and herding land (Kent 2014, 52). The whole Sámi population of Finnish Sápmi residing in war zones was evacuated and resettled over the course of the conflict. The Finnish government oversaw Sámi resettlement, making it clear that relocation was at the sole discretion of the state, and there were no guarantees for resumption of traditional livelihoods upon relocation.

While the threat of war shaped government priorities, paternal attitudes toward the Sámi continued. The outbreak of World War II interrupted Sámi livelihoods and existence, though these internal crises fell outside the state's concern. Instead, domestic policy was firmly tied to national security and internal cohesion (Kinnunen and Kivimäki 2011). War decreased support from other Nordic states, and the ineffectiveness of the League of Nations strengthened national consensus that the state was responsible for its own survival and had the purview to summon internal resources—including populations—as needed. Restricted by military strategy, state policy, and belligerent destruction, wartime organization was neither viable nor possible. The Sámi condition was effectively that of obscurity and restriction.

Norway

Germany invaded Norway on April 9, 1940. After a brief, unsuccessful military engagement with the invaders, the Norwegian royal family left for England two months later, on June 7, where they led the government-in-exile for the remainder of the war. Much like in Finland, wartime threats created a strong wave of patriotism that pushed for national consolidation during the German occupation (Sjersted 2011). Parliament was taken over by parties unsympathetic to Sámi determination and association. The pro-German puppet government recruited the Sámi as forced guides for travel in mid-Norway and Sápmi. Any ties the Sámi population had had with the legitimate government became useless, and prewar Sámi organizational gains were nullified. External group communication connections were severed, including transnational Sámi associations; therefore, Norwegian Sámi communication was limited to an intragroup level. The early war years saw an increase in such intra-Sámi communication through holiday broadcasts, regular radio programs, and print media, and the small monthly religious magazine *Nuortanaste*, with an unbroken publishing history going back to 1889, persisted throughout World War II.

Throughout the war, Norway experienced high levels of Allied support in the forms of international aid and sabotage. This physical presence and monitoring fostered greater international awareness of Norway's domestic events, such as the German-led evacuations of the Norwegian portion of Fennoscandian Sápmi region in 1940. Domestic resistance to these evacuations was widespread. Many residents tried to stay in their homes without official permission, though communities along the coasts were less capable of resisting German mandates. Inland, almost one-third of those seventy-two thousand residents evaded the evacuation by hiding in the wilderness (Kent 2014, 52).

The evacuation policy of 1940 was transformative. Up to this point, the Quisling puppet government had paid little attention to Sámi associations promoting greater autonomy within communities and significant resistance to German manipulation attempts. For the remainder of the war, there were numerous cases of Sámi aiding the Allies and Norwegian Resistance, which included stealing collaborators' funds, transporting supplies to the Resistance, and delivering injured Resistance members to Sweden (Howarth 2016; Hunt 2014).

In Norway the occupying forces threatening the Resistance and the Sámi resulted in cooperation between the two groups, given their aligning interests. This cooperation has been captured in modern media and pop culture, from the film *Den 12. mann* (*The 12th Man*) to the biographical novel *We Die Alone.* Joint missions of the Resistance and the Sámi meant that the Norway-Sweden border remained permeable for rebels and Sámi alike. German interests in munitions and heavy water oriented the puppet government's attention and energy toward weapons development and protection. Given these priorities, the Quisling government failed to advance Sámi-specific restrictions, which provided incentives for the Sámi to mobilize among themselves and with the Resistance. These motives for Sami political mobilization differed from those of the early 1930s, but internal patterns of coordination persevered. The Allied presence meant that domestic activity was visible internationally, and freedom of intragroup association remained a possibility, given the greater mobility of the Norwegian Sámi than their Swedish and Finnish counterparts.

Dawn after the Long Night

German evacuation from the North, Operation Birke, had left scorched lands in its wake across all three states, but the most devastating effects were in Finland. Communities forced to evacuate were left impoverished, with higher numbers of people lacking stable residence or means of livelihood in Finland and Norway. In Norway language assimilation policy was lax during the occupation, whereas Sweden had maintained its formal linguistic and cultural assimilation policies with the Sami. With the unconditional surrender of Nazi Germany on May 8, 1945, the long night broke in Scandinavia, and the variation in postwar conditions quickly became apparent. Exiting the war, the Sámi nations in different states found their Sápmi communities on drastically different playing fields. In Sweden the number of Sámi practicing herding fell, and reindeer stock declined over the course of the war, but in Finland and Norway the decline in reindeer stocks was far more drastic (Sustainable Reindeer Husbandry 1999). In addition, Norwegian and Finnish Sámi experienced greater loss of land farther north and significant internal displacement. They did, however, retain one distinctive characteristic: a greater capacity for intragroup association. Internal restrictions imposed by the occupying forces created incentives to express autonomy through resistance and internal organization.

During the war, areas experiencing the most active conflicts were also those of the greatest Sami repression. Finnish Sami experienced the most control by the state and the greatest destruction from invading forces; in some Sápmi regional communities, more than 80 percent of the land and infrastructure was devastated in what was effectively a prolonged war front. All houses, roads, and visible history were destroyed. Because of their prolonged military service, many Sámi were forced to forfeit herding, and many reindeer were culled. Anecdotal evidence suggests that the material wealth of many communities, combined with a sharp decrease in viable grazing land, was greatly diminished (Nilsson et al. 2011; Paine 1994; Reinert 2006). Additional threats to the survival of the nation-state, particularly from conflicts on the domestic front, resulted in the greatest levels of coercion and restrictions imposed on native Sámi across Scandinavia.

The Legacy of World War II and Minority Comparisons

The decade following World War II is widely considered a turning point for Sámi self-determination and cultural pride. Changes in domestic attitudes, coupled with broader European ideological shifts, came with an international reexamination of human rights fueled by the abuses of World War II (Lehtola 2005). As the global community examined the buildup to World War II, countries began to realize they could no longer maintain their pervasive nationalistic rhetoric. The rise of an international community composed of states, intergovernmental organizations, and nongovernmental organizations capable of espousing norms (and shaming states that failed to embody or uphold these norms) meant new capabilities for minority groups within states. For the Sámi, an international community meant a change in the way they sought to protect and advance their interests. Previously, state denial was the end of a rights campaign. An international community concerned with the treatment of domestic minority groups meant that the denied Sámi could appeal to international parties to put pressure on the state to change its behavior, a process called the "boomerang strategy" (Keck and Sikkink 1998).

This boomerang strategy created a new path of recourse for the Sámi to affect the domestic decisions made by the Nordic states. An attentive international community espousing human-centered norms meant that the Sámi had a greater ability to embarrass or shame the self-proclaimed (and self-perceived) egalitarian Nordic states when they did not recognize indigenous rights. Whereas previous rights gains could be more directly traced to individual campaigning efforts and negotiations with the state (Kent 2014), postwar rights gains were secured by Sámi associations, whose numbers continued to grow through the decades, whose members connected with other Sámi associations across borders, and who recognized that their domestic activities were visible to actors outside of the state who were capable of "naming and shaming" (Hafner-Burton 2008) the Nordic states. The international community increased its attention to the rights of individuals, minorities, and indigenous peoples, yet the Sámi residing in different states were not on a level playing field to engage and take advantage of the new normative environment (Jarratt 2014). Moving into the postwar era, they were asymmetrically positioned through varied wartime restrictions and conflicts to broadly mobilize on their own behalf.

The effects of World War II on Sámi mobilization were significant. Before the war, Sámi efforts to mobilize, while infrequent across borders, were relatively steady across Fennoscandia. As the Nordic states were drawn into the war, mobilization among the Sámi decreased in proportion to the loss of transparency of domestic conditions to the global community. At the end of World War II, political mobilization resumed, but at different rates. Sámi mobilization did not occur at similar frequencies between Norway, Sweden, and Finland, nor were Sámi communities experiencing similar success rates across borders. In Finland forced mobility had triggered a lasting sense of "placelessness," as many people were torn from the roots of their life narratives (Seitsonen and Koskinen-Koivisto 2018) and the need to reestablish one's home took precedence over politicking. While Finnish Sámi formed fraternal organizations, Helsinki was framing reconstruction of the North as a route to modernization. A "Finnish" way of life was promoted as a path to progress, and despite resistance from Sámi activists, the Sámi were further subjugated to the state (Lantto and Mörkenstam 2008).

Comparatively, Norway saw many linguistic gains for the Sámi in the postwar years. Regular news in Sámi on national radio began airing in 1946. At the same time, elementary schools began incorporating bilingual lessons in Sámi dialects and Norwegian. This was a turnaround from the considerable money and effort the government had invested in assimilation policies from 1900 to 1940, and "Norwegianization" policies gradually dissipated (Gaski 1997). Both language and political rights were formalized through ratification of the International Covenant on Civil and Political Rights, article 17, which protects indigenous peoples against discrimination and affirms their right to practice their languages and religion, while taking place in a space where the Norwegian state's commitments were on display to the international community.

Slowly, across the three states, Sámi national associations formed in the aftermath of separation. The Finnish Sámi Alliance was formed in the 1940s, the Norwegian Sámi Reindeer Herders' Association was founded in 1947, and the Swedish Sámi Association was created in 1950, highlighting national-level mobilization of Sámi culture. Each association was enabled to represent its constituents in international organizations and gatherings. In the 1950s the Swedish government slated reindeer herding as a crucial component of Sámi culture, and special measures were required to preserve reindeer husbandry as a part of the Sámi culture. A defining drawback of this policy was that non–reindeer herders were excluded as bearers of Sámi culture. Linguistic rights and recognition in Sweden also trailed behind Norwegian policies. Indeed, Sweden made little progress in terminating assimilationist policies until the late 1950s, when successor Sámi organizations from prewar local associations mobilized connections among rural and northern Sámi (Osherenko and Young 1989, 89).

Through the 1950s distinctive policy trends emerged among the Nordic states as the result of Sámi mobilization. Norway advanced linguistic rights and education. Finland experienced association building and efforts to establish municipal and federal herding associations. Sweden, which was the last to establish a national Sámi association, lagged behind its neighbors in cultural and livelihood policy. Legislation on Sámi interests, while ambitious, only began to translate into successful policy in the 1960s with the influence of the Sámi Council. This decade saw national Sámi organizations undertake greater coordinated action, and, having gathered along national lines, they soon moved to connect across borders. The Sámi Council, an umbrella organization for Sámi organizations in Norway, Sweden, Finland, and Russia, was founded in 1956 during the second Sámi Conference in Karasjok, Norway. This transboundary organization strengthened cooperation across borders, coordinated Sámi voices internationally, and fostered feelings of affinity among the Sámi people. Each function strengthened the demanding power of Sámi domestically while giving them the opportunity to represent themselves in international organizations. They also gained more visibility in the international sphere and greater access to international partners who could place pressure on the Nordic states to behave in ways consistent with the norms promoted in the international arena.

With this increased representation, the Nordic countries experienced a rapid expansion of Sámi policies. Sámi became a curriculum subject in Swedish schools in 1962, and the Swedish youth organization Saminuorra was formed. Previous Norwegian restrictions on Sámi construction and house size were lifted. With Sámi Council support, the Norwegian government accepted the International Convention on the Elimination of All Forms of Racial Discrimination (1965), which asserts that minorities shall not be denied the right to enjoy their own culture, profess and practice their religion, or use their own language.

The restriction-legacy framework from wartime devastation and state policy in Scandinavia has had long-term impacts that are reflected in the later establishment of Sámi parliaments. While Sámi parliaments are present in each Scandinavian state (and Russia), their establishment dates vary by twenty years. Furthermore, issues on which Sámi parliaments and advisory boards may consult vary by nation. Swedish Sámi bill amendments introduced in 1992 only gave Sámi municipalities power over matters of hunting, fishing, herding, and compensation caused by predator damage. No formal decision-making exists for any of the Sámi parliaments; they are merely able to make policy recommendations to the Nordic governments. Further, while the government-sponsored Strategy for National Minorities designated financial resources to preserve Sámi language, most complaints submitted to the Swedish Ombudsman for Ethnic Discrimination (established in 1986, later combined with three other offices to create the Equality Ombudsman agency in 2009) asserted the failings of these government programs (Pikkarainen and Brodin 2008, 16). Meanwhile, the Norwegian government ratified the International Labor Convention No. 169, confirming protection of the land rights of indigenous peoples (though Norway remains the only Scandinavian state to have done so). It has also made greater strides in language protection and preservation (Corson 1995). Norway is also the only state to acknowledge *siida* (local communities) as the basic unit of organization regarding land rights, herding management, and delegation (Lindqvist 2009).

Ultimately, the degree of wartime restriction experienced by the Sámi is linked to the degree of wartime violence the state faced as well as to the likelihood of later success in postwar mobilization. Higher domestic threat levels corresponded with higher levels of residential and food instability, underemployment and unemployment (especially among traditional livelihoods), and infrastructure devastation. These differences among the Sámi communities affected their ability to respond to postwar ideological changes and take advantage of an international audience capable of putting pressure on the Nordic states.

Today, the Nordic states rank highly on all accounts of transparency, whether in business, politics, or international agreement compliance (Greve and Hodge 2011; Ingebritsen 2006; Transparency International 2017). Both Sámi and immigrants benefit from and contribute to this transparency in their interactions with the state, yet we must remember that this transparency culture is a relatively recent phenomenon. World War II obscured domestic events through the occupation and the existence of war fronts. It would have been hard to predict at that time the legacy wartime changes would cause in Sámi mobilization and capability, especially given the widespread relief at the end of occupation. In Scandinavia, the war threatened not only the Nordic states but also the heart of Sámi cultural existence.

The lessons we learn about the way states respond to indigenous mobilization under normal and wartime conditions contribute to our knowledge of state interactions with many other domestic and nonstate actors, including nonindigenous ethnic minorities and civil societies. The Sámi experience has much to lend to contemporary immigration debates, as similar themes of assimilation are echoed in immigration policy. Much of the existing ethnic-politics literature has focused on restrictive and assimilatory immigration policy as a response to the rise of right-wing parties (Brochmann and Hegeland 2012; Junn and Masuoka 2013), yet few examine the legacy of Nordic colonial behavior on contemporary ethnic attitudes. Assimilation policies of the early twentieth century intended to make the Sámi less visible to the majority culture—aims that are reflected to different degrees and through different strategies in some contemporary Scandinavian policies. Not only do such policies seek to integrate immigrants into the economy and labor market to different degrees (as states sought to do with the Sámi in the nineteenth and twentieth centuries), but they have also moved to ban visible cultural practices in the public sphere. Some politicians and activists denounced fasting, for example, as "a danger to all of us" and have increasingly spoken on banning burqas and niqabs (Barry and Sorensen 2018; Laborde 2012). Yet while Sámi and immigrants share challenges of assimilatory policy, legal distinctions affect how much ethnic minorities may borrow from the successful strategies of earlier Sámi activists. Instead, it is beneficial to recognize the discursive parallels between "domestic" and "foreign" minorities. A lacking or belated recognition of migrant rights in the Nordic states can be understood as a contemporary reflection of a belated—or reluctant—recognition of assimilationist histories.

In 1987 the Norwegian Sámi Act was signed, comprehensive legislation that affirmed and articulated the existence of rights unique to Sámi because of their indigenous status. Two years later, the Norwegian Constitution itself was amended. It elaborated upon minority rights, adding that it is the "responsibility of the authorities of the State to create conditions enabling the Sámi people to preserve and develop its language, culture, and way of life" (Constitution, section A, article 108).[2] Here a crucial distinction is made that affects the ability of immigrant minorities to draw from the mobilization strategies of the Sámi: across Scandinavia, Sámi are a recognized and legally protected minority, but immigrants are not. Furthermore, indigenous groups understand their relationship with the state as nation-to-nation and therefore consider their rights protected under international law (Henderson 2006; Semb 2001). While states may adopt or ratify minority and human rights conventions that impact immigrant minorities, these conventions are voluntary, nonbinding, and difficult to monitor.

CONCLUSION

The Nazi occupation had devastating material and psychological consequences on northern residents. These influences persisted after the end of the war; however, the Sámi postwar mobilization illustrates an effort—undeterred by the asymmetric disruptions of war—to preserve the integrity of Sámi association. After World War II's tumultuous events, European ideology opened to an unprecedented degree to recognition of the role of minority identity. While debates continue today on the rights and responsibilities of immigrant and ethnic minorities, early and postwar Sámi mobilization may serve as a template for contemporary association building. The importance of this intergroup learning is significant, given the challenges of minority mobilization in homogeneous states.

Parallel themes emerge in both Sámi and immigration policy. Assimilatory policies discourage minorities from engaging in visibly distinct practices in the public sphere and push outsiders into the mainstream labor market. While themes of assimilation pervade each ethnicity's experiences, immigrants will have to develop pathways for cross-ethnic mobilization to more effectively draw from the pre- and postwar strategies of Sámi activists. Exogenous shocks and repressive state policy may cause political mobilization to waver, yet it has not been repressed. While Sámi mobilized at different postwar rates, the associations of each nation still evolved. A willingness to identify indigenous Sámi needs has the potential to translate across categories and to color immigration politics today. Coupled with greater international transparency and a developed civil society, immigration policy stands on the shoulders of the preceding indigenous policy, testifying to the influence of such mobilization in shaping state policy.

Notes

1. Established in 1935 in Germany, the *Lebensborn* project was a breeding program intended to result in the birth of "racially superior" children. In Scandinavia, Norwegian women were under pressure to have children with German men, resulting in up to twelve thousand children being born between 1940 and 1945. These children were considered to have the "purest" Aryan blood.

2. *Det påligger statens myndigheter å legge forholdene til rette for at den samiske folkegruppe kan sikre og utvikle sitt språk, sin kultur og sitt samfunnsliv*, https://lovdata .no/dokument/NL/lov/1814-05-17.

References

Barry, Ellen, and Martin Selsoe Sorensen. 2018. "In Denmark, Harsh New Laws for Immigrant 'Ghettos.'" *New York Times*, July 1, 2018.

Berg-Nordlie, Mikkel. 2015. "Two Centuries of Russian Sámi Policy: Arrangements for Autonomy and Participation Seen in Light of Imperial, Soviet and Federal Indigenous Minority Policy 1822–2014." *Acta Borealia* 32(1): 40–67.

Brochmann, Grete, and Anniken Hegeland. 2012. *Immigration Policy and the Scandinavian Welfare State, 1945–2010*. New York: Palgrave Macmillan.

Corson, David. 1995. "Norway's 'Sami Language Act': Emancipatory Implications for the World's Aboriginal Peoples." *Language in Society* 4(1): 493–514.

Coyne, Christopher, and Abigail Hall. 2014. "Perfecting Tyranny: Foreign Intervention as Experimentation in State Control." *Independent Institute* 19(2): 165–89.

Demant Hatt, Emily. 2013. *With the Lapps in the High Mountains: A Woman among the Sami, 1907–1908.* Translated by Barbara Sjoholm. Madison: University of Wisconsin Press.

Drouard, Alain. 1999. "Concerning Eugenics in Scandinavia: An Evaluation of Recent Research and Publications." *Population* 11(3): 261–70.

Ericsson, Kjersti, and Eva Simonsen. 2008. "On the Border: The Contested Children of the Second World War." *Childhood* 15(3): 397–414.

Fouche, Gwladys, and Alister Doyle. 2018. "As Arctic Warms, Reindeer Herders Tangle with New Industries." Reuters, July 9. https://www.reuters.com/article/us-arctic-economy-sami-insight-idUSKBN1JZ0CU.

Gaski, Harald. 1997. *Sámi Culture in a New Era: The Norwegian Sámi Experience.* Karasjok, Norw.: Davvi Girji.

Greve, Carsten, and Graeme Hodge. 2011. "Transparency in Public-Private Partnerships: Some Lessons from Scandinavia and Australia." Working paper, Rutgers University.

Hafner-Burton, Emilie M. 2008. "Sticks and Stones: Naming and Shaming the Human Rights Enforcement Problem." *International Organization* 62(4): 689–716.

Henderson, James. 2006. *First Nations Jurisprudence and Aboriginal Rights: Defining the Just Society.* Saskatoon, SK: Native Law Center.

Henne, Peter, and Jason Klocek. 2017. "Taming the Gods: How Religious Conflict Shapes Religious Repression." *Journal of Conflict Resolution* 1(1): 1–27.

Howarth, David. 2016. *We Die Alone: A WWII Epic of Escape and Endurance.* Guilford, NC: Lyons Press.

Hunt, Vincent. 2014. *Fire and Ice: The Nazi's Scorched Earth Campaign in Norway.* Gloucestershire, UK: History Press.

Ingebritsen, Christine. 2006. *Scandinavia in World Politics.* New York: Rowman and Littlefield.

Jarratt, Emma. 2014. "Sami Voices Not Heard in Finnmark Liberation Ceremony." *Barents Observer*, October 25.

Jentoft, Svein, Henry Minde, and Ragnar Nilsen, eds. 2003. *Resource Management and Global Rights.* Delft, Neth.: Eburon Academic Publishers.

Josefsen, Eva. 2010. "The Saami and the National Parliaments: Channels for Political Influence." Mexico City: Bureau for Development Policy.

Junn, Jane, and Natalie Masuoka. 2013. *The Politics of Belonging: Race, Public Opinion, and Immigration.* Chicago: University of Chicago Press.

Keck, Margaret, and Kathryn Sikkink. 1998. *Activists beyond Borders: Advocacy Networks and International Politics.* Ithaca, NY: Cornell University Press.

Kent, Neil. 2014. *The Sami Peoples of the North*. London: C. Hurst.

Kinnunen, Tina, and Ville Kivimäki, eds. 2011. *Finland in World War II: History, Memory, Interpretation*. Boston: Brill.

Kipling, Rudyard. 1899. "Modern History Sourcebook: Rudyard Kipling. The White Man's Burden." The Internet Modern History Sourcebook. http://source.books.fordham.edu/mod/kipling.asp.

Kulchyski, Peter. 2011. *Aboriginal Rights Are Not Human Rights*. Winnipeg, MB: Arbeiter Ring Publishing.

Kvist, Roger. 1992. "The Racist Legacy in Modern Swedish Saami Policy." In *Readings in Saami History, Culture, and Language III*, edited by Roger Kvist, 203–20. Umeå, Swed.: Department of Saami Studies, Umeå University.

Laborde, Cecile. 2012. "State Paternalism and Religious Dress Code." *International Journal of Constitutional Law* 10(2): 398–410.

Lantto, Patrik, and Ulf Mörkenstam. 2008. "Sami Rights and Sami Challenges: The Modernization Process and the Swedish Sami Movement, 1996–2006." *Scandinavian Journal of History* 33(1): 26–51.

Lawrence, Rebecca, and Rasmus Kløcker Larsen. 2017. "The Politics of Planning: Assessing the Impacts of Mining on Sami Lands." *Third World Quarterly* 38(5): 1164–80.

Lehtola, Veli-Pekka. 2005. *The Sámi People: Traditions in Transition*. Anchorage: University of Alaska Press.

Lindqvist, Johanna. 2009. "Reindeer Herding: A Traditional Livelihood." *Macquarie Journal of International and Comparative Environmental Law* 5(1): 83–103.

Mustonen, Kaisu, Tero Mustonen, Antti Aikio, and Pekka Aikio. 2010. *Drowning Reindeer, Drowning Homes: Indigenous Sami and Hydroelectricity Development in Sompio, Finland*. Vaasa: Snowchange Cooperative.

Nilsson, Lena Maria, Lars Dahlgren, Ingegerd Johansson, Margiritt Brustad, Per Sjölander, and Bethany Van Guelpen. 2011. "Diet and Lifestyle of the Sami of Southern Lapland in the 1930s–1950s and Today. *International Journal of Circumpolar Health* 70(3): 301–18.

Nordin, Dennis Sven. 2005. *A Swedish Dilemma: A Liberal European Nation's Struggle with Racism and Xenophobia, 1990–2000*. Lanham, MD: University Press of America.

Osherenko, Gail, and Oran Young. 1989. *The Age of the Arctic: Hot Conflicts and Cold Realities*. Cambridge: Cambridge University Press.

Øverland, Indra, and Mikkel Berg-Nordlie. 2012. *Bridging Divides: Ethno-political Leadership among the Russian Sámi*. New York: Berghahn Books.

Paine, Robert. 1994. *Herds of the Tundra: A Portrait of Saami Reindeer Pastoralism*. Washington, DC: Smithsonian Institution Press.

Pikkarainen, Heidi, and Björn Brodin. 2008. "Discrimination of the Sámi: The Rights of the Sámi from a Discrimination Perspective." Stockholm: Ombudsman for Ethnic Discrimination.

Ravna, Øyvind. 2015. "Recognition of Indigenous Lands through the Norwegian 2005 Finnmark Act: An Important Example for Other Countries with Indigenous People?" In *Indigenous Peoples' Governance of Land and Protected Territories in the Arctic*, edited by T. M. Herman and T. Martin, 189–208. New York: Springer.

Reinert, Erik S. 2006. "The Economics of Reindeer Herding: Saami Entrepreneurship between Cyclical Sustainability and the Powers of State and Oligopolies." *British Food Journal* 108(7): 522–40.

Seitsonen, Oula, and Eerika Koskinen-Koivisto. 2018. "Where the F . . . Is Vuotso? Heritage of the Second World War Forced Movement and Destruction in a Sami Reindeer Herding Community in Finnish Lapland." *International Journal of Heritage Studies* 24(4): 421–41.

Semb, A. J. 2001. "How Norms Affect Policy: The Case of Sami Policy in Norway." *International Journal on Minority and Group Rights* 8(2): 177–222.

Sikku, Nils-Henrik, Karin Kvarfordt, and Michael Teilus. 2005. "The Sami: An Indigenous People in Sweden." National Sami Information Centre informational paperback, Västerås, Norway.

Sjersted, Francis. 2011. *The Age of Social Democracy: Norway and Sweden in the Twentieth Century.* Princeton, NJ: Princeton University Press.

Sustainable Reindeer Husbandry. 1999. "Reindeer Husbandry in Sweden." Swedish University of Agricultural Sciences. Stockholm: Statistics Sweden.

Transparency International. 2017. "Corruption Perceptions Index 2017." https://www.transparency.org/news/feature/corruption_perceptions_index_2017.

Denmark in Miniature

The Interplay of Cosmopolitanism, Nationalism, and Exoticism in Copenhagen's Tivoli

JULIE K. ALLEN

Although the center of Copenhagen was once defined by the royal palace of Christiansborg and the Royal Theater on Kongens Nytorv, the city has shifted westward over the past century and a half, in tandem with the democratization of Danish society and the expansion of the city's borders. Today, the city center lies beyond the erstwhile ramparts of medieval Copenhagen: the main train station is the city's beating heart, nurturing a network of transport connections to the Copenhagen suburbs, rural Denmark, and the rest of the world, while across the street lies its cultural navel—the world-famous amusement park Tivoli, the most Danish of spaces, characterized by the elegant arabesques of its Orientalist architecture. In this internationally and nationally significant public space, which attracts nearly five million visitors per year—nearly equivalent to the entire population of Denmark—the harmonious coexistence of the romanticized familiar and the stylized foreign allows guests, subconsciously for the most part, to imbibe a historical fantasy of Danish cultural sophistication and tolerance that serves to brand contemporary Denmark as a cosmopolitan space while also modeling idealized Danish interactions with cultural difference.

Founded in August 1843 by the magazine editor and former lieutenant Georg Johan Bernhard Carstensen (1812–57), together with architect Harald Conrad Stilling (1815–91), the Copenhagen Tivoli was born from the same revolutionary, modernizing impulse that produced Denmark's June constitution of 1849, with its guarantees of free speech, free assembly, and the free exercise of religion. The constitution legally transformed Denmark from an absolute monarchy into a parliamentary democracy, but it was Tivoli that rendered the corresponding social transformation visible and viable as it took place over the course of the second half of the nineteenth century. Martin Zerlang explains, "It may sound a bit exaggerated to make a pleasure garden a turning point in history, but so it was: Tivoli with its roller-coaster, its merry-go-round and its bazaar marked [Denmark's] transition into Modernity. . . . A modern, liberal, democratic culture was promoted with greater force by Tivoli than by all the inflammatory political speeches" (1997, 81). Since 1843 Tivoli has represented Danish culture both outwardly and inwardly, but it has done so rather paradoxically by blending traditional Danish symbols of identity and belonging with markers of Denmark's engagement with the wider world, in particular the distant countries perceived as the exotic Orient. This chapter explores how Tivoli has facilitated ongoing negotiations of Danish cultural identity since the mid-nineteenth century, particularly with regard to managing discourses of multiculturalism in the context of Denmark's engagement with colonialism, imperialism, and globalization.

From its inception, Tivoli was designed to showcase both Danish cosmopolitanism and Danish nationalism. After an extended European tour, during which he visited both the Parisian Jardin de Tivoli (1766–1842) and the British Vauxhall pleasure gardens in London (1785–1859), Carstensen had lobbied the Danish king for permission to build an amusement park in order to help Copenhagen keep pace with such European capital cities as Paris and London. Rather than copying either French or British cultural symbols, however, the Danish Tivoli aimed to evoke the cosmopolitan sophistication of London and Paris by replicating the visual markers of imperialism from which the wealth of most Western European countries, including Denmark, was derived. Drawing on the popularity of Chinese curios among Danish merchants, aristocrats, and sailors alike, Carstensen gave Tivoli a decidedly "Orientalist" aesthetic, with a towering Chinese pagoda, Chinese lanterns, and Islamic minarets placed throughout the park. This self-consciously exotic decorative style, paired with the park's deliberate juxtaposition of natural and artificial attractions, provided inspiration, alongside the Swedish singer Jenny Lind, for Hans Christian Andersen's story "Nattergalen" ("The Nightingale"), which appeared in November 1843. Andersen attended the grand opening of Tivoli on August 15, 1843, as he noted in his almanac, and chose, as a result, to set his story dealing with the tension between nature and artifice, humility and pretension, art and artifice at the court of the Chinese emperor. Yet, as with Tivoli itself, the story's "Chinese" window dressing serves to conceal its preoccupation with its own Danish context, in particular the dangers of self-congratulatory cultural homogeneity. The story begins with the pronouncement, "In China, as you may know, the Emperor is Chinese, and everyone there is also Chinese" (Andersen 2008, 80), an obvious oversimplification that can be read as a commentary on the leveling tendencies present in Danish society against which Andersen frequently chafed.

The intersection of Tivoli's exotic Orientalism with Danish nationalism exposes the park's contributions to constructions of Danish identity from the mid-nineteenth century until today, particularly with regard to multicultural Denmark. Zerlang emphasizes the pedagogical element of the park, describing it as a "small scale big city where they [Copenhageners] would be able to develop and practice their talents for living among strangers in a public space" (1997, 86), while Elisabeth Oxfeldt concentrates on its political dimensions. She explains the park's Orientalist discourse in terms of mid-nineteenth-century political tensions about the nature of Danishness during a time of massive political, social, and economic shifts occurring within Danish society, and suggests that Tivoli enabled Danes to "enact their national group identity as a reassuring social practice" through ritualized behavior, conspicuous consumption, and visualization of the imagined national community (Oxfeldt 2005, 57).

The kind of Danish nationalism Oxfeldt and Zerlang connect with Tivoli is not strident or flashy but is simply banal nationalism, to use Michael Billig's term, reproduced in such ordinary, commonplace ways as to be entirely unnoticeable and unexceptional to the casual observer. For Billig, banal nationalism consists primarily of "ideological habits of thought" by which the nation is continually "'flagged,' in the lives of its citizenry" (1995, 6), forming the background for their political discourse and cultural products. This is a practice at which Tivoli excels. Tivoli's placement on the ramparts of the old city heralds its pioneering role in bringing Denmark into the modern age, while the layout of the park itself, with its broad central promenade flanked by important public buildings, notably the bazaar and concert hall, as well as symmetrical pairs of restaurants, is characterized, as Zerlang notes, "by an almost classicist celebration of order and regularity" (1997, 87). Tivoli is a city within a city, a model state, a celebration of Danish democracy and harmony. It has evolved considerably over the 175 years of its existence, particularly in terms of the technical sophistication of its rides, but it has maintained its focus on providing an immersive experience, an "atmosphere that greets and embraces you," as a recent commemorative volume gushes (Olsen and Schaldemose 2018, 12). This liberated, welcoming space is explicitly coded as

Denmark in Miniature

Old-fashioned Danish hard candies, known as *bolcher* or *bolsjer*, featuring the flags of the Nordic countries, are available for purchase throughout the park.

Danish in subtle ways. Throughout the park, unobtrusive visual reminders of Danish national culture shape the visitor's experience, from the ubiquitous Danish flags to Danish *smørrebrød* (open-face sandwich) restaurants, the old-fashioned alleyway (known as Smøgen) lined with shop signs from rural Danish market towns, and shops selling red-and-white kitsch and old-fashioned Danish *bolsjer* (hard candies), some imprinted with the Danish flag.

The uncommented juxtaposition of these markers of banal Danish nationalism with easily recognizable symbols of Oriental exoticism, including pagodas, minarets, and a ride called "Den flyvende kuffert" (The flying trunk), serves to incorporate them into a narrative about Danishness. The ride's name alludes to Andersen's story of the same name about an impoverished young storyteller who flew to Turkey in a magical trunk, where his dressing gown and slippers wouldn't attract attention. Upon his arrival, he tried to win the hand of a princess by pretending to be a god but was thwarted by his own arrogance. As in "The Nightingale," the exotic setting of "The Flying Trunk" veils Andersen's satirical commentary on nineteenth-century Danish colonialism and class-based identity politics, making the title's incorporation into Tivoli doubly appropriate. Tivoli is also a place where the exotic stands in for the familiar, where a modern-day Aladdin—the Algiers-born Georg

Carstensen—seduced Danes with the bewitching wonders of the Orient in order to entertain, amuse, distract, and delight them. While Carstensen's own life story functions, like the tale of Aladdin, as "a myth of social mobility cloaked in Oriental garments" (Zerlang 1997, 90), Tivoli became the magic lamp that had the power to transport visitors into pleasurable realms of fantasy while allowing them to remain safely at home.

In the Tradition of
European Pleasure Gardens

Although the Jardin de Tivoli in Paris, which Carstensen had personally visited, was likely the immediate inspiration for the name of Copenhagen's Tivoli, the pleasure garden has a much longer history that the name Tivoli is intended to evoke. Its oldest namesake is the Roman emperor Hadrian's Villa d'Este, in the hilltop Italian town of Tivoli, which H. F. Raup (1974, 36) claims as the direct origin of the name. Country villas, which were common in Rome in the first and second centuries CE, were, as art historians William Macdonald and John Pinto note, "a place for restful leisure, or *otium*, the opposite of *negotium*, business or non-rest" (1995, 3). Likewise, the Danish Tivoli offers a refuge from the noise and bustle of the city of Copenhagen, replete with swaths of green grass, meandering paths, and peaceful waterways. In both cases, "woods, meadows, and views both natural and contrived are essential to the overall effect" (3). The area of Hadrian's pleasure gardens was twice that of Pompeii and thus much larger than the Danish Tivoli, which was built on a plot of grazing land in an area outside the Copenhagen city walls known as Dronningens Enghave. Although Tivoli is now situated in central Copenhagen, between the main train station and the town hall, it was deliberately placed outside the city limits of the time in order to ensure the requisite amounts of light, green space, and water and to allow for fireworks displays (Haugsted 1993, 25). Likewise, Hadrian's villa was constructed far enough from Rome to allow the emperor to rest and relax. Food and socialization were important aspects of life at Hadrian's villa, along with music, concerts, theatrical performances, and other festivities. In the late eighteenth century, when the Ruggieri brothers named their Parisian pleasure garden Tivoli, the ruins of the Roman villa were sorely neglected, but the name, Rob Rentenaar asserts, still "reminded the educated public of the times and splendours of Maecenas, Hadrianus, Horatius, Propertius, Catullus, and Zenobia" (1976, 26). Carstensen's adoption of the name for his Danish pleasure garden evoked both these pagan archetypes and their Parisian reincarnation.

The term "tivoli" has long been used as shorthand for a place of enter-tainment. In fact, in the sixteenth-century *Ordbog over det danske sprog*, the definitions given of a "tivoli" include "fun-fair," "travelling fun-fair," and "noisy conduct, pleasure" (Rentenaar 1976, 25, 29). In the third volume of his *House-hold Words*, published in 1851, Charles Dickens reports attending several *tab-leaux vivants* that were held at a "Tivoli, a kind of Vauxhall Gardens, at the Thier Garten" in Berlin (1851, 201). Rentenaar documents the widespread use of the name Tivoli in the Netherlands, the United States, and elsewhere in the English-speaking world in reference to "theatres, cafes and restaurants, espe-cially those with garden arrangements," as well as to "settlements, natural areas and even barbershops and beauty salons" (1976, 24). Many stage and early movie theaters across the world were named Tivoli, from Sydney, Aus-tralia, to Aberdeen, Scotland, as was a famous nineteenth-century saloon in Denver, the Tivoli Club ("Tivoli" n.d.). There is even a Chateau Tivoli in San Francisco, a large Victorian townhouse once occupied by Mrs. Ernestine Kreling, owner of the city's Tivoli Opera House, "the first place where opera was performed on the West Coast" of the United States ("History" n.d.). In 1989, after housing a variety of Jewish organizations and a New Age psychology center, it became a bed and breakfast, with rooms named after such famous entertainers and guests as Mark Twain, Lily Langtry, and Enrico Caruso.

Like its name, Tivoli's function as an egalitarian *forlystelsessted* (place of pleasure) is also derivative. The earliest documented amusement park is in fact Danish, but it was not Tivoli. Instead, that distinction belongs to Dyre-havsbakken (generally known just as Bakken), founded in 1583 in the middle of the Royal Game Park in northern Zealand (Wanhill 2003, 40). Almost a century later, in 1661, a man named John Vaux established the Vauxhall Gar-dens on the south bank of the Thames in London, featuring entertainment, music, fireworks, games, and even primitive rides. In the seventeenth century, Vauxhall was considered a somewhat scandalous place, especially for young, marriageable women—it was certainly not designed for family outings—but it inspired many imitators. Vauxhall became a common term for pleasure gar-dens; several temporary Vauxhalls popped up in Denmark in the late eigh-teenth and early nineteenth centuries, whetting the Danish public's appetite for a permanent pleasure garden. Elsewhere in Europe, the Prater leisure gar-den opened in Vienna in 1766, followed by the Jardin de Tivoli in Paris in 1771, though the latter did not acquire its famous name until it came under the direction of the Ruggieri brothers in 1796. The French Jardin de Tivoli was a popular attraction for young reactionaries and visiting dignitaries, including the emperor of Austria, the czar of Russia, and the king of Prussia (Rentenaar 1976, 26). Other pleasure gardens called Tivoli were founded in Hamburg and Berlin in the first quarter of the nineteenth century, as were several Tivoli theaters and Tivoli parks in the Netherlands in the 1820s and 1830s. The Jardin de Tivoli in Paris ceased operation in 1842, the year before Tivoli in Copenhagen was established.

From its inception, Tivoli was intended to illustrate and exemplify Copenhagen's cultural sophistication. Carstensen's exposure to pleasure gardens around the world contributed to his vision for Tivoli as a showcase of Danish modernity and cosmopolitanism, well before those became widely accepted national character traits of his home country. In 1836 he traveled to Spain, Portugal, North Africa, France, England, and finally the United States, where he lived for a year and edited a few newspapers in Philadelphia (Haugsted 1993, 11). After several extended stays in Paris, he returned to Copenhagen in May 1841 and submitted an application for a five-year license to run a stationary "Tivoli or Vauxhall" that could compare to the European establishments known variously as "Vauxhall, Tivoli, Jardin-turc, Bazar, Nuit-venetienne, etc." (21). Fortuitously for Carstensen, the citizens' assembly that had been elected in April 1840 to administer the city of Copenhagen was interested in the idea of a combined amusement park and shopping bazaar near the city and approved Carstensen's application. According to historian Ida Haugsted (19), the goal, at least on the part of the city council, was to create a place that would attract tourists and showcase Copenhagen as being on par with other European capitals and as a city where commerce and culture flourished hand in hand. In order to raise Copenhagen's international profile, Carstensen's amusement park could not just be a pretty green space with some handicraft stalls. For the sake of Denmark's international renown and its own sustainability, Tivoli needed to transcend the homely Danish delights of Bakken and engage with a more internationally recognizable discourse around pleasure, leisure, and culture.

Tivoli's Oriental Imagescape

Carstensen accomplished this feat by invoking the "exotic East" as Tivoli's organizing theme and positioning the park as a meeting place between Orient and Occident, between the colorful allure of the foreign and the comfortable domesticity of the familiar. While each of its predecessor parks had offered a wide and incoherent array of attractions, Carstensen's Tivoli transformed the fundamental character of amusement parks through its unprecedented

Denmark in Miniature

thematic consistency. In this way, Tivoli anticipates the modern theme park, which the Marriott Corporation defines as "a family entertainment complex oriented towards a particular subject or historical area, combining the continuity of costuming and architecture with entertainment and merchandise to promote a fantasy-provoking atmosphere" (Wanhill 2003, 40). While this definition postdates the establishment of Tivoli by more than a century, it captures the significance of the park's deliberately Orientalist aesthetic in creating an immersive, meaningful visitor experience. According to marketing theorist Stephen Wanhill, the "key economic aspects to consider in developing any attraction are the imagescape (or a number of imagescapes, thus giving a place within a place), the location, and the market" (42). For an imagescape to succeed, it needs to "evoke known products or events in the minds of the public" (44). Since the Tivoli gardens were not built around a commercial brand, like LEGO, Universal Studios, or Disney, the imagescape of Tivoli had to be drawn from more intangible sources, primarily discourses about culture and cultural difference that reflected Danish encounters with the wider world through its merchant fleet, far-flung colonies, and intellectual engagement with images of the Orient.

Given the geopolitical circumstances of Tivoli's establishment and the biography of its founder, its Orientalist flair can illuminate Denmark's relationship to other, alien cultures at the time. In the mid-nineteenth century, Denmark's imperial adventures were drawing rapidly to a close, but the country had had more than a century of mercantile and colonial contact with China, Africa, India, the West Indies, and other distant locales. As Oxfeldt notes, the establishment of the Asiatisk Kompagni (Asiatic Company) in 1732 had ensured a steady stream of "chinoiseries—porcelain, silk, cotton, and tea" into the Danish capital city (2005, 22), with the result that Chinese pagodas appeared in parks and Chinese goods adorned even rural vicarages, as B. S. Ingemann reported of his grandmother's parlor (Zerlang 1997, 82). Literary and scholarly texts, from Danish Romantic poet Adam Oehlenschläger's play *Aladdin, eller Den forunderlige lampe* (*Aladdin, or the Wonderful Lamp*, 1805) and Andersen's travelogue *En digters bazar* (*A Poet's Bazaar*, 1840) to Rasmus Rask's treatises on Indo-European languages from Anglo-Saxon to Sanskrit, had brought Orientalist tropes into the homes and conversations of educated Danes. The British victory in the First Opium War in 1839 forced China open to Western influence and filled newspapers with accounts of the magnificence of Chinese buildings and gardens.

Born in Algeria, where his father, Johan Arnold Hieronymus Carstensen (1783–1853), was the consul general, Carstensen grew up surrounded by North

African culture. While in the Danish military, serving in the eighth company of Kongens Livjægerkorps (the Royal Life Guards), he edited and published several newspapers, including *Tusinde og een nat* (A thousand and one nights, 1832–33) (Zerlang 1997, 90). According to Zerlang, Carstensen himself was widely regarded as an Aladdin figure in Copenhagen, an image he promoted by his dandyish appearance, complete with "tight, railway-striped pantaloons, flowery jacket, pinched waistcoat, Van Dyke beard, golden pince-nez, top hat and billowing Havana cigar" (90). With so many tangible and intangible Orientalist symbols already present in the Danish environment, Carstensen needed only to transform these tropes into experiential opportunities for his countrymen. He was only the director of Tivoli for five years, until breaking his contract to fight in the first Schleswig War in 1848, but he set the tone for the Orientalist style and cosmopolitan feeling that the park retains to this day.

Theming Tivoli as an Orientalist fantasy heightened the park's entertainment value and allowed it to offer an immersive experience to its visitors in an imagined world with which they were superficially familiar. From the outset, Tivoli showcased a self-conscious exoticism that offers a playful but reductionist approach to the non-Western cultures upon whose exploitation Danish colonial wealth depended. Carstensen brought to Tivoli many of the Oriental decorations he had used for several temporary Figaro-themed Vauxhall events held in the Christiansborg castle arena in 1842 and 1843. His original plan included not only a bazaar for the selling of arts and crafts and a fireworks alley but also swings, Russian slides, and a divan for tobacco smoking. The park's original wooden roller coaster from 1843, based on a Russian design, was initially denounced by critics as "un-Danish" but was ultimately allowed to stay and has now, in its fourth iteration that dates to 1914, become "a genuine Tivoli icon" (Olsen and Schaldemose 2018, 29). Wanhill notes that "theming allows imagineers to give new meaning to attractions, park facilities and infrastructure" and that "to be effective the message is continually repeated in the imagescape of each zone so as to have the highest visitor impact and to solidify the entertainment value through the illusion and sense of role-play created by the use of different story lines and settings" (2003, 48). Tivoli has modeled this thematic repetition since the beginning.

On opening day in August 1843, the concert hall was decorated in Turkish style, with "coloured glass windows that stretched from cornice to skirting board," while the Chinese pagoda housed a Middle Eastern bazaar, which, according to the *Tivoli-Avis* on May 28, 1845, was intended to evoke the Arabian

Nights as a place "where the riches of the world are piled up, all the extravagant splendor of the Orient" (Zerlang 1997, 91). The two main restaurants, known as Divan I and Divan II, perhaps in a nod to the German author Goethe's famous 1819 poetry collection *West-östlicher Diwan* (*West-Eastern Divan*), were situated "along the vista lines of the promenade," while the bazaar, concert hall, and other public buildings are "placed at slopes in the ground in a kind of natural amphitheater" (87). Initially, the main attractions were the elaborate gardens and the pantomime theater, but new features were added regularly. Architects Ove Petersen and Vilhelm Dahlerup modeled the dragon-flanked Pantomime Theater, constructed in 1874, on the Forbidden City in Beijing, relying on drawings, paintings, and handicrafts to supply appropriate motifs (Olsen and Schaldemose 2018, 24). The Chinese Tower, also somewhat confusingly called the Japanese Pagoda, was added in 1900, a new concert hall built by Richard Bergmann and Knud Arne Petersen in 1902 featured large domes and minarets, and a Moorish bazaar constructed in 1909 became the home of the restaurant Nimb. The original entrance to the park was just a wooden gate with a ticket house on each side, but monumental gates facing Bernstorffsgade and Vesterbrogade were added in the 1890s and 1910s, though they were initially so flamboyant that they had to be toned down in the 1920s at the behest of the city ("Tivoli's History" n.d.).

NATIONAL SELF-FASHIONING AT TIVOLI

Dismissing Tivoli's Orientalist aesthetic as merely a design choice overlooks the park's involvement in constructing a sense of Danish national and cultural identity in a crucially transitional period of Danish history. Zerlang reports that Tivoli was immediately hailed by Danish and foreign observers alike as "the epitome of Danish culture" and has remained closely associated with "all the expectations attached to the development of modern Denmark since the 1840s" (1997, 81–82). The role of the park's decor in this project is not self-evident, particularly since the relationship between these two elements involves both othering and imitation. Rather than engaging directly with Denmark's exploitative and highly profitable involvement in European imperialism, nineteenth-century Tivoli offered an uncritical reproduction of Orientalist motifs that comes across today as deliberately naive, a way to showcase the riches procured through imperialist economics without acknowledging their human costs. No attempt is made to depict or explain the actual cultures or histories of China, Arabia, North Africa, or Turkey; instead, the park evokes an idealized, imaginary Oriental landscape to entertain its visitors without

This structure, known as both the Chinese Tower and the Japanese Pagoda, was built in 1900 in the heart of Tivoli gardens.

The use of Islamic domes and crescents recurs throughout the park, as on top of one of the rides depicted here.

requiring them to confront that landscape's actuality. In this way, Tivoli reinforced European constructions of the Orient as "a place of romance, exotic beings, haunting memories and landscapes, remarkable experiences" (Said 1978, 9). If one accepts the premise that Orientalism is rarely if ever about the culture being depicted, serving instead as a foil for the culture doing the depicting, Tivoli's Orientalism begs the question of how this self-conscious appropriation of Oriental motifs has facilitated the park's identification as a quintessentially Danish space from the mid-nineteenth century until today.

One way in which Tivoli fulfilled this function in its early years was by educating provincial Danes about cosmopolitan behavioral norms that borrowed their glamour from the Orient. In the words of journalist and politician Orla Lehmann, public life and entertainments in Copenhagen in the 1830s could be summed up in two words: "small and dull" (Hage 1872, 230). Unlike Bakken, which was open to all, Tivoli was an exclusive space reserved for patrons who could afford to pay admission of one mark and who likely aspired to Continental sophistication such as that represented by coffee drinking. Coffee had made its way from eleventh-century Ethiopia to the Ottoman Empire in 1655 to Venice, Paris, London, Leipzig, and Vienna in the late seventeenth century before conquering the Danish palate, but in order for the beverage to carry with it the sophistication of those European capitals, it had to be partaken of correctly. In 1842 the actor Niels Volkersen, who later played the first Danish Pierrot in Tivoli's pantomime theater until his death in 1893, criticized his countrymen in an article in the periodical *Politivennen* for drinking their coffee "with an earnestness, a reserve bordering on anxiety, as if they were treading the path of vice, as if they were doing something wrong, as if they suffered from bad conscience, or at least as if they wished to make done undone" (qtd. in Zerlang 1997, 85). Early Tivoli guests received instruction through the *Tivoli-Avis* in how to drink coffee properly. Merely making coffee available to Danes was not sufficient to liberate them, in Volkersen's opinion, from their "ingrained habit of gathering in secluded, small, and cramped circles, an absolute lack of experience with large, public gatherings, and a misplaced and ill-timed fear of approaching public gatherings" (85), but Tivoli served as a place where those kinds of provincial attitudes could be stretched enough to eventually accommodate a different, more expansive conception of Danishness. Framing such behavioral challenges within the nineteenth-century equivalent of a virtual reality created new receptivity to urbane behavioral norms and attitudes that contrasted strikingly with the rigid parochialism of early nineteenth-century Copenhagen society. Moreover,

Tivoli offered opportunities for all manner of scintillating interactions between men and women, the upper and emerging middle classes, and even people of different nationalities, free from the constraints of the bourgeois parlor. Still, when necessary, Tivoli could call on Danish nationalism to restore order, as, for example, during a brawl that erupted on the terrace in front of Restaurant Wivel in 1913, when the restaurant's orchestra repeatedly played the official Danish national anthem, "Kong Christian stod ved højen mast" (King Christian stood by the lofty mast), in order to compel everyone in earshot to stand at attention (Olsen and Schaldemose 2018, 17).

The rendering of this space of national self-discovery and education as an Orientalist fantasy suggests a great deal about Denmark's view of its own shifting positionality within Europe over the nineteenth century. Oxfeldt reads Oehlenschläger's *Aladdin* in terms of the ebullient political climate in Denmark in the early nineteenth century, noting that it "captured the spirit of Denmark when it seemed bound for fortune—before the Napoleonic War, the loss of Norway, and the loss of Slesvig-Holstein"; Aladdin himself, despite his Asian origins, was tinted with the Danish national colors of "lovely red and white, like milk and blood" (2005, 24). In 1844 Carstensen introduced the Tivoli Guard, originally a "Lilliputian military" consisting of young boys tasked with guarding the buildings. In 1872 they adopted red-and-white uniforms modeled on those of the Royal Life Guards but in the colors of the Danish flag, and in 1909 they were joined by a brass band (Olsen and Schaldemose 2018, 25). Just as Oehlenschläger's play appeared shortly before the British bombing of Copenhagen and the state bankruptcy of 1813, Tivoli was founded in the period of relative social and political calm before the storms of 1848 and 1864 that destroyed Danish nationalist illusions of restoring the grandeur of the medieval Danish Empire. Allusions to the Aladdin theme in both Carstensen's self-presentation and Tivoli's buildings evoke an era of Danish prosperity and allude to the promise of renewed riches and good fortune that the story conveys while also allowing for veiled critique of the status quo. Oxfeldt notes that, after Denmark's bankruptcy in 1813 and the political upheavals of the 1830s, comparing the aging and reactionary Danish king Frederick VI to a head-bobbing Chinese mandarin became a relatively common way of critiquing the ossification of the Danish monarchy, despite strict limits on freedom of the press, speech, and assembly. Against this backdrop, Tivoli came to function as "an Oriental lens through which Danes viewed themselves," in that viewing "the monarchy of the past and . . . the middle class democracy of the future . . . as Oriental made them tolerable because the

Oriental—whether applied to political or aesthetic representation—was by nature stripped of substance, and functioned simply as an exotic framework and fantasy space in which the Danes had enjoyed imagining themselves playing since the publication of Oehlenschläger's *Aladdin*" (Oxfeldt 2005, 57). Once Denmark sold its African and Indian colonies to Great Britain in 1845 and 1850, turned inward after its disastrous defeat by Prussia and Austria in 1864, and began to view itself as existing on the periphery of Europe, victimized by the aggressive expansion of the German Empire, the escapism that Tivoli offered took on new significance as offering a way in which Denmark could redefine itself, vis-à-vis its powerful neighbors, as less complicit in colonialism and more tolerant of other cultures.

At around the turn of the twentieth century, at a time when atrocities committed by, among others, German and Belgian colonizers in Africa were beginning to arouse public outrage, Tivoli's Orientalism took on a more pedagogical tone. This turn is evident in a series of ethnographic exhibits, commonly called "folk caravans," of Chinese, Africans, Indians, Arabs, Native Americans, and other nonwhite peoples who were put on display in Tivoli and other places in Denmark, including the Copenhagen Zoo and the city of Aarhus. By way of example, a 1902 exhibition called *Kina i Tivoli* (China in Tivoli) featured a group of twenty-six men, three women, and five children from China, nearly all of them from Canton province. The group included a lantern maker, a tailor, a doctor, a pair of actors, and several coolies. Although the prospect of putting people on display may strike modern Tivoli guests as regressive, the exhibit program touted the exhibit's innovative approach and authenticity, noting that "there has never before been shown in Europe a picture of real Chinese folk life comparable to that which 'China in Tivoli' offers so accurately, so elegantly, and in such an extraordinarily interesting manner" (*Vejleder* 1902, 3, my translation). The guide promises visitors ethnographically instructive insights into "an ancient and highly developed culture" with the intent of raising visitors' awareness of Chinese culture and customs (3). The exhibit included a theater, a kiosk, a temple, a cooking area, and a bazaar full of "very cheap, odd things, which one can bring home as a souvenir from the Chinaman city for a trifle" (5), but also "up ahead in the 'cage' a very strange 62-year-old dwarf, who is a first-rate attraction," and a woman with bound feet (7). The exhibit notes oscillate, uncomfortably for modern readers, between unabashed voyeurism and self-congratulatory solemnity about how much visitors can learn from "the diligent, hard-working sons of the blue dragon's kingdom" (8), but the exhibit undeniably succeeded at bringing

This Chinese dragon and strings of red lanterns traditionally reserved for seasonal festivals create ambience in the park year-round.

Danes face-to-face with actual representatives of a foreign culture in a potentially more meaningful way than decorative architectural flourishes.

The exhibit's expressed intent of educating visitors about the merits of a foreign culture and its explicit challenge to Victorian anthropological hierarchies at least gestures toward multiculturalism at a time when Chinese immigration to the United States was being severely curtailed and the Eight-Nation Alliance (made up of Germany, Great Britain, France, Italy, Austria-Hungary, Russia, Japan, and the United States) had just put down the Boxer Rebellion in China. Yet in many ways, the folk caravans also replicated the colonial conditions they ostensibly challenged. As Mary Louise Pratt has shown of European travel writing, these objectifying performances of ethnicity had the effect of "producing" these countries for visitors to Tivoli, implicitly engaging the Danish public with the imperialist-colonialist enterprises in which their country was involved. These exhibits created a contact zone, a space of colonial encounters where peoples "geographically and historically separated come into contact and establish ongoing relations, usually involving conditions of coercion, radical inequality, and intractable conflict" (Pratt 1992, 6). The confinement of the "performers" into a miniature city within a city within a city, as if inside a series of Chinese boxes, provided visitors with a pretense of scientific objectivity, but the viewers' position of mastery made them complicit in exercising the dominant imperial gaze. Pratt suggests that, by the very act of looking, the "imperial 'seeingman' desires, objectifies, and possesses the observed" (7). Yet despite these problematic power dynamics, the exhibits' exposure of Tivoli guests to the physical reality of the people behind the glossy facade of architectural arabesques and Romantic literary myths like *Aladdin* began to complicate its earlier, deliberately romanticized relationship to Oriental tropes in a productive way that points ahead to Tivoli's contribution to Danish attempts to manage its encounters with multiculturalism in the twenty-first century.

Conclusion

Although much has changed in Tivoli's appearance and entertainment offerings over the past 175 years, not least because of the destruction of many of its buildings by German occupying forces during World War II, a visit to Tivoli today offers a blend of Danish flags, Chinese dragons, Islamic minarets, and both foreign and traditional Danish foods reminiscent of what the park's first visitors would have encountered in 1843. The cityscape around Tivoli has been altered beyond recognition due to infrastructure changes, such as the demolition of Copenhagen's ramparts in 1867 and the ongoing expansion of the Copenhagen metro system, but Tivoli continues to function as an important branding tool for Denmark and Danishness at home and abroad. It is particularly proud of its long-standing cultural institutions, including the Tivoli Youth Guard, which admits twenty applicants per year into "one of Denmark's most ambitious music schools"; the Tivoli Ballet School; and the Tivoli Copenhagen Philharmonic Orchestra, founded by the composer Hans Christian Lumbye in the 1840s (Olsen and Schaldemose 2018, 53). Tivoli has worked to preserve its explicitly Danish associations, for example, through the construction of a Danish market town within the park in 1952 and the hosting of an annual Christmas market full of Danish holiday trinkets and treats, complete with fake snow for ambiance, while also expanding its multicultural offerings by incorporating new traditions from other cultures, such as the celebration of American-style Halloween beginning in 2006; Friday Rock concerts; and many new foods, from spring rolls, which were introduced by Chinese immigrant Sai-Chiu-Van in 1937, to Iberian-inspired churros.

Much more than the physical landscape of Copenhagen and the forms of entertainment on offer at Tivoli have changed since 1843; the makeup of Danish society and the demographics of Tivoli visitors have been significantly altered by the influx in recent decades of immigrants and refugees from many of the same countries whose cultural traditions and architectural styles were incorporated into Carstensen's designs and whose inhabitants were put on display in Tivoli in the late nineteenth century. Tivoli's deliberate blend of the familiar and the exotic—"a fairy tale at its most fun, its wildest and cosiest" (Olsen and Schaldemose 2018, 14)—has attracted millions of visitors over nearly two centuries—including Bill Clinton, Vladimir Putin, and Walt Disney, the latter of whom came several times in the 1950s in search of inspiration for his own planned themed amusement park (31)—but it is unclear how welcome new, nonethnic Danes feel in Denmark's iconic park. While Tivoli doesn't keep statistics on visitors' ethnic backgrounds, its 2017 annual report reveals that approximately 70 percent of Tivoli's 4.4 million guests in 2017 came from Denmark, while the remaining 30 percent came from all around the globe, primarily Sweden, the United States, the UK, Norway, and Germany, though visitor counts from southern Europe, India, and China show an upward trajectory (Tivoli 2017). The concentration of immigrants in greater Copenhagen makes it at least probable that they made up some sliver of those roughly three million Danish guests, though the admission fees might have put Tivoli out of reach for many.

Yet as political convulsions in Denmark in recent years over cartoons, head scarves, and school meals reveal, creating a truly multicultural Danish society will require much more of Danes than merely admiring the elegant arabesques of onion domes and consuming spring rolls. It may be that Tivoli can help both parties learn to negotiate this cultural fusion, much as it once served to help Danes acclimatize themselves to conditions of modernity, simply by exposing them to each other and giving them a place to practice intercultural communication and acceptance. Tivoli has come a long way from the days of its folk caravans, and has made efforts to foster intercultural dialogue inside the park. Tivoli's concert halls have often featured performances by African American jazz musicians, including Louis Armstrong in 1933 and 1962 and Josephine Baker on a regular basis throughout the 1960s, and its theaters have long been known for their satirical revues that poke fun at the idiosyncrasies of social and political trends. Moreover, Tivoli's commitment to facilitating immigrant integration goes beyond the stage. In the 2016 annual report, Tivoli's management describes their program for hiring sixteen refugees on a work-study basis and assigning part of their working hours to language study: "The idea is that it is easier to learn Danish when you combine learning with spending time with Danish-speaking colleagues, because you make active use of the language and develop a language practice. At the same time, the language trainees learn about the culture and norms in a Danish workplace. Each language trainee was also allocated a mentor within Tivoli, who could provide advice and guidance on finding their footing as a new arrival in Danish society" (Tivoli 2016). While the program's explicit goal is integration rather than fostering cultural exchange, the initiative reflects Tivoli's commitment to diversity in its workforce. While it is unclear whether this work-study program continued beyond 2016, the report also describes the development of a two-year "basic integration course" and a "mentoring scheme for highly educated new Danes who are having difficulties breaking into the labour market" (Tivoli 2016). All three of these programs aim to help new Danes establish themselves as contributing members of Danish society and come into contact with ethnic Danes in order to put down roots in Denmark.

By its own account, Tivoli strives to be a place where people of all ethnic backgrounds can try cultural hybridity on for size. The blend of cosmopolitanism and banal nationalism that characterizes Tivoli's design aesthetic, restaurants, and artistic performances provides proof that Danish culture can be, indeed has already been, enriched by imports—of food, music, architecture, and so on—from far-flung places. The park is proud of its reputation as a safe, tolerant space where guests of all nationalities are welcome. Lars Hedebo Olsen avers, "There is no agenda at Tivoli; there is nothing you have to do. You can do exactly as you want. . . . You would be hard-pressed to find a safer place in Copenhagen" (Olsen and Schaldemose 2018, 13). There are, of course, exceptions to this rule. In one highly publicized case in 2007, the right-wing Danish politician Morten Messerschmidt was accused of proffering a Nazi salute during a drunken dinner at Tivoli, an incident that sparked a firestorm and a court case brought by Messerschmidt against the newspaper *Berlingske* (formerly *Berlingske Tidende*). Tivoli's tolerance does not apparently extend to displays of intolerance.

Yet while the park's nostalgic elements can be co-opted to support a reactionary fantasy of reclaiming an imagined homogeneous Danish past, its tradition of deliberately juxtaposing the foreign and the familiar also has the potential to help define Danishness in positive, inclusive ways, if only because this image fits well with Danish branding efforts and makes for an effective business strategy. Olsen affirms, "Tivoli fits perfectly with the picture of Denmark that we would like to sell to the rest of the world. It's beautiful, it's safe, it's fun, it has loads of history, there is room for everyone and it has an atmosphere all of its own. . . . In general, Tivoli is a pretty tolerant place, where everyone should feel welcome, but it is also a place that demands something from its guests" (Olsen and Schaldemose 2018, 68). In Olsen's account, Tivoli envisions itself as an idealized Denmark, one where Danes are able to live up to their own ideals of tolerance and mutual respect between people. Thus, although Tivoli's performance of what Michael Haldrup and Jonas Larsen term "practical Orientalism . . . through the establishment of sensuous geographies of smells, tastes, food, sounds, embodied poses and visuality" (2009, 86) contributes in some degree to the consolidation and production of difference between the familiar and the exotic, between Danish and the Other, it also contains the potential for its own redemption. If, by blending Danish and "Oriental" elements and making that combination familiar and palatable, Tivoli can encourage visitors to move beyond stereotypes about other groups of people and discover their individuality, it can help counteract the banality of the reductionist Orientalist discourse that has become increasingly pervasive in Denmark and the violent expression of such views. The Danish flag may fly peacefully over a minaret in Tivoli while dark- and light-skinned children eat old-fashioned Danish *bolsjer* and cavort on playgrounds together, but unless Tivoli's guests take that same embrace of hybridity with them out into the city streets surrounding the park, the harmoniously multicultural Denmark it models will remain a fantasy.

REFERENCES

Andersen, Hans Christian. 1990. *H. C. Andersens almanakker 1833–1873.* Edited by Helga Vang Lauridsen and Kirsten Weber. Copenhagen: Det Danske Sprog- og Litteraturselskab.

Andersen, Hans Christian. 2008. *The Annotated Hans Christian Andersen.* Edited by Maria Tatar. New York: Norton.

Billig, Michael. 1995. *Banal Nationalism.* London: SAGE.

Dickens, Charles. 1851. *Household Words.* Vol. 3. New York: Angel, Engell & Hewitt.

Hage, Hother. 1872. *Orla Lehmanns efterladte skrifter.* Vol. 1. Copenhagen: Gyldendal.

Haldrup, Michael, and Jonas Larsen. 2009. *Tourism, Performance and the Everyday: Consuming the Orient.* London: Routledge.

Haugsted, Ida. 1993. *Tryllehaven Tivoli: Arkitekten H. C. Stillings bygninger og den ældste have.* Copenhagen: Museum Tusculanums Forlag.

"History." n.d. Chateau Tivoli. Accessed May 5, 2017. http://www.chateautivoli.com/history/.

Macdonald, William L., and John A. Pinto. 1995. *Hadrian's Villa and Its Legacy*. New Haven, CT: Yale University Press.

Olsen, Lars Hedebo, and Anne Prytz Schaldemose. 2018. *Tivoli: A Garden in the City.* Copenhagen: Gyldendal.

Oxfeldt, Elisabeth. 2005. *Nordic Orientalism: Paris and the Cosmopolitan Imagination 1800–1900*. Copenhagen: Museum Tusculanum Press.

Pratt, Mary Louise. 1992. *Imperial Eyes: Travel Writing and Transculturation*. London: Routledge.

Raup, H. F. 1974. "Tivoli: A Place-Name of Special Connotation." *Names* 22(1): 34–39.

Rentenaar, Rob. 1976. "How Danish Is Tivoli?" *Names* 24(1): 24–30.

Said, Edward. 1978. *Orientalism*. London: Routledge.

"Tivoli." n.d. Wikipedia. Accessed May 5, 2017. https://en.wikipedia.org/wiki/Tivoli.

Tivoli. 2016. *Summary of Annual Report*. https://www.tivoligardens.com/en/om/virksomheden/aarsrapporter/2016.

Tivoli. 2017. *Summary of Annual Report*. https://www.tivoligardens.com/en/om/virksomheden/aarsrapporter/2017.

"Tivoli's History." n.d. Tivoli. Accessed May 8, 2017. http://www.tivoligardens.com/en/om/tivolis+historie.

Vejleder gennem "Kina i Tivoli." 1902. Pamphlet. http://www.5.kb.dk/e-mat/cop/pamphlets/dasmaa/pamphlets-dasmaa-2012-jul-smaatryk-object83465.pdf.

Wanhill, Stephen. 2003. "Economic Aspects of Developing Theme Parks." In *Managing Visitor Attractions: New Directions*, edited by Alan Fyall, Brian Garrod, and Anna Leask, 39–57. Oxford: Butterworth/Heinemann.

Zerlang, Martin. 1997. "Orientalism and Modernity: Tivoli in Copenhagen." *Nineteenth-Century Contexts* 20:81–110.

"Musicians Find 'Utopia' in Denmark"

African American Jazz Expatriates

ETHELENE WHITMIRE

During the summer of 2013, I lived in the Nørrebro section of Copenhagen. I frequently took a shortcut through the Assistens Kirkegård (Assistens Cemetery) to the cafés on the trendy street Jægersborggade. Famous Danes such as author Hans Christian Andersen and philosopher Søren Kierkegaard are buried there. On the path back to my apartment, I noticed a rather prominent headstone with the very non-Danish name of Ben Webster. I was surprised to discover that he was one of many African American jazz musicians who had lived and were buried in Copenhagen. Pianist Kenny Drew's and trombonist Richard Boone's final resting places are with Webster in a special jazz section. Thad Jones, who was a trumpet player and leader of the legendary band at New York City's Village Vanguard, and drummer Ed Thigpen are buried side by side in Vestre Kirkegård, along with pianist Duke Jordan, interred in a different section. I did not know about these African Americans living in Denmark and was curious. While many educators, social workers, writers, diplomats, and activists lived, worked, studied, visited, and performed in Denmark, the jazz musicians comprised one of the largest groups of expatriates.[1]

Why did these African Americans go to Denmark? What were their experiences while there? And why did they stop moving to Denmark? This chapter explores how economic and social issues in the United States drove African American jazz musicians to become expatriates in Denmark and how social and economic issues in Denmark ended the influx of these expatriates.

~

Born in 1909 in Missouri, Ben Webster played with many of the great jazz legends, including Andy Kirk, Fletcher Henderson, Benny Carter, and Duke

Ellington. Webster, like the other jazz musicians who moved to Denmark, was already an established musician in the United States when he left. In 1964 he moved to Denmark and performed all over Europe. Webster liked Copenhagen: "The city was beautiful, and he found regular employment at the Montmartre club with one of Europe's best rhythm sections: pianist Kenny Drew, 18-year-old bass player Niels-Henning Ørsted-Pedersen, and 24-year-old drummer Alex Riel" (Valk 2001, 136). Beginning in 1927, jazz venues could hire foreign musicians if they employed an equal number of Danish musicians (Brown et al. 2014). This rule gave Danish musicians an opportunity to work with and to learn from the American jazz legends who played in local clubs. Webster died in 1973 while performing in Holland and was cremated and buried in Copenhagen.

American musician Stan Getz pondered, specifically, "Why did a marvelous saxophonist like Ben Webster have to waste his last years in Europe when his value as a teacher could have been put to such great use in some of our schools?" (Feather 1988, 38). Similarly, musician Phil Woods wondered, "Why did Ben Webster die in Europe alone? Why wasn't he given a post? Jazzman-in-residence—give him all the beer he wants and a room. 'Ben, you don't have to do nothing. Just stop by the jazz department if you feel like rapping with the kids'" (Knauss 1977, 233).

Webster's pianist Kenny Drew realized that although working and living in Europe would negatively impact his career in the United States, he enjoyed the opportunity to make a living performing in Europe without having to deal with racism too (Yanow 2008). Despite living as an expatriate in Denmark, pianist Kenny Drew once declared, "I still love New York ... give or take a few things, but my life is in Europe. I wouldn't want to live in the States again—too much upheaval. But I remain one hundred percent American" (Hennessey 1986, 8). Most of the musicians remained American citizens—Denmark did not offer dual citizenship until 2015 after a bill passed in Parliament in December 2014. Some expatriates did become Danish citizens, but most remained in a liminal space—not living in the United States but also not 100 percent committed to Danish life and culture.

Born in New York City in 1928, Drew first settled in Paris in 1961 before moving to Copenhagen in 1964. Drew worked with musicians such as Coleman Hawkins, Charlie Parker, and Lester Young, and, notably, he was the pianist on John Coltrane's *Blue Train* in 1957. He regularly performed at Jazzhus Montmartre as a duo with bassist Niels-Henning Ørsted Pedersen or as a trio with Alvin Queen on the drums (Yanow 2008). Drew continued performing until shortly before his death just weeks before his sixty-fifth birthday (Yanow 2008).

Lars Johansen, the owner of the Danish record label Jazzcraft, said, "For some crazy reason, American jazz musicians keep coming here to settle in Copenhagen of all places" (Nelson 1980, B12). Nic Liney (2016) argued, "Denmark, a state well known for its tolerance, egalitarianism and high standard of living, presented an easy alternative to the racial and economic problems faced by the predominantly black jazz community in the States." And "Copenhagen has become the jazz capital of Europe precisely because so many American musicians have found this Scandinavian city—and, to a lesser extent, Stockholm and Oslo—a most congenial place to live and play music" (Nelson 1980, B12).

In the past, the jazz musicians had gone to Denmark, performed, and then left. For example, in 1933 Louis Armstrong went to Copenhagen, "where 10,000 fans turned out to meet him at the railroad station. He filled the Tivoli concert hall eight evenings in a row" (Burns 2004). But musicians did not begin living in Denmark until after World War II, because "air travel changed the whole picture. No longer was it necessary to spend nearly two weeks in crossing and re-crossing the Atlantic. As a notable result, musicians living in Europe never felt cut off and far from home" (Moody 1993, 1). American jazz musicians went abroad because, "beginning in the mid-40s several jazz artists, dismayed at their prophet-without-honor status, went abroad to stake out more prosperous careers. Some who fell in love with the hospitality and newfound appreciation became fulltime expatriates" (Santosuosso 1980, C1).

As early as 1962, journalists recognized that Denmark was a haven for African American jazz musicians. Newspaper headlines declared: "Musicians Find 'Utopia' in Denmark" or "Looking for Good Jazz? Try Copenhagen" or "American Jazz Swings in Denmark." One reporter noted that "Copenhagen, a city of nearly one million people, has become a jazz center largely because of the central European location and because of the attractive way of living it offers the US expatriate. . . . The lure of far-off lands has always been fascinating for most people in general. For Negro musicians, who decide to leave the country forever, . . . the 'utopia' usually turns out to be Denmark." One expat added, "Bud Powell had intended to stay in Denmark for just one week, but hung around for a month, and finally, decided that it was the place for him" (*Chicago Daily Defender* 1962, 16).

This pattern would repeat itself. An opportunity to perform in Copenhagen would turn into months and years of living in Denmark. The musicians gave a variety of reasons for their exodus to Denmark: "tensions in America, the struggles with the booking agent, the constant fight with night club owners, the continuous move from gig to gig" (*Chicago Daily Defender* 1962, 16). In *Cool Cats*, a Danish documentary about Dexter Gordon's and Ben Webster's lives in Copenhagen, three reasons were given for why African American jazz musicians went to live in Denmark: (1) no discrimination, (2) they got paid, and (3) accessible women (Køster-Rasmussen 2015). One of the expatriates said, "There is something about it [being abroad] that makes you want to play better. . . . You're accepted more readily by the Europeans, not just for music, but for yourself." He lamented that other musicians remained in the United States dealing with discrimination (*Chicago Daily Defender* 1962, 16).

Many jazz musicians, both black and white, moved to Copenhagen. A "few have returned home but the others, to a man, say that life in Scandinavia is a hell of a lot more rewarding than the life they led in the US, even though their reasons for moving may have differed." For example, "some came because of the racial situation in the [S]tates, others to develop their music in a slower, more evenly paced atmosphere. Still others fell in love, not only with the country but with the women as well, and stayed on to raise families. Many, of course, chose Denmark for a combination of all of these" (Nelson 1980, B12).

Bill Moody, author of *The Jazz Exiles: American Musicians Abroad*, raised a series of questions, including: "Why were many of the major names in jazz spending large chunks of their lives in foreign countries performing a music that is uniquely American in origin?" (1993, xvii). Moody concluded that white jazz musicians went to Europe because their music was appreciated. Black jazz musicians went for that same reason and to escape racism. While Denmark was not free from racism, there were not legally segregated institutions in Denmark, and the musicians could dine and live where they wanted.

What attracted the musicians to Denmark? One scholar stated, "Danes have traditionally been seen as a tolerant and liberal people who place importance and value on social cohesion and equality" (Moore 2010). Denmark was the first nation to recognize gay marriage, and during World War II Danes saved nearly their whole Jewish population from the Nazis. But the 1980s and 1990s saw a rise in anti-immigration sentiment that impacted the once-warm reception received by the African American jazz musicians.

The following section includes minibiographies of the musicians focused primarily on their time in Denmark, interwoven with some context about the changes in Danish policies that impacted the livelihoods of the musicians.

Double bassist, cellist, arranger, and composer Oscar Pettiford, born in 1922 in Oklahoma, was among the first musicians to decide to make Denmark his home and the first to be buried there. Pettiford moved to Denmark in 1958 because "he found so much democracy" there (*Baltimore Afro-American* 1960, 19). He had performed with Duke Ellington and Dizzy Gillespie, Max Roach, Don Byas, and Lionel Hampton and was one of the earliest bebop musicians. After a concert at a Copenhagen art exhibition in September 1960, thirty-seven-year-old Pettiford suddenly fell ill, complained about a sore throat, and became completely paralyzed. As he lay dying in a hospital, he asked the mother of his three children to "promise me, no matter how hard it gets, that you and the children will stay here in Denmark forever. I stay here forever." He wanted her to raise their children in what he called a "color-blind" country (*Jet* 1960b, 60).

Saxophonist and flutist Sahib Shihab, born Edmund Gregory in 1925 in Savannah, Georgia, followed in Pettiford's footsteps in the late 1950s, motivated by financial concerns and racism. Shihab explained, "I was getting tired of the atmosphere around New York. . . . I wanted to get away. I was getting fed up with clubowners, most of whom are a sick lot, influenced solely by money. I was also getting disgusted with certain record companies that tried to take advantage of you—and I wanted to get away from some of the prejudice" (Lind 1963, 17–18). Another important factor: "I don't have time for this racial bit. It depletes my energies" (18). Financially, he was struggling and had to play rock and roll in order to make a living (Lind 1963). When his widow, Maiken Gulmann, was asked, "How did Sahib end up living in Denmark?" she replied, "He left the US because he was tired of being kept down as a black man" ("Maiken Gulmann" 2011).

Shihab, who performed with Fletcher Henderson, Thelonious Monk, Dizzy Gillespie, Coleman Hawkins, Sarah Vaughan, John Coltrane, and Quincy Jones, recalled in an interview that during his first trip to Europe in 1954 he had such a favorable impression that he chalked it up to his brief visit. But after a return visit, he decided to remain in Europe. When his bandmates headed to the airport, he remained behind in Paris and then went to live in Sweden for two and a half years before settling in Denmark for his last twenty years (Baggenæs 2008).

While living in Denmark, Shihab interacted with other African American expatriates, including Ed Thigpen, Thad Jones, Brew Moore, and Al Heath.

He created a record label and publishing company with Kenny Drew ("Maiken Gulmann" 2011).

A few years later, in 1962, tenor saxophonist, arranger, composer, and conductor Ray Pitts moved to Denmark and remained there until his death in 2012, with a brief sojourn to the United States. Pitts became the conductor for the Danish Radio Big Band and also wrote compositions and arrangements for the orchestra. In 1961 Pitts went to Copenhagen and performed at Jazzhus Montmartre, where he met his future wife, Grethe Kemp. He became integrated into Danish life and culture. Pitts said, "I put a lot of effort into learning Danish as quickly as possible" (Wiedemann 1997). In a 1997 interview, Pitts declared, "I do not feel like a stranger here. I am American, but I feel at home in both the United States and Denmark" (Wiedemann 1997). He died in 2012 on the day he was to receive an award recognizing his achievements, the Leo Mathisen Prize, in Copenhagen.

Around the same time Pitts moved to Denmark, saxophonist Dexter Gordon also arrived in Copenhagen. Gordon loved Denmark. "'It was love at first sight,' he recalled. 'Imagine the feeling. Imagine the feeling. Jazz music was really low man on the totem pole in America, except in a particular circle. Over there, it's that feeling for the artiste the Europeans have'" (Freedman 1986, 2). In 1964 Gordon said, "Since I've been over here [in Denmark], I felt that I could breathe, you know, and just be more or less a human being white or black, green or yellow, whatever" (Lind 1964, 69).

Gordon was born in 1923 in Los Angeles. He left high school to perform with Fletcher Henderson, Louis Armstrong, Nat King Cole, Billy Eckstine, and Lionel Hampton for three years. During the 1960s he struggled with heroin addiction ("Gordon, Dexter" n.d.). A consequence of his drug use, arrests, and imprisonments was his inability to get a cabaret card, needed to perform in the United States. In 1962 club owner Ronnie Scott told Gordon that he could work in England on and off during a month and that he could get him gigs in other countries for two additional months. Biographer Stan Britt (1989) said Gordon was surprised to see that he was referred to as an expatriate in an article. He had not thought of himself as one.

Gordon was not the only musician to suddenly realize that he was now an expatriate. Arthur Taylor in *Notes and Tones: Musician-to-Musician Interviews* stated, "Few of the jazz musicians who moved to Europe initially intended to do so. Most visited the Continent for limited tours and, finding an appreciative atmosphere, decided to stay. From overseas, the problems of America stood

"Musicians Find 'Utopia' in Denmark"

in painfully clear relief" (qtd. in Freedman 1986, 2). Britt said Gordon's lengthy European residence was "comprehensively a happy and fulfilling period in his life; in many ways, the peace of mind, tranquility and all-around acceptance he discovered wherever his travels took him, combined to make the years 1962 to 1976 as rewarding as any other previous portion of an already eventful life" (Britt 1989, 99).

In 1976, after living for fourteen years in Copenhagen, Gordon returned to the United States and had an acclaimed show at the Village Vanguard (Watrous 1990). Gordon permanently returned to live in the United States in 1977. Later, he starred in the movie *'Round Midnight* in 1986 and was nominated for a Best Actor Academy Award. He died in Philadelphia in 1990 at the age of sixty-seven from cancer of the larynx. His widow, Maxine Gordon, recently chronicled his life in a critically acclaimed biography, *Sophisticated Giant: The Life and Legacy of Dexter Gordon*.

Before moving to Denmark, "Stuff" Smith, born Hezekiah Leroy Gordon Smith in Portsmouth, Ohio, in 1909, was a composer, singer, and violinist. He was called "the mad genius of the violin. . . . He was said to have broken all of the traditional violin rules with his amplified violin" (*Philadelphia Tribune* 1967, 13). Like Webster, Smith performed at the Jazzhus Montmartre with Drew, Ørsted-Pedersen, and Riel. Like Pettiford, Smith only lived in Denmark for two years before dying in 1967 at the age of fifty-eight, after appearing on television and performing in Munich, Germany (*Los Angeles Sentinel* 1967, 4). His body was returned to Denmark and buried there.

When drummer Ed Thigpen was asked why he moved to Denmark, he said racism was one factor but also "the love of a woman" (Vacher 2010). While Thigpen lived in Denmark, his career continued to flourish: he worked as a recording artist, a bandleader, and a mentor to young Danish musicians (Vacher 2010). He also wrote instruction books about drumming and taught at the Danish Conservatory. Thigpen was most famous as a member of the Oscar Peterson Trio from 1959 to 1965. From 1968 until 1972 he performed around the world with Ella Fitzgerald, who had herself moved to Denmark for several years in the early 1960s. Thigpen died in 2010 at the age of seventy-nine (Heckman 2010).

Pianist Horace Parlan became good friends with Thigpen when he moved to Denmark. Parlan performed with Charles Mingus in the late 1950s, then with saxophonist and flautist Rahsaan Roland Kirk and saxophonist Archie Shepp in the late 1960s and early 1970s. However, by then Parlan had seen several of his friends succumb to alcohol and drugs. He was getting less work, too. The final straw was when he was mugged at gunpoint. Parlan said, "I was living in Harlem at the time and I had the misfortune to be mugged by three men, two with knives, one with a pistol. . . . That's a kind of traumatic experience" (Nelson 1980, B12). He said, "When that happened I said, 'That's it. I gotta get out of here'" (Houd 2016). Parlan also said he was frustrated by the lack of opportunities for jazz musicians and what he called "a rise in overt racism" (Keepnews 2017).

Parlan moved to Denmark in 1972 after having heard from many musicians about their experiences working and living in Europe. His first gig was at Jazzhus Montmartre in April 1972. He liked Copenhagen and said he liked being in Europe—he could give his pistol away before he left the United States (Parlan and Barfod 2011). Parlan recalled, "I was happy in Europe, and it was clear to me that you can't create good music in an atmosphere full of tension with drugs and crime in the streets. I was straight, but many of my colleges [*sic*] were drug addicts and several had died from it" (122). He became a Danish citizen in 1995 ("Dansk jazzlegende" 2017). Parlan would eventually live more than half of his life in Denmark (Houd 2016).

Akbar DePriest also moved to Denmark in 1972 and chronicled his adventures in Copenhagen in the *New York Times*. He viewed Copenhagen as an "Impossible Dream," "a Western World city in which a member of a racial minority is respected as a human being. . . . It's a place where a jazzman is appreciated as an artist, even treated like a celebrity sometimes—and where, just maybe, he can eke out a living playing his music" (DePriest and Nellhaus 1975, 1). He wanted to escape the United States and the "white and black club owners who cheat their musicians, pushers and hoods who try to latch on the jazzmen, musician working against musician over a few available gigs" (1). The day after he arrived, he headed to the Jazzhus Montmartre and played and then got other gigs after mentioning the still-existing venues Dropp Inn and La Fontaine and the defunct Casanova, all in Copenhagen.

Ultimately, Akbar DePriest left Copenhagen after one year, stating, "I never did find the rainbow." He said, "The Montmartre, for instance, cut the pay of musicians who lived in Copenhagen on the grounds we were 'local,'" which impacted the African American expatriates. DePriest continued, "As foreigners we weren't allowed to work at other jobs. And Danish club owners had a nasty habit of taping your performances, leaving you wondering what happens to those tapes, which you have no control over" (DePriest and Nellhaus 1975, 1). Despite these difficulties, jazz musicians continued to move to Denmark.

It was around this time, in 1973, that Denmark changed its immigration policies, after initially accepting laborers in the late 1960s from Turkey, Pakistan, Yugoslavia, and Morocco (Mouritsen and Olsen 2013). Even with the influx of these guest workers, Denmark had remained very homogeneous. The laborers were doing undesirable work that did not interest most Danes. But at the same time, the African American jazz musicians still received a warm welcome because of their specialized skills.

Pianist Duke Jordan, born in 1922 as Irving Sidney Jordan in New York City, was considered one of the great early bebop pianists. He performed in Copenhagen in 1973 and moved to Denmark in 1978 in a "self-imposed exile" (Weiner 2006, 1). Beginning in the late 1940s, he played in the Charlie Parker Quintet with Miles Davis, Max Roach, and Tommy Potter and later with Coleman Hawkins, Stan Getz, and Sonny Stitt in New York City. But Jordan got hooked on heroin and began driving a taxi in the 1960s. After a stint in rehab in the 1970s, he organized "trios and quartets in Copenhagen . . . recorded more than 30 albums for the Danish label steeplechase records, and performed in concerts and at jazz festivals worldwide" (1). Jordan died in Valby in 2006 at the age of eighty-four, leaving behind a daughter, Traci, from his 1952 marriage to jazz singer Sheila Jordan.

Thad Jones, a bandleader, self-taught trumpet and flugelhorn player, composer, and arranger, had a more dramatic move to Denmark. Born on March 28, 1923, in Pontiac, Michigan (Orsted 1980, 32), Jones created "syncopated, intricately harmonized arrangements [that] became an ideal for a new generation of arrangers" (Hevesi 1986, D23). Jones was famous for the Thad Jones–Mel Lewis Orchestra, which performed on Monday nights at the Village Vanguard (D23). The eighteen-piece band performed for thirteen years.

In 1979 Jones abruptly decided to live in Copenhagen. *Melody Maker's* headline said, "Thad & Mel's Shock Split." The article announced, "The principal reason appears to be Jones's increasing involvement with commitments to compose and conduct music for European radio stations" (*Melody Maker* 1979, 57). Additionally, referring to the Thad Jones–Mel Lewis Orchestra, Jones said, "Financial considerations had much to do with that decision. . . . I was probably losing as much money as I was making by turning down so many outside writing assignments." In Denmark, Jones argued, "At least the people around me appreciated the fact that I was not just a 'jazz musician,' but a jazz artist. They afforded me that respect" (*Los Angeles Times* 1986, 28).

Jones was remarried in Denmark to a Danish woman, Lis, and they had a son, Thaddeus Jr. (Orsted 1980, 32). In Denmark, Jones conducted the

Danish Radio Big Band. His also formed Eclipse, a twenty-piece band with a nucleus of expatriate American musicians: Horace Parlan, piano; Richard Boone, trombone; Sahib Shihab, baritone saxophone; and Ed Thigpen, drums. The remainder of the band consisted of Danish musicians and two Swedes. Like Jones's previous band in the United States, this band also performed on Monday nights at Copenhagen's Vognporten Club (32). Jones also composed and arranged music for the Danish Radio Orchestra (Hevesi 1986, D23). He taught jazz at the Royal Conservatory in Copenhagen (Carlin 2008).

In 1985 Jones returned to the United States to lead the Count Basie Orchestra. He was only there for a year before returning to Denmark, denying that he was ill. He said he wanted to continue composing and conducting bands in Europe (Heckman 2010). But a year later he was dead in Denmark at the age of sixty-three after a battle with cancer (Hevesi 1986, D23).

Ernie Wilkins also moved to Denmark in 1979 and created his own band. He declared, "Forming the Almost Big Band and writing for it as a composer and arranger is the best thing I've ever done in my life, in my entire career. It has made me happier than anything else I've ever done" (Baggenæs 2008, 97). For Wilkins, Denmark represented a change of venue after he succumbed to drug addiction. Wilkins had developed a drug habit after becoming a famous jazz musician. He entered rehab in 1966, and later, musician Clark Terry supported Wilkins's return to the business. Wilkins recalled, "What was so gratifying was when I found . . . out that everybody still loved me and was really so happy to see me come back. I didn't . . . think I would ever be able to" ("Ernie Wilkins" 1977, 4).

A few years after a 1977 interview with Bob Rusch, Wilkins moved to Denmark. Being in Denmark transformed his music: "I must brag a little bit, too. I'm writing, composing, and arranging better since I've had this band than I ever did in my life. I like what I'm doing now and I think that I'm more creative and a little more adventurous in my writing. I take a few more chances harmonically, rhythmically, and melodically, and I think it's because of the inspiration from my band. . . . I certainly consider their particular gifts when I was writing" (Baggenæs 2008, 98). He also recorded albums for Storyville and for Matrix Records, which he co-owned with Kenny Drew and Sahib Shihab.

Wilkins was fifty-seven years old when he moved to Denmark. He later said, "Denmark is going to be my home from now on. Even if I go back to the States for a period of time, this will still be a home. Only if I was very young I might consider to go back to live. But now I can't pull up my roots anymore" (Baggenæs 2008, 104). The final chapter of Wilkins's career was a happy one. In 1981 he received the Queen of Denmark's Ben Webster Jazz Award. He continued leading the Almost Big Band and recording albums until he suffered a stroke in 1991. Wilkins died in 1999, leaving behind his widow and second wife, Jenny Mikkelsen, whom he married in 1975. John Wriggle (2008) concluded, "The success of Wilkins's comeback career remains one of jazz's most inspirational stories."

Wilkins was one of the last African American jazz musicians to move to Denmark. In the 1980s Denmark was "more insular and exclusive" (Moore 2010, 357). During this time "the inexpensive immigrant laborers were replaced with asylum seekers and refugees" (358). These new types of immigrants needed aid from the Danish government, which caused resentment among some of the Danish people (Moore 2010, 358). During this time and continuing into the early 1990s, asylum seekers and refugees fleeing wars in Iran, Iraq, Sri Lanka, and Yugoslavia increased concerns that these immigrants could not assimilate or integrate into the Danish culture and that they would be an economic burden on the government, since they arrived not as workers but as people in need of services. There were escalating concerns about religion (many refugees were Muslim) and demands that they learn the language, become "self-supporting, acquire (knowledge of) Danish values, and participate in society—all for their own benefit" (Mouritsen and Olsen 2013, 695). In this atmosphere, few African American jazz musicians migrated to Denmark.

In 1995 the Far Right anti-immigration political party, the Dansk Folkeparti (Danish People's Party, DPP), was formed. Immigration concerns, especially regarding immigrants from non-Western countries, became part of platforms and political discussions. Immigrants were expected to demonstrate knowledge and respect for Danish culture.

Jazz musician Ray Pitts offered a unique perspective on Danes and immigration. He arrived in Denmark in 1962, and thirty-five years later, in 1997, a reporter from Information.dk asked him about Danes' perceptions of foreigners. He replied, "I think probably the Danish attitude to strangers, to people who are different, has developed poorly. There is so much talk about Danishness and Danish identity. . . . I come from a nation of immigrants, so the things I see here, I have all experienced before. It is curious that the Danes have not learned from the Americans' mistakes but repeat the same stupidities" (Wiedemann 1997).

After the 2001 elections, the "'immigrant question' topped the Danish agenda, and parties competed at being tough on immigration. . . . In a series of steps, all forms of immigration were restricted as much as possible and onerous obligations were placed on immigrants to adopt Danish values in order to remain in the country and obtain permanent residence and citizenship" (Mouritsen and Olsen 2013, 692). A change in the government from 2011 to 2015, led by the Social Democrats, briefly eased some of these restrictions (Hercowitz-Amir, Raijman, and Davidov 2017).

A recent study can provide insight into why the African American jazz musicians were initially accepted by the Danes. Andrea Bohman's article "Who's Welcome and Who's Not? Opposition towards Immigration in the Nordic Countries, 2002–2014," published in 2018, found that the race or ethnicity of the immigrants did not matter. What mattered were immigrants' abilities to contribute to the Danish economy.

In the mid-1980s Denmark established professional jazz education programs, and by the 1990s these musicians were ready to perform and compete with their American counterparts (Washburne 2010, 122). The Danish government and the Danish Jazz Federation provided support for these Danish musicians to promote their concerts. It subsidized their tours and provided funds for travel expenses, along with the union Dansk Musiker Forbund, which provided opportunities for Danish jazz musicians to perform in Denmark. All of these things resulted in the loss of opportunities for American jazz musicians in Denmark (150, 151). The creation of the European Union also increased the opportunities for Danish jazz musicians to perform in many countries throughout Europe. The Americans would not benefit from these opportunities. Most importantly, "Danish jazz musicians, producers, and institutions, in collusion with governmental agencies, have been advocating for—and implementing more—nationalistic policies in support of Danish jazz" (123).

Christopher Washburne argues that "state-sponsored cultural policies, an upsurge in nationalistic fervor, . . . as well as the economic prosperity in the US in the mid-1980s are tied to striking changes in the jazz performed and produced in Denmark" (2010, 123). One goal was to create a distinctive brand of Danish jazz that was not based on the influence of jazz from the United States. The American jazz musicians living in Denmark were no longer considered to be stars (Larsen 2004). They were not immune from the Right-leaning governmental policies that applied restrictions to asylum seekers and refugees. Washburne argues that "politicians have initiated a push to define and delineate Denmark's finest cultural achievements in order to establish a 'Danish space' within global economic and cultural spheres" (2010, 135). In fact, Danish musicians soon learned that in order to obtain subsidies and grants, they needed to demonstrate originality. It was not advantageous for a musician to say, for example, that they were the next Danish Miles Davis (143).

CONCLUSION

Beginning in the late 1950s and through the 1960s and 1970s, African American jazz musicians prospered professionally and personally in Denmark. They were welcomed for their skills and knowledge as musicians and instructors. But by the 1980s, with the rise of nationalistic sentiments in Denmark, the jazz musicians' livelihoods were as negatively impacted as those of low-skilled laborers from other countries in eastern Europe and the Middle East. Preference was given to hiring native Danes for jazz bands. As opportunities dwindled or ceased to exist, the influx of African American jazz musicians to Copenhagen ended.

An April 2016 episode of the podcast *Unfictional*, "A Portrait of Horace Parlan," said, "Denmark was once home to many expatriate American jazz musicians. These days, Horace Parlan is one of the only ones left" (Houd 2016). At the time of the podcast, Parlan was blind from diabetes and confined to a nursing home. He was living in a coastal town in Denmark near a body of water where he liked to sit. He still went to Copenhagen, about an hour away, on occasion to listen to jazz music in Jazzhus Montmartre, where he had met his wife of thirty-seven years; she had died two years earlier (Houd 2016). Horace Parlan died in February 2017 in Denmark ("Dansk jazzlegende" 2017). He was the last of the great musicians who made their journey to Copenhagen in the second half of the twentieth century.

In the southern harbor of Copenhagen there are seven streets in a residential complex in Sluseholmen named after African American jazz musicians: Richard Boone Vej, Kenny Drew Vej, Dexter Gordon Vej, Thad Jones Vej, Oscar Pettiford Vej, Ben Webster Vej, and Ernie Wilkins Vej. In 2019 the Copenhagen Jazz Festival celebrated its fortieth anniversary with about 1,200 concerts in 120 venues with an audience of approximately a quarter of a million people (Copenhagen Jazz Festival 2019). Many African American jazz musicians and singers performed in Denmark in July 2019, but they have gone back to the former model of performing in Denmark and then returning to the United States. Horace Parlan's death signaled the end of an era.

Note

1. I purposefully use the term "expatriates" because the subjects were often referred to using that term. I acknowledge that this term sometimes denotes a privilege often afforded to wealthy and famous immigrants from Western countries.

References

Baggenæs, Roland. 2008. *Jazz Greats Speak: Interviews with Master Musicians*. Lanham, MD: Scarecrow Press. Kindle.

Baltimore Afro-American. 1960. "Deaths at Large." September 24, 1960, 19.

Bohman, Andrea. 2018. "Who's Welcome and Who's Not? Opposition towards Immigration in the Nordic Countries, 2002–2014." *Scandinavian Political Studies* 41(3): 283–306.

Britt, Stan. 1989. *Dexter Gordon: A Musical Biography*. New York: Da Capo Press.

Brown, Cecil, Anne Dvinge, Petter Frost Fadnes, Johan Fornäs, Ole Izard Høyer, Marilyn Mazur, Michael McEachrane, and John Tchicai. 2014. "The Midnight Sun Never Sets: An Email Conversation about Jazz, Race and National Identity in Denmark, Norway and Sweden." In *Afro-Nordic Landscapes: Equality and Race in Northern Europe*, edited by Michael McEachrane, 57–83. New York: Routledge.

Burns, Ken. 2004. "Louis Armstrong Returns to Europe." In *Jazz: A Film by Ken Burns*, clip from season 1. Hollywood, CA: PBS Home Video, distributed by Paramount Home Entertainment. https://www.pbs.org/video/jazz-louis-armstrong-returns-to-europe/.

Carlin, Richard. 2008. "Jones, Thad." In *African American National Biography*, edited by Henry Louis Gates Jr. and Evelyn Brooks Higginbotham. Oxford African American Studies Center. http://www.oxfordaasc.com/article/opr/t0001/e1099.

Chicago Daily Defender. 1962. "Musicians Find 'Utopia' in Denmark." November 7, 1962, 16.

Copenhagen Jazz Festival. 2019. Concerts. https://jazz.dk/en/copenhagen-jazz-festival-2019/concerts/.

"Dansk jazzlegende er død." 2017. *DR*, February 25. http://www.dr.dk/nyheder/kultur/musik/dansk-jazzlegende-er-doed.

DePriest, Akbar, with Arlynn Nellhaus. 1975. "The Impossible Dream: A Cat's View of 'Cope.'" *New York Times*, November 9, 1975, 1.

"Ernie Wilkins: Oral History." 1977. Transcribed by Bob Rusch. *Cadence* 2(6–7): 4.

Feather, Leonard. 1988. "A Master at Work." *Jazz Times* 18 (October): 38.

Freedman, Samuel G. 1986. "The Blues of Expatriate Paris: Recalling America's Jazz Exiles." *New York Times*, October 12, 1986, 2.

"Gordon, Dexter." n.d. In *Encyclopedia of African American History, 1896 to the Present: From the Age of Segregation to the Twenty-First Century*, edited by Paul Finkelman. Oxford African American Studies Center. http://www.oxfordaasc.com/article/opr/t0005/e0483.

Gordon, Maxine. 2018. *Sophisticated Giant: The Life and Legacy of Dexter Gordon.* Berkeley: University of California Press.

Heckman, Don. 2010. "Ed Thigpen Dies at 79; Jazz Drummer." *Los Angeles Times,* January 15.

Hennessey, Mike. 1986. "Europajazzz." *Jazz Times,* June, p. 8.

Hercowitz-Amir, Adi, Rebeca Raijman, and Eldad Davidov. 2017. "Host or Hostile? Attitudes towards Asylum Seekers in Israel and in Denmark." *International Journal of Comparative Sociology* 58(5): 416–39.

Hevesi, Dennis. 1986. "Thad Jones Dies in Denmark; Trumpeter and Band Leader." *New York Times,* August 21, D23.

Houd, Rikke. 2016. "A Portrait of Horace Parlan." *Unfictional* podcast, KCRW, April 8. https://www.kcrw.com/culture/shows/unfictional/a-portrait-of-horace-parlan.

Jet. 1960a. "Danish Concert Raises $4,350 for Pettiford Family." October 27, p. 61.

Jet. 1960b. "Oscar Pettiford's Estate." November 3, pp. 60–61.

Keepnews, Peter. 2017. "Horace Parlan, Jazz Pianist, Dies at 86." *New York Times,* March 1.

Knauss, Zane. 1977. *Conversations with Jazz Musicians.* Detroit: Gale Research.

Køster-Rasmussen, Janus. 2015. "Cool Cats." Video recording. *DR.* CPH DOX. https://www.youtube.com/watch?v=hmtTYezjotU.

Larsen, Peter H. 2004. "Jazz, Rock, Pop and Techno." Ministry of Foreign Affairs, Denmark. http://www.netpublikationer.dk/um/8903/html/chapter01.htm?&searchword=peter%20+larsen%20+jazz%20+same%20+star%20+status.

Lind, Jack. 1963. "Sahib Shihab's Expatriate Life." *Down Beat,* March 14, pp. 17–18.

Lind, Jack. 1964. "Americans in Europe, a Discussion." *Down Beat,* July 2, pp. 64–73.

Liney, Nic. 2016. "When the Village Vanguard Came to Denmark." *The Local,* July 1.

Los Angeles Sentinel. 1967. "'Stuff' Smith, Jazz Great, Dies in Europe." October 5, p. 1.

Los Angeles Times. 1986. "Thad Jones, Arranger for Basie, Dies." August 21.

"Maiken Gulmann about Sahib Shihab." 2011. *Othersounds,* September 18. http://othersounds.com/interview-maiken-gulmann-about-sahib-shihab/.

Melody Maker. 1979. "Jazz News: Thad & Mel's Shock Split." March 24, p. 57.

Moody, Bill. 1993. *The Jazz Exiles: American Musicians Abroad.* Reno: University of Nevada Press.

Moore, Harald F. 2010. "Immigration in Denmark and Norway: Protecting Culture or Protecting Rights." *Scandinavian Studies* 82(3): 355–64.

Mouritsen, Per, and Tore Vincents Olsen. 2013. "Denmark between Liberalism and Nationalism." *Ethnic and Racial Studies* 36(4): 691–710.

Nelson, Don. 1980. "Looking for Good Jazz? Try Copenhagen." *Boston Globe,* February 24, B12.

New York Times. 1960. "Oscar Pettiford, Bassist, 37, Dies." September 9.

Orsted, Knud. 1980. "Jazz: THAD JONES: Popular U.S. Jazz Musician Is Now Residing and Working in Denmark." *Billboard* 92(8): 32 (Archive: 1963–2000).

Parlan, Horace, and Hans Barfod. 2011. *My Little Brown Book: Seventy Years of Jazz Life*. Karrebæksminde: Saxart.

Philadelphia Tribune. 1960. "Mourn Pettiford—Bassist Died in Copenhagen." September 20, 1960, 5.

Philadelphia Tribune. 1967. "Jazz Violinist 'Stuff' Smith Dies." October 17, p. 13.

Santosuosso, Ernie. 1980. "No Gigs at Home: The Jazzman's Testifyin' Heard Mostly Overseas." *Boston Globe*, January 13, C1.

Spies, David. 2008. "Pettiford, Oscar." In *African American National Biography*, edited by Henry Louis Gates Jr. and Evelyn Brooks Higginbotham. Oxford African American Studies Center. http://www.oxfordaasc.com/article/opr/t0001/e1159.

Stewart, Ollie. 1960. "Report from Europe: Musicians Honor Pettiford." *Baltimore Afro-American*, October 22, p. 4.

Taylor, Arthur R. 1982. *Notes and Tones: Musician-to-Musician Interviews*. New York: Coward, McCann & Geoghegan.

Vacher, Peter. 2010. "Ed Thigpen Obituary." *The Guardian*, February 24.

Valk, Jeroen de. 2001. *Ben Webster: His Life and Music*. Berkeley, CA: Berkeley Hills Books.

Voce, Steve. 1999. "Richard Boone." *Independent*, February 24.

Washburne, Christopher. 2010. "Jazz Re-bordered: Cultural Policy in Danish Jazz." *Jazz Perspectives* 4(2): 121–55.

Watrous, Peter. 1990. "Dexter Gordon Dies at 67; a Charismatic Jazz Figure." *New York Times*, April 26, p. 1.

Weiner, Tim. 2006. "Duke Jordan, 84, Jazz Pianist Who Helped to Build Bebop." *New York Times*, August 12, p. 1.

Wiedemann, Erik. 1997. "Danmark er blevet mere råt." *Information*, November 22. https://www.information.dk/1997/11/danmark-blevet-mere-raat.

Wriggle, John. 2008. "Wilkins, Ernie." In *African American National Biography*, edited by Henry Louis Gates Jr. and Evelyn Brooks Higginbotham. Oxford African American Studies Center. http://www.oxfordaasc.com/article/opr/t0001/e1820.

Yanow, Scott. 2008. "Drew, Kenny." In *African American National Biography*, edited by Henry Louis Gates Jr. and Evelyn Brooks Higginbotham. Oxford African American Studies Center. http://www.oxfordaasc.com/article/opr/t0001/e5778.

Finnish War Children in Sweden after World War II and Refugee Children of Today

BARBARA MATTSSON

This chapter opens with an account of events in Finland's history leading to the evacuation of seventy thousand Finnish children to Sweden during World War II. It then presents an interview study with evacuated children who did not return to their homeland after the war. Ten of them were interviewed in Stockholm in 2007 by two Finnish psychologists. The aim of the study was to deepen the understanding of the psychic consequences of the evacuation for small children. The chapter also addresses the debate about refugees of today who come to Sweden to strive for a new life. It also notes psychological hardships connected to the asylum process and discusses the "apathetic child syndrome."

HISTORICAL BACKGROUND TO THE EVACUATION OF FINNISH CHILDREN

Finland made up the eastern part of Sweden for about seven hundred years, but in 1809 Finland was annexed as part of Russia, becoming the autonomous Grand Duchy of Finland. In 1917, at the time of the turbulent revolution in Russia, Finland declared its independence.

However, on November 30, 1939, the Soviets, who wanted to reclaim Finland as a buffer against the threat of German expansion, bombed Helsinki, beginning the Finnish Winter War. This war had an interim period of peace from March 13, 1940, to June 25, 1941, at which time the Continuation War began. Finland fought in the hope of pushing back against the Soviets with German backing until the autumn of 1944, when the tide turned against Germany. At the end of World War II, Finland remained independent but was forced to relinquish Karelia, the easternmost part of the country, to the Soviet Union.

This transfer of land meant that the entire Karelian population, around 410,000 people, was moved to the remaining parts of Finland. During Finland's independence, ties between Finland and Sweden had remained strong.

Almost immediately after the outbreak of the Winter War, various Swedish women's organizations became involved in the plight of Finland under the motto "Finland's cause is ours." They proceeded with a campaign to help by opening their homes to Finnish children to keep them out of harm's way. In Sweden there was a massive and positive response to this call.

The generous posture of Sweden toward its Nordic neighbors has been partly attributed to the Lutheran ethic of solidarity with the poor, whereby taking a Finnish child into one's home could be seen as an altruistic deed (Sköld, Söderlind, and Bergman 2014). Sweden had a tradition of helping children from different war zones. For example, after World War I, undernourished children from Central Europe and the Baltic states were temporarily transported to Sweden for restorative health care (Kavén 1985).

Norway and Denmark also took in Finnish children, but on a smaller scale than Sweden. The 109 Finnish children who were evacuated to Norway were sent back to Finland immediately after the German invasion, which the Norwegians decided to resist, while the 4,200 Finnish children who were in Denmark stayed until the end of the war, even though Denmark was occupied by Germany.

The children sent out of the country were collectively referred to as "Finnish war children." There are no exact figures as to how many children came to Sweden, since a number of children came to Sweden by means of their own, apart from the official transports, but there were most probably around seventy thousand. The authorities in Finland actively encouraged families to send their children to the other Nordic countries. Food and medicine shortages were a strong argument. The transports were managed by the Finnish state. Some researchers have understood these actions to have been not only a humanitarian matter but also a population policy effort to save the lives of Finnish children in the event of a successful Soviet invasion of Finland. While this fear was not realized, 7,100 Finnish children remained in Sweden after the war ended, so it can be said that Finland did lose a share of its children to Sweden (Kavén 2010).

Transport and Arrangements for Finnish Children during the War

The Finnish war children were transported to Stockholm by boat and later by train via Tornio. The latter route was safer but longer. In some individual

Finnish War Children in Sweden

cases, the children were sent by plane. The transports to the Finland-Sweden border were supervised by members of the Finnish Lotta Svärd (a women's voluntary paramilitary organization). Since there was one nurse per thirty children at the departure from the border station, it is understandable that the children did not have access to an adult who could be conscious of or respond to their individual needs during the transport. On the Swedish side, Swedish nurses took over.

In Sweden the children were first put in quarantine and their health status was determined, after which most were placed in Swedish families. The routine preceding the placement itself could be stressful. When Swedish families came to choose a child, it became apparent that little girls were popular, while older boys were harder to place. Even when children from the same family were placed in the same general area, they were often kept separated from their siblings with the reasoning that they would then be sure to acclimatize themselves and learn Swedish.

Most of the evacuated children came to Swedish families whose socio-economic status was higher than that of the children's Finnish parents. The Swedish foster parents were in general older than the Finnish parents, and most of them had children who were older than the war child (Kavén 2010). The Swedish families usually treated their Finnish foster children as members of the family. Children of school age attended Swedish schools together with Swedish children. However, as mentioned above, older boys could be hard to place. Some of them were sent to orphanages, and some were sent to farms, where they could help with the farmwork. Boys at orphanages were sometimes given schooling in Finnish. When peace was proclaimed in 1944, the return of children did not take place on an especially large scale, since the political situation in Finland was unstable. Many of the war children returned to Finland first in 1946, but about 7,100 children remained in Sweden (Kavén 2010). The children who returned to Finland for the most part kept up a continued contact with their Swedish family, and many of them would travel to Sweden for a summer visit with this family. They could also receive packages from Sweden containing, for example, clothes. These packages were highly appreciated, owing to the great shortage of various necessities in postwar Finland.

TRANSPORT AND ARRANGEMENTS FOR OTHER CHILDREN DURING THE WAR

During World War II, many children in Europe were evacuated from their home areas to safer places. One well-known example is the so-called *Kindertransport*, whereby Jewish children were sent from Austria to England before the outbreak of the war (Fast 2011).

In spite of many explicit protests by pediatricians, the British authorities, even before the war broke out for England, carried out their plan to move schoolchildren from London and other large cities to the countryside to protect them from the dangers of war. Around 1.5 million children were evacuated (Parsons 1998), but many of the evacuees to the countryside suffered harm. When this fact finally became an object of scrutiny about sixty years later, it stirred up strong feelings, since the evacuation of these children had been a source of national pride for the English nation (Parsons 1998). In England as in Finland, it was taboo after the war to criticize the decisions of the authorities.

At the end of the Vietnam War in 1975, the US government moved Vietnamese orphans to the United States for adoption. This was called Operation Babylift and involved 2,547 children (Kavén 2010), although 178 children died when their airplane crashed.

Research Concerning Finnish War Children

Children's experiences of war had long been relegated to silence not only in Finland but also in other European countries involved in World War II. The children faded into the shadow of war events, and their experiences were therefore not considered to be of general interest. Since around the beginning of the twenty-first century, however, the Finnish war children have been taken up in both historical and psychological research (Heilala 2016; Kavén 2010; Mattsson 2018).

Being an evacuated child has been associated with early life stress (ELS), a vulnerability that follows difficult experiences in early childhood. Medical research on war children has uncovered surprising results, showing that, compared with nonevacuated siblings, evacuated children who returned to Finland after the war experienced an increased risk for depression and other mental health disturbances later in life (Eriksson, Räikkönen, and Eriksson 2014). The same study showed that the war children who returned to Finland had an increased risk for ELS with long-term symptoms, cognitive functioning disorders, and physical and psychosocial disorders. The results show that the war children who came back to Finland had poorer health and poorer school results than those who were not evacuated.

The latest finding on the research front is that female (but not male) offspring of mothers who had been placed in Swedish foster families during the war had a significantly higher risk of hospitalization attributable to mood disorders than did female cousins who were not evacuated (Santavirta, Santavirta, and Gilman 2017). It seems that separation experiences early in a child's life may be passed down from one generation to another.

Children and Separation

Today there is a great deal of knowledge available about the impact and consequences of separating children from their parents that was not widespread at the time of World War II. It was more common to believe that children would forget unpleasant experiences and that separation therefore had no significance later in life.

Anna Freud and Dorothy Burlingham (1943) were among the first to underscore the risks when young children were separated from their mothers for a long period of time. Later, John Bowlby (1960) especially emphasized how difficult it can be for an outsider to understand the depth and seriousness of the pain that a child can feel upon separation, whether from placement with strangers or during a hospital stay, for example. The harmful consequences of early separation are now well known.

Trauma

For young children, a traumatic experience means total helplessness, so-called mortal fright. A child's permanent separation or long-term separation from its parents can be seen as the prototype of a traumatic experience. An early separation means that the trust experienced by the child disappears. Continuity is thereby destroyed, along with expectations of the presence of a possibility for linkage and empathetic understanding (Laub and Auerhahn 1993).

A central feature in a traumatic experience is a perception of having been abandoned by outer and inner protective forces, which can lead to impairment in the ability to trust others. Because separation from the parents interferes with children's developmental processes and can lead to a partial inability to reflect on their own mental states (Fonagy 2001), such children can be unable to integrate the reality of the traumatic experience, which results in the repetition of the trauma in images, acting out, and abnormal physiological states (Varvin 2003). When a child's attention is turned to a feeling of being threatened, the child can find it difficult to focus on play and learning. Early traumatic experiences influence thinking and emotional life even in adulthood.

From a neuroscientific perspective, Onno van der Hart, Ellert Nijenhuis, and Kathy Steele (2006) emphasize that a trauma may split the personality into a so-called normal part and a traumatized one. A traumatized person has a tendency to hide his pain and anger behind a veneer of normality. That defense maneuver, which can be helpful for the moment, hides feelings that could be difficult to control.

An Interview Study with
Finnish War Children in Sweden

As part of a larger study of Finnish war children carried out by the Department of Education at the University of Helsinki, a questionnaire was sent to the 202 members of the Stockholm branch of the Finnish War Child Association. There was also a question about interest in participating in an interview study. Of those 202 members, 144 said they were willing to participate in a personal interview.

Out of this sample, the researchers from Finland chose ten people for a personal interview. The interviewees had been between two and five years of age, with one seven years old, at the time of the transport to Sweden. Seven of them were women, and three were men. At the time of the interview, they were about sixty-five years old.

The interviews were carried out in 2007 in Stockholm at the Karolinska Institute by two Finnish researchers, a psychotherapist and a psychoanalyst, the author of this chapter.

The interviews started with the request "Tell me about your life." The interviews took in most cases approximately two hours. They were taped and transcribed.

During the interview, many contradictions came to light in the war children's narratives. Language usage was a core source of information about the war children's inner world. When individuals express themselves, their verb tense changes, and word choices can provide an image of their psychic state (Crittenden and Landini 2011), and so it was with these interviewees. On the one hand, they said that they did not remember anything from their early childhood or the evacuation, while on the other hand, they could express different feelings about the evacuation as if it were something going on right at the present moment. This contradiction came out clearly when they changed verb tense to the present while speaking about the evacuation, which they could not remember but which nonetheless awakened strong feelings about life (Mattsson 2018).

The interviewees' way of telling their stories at the beginning of the interview conveyed a sense of loneliness and desolation, and they did not direct their words to the interviewer. This phenomenon bears witness to the nature of trauma: early experiences of loneliness were present as if they were experiences in the now. Thus, during the interview, they were visibly affected by their early experiences, discernible in both the form and the content of the language but also in their way of neglecting the listener. In that moment they were alone (Mattsson 2018). When they spoke about their adult lives, the nature of their language changed. They communicated directly with the interviewer, did not have a desolate tone, and did not switch tenses.

Many of the interviewees had lost their curiosity about their earlier life in Finland. In this way they had lost the possibility of reflecting over what it could have meant to them to grow up with their family of origin. For those who did mention their mother, she remained a distant person during the interview. Their feelings of having been abandoned were presumably a reason for the war children's difficulties in thinking about her (Mattsson, Maliniemi-Piispanen, and Aaltonen 2017). Similar observations have also been made about adopted children (Hodges 1989). A lack of curiosity is an obstacle against testing different alternatives and affects one's thinking ability (Bion 1962). The war children's trauma was manifested in their stance of indifference toward the past. However, they agreed to tell their stories.

EXAMPLES FROM THE INTERVIEWS

Pirjo, evacuated at four years of age, loved her foster mother in Sweden, but by doing so she felt she had abandoned her Finnish mother. She became convinced that either her foster mother or Pirjo herself could die or that she would become blind. She developed different compulsive symptoms trying to prevent the future catastrophe she imagined. Pirjo was the only one in this sample who explicitly spoke about psychic symptoms (Mattsson and Maliniemi-Piispanen 2011). Pirjo lived with a burden of guilt.

Eeva, evacuated at four years of age, began her narrative with a long sequence about her brother. "Myself, I came to Stockholm then, I do not know, I think, I have repressed most of it, so I do not remember anything special [*crying*] . . . I do not know." Her narrative was about the never-ending conflict with her foster mother: "I have never had a close mother-daughter relationship." She did not mention her Finnish mother, but she told the interviewer about her first visit to Finland after the war: "I could not talk to them. . . . It was so hard for me" (Mattsson and Maliniemi-Piispanen 2013, 37–38; Mattsson, Maliniemi-Piispanen, and Aaltonen 2017, 133). Eeva did not speak about her Finnish parents.

Olli, evacuated at three years of age, explained, "I was born in Kotka at the height of the war, so to say, to an unmarried mother, yeah, so to say, and while bombs were falling, I was taken by train . . . to Haparanda . . . and to a delousing camp and . . . by and by I was placed in a foster family." "Delousing camp" indicated strong feelings of anger and shame. When he came to Sweden, he was seriously undernourished. "I do not have so many memories from my childhood, but, yeah, I mean that they are hidden, but the feeling can sometimes get triggered. Yeah, triggered, what's it called? I got some triggers in my personality, and then they awaken feelings in me" (Mattsson, Maliniemi-Piispanen, and Aaltonen 2015, 132, 134). Olli struggled with anger issues.

Seeming indifferent to or unknowing of the past can be seen as a strong defense mechanism, since we know that a mother always leaves traces even if the child cannot remember her (Bollas 1987; Stern 1985). A child's language comes into being in its early relation to its mother and forms the root of its identity (Matthis, Kaplan, and Varvin 2006). By forgetting its mother, a child loses a part of itself. The father is of importance as well, but for these interviewees he was more or less absent, since most men were stationed at the front.

The Finnish children who remained in Sweden after the war could express feelings of abandonment and of being left behind. The feeling of being "different" could, even in adulthood, evoke feelings of shame and anger in the war child. One strategy for trying to escape such feelings can be doing one's utmost to conform to the majority society, to act as "ordinary" as possible. The desire to be "ordinary and normal," especially for children who have felt strange and different, is a common phenomenon, but it can also be seen as a diagnosis, "normopathy" (Bollas 1987; McDougall 1990), an illusion that can give a feeling of competence and security. It provides protection from feelings that otherwise could be overwhelming. The quest to be normal can be interpreted as a desire to be like everyone else. Traumatized people have a tendency to want to forget their past, while at the same time the historical truth can be important to them.

Discussion and Conclusions

The aim of the study with ten Finnish war children was to trace the after-effects of the evacuation to Sweden as well as to find out what it can mean for a child to be moved from one country to another, to complete strangers and to a new language. The interviewees were all members of the Stockholm branch of the Finnish War Child Association in Sweden and thus a select group.

The theoretical background for the study was grounded theory (Glaser 1992, 1994), that is, a study without readymade hypotheses, which is suitable in areas where there is not much other research. Adult attachment theory (AAI) and psychodynamic thinking and interpretation were tools for understanding. The researchers listened to the explicitly stated content of the life-story narrative but also to that which remained unsaid but nevertheless was present. The interviewees' way of relating to the interviewer was also noted.

What one remembers or does not remember of difficult childhood experiences affects one's mental and emotional life even in adulthood and, as has been shown, can even affect the next generations (Santavirta, Santavirta, and Gilman 2017). Many of the interviewees seemed to have lost interest in their earlier life, yet they could still feel abandoned by their Finnish homeland. During the interview, when the circumstances around their transport to Sweden came up, they were deeply affected. Trauma is by its very nature timeless. The traumatized person deals with what has been overwhelming not as a memory but as an action in the now (Eriksson 2014).

The Finnish war children adapted themselves to their new life by forgetting the past. They were said to have learned Swedish within some months. In contrast, other children, those who returned to Finland, paradoxically had a hard time learning Finnish anew, which affected their schooling, not to mention their communication with their family. The effects of the traumatic displacements were actively present during the interview itself, manifesting themselves in the interviewees' manner of speaking, in their grammar, and in their approach to communication with the interviewers, who at times were put into different roles, such as the one who understood and the one who did not understand. The feeling of having been abandoned by their Finnish parents had not changed over the course of the years. Most of them met their relatives later in life, but communication relied on a translator (Mattsson 2018). Whatever the case, there is evidence that a mother can never disappear entirely from her child's inner world (Bollas 1987; Botella 2014; Hodges 1989). A traumatic experience from early life continues to have an influence later in life (Botella 2014; Eriksson 2014). "As trauma traces for a child are non-verbally encoded, they cannot be accessed by conscious recollection. Instead, the traumatic experiences leave action tendencies, sensations, affected states and images, which tend to re-appear out of context later in adult life" (Habermas 2014, 952).

The interviewees conveyed what had been difficult in their psychic development. At the same time, they gave a picture of ten people who had been struggling throughout their entire lives to master their early experiences and who had succeeded in settling down and adapting themselves in Sweden. Their participation in the meetings of the Stockholm Finnish War Child Association proved to be of great importance. The association offers meetings with like-minded people as well as possibilities for discussions in smaller groups. It also provides insight into larger contexts, conditions of war, and historical events (Mattsson 2018).

Today's World

Like many other European countries, Sweden and Finland have taken in refugees, including young children.

When children of today are sent away, with or without their parents, from their homeland to foreign countries, they can have problems with adjustment, emotional life, and identity. However, the newcomers who arrive alone are seldom as young as the Finnish children who were sent away during World War II.

Refugees from faraway countries, where customs are different from those in the Nordic countries, can experience an even greater change in their life than did the Finnish war children in Sweden in their time. The refugees also face a significantly tougher situation than that of the Finnish war children who, over half a century ago, were invited to Sweden.

Language, values, customs, food, and climate are sometimes vastly different from what refugee children have known all their lives, while the Finnish children came to a culture where, except for language, they could find some familiarity with what they were used to. In addition, the placement of the Finnish children in Swedish homes as a family member gave them a push into Swedish society. They went to school with Swedish children. In contrast, those children who were placed in orphanages had their schooling in Finnish.

Refugees today come from zones of war, chaos, and deprivation, but for them the journey is often more dangerous and insecure than the one the Finnish war children had to endure. In addition, they cannot be sure that they will be granted asylum. Children and youths who arrive in Sweden without their parents are placed in some form of dormitory living. The loss of roots, the abrupt change of language, and the absence of another human being to whom one can express disappointment or anger are probably common experiences for both children and adults who come to a new country. The feeling of being abandoned and of being an outsider can also strike if a refugee returns home after a prolonged stay in the receiving country. This is well documented in the case of teenage Finnish boys who returned to Finland from Sweden after the war. Compared with peers who weren't war children, they felt lost in Finland and ran an increased risk of being placed in juvenile detention (Westling 1956). They were also rebellious when they were expected to do military service in Finland (Mattsson 2018). In Sweden today, in contrast to the Finnish war children in the 1940s, refugee children are given help in school to maintain and develop their mother tongue (Bylund and Diaz 2012).

Related to the topic of refugee children's psychological and physical wellbeing is the issue of so-called apathetic children, which has caused a heated and still ongoing debate in Sweden. The long waiting period and uncertainty about the asylum decision are extremely stressful for today's refugees, and in Sweden some refugee children have developed a puzzling apathetic child syndrome, manifested as a devitalized or sleeplike state. These children have become bedridden and stopped eating, drinking, and communicating.

The phenomenon has proven difficult to interpret. Many see it as a psychosomatic reaction in which children in their insecurity and helplessness regress to an earlier level of development where depression, lethargy, eating disorders, and nightmares occur. Aggressive outbursts could also be observed, after which the children returned to the sleeplike state (Bodegård 2004). Could it also be that the helpless and anxiety-ridden parents, because of their own stress, do not have the resources to give their children what they need? Or, as lately has been claimed, do some parents force their children to play up different scenarios in a desperate attempt to influence the asylum decision?

Others have interpreted the syndrome as an attempt to evoke compassion that could contribute to a positive asylum decision for the children and their families. For example, journalist Ola Sandstig (2019) claimed in an issue of the Swedish magazine *Filter* that children had been forced by their parents through physical violence and starvation to act sick. Two women interviewed by Sandstig claimed that they as children had been coerced by their parents to stage different symptoms. If this syndrome was in fact a bluff, it would indicate the desperation refugees are feeling, even to the extent of jeopardizing their child's physical and psychic health. On the other hand, Gellert Tamas (2019) has claimed that the facts about the apathetic children are distorted. In September 2020 physicians and police described the cases of apathetic children as a bluff (Lapidus 2020). The debate around these children is, in other words, still ongoing.

CLOSING WORDS

At times of war or other catastrophes, children are the most vulnerable. The displacement of young children, without or together with their parents, from one country to another, even if the move takes place under well-organized conditions, can be an overwhelming experience that leaves a mark on the child, a mark that can even be passed on to the generations that follow. When children have to witness their parents' panic, as has been the case for at least some of the apathetic children, they are also permanently marked by this experience, even if the parents have not meant to do harm. From a psychological view, it may also be hard for a child to feel responsible for the family's future life.

The Finnish children who remained in Sweden after the war received an opportunity to have a safe life and gained access to advanced education. It is questionable whether most of them, who came from more limited circumstances in Finland, would have had such opportunities in their former homeland. When the war children were asked to tell about their lives, they replied that they had a good life, which did not mean, however, that they lacked feelings of abandonment and anger, often directed toward the former homeland.

At the beginning of the twenty-first century, the former war children, as members of the War Child Association in Sweden, approached the Finnish authorities with a request to be granted dual citizenship. Their argument was that they had not chosen their fate when they were moved to Sweden by the request of the Finnish state. After many setbacks, the war children were finally given back their Finnish citizenship, effective from 2011, and free of charge through a simple application procedure. Thus, they now had two homelands.

References

Bion, Wilfred Ruprecht. 1962. "The Psychoanalytic Study of Thinking." *International Journal of Psychoanalysis* 43:306–10.

Bodegård, Göran. 2004. "Fallbeskrivning av depressiv de-vitalisering: Asylsökande flyktingbarn utvecklar livshotande funktionsbortfall" [Case description of depressive devitalization: Asylum-seeking refugee children develop life-threatening functional failures]. *Läkartidningen* 101(19): 1696–99.

Bollas, Christopher. 1987. *The Shadow of the Object: Psychoanalysis of the Unthought Known.* London: Free Association Books.

Botella, César. 2014. "On Remembering: The Notion of Memory without Recollection." *International Journal of Psychoanalysis* 95(5): 911–36.

Bowlby, John. 1960. "A Psychoanalytic View of Consequences of Separation and Loss." *International Journal of Psychoanalysis* 41:89–113.

Bylund, Emanuel, and Manuel Diaz. 2012. "The Effects of Heritage Language Instruction on First Language Proficiency: A Psycholinguistic Perspective." *International Journal of Bilingual Education and Bilingualism* 15(5): 593–609.

Crittenden, Patricia McKinsey, and Andrea Landini. 2011. *Assessing Adult Attachment: A Dynamic-Maturational Approach to Discourse Analysis.* New York: W. W. Norton.

Eriksson, J. 2014. "Att minnas—om erinring, upprepning och genomarbetning" [Remembering—about recalling, repeating, and working through]. *Divan* 3–9: 74–85.

Eriksson, Mia, Katri Räikkönen, and Johan Eriksson. 2014. "Early Life Stress and Health and Later Health Outcomes: Findings from the Helsinki Cohort Study." *American Journal of Biology* 26(2): 111–16.

Fast, Vera K. 2011. *Children's Exodus: A History of the Kindertransport.* London: I.B. Tauris.

Fonagy, Peter. 2001. *Attachment Theory and Psychoanalysis.* London: Karnac.

Freud, Anna, and Dorothy Burlingham. 1943. "War and Children." *Social Service Review* 17:518–19.

Glaser, Barney G. 1992. *Basics of Grounded Theory Analysis.* Mill Valley, CA: Sociology Press.

Glaser, Barney G. 1994. *More Grounded Theory: A Reader.* Mill Valley, CA: Sociology Press.

Habermas, Tilmann. 2014. "Dreaming the Other's Past: Why Remembering May Still Be Relevant to Psychoanalytic Therapy, at Least in Some Traditions." *International Journal of Psychoanalysis* 95(5): 951–63.

Heilala, Cecilia. 2016. "The Child in the Eye of the Storm: Unveiling the War Child Syndrome." PhD diss., University of Helsinki.

Hodges, Jill. 1989. "Aspects of the Relationship to Self and Objects in Early Maternal Deprivation and Adoption." *Bulletin of the Anna Freud Centre* 12(1): 5–27.

Kavén, Pertti. 1985. *70,000 pientä kohtaloa* [70,000 small destinies]. Helsinki: Otava.

Kavén, Pertti. 2010. "Humanitaarisuuden varjossa: Poliittiset tekijät lastensiirroissa Ruotsiin sotiemme aikana ja niiden jälkeen" [The shadows of humanity: Political factors regarding the evacuations to Sweden during our wars and after them]. PhD diss., University of Helsinki.

Lapidus, Arne. 2020. "Läkare och polis vittnar om bluffar med apatiska barn." *Expressen*, September 25.

Laub, Dori, and Nanette C. Auerhahn. 1993. "Knowing and Not Knowing of Massive Psychic Trauma: Forms of Traumatic Memory." *International Journal of Psychoanalysis* 74:287–302.

Matthis, Irén, Suzanne Kaplan, and Sverre Varvin. 2006. "Trauma i vår tid" [Trauma in our time]. In *Svenska psykoanalytiska föreningens skriftserie 9.* Stockholm: Svenska Psykoanalytiska Föreningen.

Mattsson, Barbara. 2018. "A Lifetime in Exile: Finnish War Children in Sweden after the War; An Interview Study with a Psychological and Psychodynamic Approach." PhD diss., University of Jyväskylä.

Mattsson, Barbara, and Sinikka Maliniemi-Piispanen. 2011. "An Interview Study with a Finnish War Child." *Scandinavian Psychoanalytic Review* 34(1): 31–40.

Mattsson, Barbara, and Sinikka Maliniemi-Piispanen. 2013. "Thinking about the Unknown: An Interview Study of Finnish War Children." *Trauma and Memory* 1(1): 34–46.

Mattsson, Barbara, Sinikka Maliniemi-Piispanen, and Jukka Aaltonen. 2015. "The Lost Mother Tongue: An Interview Study with Finnish War Children." *Scandinavian Psychoanalytic Review* 38(2): 128–39.

Mattsson, Barbara, Sinikka Maliniemi-Piispanen, and Jukka Aaltonen. 2017. "Traces of the Past: An Interview Study with Finnish War Children Who Did Not Return to Finland after the War." *Scandinavian Psychoanalytic Review* 40(2): 129–37.

McDougall, Joyce. 1990. *A Plea for a Measurement of Abnormality*. London: Free Association Books.

Parsons, Martin L. 1998. *"I'll Take That One": Dispelling the Myths of Civilian Evacuation 1939–45*. Peterborough: Beckett Karlson.

Sandstig, Ola. 2019. "Ohörda rop." *Magasinet Filter* 70:46–69.

Santavirta, Torsten, Nina Santavirta, and Stephen E. Gilman. 2017. "Association of the World War II Finnish Evacuation of Children with Psychiatric Hospitalization in the Next Generation." *JAMA Psychiatry* 75(1): 21–27.

Sköld, Johanna, Ingrid Söderlind, and Ann-Sofie Bergman. 2014. *Fosterbarn i tid och rum* [Foster children in time and space]. Stockholm: Carlsson.

Stern, Daniel N. 1985. *The Interpersonal World of the Infant: A View from Psychoanalysis and Developmental Psychology*. New York: Basic Books.

Tamas, Gellert. 2019. "Förvrängda fakta om de apatiska barnen." *Dagens Nyheter*, September 30.

van der Hart, Onno, Ellert R. S. Nijenhuis, and Kathy Steele. 2006. *The Haunted Self: Structural Dissociation and the Treatment of Chronic Traumatization*. New York: W. W. Norton.

Varvin, Sverre. 2003. *Mental Survival Strategies after Extreme Traumatization*. Copenhagen: Multivers Academic.

Westling, Achilles. 1956. "Juurettomana omassa maassa" [Without roots in one's homeland]. *Lapsi ja Nuoriso* 15:1.

Afterword

SHERRILL HARBISON

Of course, there is no "conclusion" to the discussions in this volume; perhaps "direction" is a better term for closing remarks. And that direction is full of unprecedented and serious challenges, perhaps also unprecedented opportunities.

The history of ethnic and cultural pluralism in Scandinavia is long, as both the introduction and Önnerfors have made clear. It originates partly from a colonial past, in which both Denmark and Sweden participated in the plantation economy and slave trade in the Caribbean.[1] Denmark and Sweden also have histories of territorial conquest within Europe, including claiming parts of each other's territory and both of them adopting Norway altogether at different times. Finland, Pomerania, Schleswig-Holstein, Iceland, the Faroe Islands, and Greenland have all been subjected to their Scandinavian neighbors, and in all these cases, exchanges of language and culture (in both directions), as well as of labor, have been integral to these expansions.

Furthermore, indigenous populations in the Arctic region have been subject to colonialist policies and attitudes—the Sámi in Norway and Sweden, the Greenlanders by the Danes. In earlier centuries this meant evangelizing the heathen to Christianity, stigmatizing languages, and contesting land claims and migration patterns. Today, suppression of minority religious practices has ended, and in Norway and Greenland indigenous peoples have degrees of self-governance, but the struggle over land rights and cultural imperatives continues, as both Ahlness and Heith illustrate for the Sámi.

And herein lies an important distinction. The introduction and Brochmann have explained how welcome and important Finnish migrants were after 1945 to the economy of Sweden, whose wartime nonalliance had allowed its cities and industries to survive the war unmolested. The Finns, ethnically and culturally similar to the Swedes, integrated relatively easily and contributed to the country's postwar economic boom; Finland also established important regulations favorable to immigrant labor.[2] Nonetheless, Mattsson's psychological study of Finnish children sheltered by Swedish families during the war years (1939–45) reports on children who did not return to their families after the war but remained in Sweden and became citizens there. The trauma of their separation and the loss of their homeland and language were significant and often repressed in adulthood, which speaks to their age at the time of separation and sheds light on the far greater trials for children migrating today.

Brochmann describes the "new immigration," starting in the 1970s and 1980s, as being only partly economic in nature, as it included increasing numbers of political refugees seeking asylum from wars, terrorism, or despotism in eastern and southeastern Europe, Latin America, Africa, and the MENA region (the Middle East and North Africa) and who were drawn to the Nordic countries by their humanitarian reputations. Since the attack on the World Trade Center in New York and the subsequent "war on terror" began in 2001, spreading conflicts in Asia and the Middle East have led thousands of refugees from those regions to seek asylum in Europe. Scandinavia's liberal welfare policies, particularly Sweden's, have attracted a disproportionate share of these refugees, to the point of overwhelming local services designed to accommodate them.

There is no question that part of the problem for the "new immigrants" was their sheer numbers. There is also no question that these numbers, combined with cultural customs and religions very different from and at times conflicting with secular or Lutheran Scandinavian social liberalism, have created the greatest alarm and resistance among native Scandinavians. The "new immigrants," like the indigenous Sámi and Greenlanders, are Other in a way that neighboring European immigrants are not. Conservative Catholics from Poland and Latin America were one thing, but Muslims from Bosnia, Afghanistan, Iraq, North Africa, and Syria have increasingly unnerved their hosts for reasons that are somewhat obscure to the Scandinavians themselves. Teitelbaum explains how the Nordics have long prided themselves on being open-minded and welcoming of difference to the degree that the term "race" was banned from public discourse in Sweden after being deemed "nonscientific," merely a "cultural construct." This "color-blind antiracism," also discussed by Schall and Skinner, is belied by the fact that the new immigrants, often easily identifiable by their skin color or phenotype, encounter widespread social and civil discrimination in ways more similar to the treatment of indigenous peoples (who are *not* newcomers) than to new arrivals from Protestant northern Europe. As Törngren and Sandset discuss, even native-born citizens of mixed race experience this discrimination—unless they can "pass" as ethnic Scandinavians.

How have actors on both sides processed the integration experience? Allen's essay on the creation of Copenhagen's Tivoli gives instructive historical context about the Danes' self-image as cosmopolitan and open-minded, which is not always borne out in today's multicultural Copenhagen. Created during the Romantic era, the amusement park's design combined Oriental exoticism with "banal Danish nationalism" to create a "historical fantasy of Danish cultural sophistication and tolerance," combining entertainment value with domestic education about the wider world. Later in the century, Tivoli offered live ethnographic exhibits—today a wince-inducing example of the imperial gaze but in the late nineteenth century presented as pedagogy. Today the park's "playful but reductionist" approach to pluralism contrasts with Denmark's strict demands of immigrants for cultural conformity. Whitmire describes the relatively warm welcome Danes gave to African American jazz musicians who worked and settled in Denmark between the 1940s and 1960s, a period when their music was highly prized and Danish cultural norms were an appealing alternative to Jim Crow laws at home. But starting with the "new immigration" in the 1970s, they began to be stigmatized together with other newcomers of color.

McKowen's anthropological study of immigrants' experience of acceptance in Norway gives a mixed report, as unemployed newcomers puzzle over domestic attitudes toward work in a welfare state where universal labor participation is key to the social contract, yet rest and leisure are valued just as highly. Locals' complaints that "migrants do not understand and properly value Norway's welfare system" offend immigrants who have experienced desperate and punitive work environments elsewhere; on the contrary, they feel they value it *more* highly than their hosts, who seem unaware of how discrimination affects immigrants' employment opportunities. Reception also figures in Skodo's article about the 2015 influx in Sweden, where he sees a discrepancy between the official state narrative, clothed in the language of crisis, and the reality on the ground, which revealed the extensive control the state exerts over certain asylum seekers. Using the case of Afghans, he argues that the experiences, narratives, and skills of this group were discredited through a pattern of official preferences, assumptions, and policies about asylum worthiness that structurally disfavors Afghans.

Artists have particularly potent ways of addressing such issues. Through works by Swedish artists of color, Leonard illustrates their responses to the disconnect between the country's "antiracist" self-image and their personal experiences of racism by using art strategically to jolt cultural norms and to "consciously examine the tension between identity politics and egalitarianism." At the same time, Oxfeldt examines two novels by contemporary Nordic women to show how their privileged status, endorsed by neoliberal individualism, allows them to pursue careers as artists while also corroding feminist solidarity with their struggling immigrant neighbors. Although earlier generations of women had fought for privileges they now enjoy, these independent women distance themselves from their immigrant tenants and in exchange feel discomfort, guilt, and doubt about the value of the creative class. In this postfeminist world, Oxfeldt argues, "the haves may have capitalism, laws, and regulations on their side, but these do not safeguard them emotionally and ethically."

It is a short step from discomfort with the self to projection of that discomfort onto the Other, and the fruits of this projection are something the Nordic countries now bear. The real and practical problems for overburdened welfare systems—to integrate thousands of newcomers who do not speak the local language and are sometimes untrained, illiterate, or undereducated in their own tongues—are a huge challenge in themselves. Adjusting to each other's radically different customs with regard to religion, diet, dress, and gender politics is challenge enough. To this has been added resentment, fear, and native Scandinavian identity crises, which have found expression in New Right theories and populist political movements in Scandinavia and throughout Europe.

Policies on qualification, integration, and naturalization are volatile and fraught in each country. Önnerfors documents the way nostalgia, or a "retrotopian longing" for an imagined golden age of the Swedish welfare state (*Folkhemmet*, which was shaped by the Left since the 1930s), has allowed the Far Right Sweden Democrats to win significant numbers of seats in parliament, appropriating the *Folkhemmet* mystique for the Right by using rhetoric adapted to its program of excluding outsiders. With the Left's misguided emphasis on multiculturalism, they argue, it has abandoned native Swedes to hoards of indigent Others who threaten Swedish culture and traditions. As Benjamin Teitelbaum (2017) documents elsewhere, the Sweden Democrats' emphasis on folk culture is pronounced and popular, even though the neo-Nazi roots of the party are well known and have not been explicitly denounced.

On the same theme, Schall emphasizes how "the blind spots of the neo-liberal Left created space for resurgences of Far Right racism" in Sweden (and also in the United States). Neoliberalism spread in Europe after the fall of the Berlin Wall and the presumed triumph of liberal democracy and global capitalism. By turning to an emphasis on individualism over collective responsibility in the economic sphere, she points out, Social Democrats abandoned full employment as their primary policy goal, and "previously loyal working-class Left voters began to understand migrants, particularly the new Muslim nonwhite asylum seekers, as threats." Neoliberalism thus relegated racism to "a problem of individual, anomalous cases of interpersonal racism" rather than "the racial inequalities inherent in systems," creating the peculiarly Swedish ideology of "color-blind racism."

Once again, artists give this matter pungent expression. Skinner examines literature, performance, and the visual arts by Afro-Swedes who, with their audiences, "significantly contribute to Sweden's 'cultural life' (*kulturliv*) while confronting endemic racism." He discusses works that deliberately illuminate the reality of *race* in a "color-blind," antiracist society. Their message, "We're here. We're strong. We're beautiful. And we aren't going anywhere," is able to stir public imagination, Skinner argues, while at the same time "resisting assumptions of exoticism and foreignness." The Afro-Swedish artistic movement "insists that it is Sweden that can—*and must*—be reborn in order to embrace and cultivate a social and cultural heterogeneity that is always and already present."

Although the influx of immigrants into Scandinavia has slowed since the border closings prompted by the 2015 refugee surge, the presence of large nonethnic populations in the Nordic countries remains divisive and challenging to social and political stability. In Sweden's 2018 national election, the Far Right Sweden Democrats won 17.5 percent of the vote—the highest ever, though not as high as some had predicted. The Sverigedemokraterna (Sweden Democrats), with the Norwegian Fremskrittspartiet (Progress Party) and the Danish Dansk Folkeparti (Danish People's Party), are part of the political family of European New Right parties, and all have made significant gains in their respective governments in the early twenty-first century. Their participation in coalition governments helps tilt Europe in an increasingly illiberal and anti-immigrant direction.

What lies ahead? Tamir Bar-On points out that left-wing intellectuals frequently use the European New Right as "a convenient scapegoat for the left's demise after the fall of the Berlin Wall in 1989" (2007, 3), but as we are learning, the situation is complex. The Left, too, is searching for an ideological synthesis to combat the spiritual desert of modern technocapitalist culture, as well as its own growing reputation as "the politically correct elite"—a broad, indeterminate amalgam of political, economic, and cultural actors and technocrats unconcerned with ordinary people (Bangstad 2014, 128). Strategically, the Right has claimed this constituency's concern with jobs, wages, poverty in old age, and insufficient benefits that are traditionally the Left's domain. Önnerfors's detailed analysis of the Sweden Democrat leader Jimmie Åkesson's speech from 2017 is a case study of this strategy: leftists' failure to protect the cherished welfare state from corruption by capitalist neoliberalism means they have failed their proper constituents, Åkesson argues. The Left has focused on the rights of strangers who are disrupting the labor market and robbing ethnic Swedes of their proper due.

Because human dislocation, anxiety, and alienation are real both for migrants and for those in receiving countries, the appeal of populist promises for a quick fix means risk of compromised democratic processes and demagoguery, as recent elections in the United States, Hungary, Brazil, and Italy make clear. Elections in Britain, Sweden, and Germany illustrate how the "center" has moved to the right in European parliaments. Bar-On sees this "steady slide toward . . . an anti-immigrant, white, fundamentalist, protectionist Europe through metapolitical, democratic and legal means" as constituting the threat of authoritarianism from *within* (2007, 3).

Kierkegaard once said that while life can only be understood backward, it must be lived forward. Because we can never stand in the same river twice, the New Right's dream of returning to the past cannot be a solution to the global challenges ahead. If there is to be a "postmodern synthesis," it must address the shared Left and Right concerns about modernist isolation, alienation, and loss of community in new policy configurations that take multicultural realities and economic globalism—and modern technology—into account. As always, the one certain thing about the future is change, and all indicators point not to decreasing but to increasing human migration worldwide, whether from political and civil unrest or from climate change. The Nordic countries will be attractive destinations on both fronts, which means that in spite of New Right wishes to return to earlier regional ethnic enclaves, multicultural Scandinavia will be here for the long term.

Notes

1. Though they participated in the slave trade and plantation economy, they had little human or cultural exchange with these regions themselves.

2. Swedes generally considered immigrant Finns to be an inferior social class. They were also regarded as problematic in the 1970s and 1980s due to a sizable group of Finnish immigrants with social problems (mostly alcoholism). See the the Swedish National Council for Crime Prevention report (Olsson 1986).

References

Bangstad, Sindre. 2014. *Anders Breivik and the Rise of Islamophobia.* London: Zed Books.

Bar-On, Tamir. 2007. *Where Have All the Fascists Gone?* London: Routledge.

Bar-On, Tamir. 2013. *Rethinking the French New Right: Alternatives to Modernity.* New York: Routledge.

Olsson, Monika.1986. *Finland tur och retur: Om utvisning av finska medborgare* [Finland round trip: On deportation of Finnish citizens]. Stockholm: Swedish National Council for Crime Prevention.

Teitelbaum, Benjamin R. 2017. *Lions of the North: Sounds of the New Nordic Radical Nationalism.* New York: Oxford University Press.

Contributors

ELLEN A. AHLNESS is a political science doctoral candidate at the University of Washington. She is a graduate fellow for the UW International Security Colloquium and the Washington Institute for the Study of Inequality and Race. Her work on Scandinavian military and war history is on file at the Norwegian Home Guard and Minnesota National Guard libraries, and appears in *Arctic Yearbook* and *On Contested Shores*, among other journals.

JULIE K. ALLEN is a professor of comparative arts and letters at Brigham Young University. She works on questions of cultural identity in nineteenth-, twentieth-, and twenty-first-century northern Europe, particularly with regard to literature, religion, silent film, and migration in Denmark and Germany. She is the author of *Icons of Danish Modernity: Georg Brandes and Asta Nielsen* (2012), *Danish but Not Lutheran: The Impact of Mormonism on Danish Cultural Identity, 1850–1920* (2017), and *Screening Europe in Australasia: Transnational Silent Film before and after the Rise of Hollywood* (2022).

GRETE BROCHMANN is a professor of sociology in the Department of Sociology and Human Geography at the University of Oslo. She has published several books and articles on international migration, sending and receiving country perspectives, EU policies, welfare state dilemmas, as well as historical studies on welfare policy and immigration. She has served as a visiting scholar in Brussels, Berkeley, and Boston. In 2002 she held the Willy Brandt visiting professorship in Malmo, Sweden. She has been head of two national commissions on immigration and the sustainability of the Norwegian welfare model. Brochmann has held various positions in the Norwegian Research Council and is member of the Norwegian Academy of Science.

ERIC S. EINHORN is professor emeritus of political science, University of Massachusetts Amherst. His recent publications include "Is Scandinavia Still Social Democratic?" (*Scandinavian Review*, 2015), and he coauthored "Can Welfare States Be Sustained in a Global Economy? Lessons from Scandinavia" (*Political Science Quarterly*, 2010) and *Modern Welfare States: Scandinavian Politics and Policy in the Global Age* (2003).

SHERRILL HARBISON is a senior lecturer emerita at the University of Massachusetts Amherst, where she was the director of Scandinavian studies for twelve years. She was co-organizer of the international symposium "Managing Multicultural Scandinavia" there in 2017. She has edited Penguin editions of Sigrid Undset's *Gunnar's Daughter* and Willa Cather's *The Song of the Lark* and was coeditor of *Vox Germanica: Essays in Germanic Languages and Literature in Honor of James E. Cathey* (2013), in which she published "Willa Cather and the Scandinavian Revival." Her current book project expands that subject.

ANNE HEITH is an associate professor of comparative literature in the Department of Culture and Media Studies, Umeå University. She is the author of *Laestadius and Laestadianism in the Contested Field of Cultural Heritage: A Study of Contemporary Sámi and Tornedalian Texts* (2018) and *Experienced Geographies and Alternative Realities: Representing Sápmi and Meänmaa* (2020). Her current research project is titled "Indigeneity, Ecocriticism and Critical Literacy."

MARKUS HUSS is an assistant professor of German in the Department of Slavic and Baltic Studies, Finnish, Dutch and German, Stockholm University. In 2017 he taught The Making of Multicultural Sweden as visiting Fulbright Hildeman Fellow at the Program in German and Scandinavian Studies, University of Massachusetts Amherst. His research interests include literature and migration, exile literature, literary multilingualism, and intermedial studies. His dissertation, "Motståndets akustik" (The acoustics of resistance, 2014), investigates the bilingual author Peter Weiss's return to German as literary language in Sweden.

KELLY MCKOWEN is an assistant professor in the Department of Anthropology at Southern Methodist University. His research on Nordic welfare regimes, morality, and migration has been published in *Economic Anthropology*

Contributors 321

and the *Anthropology of Work Review*. He is also the coeditor of a recent volume, *Digesting Difference: Migrant Incorporation and Mutual Belonging in Europe* (2020).

PETER LEONARD is the director of the Digital Humanities Lab at Yale University. He received his PhD in Scandinavian literature from the University of Washington and served as a Fulbright Scholar during 2007–8 at Uppsala University. His research and publications focus on "postethnic" figurations of national belonging in European fiction, with an emphasis on Scandinavian literature. Leonard also works with digital and quantitative methods in the humanities, including text mining, network analysis, image analysis, and corpus query engines.

BARBARA MATTSSON has been a practicing psychologist and psychoanalyst and has also taught psychotherapy. In 2018 she received a PhD in psychology from the University of Jyväskylä, Finland; her dissertation is titled "A Life Time in Exile: Finnish War Children in Sweden after the War."

ANDREAS ÖNNERFORS is a professor in intellectual history and affiliated with the European Academy of Sciences and Arts in Salzburg, Austria. His main area of research is the cultural history of the European Enlightenment. However, since the Norwegian terror attacks in 2011, he has also specialized in studying the worldview and ideology of the European New Right, particularly in Germany (PEGIDA and other right-wing movements), as well as conspiracy theories. He has coedited *Expressions of Radicalization: Global Politics, Processes and Politics* (2018) and is the author of *Freemasonry: A Very Short Introduction* (2017) and *Europe: Continent of Conspiracies: Conspiracy Theories in and about Europe* (2021). Please consult https://uni-erfurt.academia.edu/professorAndreasÖnnerfors for more information.

ELISABETH OXFELDT is a professor of Nordic literature at Oslo University. Among her current projects are "Unashamed Citizenship: Minority Literary Voices in Contemporary Scandinavia" and "Scandinavian Narratives of Guilt and Privilege in an Age of Globalization." Relevant publications include *Åpne dører mot verden: Norske ungdommers møte med fortellinger om skyld og privilegier* (editor with Jonas Bakken, 2017), *Skandinaviske fortellinger om skyld og privilegier i en globaliseringstid* (editor, 2016), and *Nordic Orientalism: Paris and the Cosmopolitan Imagination 1800–1900* (2005).

322   Contributors

TONY SANDSET is a research fellow at the Center for Sustainable Health-care Education, Faculty of Medicine, University of Oslo, where he received his PhD in cultural history. His current research focus is on social dispari-ties in HIV care and prevention, with a focus on the intersection between race, gender, class, and HIV care and prevention. He is the author of *Color That Matters: A Comparative Approach to Mixed Race Identity and Nordic Exceptionalism* (2018) and *"Ending AIDS" in the Age of Biopharmaceuticals: The Individual, the State and the Politics of Prevention* (2020). He has been a visiting postdoc at UC Berkeley.

CARLY ELIZABETH SCHALL is an associate professor in the Department of Sociology, Indiana University–Purdue University Indianapolis. In 2009–10 she served as Fulbright IIE Scholar in the Department of History at Stock-holm University. Her research interests include social policy, health policy, political sociology, immigration, and citizenship. Her book, *The Rise and Fall of the Miraculous Welfare Machine: Nation, Immigration and Social Democracy in Twentieth-Century Sweden*, was published in 2016.

RYAN THOMAS SKINNER is an associate professor of ethnomusicology in the School of Music and the Department of African American and Afri-can Studies at the Ohio State University. He is the author of *Bamako Sounds: The Afropolitan Ethics of Malian Music* (2015) and *Yellow, Blue, and Black: Remembering and Renaissance in Afro-Sweden* (2022). Recent articles include "Walking, Talking, Remembering: An Afro-Swedish Critique of Being-in-the-World" (*African and Black Diaspora: An International Journal*, 2019), "Afro-Swedish Artistic Practices and Discourses in and out of Sweden: A Conversation with Ethnomusicologist Ryan T. Skinner" (coauthored with Beth Buggenhagen, *Africa Today*, 2017), and "Why Afropolitanism Matters" (*Africa Today*, 2017).

ADMIR SKODO is an instructor at the Stanford Continuing Studies Pro-gram. His research focuses on historical and contemporary links between forced migration, geopolitics, state building, diaspora politics, and migration policy and how these links play out in the lives of Afghan migrants in Sweden and the United States. His work has been published by the *Journal of Refu-gee Studies, History of Political Thought*, the Migration Policy Institute, the *Times Literary Supplement*, and *The Independent*, among others. In 2017–18 he was a commissioned instructor for the Swedish Migration Agency. He has

Contributors

been an expert witness on Afghanistan in US immigration court and consults immigration attorneys on the use of country condition information in asylum cases.

Benjamin R. Teitelbaum is a scholar of the contemporary radical right and an assistant professor of ethnomusicology and international affairs at the University of Colorado, Boulder. His books include *Lions of the North: Sounds of the New Nordic Radical Nationalism* (2017) and *War for Eternity: The Return of Traditionalism and the Rise of the Populist Right* (2020). His public commentary on immigration and extremism has appeared in the *Wall Street Journal, The Atlantic, The Nation, Foreign Policy, Dagbladet, DN,* and the *New York Times.*

Sayaka Osanami Törngren is an associate professor and senior researcher at Malmö Institute for Studies of Migration, Diversity and Welfare (MIM) at Malmö University. She has published widely in the field of international migration and ethnic relations, especially on issues concerning race and racialization in the Swedish context. Recent publications include "Challenging the 'Swedish' and 'Immigrant' Dichotomy: How Do Multiracial and Multiethnic Swedes Identify Themselves?" (*Journal of Intercultural Studies,* 2020) and "Racial Appraisal and Constraints of Identity among Multiracial and Multiethnic Persons in Sweden and Japan" (*Ethnicities,* 2021).

Ethelene Whitmire is chair and professor of Afro-American studies at the University of Wisconsin–Madison affiliated with the Department of German, Nordic, and Slavic. She was a Fulbright Scholar at the University of Copenhagen's Center for Transnational American Studies and an American-Scandinavian Foundation Fellow. She is currently writing a book about the experiences of African Americans in Denmark in the twentieth century with funding from the ScanDesign Foundation and the Lois Roth Endowment. She is the author of "Those Happy Danes" (*Scandinavian Review,* 2018) and *Regina Anderson Andrews, Harlem Renaissance Librarian* (2014).